UNIONS, EMPLOYER
CENTRAL BANKS

D0260378

This book focuses on some of the most important political-economic changes in advanced industrialized countries over the past two decades, namely, the sharp rise in unemployment in some countries and the growth of inequality in others.

Using a

to this

nomic

Northe

politics

Torben

the Ce

research

politics

The Pol

bridge

journal

Jonas

Institu

search

omy, a

Democr

of *Bar*

Univer

and ed

David

Univer

ployme

researc

trainin

behavi

Prime

Unioni

Institu

Employ

have a

CAMBRIDGE STUDIES IN COMPARATIVE POLITICS

General Editor
PETER LANGE Duke University

Associate Editors
ROBERT H. BATES Harvard University
ELLEN COMISSO University of California, San Diego
PETER HALL Harvard University
JOEL MIGDAL University of Washington
HELEN MILNER Columbia University
RONALD ROGOWSKI University of California, Los Angeles
SIDNEY TARROW Cornell University

OTHER BOOKS IN THE SERIES

Carles Boix, *Political Parties, Growth and Equality: Conservative and Social Democratic Economic Strategies in the World Economy*
Catherine Boone, *Merchant Capital and the Roots of State Power in Senegal, 1930–1985*
Michael Bratton and Nicolas van de Walle, *Democratic Experiments in Africa: Regime Transitions in Comparative Perspective*
Valerie Bunce, *Leaving Socialism and Leaving the State: The End of Yugoslavia, the Soviet Union, and Czechoslovakia*
Donatella della Porta, *Social Movements, Political Violence, and the State*
Gerald Easter, *Reconstructing the State: Personal Networks and Elite Identity*
Roberto Franzosi, *The Puzzle of Strikes: Class and State Strategies in Postwar Italy*
Geoffrey Garrett, *Partisan Politics in the Global Economy*
Miriam Golden, *Heroic Defeats: The Politics of Job Loss*
Frances Hagopian, *Traditional Politics and Regime Change in Brazil*
J. Rogers Hollingsworth and Robert Boyer, eds., *Contemporary Capitalism: The Embeddedness of Institutions*
Ellen Immergut, *Health Politics: Interests and Institutions in Western Europe*
Torben Iversen, *Contested Economic Institutions*
Thomas Janoski and Alexander M. Hicks, eds., *The Comparative Political Economy of the Welfare State*
Robert O. Keohane and Helen B. Milner, eds., *Internationalization and Domestic Politics*
Herbert Kitschelt, *The Transformation of European Social Democracy*
Herbert Kitschelt, Peter Lange, Gary Marks, and John D. Stephens, eds., *Continuity and Change in Contemporary Capitalism*
Herbert Kitschelt, Zdenka Mansfeldova, Radek Markowski, and Gábor Toka, *Post-Communist Party Systems*
David Knoke, Franz Urban Pappi, Jeffrey Broadbent, and Yutaka Tsujinaka, eds., *Comparing Policy Networks*
Allan Kornberg and Harold D. Clarke, *Citizens and Community: Political Support in a Representative Democracy*
David D. Laitin, *Language Repertoires and State Construction in Africa*
Mark Irving Lichbach and Alan S. Zuckerman, eds., *Comparative Politics: Rationality, Culture, and Structure*
Doug McAdam, John McCarthy, and Mayer Zald, eds., *Comparative Perspectives on Social Movements*
Scott Mainwaring and Matthew Soberg Shugart, eds., *Presidentialism and Democracy in Latin America*
Anthony W. Marx, *Making Race, Making Nations: A Comparison of South Africa, the United States, and Brazil*
Joel S. Migdal, Atul Kohli, and Vivienne Shue, eds., *State Power and Social Forces: Domination and Transformation in the Third World*
Paul Pierson, *Dismantling the Welfare State?: Reagan, Thatcher, and the Politics of Retrenchment*
Marino Regini, *Uncertain Boundaries: The Social and Political Construction of European Economies*

List continues on first page following index

UNIONS, EMPLOYERS, AND CENTRAL BANKS

MACROECONOMIC COORDINATION AND INSTITUTIONAL CHANGE IN SOCIAL MARKET ECONOMIES

Edited by
TORBEN IVERSEN
Harvard University

JONAS PONTUSSON
Cornell University

DAVID SOSKICE
Wissenschaftszentrum, Berlin

CAMBRIDGE
UNIVERSITY PRESS

PUBLISHED BY THE PRESS SYNDICATE OF THE UNIVERSITY OF CAMBRIDGE
The Pitt Building, Trumpington Street, Cambridge, United Kingdom

CAMBRIDGE UNIVERSITY PRESS
The Edinburgh Building, Cambridge CB2 2RU, UK   www.cup.cam.ac.uk
40 West 20th Street, New York, NY 10011-4211, USA   www.cup.org
10 Stamford Road, Oakleigh, Melbourne 3166, Australia
Ruiz de Alarcón 13, 28014 Madrid, Spain

First published 2000

Printed in the United States of America

Typeface Garamond #3 10.5/12 pt.   *System* DeskTopPro$_{/UX}$® [BV]

A catalog record for this book is available from the British Library.

Library of Congress Cataloging in Publication Data

Unions, employers, and central banks : macroeconomic coordination and
    institutional change in social market economies / editors, Torben
    Iversen, Jonas Pontusson, David Soskice.
        p.   cm. – (Cambridge studies in comparative politics)
     1. Europe, Northern – Economic policy.   2. Trade-unions – Europe,
    Northern.   3. Collective bargaining – Europe, Northern.   4. Banks and
    banking, Central – Europe, Northern.   5. Monetary policy – Europe,
    Northern.   6. Unemployment – Europe, Northern.   7. Wages – Europe,
    Northern.   I. Iversen, Torben.   II. Pontusson, Jonas.
    III. Soskice, David W., 1942–   .   IV. Series.
    HC243.U55   1999
    339.5'0948–dc21   99-18002
                                                                          CIP

ISBN 0 521 65039 9 hardback
ISBN 0 521 78884 6 paperback

CONTENTS

FIGURES AND TABLES

FIGURES

TABLES

CONTRIBUTORS

Robert J. Franzese, Jr.
Department of Political Science
University of Michigan
Ann Arbor, Michigan

Geoffrey Garrett
Department of Political Science
Yale University
New Haven, Connecticut

Miriam Golden
Department of Political Science
University of California
Los Angeles, California

Peter A. Hall
Department of Government
Harvard University
Cambridge, Massachusetts

Torben Iversen
Department of Government
Harvard University
Cambridge, Massachusetts

Andrew Martin
Minda de Ginzberg Center for Euro-
  pean Studies
Harvard University
Cambridge, Massachusetts

Jonas Pontusson
Department of Government
Cornell University
Ithaca, New York

David Soskice
Wissenschaftszentrum, Berlin
Berlin, Germany

Peter Swenson
Department of Political Science
Northwestern University
Evanston, Illinois

Kathleen Thelen
Department of Political Science
Northwestern University
Evanston, Illinois

Michael Wallerstein
Department of Political Science
Northwestern University
Evanston, Illinois

Christopher Way
Department of Government
Cornell University
Ithaca, New York

PREFACE

This volume has its origins in a workshop on the "Swedish model" organized by David Soskice at the Wissenschaftszentrum, Berlin, in 1992. From the beginning, our concerns were analytical and comparative rather than descriptive and narrative and, over time, the collective deliberations that went into this volume became less "Swedocentric." As it now stands, the volume includes quantitative analyses that encompass the entire range of OECD countries as well as single-case studies of the evolution of Swedish wage bargaining and macro-economic policy and qualitative analyses that compare the Swedish experience to that of other Northern European cases. Motivated in large measure by David Soskice's distinction between "coordinated" and "liberal" market economies, the contributors focus on differences among and the dynamics of change within coordinated market economies. The Swedish case still figures prominently in most of the chapters that follow – it is seen by most as a central puzzle in the political economy of advanced democracies – but all the contributors are broadly concerned with the political economy of organized capitalism, including the causes of institutional change in wage bargaining, the rise of monetarist macro-economic policies, and the politics of wage and income equality.

A distinction that is quite central to this volume is that between centralized and decentralized coordination, the former epitomized by Sweden and the latter by Germany. Applied to the collective endeavor of this project, this is clearly a case of decentralized coordination. Although all contributors broadly agree what the important research questions are, and although we share a common concep-tual framework, there is too much disagreement about the facts and too many conflicts in our understanding of theoretical mechanisms to warrant a single overarching theoretical model. Nevertheless, the chapters in this volume are the result of a continuous collective enterprise in which ideas and data have been freely shared, and in which theoretical puzzles and answers have been bounced back and forth between different authors. We all reject the notion that changes in institutions and economic policies over the past two decades can be adequately understood within either a neo-corporatist or a new classical framework, and we all accept the idea that the patterns of change and stability are the result of distinct sets of interactions between economic institutions and actors, including employers, unions, state bureaucracies, and governments. We also broadly agree with the distinction between coordinated and uncoordinated market economies, but we cannot agree on the precise nature of institutional interactions within each category, or the extent and exact character of change. This is not surprising because the comparative study of modern capitalism is undergoing a major reconceptualization that is bound to involve controversy. By offering different points of view in this controversy, and by engaging in constructive debate, we hope to create a set of shared empirical puzzles, research questions, and theoretical conjectures that, despite differences in the answers that are given, constitute a clear alternative to both neo-corporatist theory and new classical economics.

We are grateful to the Wissenschaftszentrum, Berlin, for sponsoring the initial workshop that stimulated this collective endeavor and to the Institute for European Studies at Cornell for sponsoring a follow-up workshop, held in November 1996.

COMPARATIVE POLITICAL ECONOMY: A NORTHERN EUROPEAN PERSPECTIVE

Torben Iversen and Jonas Pontusson

Whereas the golden age of postwar economic expansion was a period of relative economic and institutional stability among the advanced democracies, the 1980s and early 1990s marked a period of policy experimentation and attempts at institutional reform. The rise of monetarism in Britain and the United States, the famous U-turn of the French socialists, and the collapse of the Government of National Unity in Italy all represented significant departures from the "post-war settlement" or, alternatively, from the corporatist trajectory of advanced capitalist political economies in the 1970s. The apparent crisis of tripartite or social democratic corporatism since the late 1970s might be attributed to the failure of corporatist experiments in countries, such as France and the UK, which never had the institutional preconditions necessary to the success of corporatist bargaining. Subjected to great political-economic stress, so the argument goes, corporatist arrangements collapse unless they have been consolidated through a long history of organizational adaptation and trust building (cf. Crouch 1993). However, such a view fails to take into account the manifest pressures for change in some of the small corporatist countries of Northern Europe.

The Swedish case stands out in this context. On the one hand, Sweden's postwar development embodied an extraordinarily coherent "model," linking wage bargaining, macro-economic policy, selective state intervention in labor markets, and a variety of social policy measures. (At least, this is how Sweden came to be conceived by Swedish policymakers as well as foreign observers in the 1960s and 1970s.) On the other hand, Sweden represents one of the most obvious instances of "paradigmatic realignment" or "regime change" among

For comments on previous drafts of this chapter, we thank Miriam Golden, Andrew Martin, Paul Pierson, John Stephens, Peter Swenson, and Kathleen Thelen.

OECD countries over the last 10 to 15 years. In terms of partisan politics, the abandonment of the postwar consensus has been much less confrontational than in the British case. As in the British case, however, we observe a reordering of basic policy priorities and a change in the way that policy makers think about the relations among the principal coordinates of economicpolicy (cf. Hall 1993). The goal of price stability has been upgraded relative to the goal of full employment, and policy deliberations have increasingly come to be informed by the notion of a trade-off between efficiency and equality and by the concomitant idea of public-sector spending and employment as an obstacle to competitiveness and growth.

The Swedish case also resembles the British case in that policy changes have been accompanied by institutional changes, rendering a reversal of policy priorities more difficult. While monetary policy has gained importance relative to other instruments of macroeconomic management, the Central Bank has gained autonomy vis-à-vis the government, and especially Parliament. The deregulation of financial markets and the decentralization of wage bargaining constitute other instances of institutional change that will be explored at some length in this volume.[1] For the time being, suffice it to say that the Swedish experience of the last 15 years does not exactly bear out Peter Katzenstein's (1985:198) thesis that "more severe international constraints [would] make the domestic politics of the small European states more cohesive." But is the Swedish case representative of a general trend among the corporatist countries of North-Central Europe or even a general trend among OECD countries? In recent years, many students of comparative industrial relations (e.g., Traxler and Crouch 1995) and comparative political economy (e.g., Berger and Dore 1996; Crouch and Streeck 1997) have challenged the popular notion that globalization has been a source of neo-liberal convergence among advanced capitalist political economies, emphasizing instead the persistence of national diversity in terms of both policy choices and institutional arrangements.

The contributions to this volume are quite different in terms of specific research questions, empirical methodologies, and analytical perspectives, but, in one way or another, they all address the issue of convergence and the politics of institutional change. Considering the volume as a whole, we (the editors) believe that our approach to these matters stands out on three counts. To begin with, our approach emphasizes institutional interaction across different political-economic arenas. In the first instance, this is a volume about the linkage(s) between wage-bargaining practices and outcomes, on the one hand, and macro-

---

1 A complete list of recent institutional changes that affect the functioning of the Swedish political economy would also include the dismantlement of the system of interest-group representation on the boards of state agencies (Ahrne and Clement 1994), the ascendancy of the Ministry of Finance within the central government (Schwartz 1994), and a host of more "subterranean" changes having to do with the organization of the public sector and the delivery of public services (Clayton and Pontusson 1998).

economic management, on the other, but linkages to social policy regimes also come into play, most explicitly in Torben Iversen's contribution. In exploring the linkages between wage bargaining and macroeconomic policy, we seek to bridge two quite separate literatures and theoretical orientations: the corporatism literature, distinguished by its concern with the effects of labor organization (encompassment), and the literature on macroeconomic performance, inspired by neoclassical economic theory, in which the autonomy of central banks emerges as the key institutional variable. In Chapter 2, David Soskice provides a comprehensive introduction to the macroeconomics of this interaction, written in a mode that is accessible to all interested political scientists. Soskice shows how, contrary to the conventional view, macroeconomic policies are essential for understanding real economic outcomes such as unemployment. This is an exciting new development in macroeconomics with multifaceted implications for political scientists interested in the politics of economic performance. It is also central, we think, for explaining institutional change.

Second, our approach stands out in that we separate two analytical issues that existing literatures tend to conflate: the question of common trends and the question of cross-national convergence. To illustrate, suppose that we are interested in some unidimensional and readily measurable feature, such as the level of social spending. Clearly, it is perfectly conceivable that two countries would partake in a common trend (decline) without becoming more alike. In this case, convergence presupposes that the rate of change is greater in the country that started with the higher level of social spending.

Third, and related to the previous point, we want to move beyond the current state of debate between proponents and opponents of the convergence thesis by introducing the idea of convergence among subsets of advanced capitalist political economies, as distinct from generalized (OECD-wide) convergence. Specifically, we want to suggest that one can make sense of the politics of institutional change in terms of "dual convergence" (or co-convergence). Among coordinated market economies, to use David Soskice's terminology (1990, 1992, this volume), we observe some cases of institutional stability and other cases of significant institutional change, and this also holds for liberal market economies. Among the former economies, Sweden, Denmark, the Netherlands, and perhaps Belgium as well might be said to have converged on the German model with respect to wage-bargaining practices, macroeconomic management, and the organization of the welfare state. And among liberal market economies, New Zealand and the UK (possibly other cases as well) might be said to have converged on the American model. One would be hard put however, to argue that coordinated and liberal market economies have become more alike.[2] To be developed in the pages that follow, this conceptualization poses

2 See Pontusson (1997) for a more sustained and comprehensive discussion of Swedish convergence on the German model. In seeking, much like us, to pull together a volume with chapters on continuity

two empirical problems: First, to explain why change has been much more extensive in some countries than in others – say, Sweden versus Germany–and, second, to explain different trajectories of change – say, Sweden versus the UK.

PATTERNS OF CHANGE IN WAGE BARGAINING

If Sweden represents one of the most obvious instances of regime change among advanced capitalist political economies, wage bargaining in turn represents one of the most obvious instances of regime change within the Swedish case. From 1956 to 1983, the Swedish system of wage bargaining pivoted on direct negotiations between the powerful confederation of blue-collar unions, Landsorganizationen (LO), and its private-sector counterpart, Svenska Arbetsgivareföreningen (SAF). As Peter Swenson and Jonas Pontusson describe in their contribution to this volume (see also Iversen 1996), the association of engineering employers, a key SAF affiliate, became increasingly disgruntled with centralized wage bargaining in the course of the 1970s and broke away to strike a separate agreement with its LO counterpart, the Metalworkers' Union, in 1983. In the decade that followed this dramatic turn of events, wage bargaining sometimes occurred exclusively on an industry-by-industry basis and at other times involved peak-level bargaining. The see-saw between industry-level and peak-level bargaining ended in the early 1990s when the SAF came out decisively against peak-level bargaining. In the wage rounds of the mid-1990s, the central institutional issue of contention – between the SAF and the unions, but also within the SAF – was no longer whether there would be peak-level bargaining, but rather how much room industry-level agreements would leave for firm-level bargaining. In the wake of the breakdown of peak-level bargaining, the question of whether industry-level contracts would have the same duration, so as to allow for coordination of bargaining across sectors, has also emerged as an issue of contention.

With Swedish employers pushing for more decentralized forms of wage bargaining in the name of "wage flexibility" conducive to productivity growth and competitiveness, the Swedish story appears to be emblematic of a common trend across advanced capitalist countries since the early 1980s. The commonality of employer rhetoric across these countries, however, may be misleading, masking different practices and trajectories. Measuring the degree of confederal and government involvement in wage bargaining according to specific criteria, Michael Wallerstein and Miriam Golden's contribution to this volume finds no evidence of a secular decentralization trend in Norway or in Finland. In the

and change in contemporary capitalism, Kitschelt et al. (in press) also arrive at the idea of dual convergence.

Danish case, Wallerstein and Golden argue, the demise of peak-level bargaining in the 1980s has been followed by the formation of subconfederal bargaining cartels, as well as wage settlements that are more encompassing than traditional industry agreements (cf. also Due et al 1995). By their account, Sweden stands out among the four Nordic countries as the only unambiguous instance of decentralization.

Wallerstein and Golden's chapter forms part of a larger, ongoing effort to map changes in industrial relations, and wage-bargaining practices in particular, across the OECD area (Lange, Wallerstein, and Golden 1995; Golden and Wallerstein 1996; Wallerstein, Golden, and Lange 1996). In all their writings, Wallerstein and Golden not only challenge the idea of neo-liberal convergence among advanced capitalist countries, but also argue against the idea of any "uniform trends" among these countries (cf. Hyman 1994; Traxler 1995a). Their work represents an important corrective to ad hoc, often impressionistic assessments of national and international trends in the existing literature. At the same time, however, there are some obvious limitations to Wallerstein and Golden's quantitative measures of wage-bargaining arrangements, which are based on procedural considerations and pertain entirely to confederal and government involvement in wage setting.

As Wallerstein and Golden themselves point out, there are only handful of countries in which peak associations regularly engaged in direct wage bargaining during the heydays of postwar corporatism. In the majority of OECD countries, the involvement of peak associations in wage bargaining was informal and/or intermittent, if not nonexistent. For these countries, it is hardly appropriate to deduce the absence of "decentralization" from the absence of any measurable change in the level of confederal involvement. To assess the extent of decentralization of wage bargaining across the OECD area, we also need information about change over time in the scope of multiemployer bargaining and in the relationship between industry-level and firm- or plant-level bargaining. For the United States and the UK, there can be little doubt that a significant decline of multiemployer bargaining has occurred since the 1970s (Katz 1993; Purcell 1995), and such a trend also appears to have characterized France in the 1980s (Howell 1992:ch. 8).

As Kathleen Thelen documents in her contribution to this volume, institutional stability represents the outstanding feature of the German case, but even here, we observe some firms leaving employer associations, thereby opting out of multiemployer bargaining. Moreover, Thelen's earlier conclusion that "the balance within the dual system is shifting toward plant-level bargaining" (Thelen 1991:155) remains valid. In Germany, plant-level bargaining focuses on non-wage issues, such as work time and work organization, and it is the growing salience of these issues that lies behind the shift toward plant-level bargaining that she describes (cf. also Thelen 1993). It is possible to imagine that wage bargaining remains formally centralized while other forms of collective bargaining become decentralized, but local-level bargaining over non-wage issues is bound to affect the substantive provisions of multiemployer wage contracts and/or their implementation.[3]

Concerning confederal involvement, Wallerstein and Golden's measures are in turn limited by their focus on procedural issues: whether bargaining occurs at the peak level, and whether sanctions exist to enforce peak-level settlements. In the Swedish case, the implementation of solidaristic wage policy through peak-level provisions from 1966 onward represents a process of centralization that did not entail any alteration of the formal relationship between peak-level and industry-level bargaining and hence does not register as a change on Wallerstein and Golden's index. For Swedish peak-level settlements after 1983, their index captures the fact that these settlements did not impose a peace obligation on industry-level bargaining, but misses the crucial point that they were primarily about average wage increases and, by comparison to peak-level settlements prior to 1983, left much more room for lower-level bargaining over the distribution of wage increases. Similarly, in the Danish case, the "cartelization" of the early 1990s was accompanied by a greatly expanded use of collective minimum-wage agreements, providing greater scope for wage increases at the plant level than did the old "normal wage" system.

Turning to the question of government involvement in wage bargaining, the retreat from incomes policy or, at least, from highly publicized government efforts to steer to the wage-setting process would appear to have been a fairly pervasive trend in Western Europe since the 1970s. Certainly, such a retreat occurred in Denmark, Belgium, and the Netherlands as well as in Thatcherite Britain in the 1980s. Also, the Italian Parliament's decision to scrap the *scala mobile* in 1991 might be seen as a retreat from government regulation and clearly represents a decentralization of the wage-setting process (Erickson and Ichino 1995:277–281). In the Netherlands, the break with incomes policy in 1982 marked the beginning of a new era of consensual coordination of industry-level and company-level bargaining by union and employer peak organizations and, as a result, the Netherlands has often come to be invoked as a case of reborn corporatism (Hemerijck 1995; Visser 1997; cf. also Rhodes 1997). Even in Sweden, a new consensus around coordinated industry-level bargaining appears to have emerged in the mid-1990s. Although the unions have abandoned their calls to reinstitute peak-level bargaining, employer advocates of decentralization seem to have abandoned the idea that wage bargaining might be organized exclusively on firm basis. The Dutch case, however, suggests that this political consensus does not necessarily preclude further decentralization of wage-bargaining practices. According to Jelle Visser (1997), "while it was fifteen years ago possible to evaluate the content of collective agreements on the

3 Traxler's (1995b) summary of recent changes within Austria's system of coordinated industry-level bargaining echoes Thelen's discussion of Germany.

basis of a few leading ones . . . , since they all copied each other, this is no longer the case. Moreover, many agreements are now concluded for two, three, sometimes even four years, upsetting any common timing in the negotiations."

In characterizing Austria as a case of "organized decentralization," Traxler (1995b) distinguishes the experience of Austria and other corporatist countries from that of countries like the United States and the UK, which he refers to as cases of "disorganized decentralization." In the corporatist countries, we observe changes in relations among different bargaining levels within a system of collective bargaining that remains highly institutionalized and encompassing. In the United States and the UK, by contrast, the decentralization of wage bargaining has been associated with a generalized decline of associational governance of labor markets. This conceptualization enables us to move beyond the debate over convergence or, in Wallerstein and Golden's words, "uniform trends," for it becomes possible to speak of decentralization of wage bargaining as a more or less common trend among advanced capitalist countries while recognizing different starting points and different forms of decentralization.

As Traxler's distinction between organized and disorganized decentralization corresponds rather closely to Soskice's distinction between coordinated and liberal market economics, we might say that organized decentralization represents the dominant pattern of institutional change in coordinated market economies.[4] At the same time, it is important to recognize that the degree of change differs among both coordinated and liberal market economies. In terms of wage-bargaining practices, Sweden, Denmark, Belgium, and the Netherlands have certainly undergone more change (more decentralization) than Germany, Austria, or Switzerland, let alone Norway and Finland. Because they have always been characterized by a more fragmented process of wage formation, liberal market economies are less comparable to each other in these terms, but in general, it seems fair to say that recent changes represent a more radical departure from the postwar system in the UK than in the United States. Also, it is clear that decentralization has been more far-reaching in New Zealand than in Australia, and that stability characterizes Canada by comparison to the United States.

Again, these considerations suggest a modified convergence thesis. As a working hypothesis, we want to propose that there is trend toward convergence on the German model of coordinated industry-level bargaining among the coordinated market economies (the corporatist countries of North-Central Europe) and, similarly, a trend toward convergence on the dual American model of firm-level bargaining and a large non-union sector among the liberal market economies (the Anglo-Saxon countries). For each set of countries, there are some

---

4 With the exception of Japan, the countries that Soskice designates as coordinated market economies are the same countries that political scientists typically designate as "corporatist political economies" (e.g., Katzenstein 1985).

cases (Norway and Finland for the coordinated market economies, Australia for the liberal market economies) that buck the trend, and these exceptions need to be explained, but the principal analytical challenge is to explain the pressures for change (convergence) within the two sets of advanced capitalist political economies, as well as the persistence of divergence between them. As indicated already, the empirical focus of the present volume is on convergence among coordinated market economies and on the contrast between coordinated market economies that have undergone major changes and those characterized by institutional stability.

Trade-union membership trends deserves some brief discussion in this context. As Harry Katz (1993) suggests, deunionization can be seen as the most extreme form of decentralization, since, in the absence of any collective representation, wages will be set at the lowest possible level (direct "bargaining" between the firm and individual employees). Table 1.1 provides an overview of the evolution of union density in 19 OECD countries from 1970 to 1993. In 13 of these countries, we observe a decline of union density since its peak, which usually occurred between 1975 and 1981. In Belgium, the decline was quite small (5.9%), and this could perhaps be said of Germany (11.5%) and Ireland (14.6%) as well, but in many countries, union density has declined by about one-third and, in France, it has declined by nearly two-thirds.[5] Does trade-union decline constitute a common trend across OECD countries? Suffice it to note here that the six countries that have not experienced any decline of union density (Norway, Canada, Denmark, Sweden, Finland, and Spain) together account for only 10 percent of the total OECD labor force.

Among liberal market economies, there would appear to be a fairly consistent association between the decline of union density and decentralization of wage bargaining and, more generally, deregulation of labor markets, but this is decidedly not the case for coordinated market economies. Among the latter, we find two cases, Sweden and Denmark, that combine decentralization of wage-bargaining practices with continued union membership growth and, on the other hand, several cases, most obviously Austria and Switzerland, that combine institutional stability with significant union membership losses. Whereas in the United States and the UK, unionization and the scope of multiemployer bargaining are closely tied to each other, legal arrangements that provide for the extension of collective contracts to non-union members constitute a prominent feature of industrial relations in many continental European countries, such as Austria and Switzerland (see OECD 1994, 1997). These arrangements have clearly been a source of institutional stability. As for the Scandinavian cases, their distinctive combination of decentralization and union membership growth

---

5 It is a bit awkward to speak of a percentage change in union density, since union density is itself a percentage, but this is unavoidable: Clearly, a decline of 2 percentage points would have a very different meaning for Sweden (with union density at 90.5%) than France (8.8%).

Table 1.1. *Union density (employed union members as percentage of employed labor force) in OECD countries, 1970–93*

	1970	Peak	Most recent	% change since 1970	% change since peak
France	22.0	22.5 (1975)	8.8 (1992)	−60.0%	−60.9%
New Zealand[a]		54.1 (1986)	30.0 (1993)		−44.5
United States	27.3	27.3 (1970)	15.3 (1993)	−44.0	−44.0
Netherlands	38.0	38.5 (1975)	25.5 (1993)	−32.9	−33.8
Australia	44.2	51.0 (1976)	35.0 (1994)	−20.8	−31.4
Austria	62.2	62.2 (1970)	43.2 (1992)	−30.5	−30.5
Japan	34.7	34.7 (1970)	24.2 (1993)	−30.3	−30.3
UK	44.8	51.8 (1977)	36.3 (1993)	−19.0	−29.9
Switzerland	28.3	33.7 (1976)	25.7 (1992)	−9.2	−23.7
Italy	36.3	49.9 (1978)	38.8 (1992)	+6.9	−22.2
Ireland	53.1	57.6 (1981)	49.2 (1992)	−7.3	−14.6
Germany[b]	33.0	37.5 (1981)	33.2 (1993)	+0.6	−11.5
Belgium	45.5	56.2 (1981)	52.9 (1992)	+16.3	−5.9
Norway	54.9		58.1 (1993)	+5.8	0.0
Canada[c]	31.0		37.4 (1993)	+20.6	0.0
Denmark	60.0		76.3 (1993)	+27.2	0.0
Sweden	67.7		90.5 (1993)	+34.7	0.0
Finland	51.4		80.5 (1993)	+56.6	0.0
Spain[d]	12.5		22.0 (1993)	+76.0	0.0

[a]Many years are missing from the New Zealand data: the real peak and the decline since the peak may have been greater than indicated here.
[b]The 1970 and 1981 figures refer to West Germany; the 1993 figure, to unified Germany.
[c]Union membership figures include retired union members; hence Canadian density ratios are not strictly comparable to those of other countries (but rates of change over time are comparable).
[d]For Spain, the benchmark (first column) is 1980 rather than 1970.
Source: Jelle Visser, "Unionisation trends revisited," Centre for Research for European Societies and Industrial Relations, Amsterdam, research paper 1996/2 (February 1996).

might be conceived in terms of an implicit compromise between unions and employers. Arguably, the unions have conceded to employer demands for more decentralized bargaining arrangements and more wage flexibility (wage differentiation) in return for continued employer support for unions and collective bargaining, including the continuation of checkoff arrangements whereby employers collect membership dues on behalf the unions.

WAGE BARGAINING AND ECONOMIC PERFORMANCE

The picture of how wage-bargaining practices have changed presented above poses a noteworthy challenge to Lars Calmfors and John Driffill's (1988) well-known analysis of the relationship between bargaining centralization and economic performance. Calmfors and Driffill posit a U-shaped relationship between centralization and performance, predicting that the performance of countries where wages are determined at the firm level or at the national (peak) level will be superior to that of countries where wages are primarily determined at the industry level. Essentially, their argument is that workers/unions do not have the capacity to alter the market determination of wages as long as bargaining is restricted to the firm level (and firms operate in competitive markets) and that national union leaders have an incentive to take the inflationary and unemployment-producing effects of their wage demands into account. When wages are set at the industry level, unions have the power to create wage-push inflation, and have little incentive to avoid doing so.

Presumably, Calmfors and Driffill had the UK in mind as the perfect example of an intermediately centralized system, combining the worst features of centralization and decentralization, but Germany also falls into this category, and so do Austria and Switzerland and, arguably, Japan as well.[6] Based on Calmfors and Driffill's reasoning, we would expect these countries to have experienced high wage inflation and, as a consequence, institutional instability.[7] With the possible exception of the UK, which perhaps did not belong in the intermediate category to begin with, this expectation is not borne out by recent developments. On the contrary, intermediately centralized systems appear to have been more stable than either centralized systems or decentralized systems.

Soskice (1990, this volume) argues that Calmfors and Driffill's concept of centralization fails to capture the features of wage-bargaining systems that are crucial to macroeconomic outcomes and results in misleading categorizations of countries. For Soskice, the crucial issue is the ability of collective actors, especially employers, to coordinate their behavior across sectors of the economy, and such coordination need not necessarily involve peak-level bargaining. (Coordinating capacity may also vary considerably among countries with industry-level bargaining.) For Soskice, the stability of the German and Austrian wage-bargaining systems is not at all puzzling: highly coordinated, these systems have performed very well in containing inflationary wage pressures. Likewise,

---

6 Undoubtedly influenced by the corporatism literature, Calmfors and Driffill mistakenly code Austria as a highly centralized bargaining system, and Japan and Switzerland as very decentralized ones. A new consensus about these cases has emerged in recent literature: See Traxler (1992), Wallerstein, Golden, and Lange (1996), Iversen (this volume), and Pontusson (this volume).

7 With some qualifications, this also applies to Alvarez, Garrett, and Lange's (1991) analysis.

high performance in Switzerland and Japan is not the result of decentralization but rather of effective coordination.

Soskice's discussion raises the question whether the (organized) decentralization of wage bargaining that we observe in countries such as Sweden and Denmark really represents such an important change. After all, Swedish and Danish unions and employers retain very significant coordinating capacities. The question of how the outcomes of informally coordinated industry-level (or firm-level) bargaining differs from those of centralized bargaining is addressed most explicitly by Iversen's and Pontusson's contributions to this volume. Both chapters argue that the implications of these different forms of coordination are primarily distributive. Exemplifying "covert coordination by employer organizations alone" (Pestoff 1995:171), the Japanese case is comparable to that of more centralized Northern European systems with respect to the trade-off between inflation and employment, but Japan's performance with respect to wage-distributive outcomes (gender differentials and intersectoral differentials) is very different indeed. The relative utility of "coordination" and "centralization" as conceptual categories, then, depends on exactly what it is that we want to explain.

MACROECONOMIC POLICY REGIMES

Most analyses of wage-bargaining structures and processes, including analyses of their consequences for economic performance, treat wage setting either in isolation from macroeconomic policy-making or as embedded in a macroeconomic context that is exogenously given. Soskice (this volume) shows, for example, that the Calmfors–Driffill model implicitly assumes that the central bank follows a nonaccommodating monetary rule. This assumption is presumably justified by the so-called money neutrality thesis, which states that "nominal" variables, such as the quantity of money, are irrelevant for explaining "real" variables, such as equilibrium rates of unemployment. As Soskice explains, in the new classical model any incentive that the monetary authority has to inflate will rationally be anticipated by workers and firms, who will set their wages and prices accordingly. Since economic agents only care about real outcomes, they simply adapt their nominal behavior to the anticipated level of inflation. Crucially, however, this logic assumes that wage–price decisions are made at the firm level, where individual wage contracts have no effect on the general price level – an assumption that is deliberately abandoned in the Calmfors–Driffill model.

If wages (and by implication prices) are set above the firm level, agreements will have at least *some* effect on the general price level, and monetary policies will consequently influence the capacity of unions and employers to externalize wage costs. From Calmfors and Driffill's own model we know that capacity for cost externalization is important for real-wage behavior and unemployment. As Soskice would have it, the monetary rule determines the extent to which union wage behavior affects the real money supply (demand), and hence the incentive for unions to exercise restraint (see also Iversen 1998; Soskice and Iversen forthcoming). When we leave the world of perfect competition – or at least a world of highly fragmented forms of bargaining – it is therefore no longer justified to treat monetary policies as an exogenous variable in the wage-bargaining game. By the same token, the effects of monetary policies cannot be understood without paying attention to the conditioning influences of wage-bargaining structures and processes. In short, wage bargaining and monetary policy-making interact.[8]

If this thesis is correct, macroeconomic regimes should have behavioral, and possibly also institutional, consequences for the wage-bargaining process. It is therefore of considerable interest to the analysis of wage bargaining that monetary regimes vary significantly across countries and time. According to one often used indicator for the orientation of monetary policies – central bank independence – the European countries represent a wide range of regime types, ranging from politically controlled, and presumably accommodating, central banks in countries such Italy, Belgium, and Sweden, to highly independent, and presumably non accommodating, banks in countries such as Germany, the Netherlands, and Switzerland.[9] Of course, central bank independence, like wage-bargaining centralization, is merely one of several useful indicators for the character of the macroeconomic regime, and it is not a very helpful one in analyzing changes in policy regimes over time. Changes in monetary policy priorities do not immediately translate into formal institutional structures. Indeed, a broad policy consensus and a strong reputation may make formal changes in central bank statutes altogether unnecessary.[10] Considering the fundamental reorientation of economic policy priorities that many countries undertook in the 1980s, the limitations of existing indices of central bank autonomy are severe.

Table 1.2 shows that as governments became increasingly concerned with price stability, interest rates rose sharply and a very notable reduction in inflation rates occurred in the 1980s. Belgium, Italy, Norway, and Sweden are partial

---

8 The underlying economic reason for real wage behavior being affected by monetary policy regimes is that large unions can have an effect on the real money supply when the monetary authority is not completely accommodating. See Iversen (1998), and Soskice and Iversen (forthcoming) for details.
9 Central bank indices typically combine information about the capacity of banks to make autonomous decisions, the scope of their control over monetary policy instruments, and the extent to which their mandate emphasizes low inflation over other policy goals. See Cukierman (1992) and Grilli, Masciandoro, and Tabellini (1991) for the most widely used indices.
10 Japan is good example of this: Although the Bank of Japan is usually coded as highly dependent, monetary authorities began to adhere to an unambiguously nonaccommodating role after 1973. See Cargil, Hutchison, and Ito (1997).

Table 1.2. *Background data on economic policies and outcomes, 1973–95*

	Real interest rates[a]			Inflation[b]			Change in deficit[c]			Unemployment[d]		
	73–79	80–89	90–95	73–79	80–89	90–95	73–79	80–89	90–95	73–79	80–89	90–95
Austria	2.3	4.4	4.4	6.5	3.8	3.2	−0.5	0.1	−0.4	1.5	3.7	5.5
Britain	4.9	6.3	4.7	8.3	4.9	4.4	0.1	0.4	−1.0	5.8	10.8	9.1
Belgium	−6.2	3.2	5.8	14.8	7.4	2.6	−0.5	0.6	0.2	4.7	10.0	8.3
Canada	−0.0	5.2	6.3	9.0	6.5	2.7	−0.2	0.2	−0.1	6.9	9.3	10.1
Denmark	3.1	6.8	6.5	10.6	6.9	2.1	−1.0	0.6	−0.2	4.8	8.9	8.5
Finland	−2.7	2.8	8.3	12.5	7.3	2.9	−0.9	0.3	−1.6	4.1	4.9	12.8
France	−0.9	4.4	5.8	10.2	7.4	2.4	0.0	0.1	−0.4	4.3	9.0	10.7
Germany	2.9	4.6	4.3	5.0	2.9	3.4	−0.5	0.4	−0.5	2.9	5.9	5.6
Italy	−3.9	3.2	6.8	15.9	11.3	5.2	−1.1	0.4	0.9	6.5	9.5	10.7
Japan	−2.4	4.0	3.1	10.3	2.5	1.7	−0.6	0.7	−1.1	1.8	2.5	2.5
Netherlands	1.3	5.4	5.1	7.3	2.9	2.7	−0.8	0.1	0.2	4.5	9.7	6.6
Norway	−1.0	4.0	5.8	8.5	8.4	2.7	−0.4	−0.2	0.6	1.7	2.8	5.5
Sweden	−0.2	4.1	4.8	9.3	7.9	5.5	−1.3	1.0	−1.9	2.0	2.7	6.6
Switzerland	0.3	1.3	1.8	4.7	3.3	3.5	−0.2	0.2	−0.3	0.3	0.6	3.7
United States	−0.3	5.1	3.7	8.2	5.5	3.5	0.0	−0.1	0.0	6.4	7.2	5.4
Average	**−0.2**	**4.3**	**5.1**	**9.4**	**5.9**	**3.2**	**−0.6**	**0.3**	**−0.4**	**3.9**	**6.5**	**7.3**
Std. deviation	2.8	1.3	1.6	2.0	1.4	1.0	0.4	0.3	0.7	1.6	1.8	1.4

[a] Average yearly yield on government bonds minus inflation IMF (various years). *International Financial Statistics Yearbook.* Washington DC.: IMF.

[b] Average annual change in the consumer price index OECD. Various years. *OECD Economic Outlook.* Paris: OECD.

[c] Average yearly change in the general government financial (before 1978) or primary balances (from 1978) (*OECD Economic Outlook*).

[d] Standardized unemployment rates (whenever available) (*OECD Economic Outlook*). For Denmark and Switzerland standardized rates are available for only 1993–95, whereas no standardized data are available for Austria.

exceptions to this pattern in that inflation remained relatively high, while interest rates were below average through the 1980s. In the first half of the 1990s, however, all OECD countries experienced convergence, not simply a parallel movement, toward a very low level of inflation. In terms of fiscal policy, expanding public deficits during the 1970s were followed by a period of consolidation in the 1980s. This turnaround was particularly dramatic in Denmark, Belgium, and Italy, where debt accumulation had been very substantial during the 1970s, but consolidation also occurred with force in Japan and Sweden. The only two countries that increased public deficits (or reduced surpluses) in the 1980s were Norway and the United States. Of these, only Norway can be said to have conformed to a Keynesian pattern by supporting the expansion with relatively lax monetary polices. Concerning the 1990s, the figures are not entirely comparable to the previous periods because they cover a downturn in the international business cycle (while the previous periods includes both up- and downturns), but it appears that some relaxation in fiscal, though not monetary, policy took place.

The overall impression from the data is that the 1980s were associated with convergence in fiscal, and especially monetary, policies to a considerably more restrictive regime, while the 1990s saw a certain relaxation and diversification in fiscal policies (see the figures for standard deviations at the bottom of Table 1.2). The divergence in fiscal policies, however, can be largely attributed to the kick-in of "automatic stabilizers" in Finland and Sweden, where unemployment rose dramatically, and to a very considerable consolidation of public finances in Norway and Italy (in the latter case as a result of trying to meet the Maastricht criteria for monetary union). Cross-national variation in unemployment increased from the 1970s to the 1980s, and then returned to the level of the 1970s. So while monetarist policies seem to have triumphed everywhere – causing a considerable convergence in interest and inflation rates – countries continue to diverge sharply in terms of real economic variables. The interaction of macroeconomic regimes with wage-bargaining institutions and practices provides a plausible explanation of this divergence.

A closer look at specific country experiences reveals a pattern that supports this general idea, although there is obviously room for disagreement about particular cases and the broader theoretical implications of these patterns. In the case of Britain, macroeconomic policies failed both before and after the "regime shift" of 1979 for reasons that are clearly related to the organization of wage bargaining. Under Labour governments in the 1970s, traditional countercyclical fiscal policies were associated with accelerating inflation, and attempts to deal with the problem by negotiated wage restraint in exchange for employment and social policy commitments (the "Social Contracts") failed. In some measure, at least, this had to do with the inability of the labor confederation (TUC) to enforce wage restraint among its members, as well as the government's dereliction in making good on either its employment or social policy promises (Regini 1984; Scharpf 1991:ch. 5). Neo-liberal policies under the Conservative government, however, did little to improve economic conditions. Although the government succeeded in weakening unions organizationally and politically, and despite fiscal retrenchment and an explicit commitment to monetarism, growth rates remained low and unemployment rose to even higher levels. The only lasting effect of the Conservative policy seems to have been a substantial rise in wage and income inequality (Hall 1986:ch. 5; Pontusson, this volume).

The British experience with monetarism is not universal, however. This is perhaps best seen if we compare the British case to the experience of Japan in the wake of the first oil crisis. If anything, the oil shock was more traumatic in Japan than in Britain. Accustomed to double-digit real growth rates, low inflation, and labor shortages, Japan saw growth rates drop below zero in 1974, wholesale price inflation increase to more than 31 percent, and labor redundancies emerging everywhere, although "disguised" inside large companies committed to lifetime employment (Pempel 1982:105–7). As in Britain, one of the core problems in the Japanese economy was the speed with which unions updated their inflation expectations, as well as their capacity to press for compensating wage increases. The Japanese case clearly diverges from the British, however, in terms of the effects of the deflationary monetary program that was put in place after 1974 (following a short period of failed price controls). Not only was inflation successfully brought under control, but real wages simultaneously started to adjust downward to a level that was compatible with full employment. The price–wage restraint observed in the annual collective bargaining rounds in the years following the policy reversal seems to have been the key to its success. While the dominant export-oriented employers, organized in the Federation of Economic Organizations and the Japan Federation of Employers' Associations, adopted a much more aggressive bargaining position, wage moderation gradually carried the day among the unions, led by the steel and the metalworking industries (Pempel 1982:104). In Japan, monetarism accomplished what a similar policy was unable to achieve in the UK. Again, the organization of wage bargaining seems to be the key to this contrast.

In the European context, the case that comes closest to a successful conversion to monetarism is probably Denmark (although the Dutch case is very similar). After a decade of largely failed attempts by a social democratic government to coordinate wage and economic policies centrally, a reform-minded bourgeois coalition government (coming to power in 1982) embarked on a new policy course by pegging the currency to the deutschmark, liberalizing capital markets, and initiating a radical program of fiscal retrenchment. The effect of these policies was a gradual reduction of inflation and (real) interest rates. Led by the metalworking industries, wages were held competitive in a reformed and more decentralized bargaining system, and when such restraint was coupled with the expansionary effect of lower interest rates, the policy produced a remarkable recovery of the Danish economy, expanding employment by nearly 10 percent from 1983 and 1988 (Iversen and Thygesen 1998).

These examples of successful "monetarist conversion" lead us to the German case, where the practice of monetarism has a long history. As documented by Fritz Scharpf (1984, 1991), Keynesianism never really took hold in Germany after the Second World War due to a combination of public fear of hyperinflation and the "institutionalization" of these fears through the creation of one of the world's most independent central banks. Although restrictive fiscal policies were not always applied with conviction, the government could usually count on the central bank to do the job. The only partial exception to this rule came during the Concerted Action period (1967–77), when the bank was placed under pressure to coordinate its monetary policies with fiscal and wage policies (Scharpf 1991:chs. 9–10). But when it came to a real test in 1974, as widespread strikes broke out in the public sector, the bank responded with an aggressive deflationary program, and this pattern was repeated after the second oil shock (Scharpf 1991:128–30; Goodman 1992; Soskice, this volume). What is noteworthy about these episodes (and similar to the situation that came to prevail in Japan) is that employers and unions seem to have learned from history and adopted more moderate wage–price strategies (cf. Hall 1994). Without doubt, such moderation contributed to the good economic performance in Germany during most of the 1980s, when unemployment rates stayed well below the European average.

But there are clearly also significant drawbacks to German-style monetarism. In the short and medium term, breakdown of coordination can have very substantial costs, as illustrated by the events following German unification. In this case, expansionary fiscal policies tempted unions to be more aggressive and simultaneously triggered a deflationary response by the central bank, which caused not only a sharp rise in unemployment, but also turmoil within the European Exchange Rate Mechanism. These are rather exceptional circumstances, but the deleterious effects of restrictive monetary policies can reach beyond the short and medium term and turn into structural economic problems, when they occur in an international trading system with integrated capital markets. The explanation for this is laid out in the contribution by Soskice, and it involves an international collective-action problem.

When a large country like Germany deflates, real exchange and interest rates in that country will rise, while other countries' trade balance with Germany will deteriorate. With integrated capital markets the combination of these effects will trigger an outflow of short-term capital from other countries into Germany. For governments in the deutschmark-dominated currency area, the only way for governments to arrest such an outflow is to raise interest rates and thus unemployment. In turn, this will cause budget deficits to rise and these deficits to be met with fiscal retrenchment to prevent a further increase in interest rates. The budgetary restraint has been particularly severe in countries trying to meet the Maastricht convergence criteria. The international contagion effects of fiscal contraction will lead to another round of deflation, and so on, until the entire system reaches a new, higher unemployment, equilibrium. Small individual countries, such as Denmark and the Netherlands, may buck the trend by essentially undercutting wages in larger countries, but the only means to restore full employment to the whole system would be to instigate a coordinated expansion of demand – something that has thus far proved infeasible.

Of course, restrictive German policies in the 1980s were themselves partly a response to the sharp rise in U.S. interest and exchange rates following the tightening of Federal Reserve policies in 1978. As deflationary policies spread from the United States and Germany to other large countries like Britain and Japan, international contagion effects from capital flows made it difficult or considerably more costly for other countries to pursue expansionary policies. The reversal of French macroeconomic policies in the early 1980s is perhaps the most dramatic example. Elected on a full-employment platform, the Socialist government embarked on expansionary macroeconomic policies in the expectation of an imminent international economic recovery. When that premise failed to materialize, and when three consecutive devaluations proved insufficient to reverse a growing current account deficit, the government soon faced the choice between leaving the Exchange Rate Mechanism of the European Monetary System (EMS) and imposing draconian capital controls or of reversing macroeconomic policies to make the French macroeconomy compatible with continued membership in the EMS.

As we all know, the French government chose the latter option, and most economists would probably agree that this was the only viable choice at the time. Yet the fate of the French strategy seems to have been sealed as much by a lack of appropriate institutions for controlling wages and prices as by the internationalization of financial markets. The Swedish experience illustrates this point nicely. Compared to France, occasional currency devaluations in the mid-1970s and early 1980s had been followed by negotiated wage restraint, which prolonged the competitive effect of the devaluations and helped diffuse speculative attacks on the currency (which were also made more difficult by relatively extensive financial market controls). The "Third Way" strategy adopted by the Social Democratic government in 1982, for example, involved a large currency devaluation designed to improve competitiveness (which had been lacking from the expansionary fiscal policy in France) while simultaneously restoring full employment (which had been undermined by monetarist policies in Britain). Though the strategy was guided by a commitment to full employment, and although it presupposed considerable exchange controls, it was not Keynesian in origin: Rather it was aimed at facilitating real-wage adjustment, and was therefore perfectly consistent with a restrictive fiscal policy stance (Martin 1979; Pontusson 1992).

Like German policy, the Swedish policy was thus directed at the supply side, but in Sweden monetary policies involved a coordinated accommodation to union wage strategies. Only since 1991 has monetary policy turned in a decidedly nonaccommodating direction, while the collapse of the centralized bargaining system has ended all pretenses to coordinate wage and macroeconomic policies. Although the currency has been depreciating after the failed attempt to peg it to the ECU in 1991, inflation has been brought down from a level exceeding the German rate by more than 5 percent (during the 1980s) to a level that is now below the German (which currently stands at 1.4%). Yet, having liberalized capital markets during the 1980s, Sweden is paying a price for past inflationary policies in the form of a long-term interest rate premium that currently amounts to several hundred basis points. The government is clearly trying hard to establish credibility for an antiinflationary policy to eliminate this premium. This includes a de facto strengthening of the power of the central bank over monetary policies, plus legislative initiatives to formalize central bank autonomy. Sweden is becoming another player in the European process of competitive deflation.

The cases of changing macroeconomic policies and outcomes discussed above do not support any simple "linear" interpretation of the relationship between institutions, policies, and outcomes. This impression is confirmed by looking at more quantitative indicators for a larger sample of countries. For example, although the average score for 15 countries on Iversen's time-sensitive index of wage-bargaining centralization (presented in his contribution to this volume) is strongly negatively related to unemployment over time ($r = -.78$ for the period 1973–93), the cross-national relationship is much weaker ($r = -.4$) and exhibits no obvious pattern (such as the hump-shape predicted by Calmfors and Driffill 1988). An even more striking result emerges if we consider the relationship between inflation and unemployment. Across time there is a very strong negative correlation between the two variables ($r = -.81$), but when we look at the cross-national pattern the relationship is actually reversed, although relatively weak ($r = .46$). The shift in macroeconomic priorities in most OECD countries over the 1980s has thus been associated with a general rise in unemployment, which can be explained by Soskice's contagion logic, but several countries have been relatively successful in combining low inflation with low unemployment.

Noting this "reversed Phillips curve" phenomenon more than a decade ago, David Cameron (1984) was too quick to attribute it to corporatism. As Table 1.2 shows, some of the most corporatist countries – Sweden, Norway, and Finland in particular – have performed poorly in terms of inflation since 1980. In fact, the relationship between centralization and inflation is U-shaped with countries such as Sweden, Norway, and Finland performing no better than liberal market economies such as Italy and Britain, and much worse than intermediately centralized ones such as Austria, Switzerland, Germany, and the

Netherlands. In this respect, new classical theory seemingly does a much better explanatory job since there is a strong negative link between a composite index of central bank independence – as an indicator for the monetary regime – and inflation ($r = -.74$).

New classical economic theory also receives some scattered support for the notion that heavy regulation of labor and product markets, and a high social wage, inhibit the expansion of employment while increasing unemployment. Thus, Richard Layard, Stephen Nickell, and Richard Jackman (1991) find that generous unemployment benefits tend to lengthen unemployment spells, and a recent OECD study suggests that egalitarian social policies contribute unemployment (OECD 1994). Iversen and Anne Wren (1998) have detected a negative relationship between wage equality and private service-sector employment, and Andrew Glyn (1997) has similarly documented a trade-off between wage equality and total work time. Yet, during the 1970s and into the 1980s, countries with highly regulated labor and product markets – Austria, Sweden, Norway, and Germany in particular – performed as well as (or better than) countries that followed a strategy of deregulation and labor market flexibilization (such as Britain and the United States). Moreover, although the politics of the welfare state has shifted from one of expansion to one of retrenchment, social spending has proven quite resilient to rollback, at least until recently.[11] Again, the effects of social policies seem to be period-specific and conditional on particular policies and institutions.

INSTITUTIONAL INTERACTION

A central claim in this volume is that "linear" models fail because they are not sufficiently attentive to the consequences of institutional interactions. Political economies are complex systems of interlocking institutions that mutually reinforce and condition the effects of each other. But recognizing this is not the same thing as saying that there are no systematic patterns. For example, it appears to be a precondition for a monetarist strategy to "work" – in terms of simultaneously producing low inflation and low unemployment – that wage bargainers be sufficiently "large" – in the sense of their behavior having macroeconomic effects – for the responses of monetary policymakers to be rationally taken into account in the bargaining process. The contrast between the relatively "benign" experiences of Japan and Germany, on the one hand, and the relatively acrimonious experiences of Britain and France, on the other, is instructive in this respect.

On the other hand, for highly centralized bargaining systems in countries

---

11 Pierson (1994, 1996) emphasizes the resilience of the welfare state; see Clayton and Pontusson (1998) for a different, less sanguine assessment of recent trends.

where solidaristic wage policies have historically played an important role, the "discipline" of strict monetarist policy rules appears to be not only unnecessary, but potentially harmful to the achievement of effective real-wage restraint as well as the successful reconciliation of conflicting distributive interests within the confederated union structure. During the 1970s and 1980s, Sweden successfully used an accommodating exchange-rate policy to achieve a downward real-wage adjustment, even though it paid a price in terms of inflation. This success contrasts with the experience of the 1970s in Denmark, where inflationary pressures in the centralized bargaining system collided with relatively restrictive exchange rate policies.

It is also conceivable that wage-bargaining institutions and macroeconomic regimes are causally related (Soskice this volume; Iversen this volume). Both Denmark and Sweden experienced a tightening of monetary policies when they went from highly centralized to more decentralized forms of bargaining, and in Denmark decentralization may itself have been precipitated by insufficient exchange rate flexibility. We do not want to take this idea too far, however. Both wage bargaining and monetary policy-making constitute partially autonomous institutional arenas, and they respond to forces of change that are exogenous to the interaction between these arenas. For example, the introduction of new technology and work organization has undoubtedly been important for changes in the form of wage bargaining, as argued by Swenson and Pontusson (this volume), and capital market integration has surely also affected the capacity for governments to pursue flexible and accommodating monetary policies. In addition, we do not claim that there is consensus in the literature, or in this volume, about the best way to conceptualize the interaction between wage bargaining and macroeconomic policy-making. Indeed, one of the purposes of this volume is to present this diversity of views.

One view is represented by the contribution by Franzese and Hall (this volume), who argue that central bank independence is only compatible with *both* low inflation *and* low unemployment when wage bargaining is highly coordinated (as in Germany). The reason is that wage bargainers are much more prone to pay heed to the threats of a central bank not to accommodate inflationary wage bargains if they know that their behavior has an appreciable effect on the price level and the actions of the central bank. In uncoordinated systems, by contrast, the signals from central bankers become "noisy" because the number of bargaining areas, and hence the sources of inflation, multiply, and because individual bargainers cannot rationally expect their wages to influence the behavior of other bargainers or the central bank. To hedge against such uncertainty, each bargainer in uncoordinated systems demands a wage "premium" that will be inflationary in the aggregate. If the bank therefore embarks on restrictive policies, the result will be higher unemployment.

The capacity for strategic behavior is also essential to the arguments of Iversen and Soskice. Like Franzese and Hall, Iversen argues that independent central banks are associated with good employment performance only if wage negotiators can rationally anticipate that their own actions will influence the behavior of the monetary authority. In fact, there may be a positive deterrence effect of a credible commitment to an nonaccommodating policy because wage bargainers will know in advance that higher wages cannot be externalized through higher prices (see also Soskice, this volume). In contrast to Franzese – Hall and Soskice, Iversen identifies a countervailing effect that is a result of unions pursuing egalitarian wage objectives. In the presence of "wage drift" (i.e., wage increases exceeding bargained rates) such distributive preferences shape not only the structure of wage demands but also overall wage claims. Specifically, because solidaristic wage policies systematically reduce the relative wages of high-paid workers – when market forces would not – wage drift tends to favor better-paid workers. Anticipating this, confederal union leaders will seek to counteract the inequalizing effects of drift by raising bargained wages, thereby increasing nominal wage pressure (see also Hibbs and Locking 1996; Calmfors 1993). Since the strength of this effect is rising with the heterogeneity of groups subjected to the same agreement, centralized and "encompassing" bargaining tends to be associated with higher nominal wage pressure. If the monetary authority refuses to accommodate such pressure, the result will be higher unemployment. Iversen consequently distinguishes between two "models" of coordinated wage bargaining systems: the German(ic) model of "monetarist" coordination of industry-level bargaining, and the Swedish model of coordination through peak-level accommodation. This distinction may help us to understand why highly centralized systems tend to be more inflationary than intermediately centralized systems (contrary to the prediction by Calmfors and Driffill), but also why the Nordic countries, especially Norway, Sweden, and Finland, refrained from adopting restrictive monetary regimes until very recently.

Switching the causal arrows, Martin (this volume) suggests that macroeconomic policy decisions in the 1980s – in essence, an excessively expansionary policy stance – contributed significantly to the decentralization of wage bargaining in Sweden. Iversen and Martin thus diverge on the issue of which comes first – change in wage-bargaining arrangements or change in macroeconomic policy – but more importantly, perhaps, they also disagree on what kind of macroeconomic regime fits best with decentralized wage bargaining. In Iversen's (1996) account of the Danish case, macroeconomic policy change paved the way for decentralization of wage bargaining, as it did in Martin's account of the Swedish case, but it was the turn to a hard-currency stance (and central bank independence) that generated this effect rather than macroeconomic expansion.

Whereas Iversen's interpretation hinges on the proposition that employers do not need to engage in peak-level bargaining with unions to secure wage restraint under a nonaccommodating macroeconomic regime, Martin's interpretation states that rapid expansion of demand and high corporate profits lead to intensified employer competition for labor, and hence decentralization. Both claims are plausible; taken together, they suggest that the relationship between wage bargaining and macroeconomic regimes is complex, and perhaps contradictory.

PRESSURES FOR CHANGE

This volume features a number of different approaches to the problem of explaining the common trends and cross-national variations that we observe. In terms of research methodologies and evidence, some of the chapters that follow belong to the tradition of qualitative case studies, whereas others engage in quantitative analysis of many OECD countries. As far as causal arguments are concerned, all of our contributions conceive of the politics of institutional stability and change in terms of some form of strategic interaction between political-economic actors with distinct material interests, but they differ in terms of how they conceive the relevant actors and their interests as well as the structural context of their interaction. In short, our contributors share a common research agenda, but not a common explanatory framework, let alone a common explanation of the outcomes we observe. Despite differences in emphasis and argumentation, however, our volume does point to a set of forces of change that might be usefully highlighted and related to existing literature. In this section, we focus on issues pertaining to the structural context or, if you wish, changes in the structure and dynamics of advanced capitalism; in the next section, we address issues pertaining to the actors, their interests, and strategic interaction.

INTERNATIONALIZATION

Many authors who perceive a more or less generalized decline of social democratic corporatism invoke accelerated economic integration among advanced capitalist economies – in particular, the internationalization of capital – as the principal culprit (e.g., Scharpf 1991; Kurzer 1993; Schwartz 1994). We can distinguish several arguments to this effect. First, internationalization can be said to have increased the "exit options" of capital, and thus strengthened its bargaining power relative to both unions and governments. This version of the internationalization thesis implies that social democratic corporatism should first and foremost be understood as an expression of labor power. A different version states that the commonality of interests between labor and capital has diminished as capital has become more mobile and more dependent on world markets. Here the premise is that the politics of class compromise in the postwar period pivoted on domestic demand stimulation. Roughly in this vein, Fritz Scharpf (1991) argues that internationalization sharply restricts the ability of governments to engage in Keynesian macroeconomic management and, as a result, the incentives for unions to exercise wage restraint diminish. Wolfgang Streeck and Philippe Schmitter's (1991) version of the internationalization thesis adds a supranational twist to this reasoning: As politicians seeks to regain political control over market forces, the European Union gains political authority relative to national governments and, for a number of reasons, the institutional configuration of the European Union is much less favorable to labor.

Clearly, it is necessary to distinguish different forms of economic integration or internationalization in this context – specifically, to distinguish between trade and capital mobility. As everyone recognizes, small, trade-dependent economies were the principal breeding ground of social democratic corporatism in the postwar era. Following Katzenstein (1985), the policies and institutional practices associated with social democratic corporatism can been as mechanisms to compensate domestic groups for the disruptive effects of economic openness. By attenuating, if not eliminating, political resistance to competitive adjustment, social democratic corporatism contributed to efficiency improvements and high rates of economic growth. In a slightly different vein, the corporatist countries would appear to be particularly capable of generating collective goods – physical infrastructure, education and training, and so on – that contribute positively to growth (cf. Garrett 1998). If these were indeed competitive advantages of social democratic corporatism 20 years ago, why would this no longer be the case?

The case for internationalization as a pressure for deregulation and reorientation of macroeconomic priorities in the social market economies of North-Central Europe hinges primarily on the effects of capital mobility. Though these economies have traditionally been distinguished by liberal trade policies, they have also been distinguished by relatively stringent capital controls. As Jeffrey Frieden (1995) argues, the removal of capital controls and the integration of financial markets means that governments must choose between monetary policy autonomy and a stable exchange rate. Also, most observers seem to agree that these developments constrain the ability of governments to engage in deficit financing or, more accurately put, increase the costs of government borrowing. The question is whether the consequences of capital mobility account for the apparent retreat from traditional macroeconomic policy priorities in Sweden and other countries.

David Soskice's chapter does not directly address this question, but underscores the contagion effects of deflationary German policies in a fixed exchange rate system with capital mobility. This is important to understand the general rise in European unemployment. Restrictive fiscal and monetary policies in one country have negative externalities in other countries because they reduce demand for exports, thereby raising unemployment and government spending in these countries. Because deficits are punished by capital flight, governments will cut back, thereby reducing demand for foreign goods and triggering further fiscal retrenchment. Countries in a highly interdependent trading system with capital mobility can thus be dragged into a deflationary spiral, with rising unemployment, by a single dominant economy committed to a restrictive policy.

It is less clear that globalization threatens the broader set of institutions associated with social democratic corporatism. Based on an elaborate quantitative analysis of OECD countries over the period 1966–90, Geoffrey Garrett (1998) concludes that it does not. His analysis shows that neither increased trade nor increased capital mobility has diminished the association between, on the one hand, Left control of the government and union strength and, on the other hand, policy priorities and economic outcomes traditionally associated with social democracy (high levels of spending, income redistribution, low rates of unemployment, etc.). In many instances, the association has actually grown stronger over time, along with increased capital mobility. This is an important finding, but it is a finding that speaks primarily to the question of OECD-wide policy convergence, and not directly to the implications of the internationalization of capital for social democratic corporatism. It may be that increased capital mobility is associated with retreat from social spending and expansionary macroeconomic policies everywhere, but more so in countries with Right governments and weak unions. Indeed, there is no reason to suppose that countries with Left governments and strong unions would be *particularly responsive* to the pressure of international financial markets.[12]

As Garrett points out, deficit spending did not use to be a distinctive characteristic of high-spending, social democratic governments in North-Central Europe. At least in Norway and Sweden, social democratic governments actually ran budget surpluses for most years between 1950 and 1970. But this does not mean that their overall macroeconomic policy stance was not expansionary. Rather, these governments relied on low interest rates as the principal instrument to stimulate economic growth, and the relative insularity of domestic financial markets was, arguably, a crucial precondition for this policy. Not only did controls on the export of capital restrict available financial investment opportunities: Perhaps more importantly, the insularity of domestic financial markets was a precondition for the central bank's ability to contain the inflationary effects of low interest rates and to direct credit to targeted sectors, such as housing, through a system of quantitative credit regulation, based on ongoing bargaining with a small number of lending institutions (banks, insurance companies, and public pension funds) with close ties to each other, and deeply embedded in the political system (see Werin 1993).

This point constitutes an important backdrop to Andrew Martin's discus-

---

12 From the point of view adopted here, the interesting question is not how the level of capital mobility affects the association between Left/labor power and "social democratic outcomes," but rather whether and how it is itself associated with "social democratic outcomes." In most of Garrett's regressions, the association is negative. See Swank (1998) for an analysis of how the effects of capital mobility (and other forms of globalization) vary across political–institutional contexts.

sion of Sweden's deregulation of financial markets in the 1980s (this volume). The other chapters on the politics of macroeconomic management also address the effects of internationalization: The loss of monetary policy autonomy figures prominently in Iversen's analysis of recent political realignments in Sweden and Denmark, and the implications of European Monetary Union for unemployment and inflation are examined at some length by Franzese and Hall. The other contributions to our volume do not pursue the causal role of internationalization in any direct or sustained fashion, however. While recognizing the need for further work in this area, we believe that this relative neglect of the forces of internationalization can be justified on two grounds. To begin with, the deregulation of financial markets is, in large measure, a product of policy choices made by governments and hence a part of the political realignments that we seek to explain rather than an exogenous variable that can be invoked to explain these realignments (cf. Notermans 1993). To the extent that the integration of financial markets and increased mobility of financial capital do indeed represent an exogenous force, moreover, these trends would appear to be too pervasive and too uniform to provide much explanatory leverage on the cross-national variations in policy and institutional change that constitute our principal concern in this volume.[13]

DEINDUSTRIALIZATION

Another set of structural changes that figures prominently in the literature on the decline of social democratic corporatism has to do with the growth of service-sector employment at the expense of industrial employment (at least in relative terms) and attendant changes in the occupational structure of employment – broadly, the growth of white-collar employment at the expense of blue-collar employment. As with financial liberalization, one might be tempted to dismiss the causal role of these trends on the grounds that the trends apply to all countries while the nature and extent of political changes differ across countries. But such reasoning, common among political scientists who wish to emphasize the "autonomy of politics," is less compelling in this instance, for the employment trajectories of advanced capitalist economies clearly vary a great deal (cf. Esping-Andersen 1990; Iversen and Wren 1998). At opposite ends of the spectrum, British industrial employment fell from 45.2 percent of total employment in 1968 to 29 percent in 1990 while Japanese industrial employment fell by less than a percentage point over the same period (from 34.6% to 34.1%). Equally important, the extent to which the growth of service employ-

---

13 Garrett's analysis is representative of the emphasis on financial markets, as well as the relative neglect of foreign direct investment in recent discussions of globalization and its effects. Quite possibly, the mobility of productive capital provides more leverage on the problem of understanding different national trajectories, especially in the sphere of industrial relations.

ment occurred under public or private auspices constitutes a major dimension of variation among the OECD countries. In 1990, government employment ranged between 6 percent of total employment in Japan and 31.7 percent in Sweden.[14]

The transition to a "postindustrial economy" may be linked to the decline of centralized wage bargaining or, more generally, social democratic corporatism via changes in societal values. In an article on the decline of corporatism, Streeck (1993:84) summarizes the value shift that apparently occurred in the 1970s and 1980s as follows: "the substantive content of interest conflicts and the focus of policy attention shifted away from class-based lines of cleavage toward a panoply of discrete issues focusing on consumer protection, quality of life, gender, environmental, ethical, and other problems." Much of the literature dealing with this value shift also suggests that the new generation(s) of "postmaterialists" display a distinctive orientation to politics, highly critical of the hierarchical, elite-centered practices associated with corporatism. In identifying such values and political disposition with well-educated service-sector employees, engaged in "people processing" as distinct from "commodity production," Herbert Kitschelt (1994) articulates an important tenet of this literature.[15]

Our volume does not engage the issue of postmaterialism in any systematic fashion, but it should be clear that its contributors are committed to the proposition that the dynamics of change and stability in advanced capitalist political economies can and should be understood in terms of materialist concerns, such as growth, unemployment, inflation, and income distribution. Swenson and Pontusson (this volume) make this point most explicitly, stressing that employers initiated the breakup of centralized bargaining in Sweden in response to changes in technology and market pressures for greater flexibility and productivity. Also, Swenson and Pontusson point out that employers in retail and other service sectors, with a higher proportion of white-collar personnel than industry, were the principal opponents of decentralization within the Swedish employer confederation. In this sense, the Swedish story contradicts the expectations of those who invoke the growth of service employment and postmaterialist values to explain the decline of social democratic corporatism.

We do not wish to deny the significance of changes in the structure of

---

14 Many comparativists end up emphasizing the causal significance of political–institutional variables because they assume that economic structures (or dynamics) are essentially the same across advanced capitalist countries and therefore cannot explain cross-national variations in outcomes. As Pontusson (1995a) argues, this conventional assumption is highly dubious, and the relative significance to be assigned to economic structures and political institutions is an empirical question. Here we are suggesting that "economic structural variables" ought not be lumped together: Some (in this case, employment structure) may vary more than others (e.g., internationalization of finance) on a cross-national basis.

15 In essence, Kitschelt adds an analysis of sectoral–occupational employment structure to Inglehart's (1977, 1990) interpretation of the rise of postmaterialism as a function of societal affluence.

employment; rather, we want to suggest that their significance (for our purposes) does not necessarily or primarily involve the rise of postmaterialist values. The effects of structural change on union density, and hence the bargaining power of unions relative to employers, constitute an alternative and perhaps more important mechanism of causation. In most countries, union density is considerably higher in manufacturing industry than in private services (see OECD 1991), and in some countries, such as the UK, the decline of union density since the late 1970s is largely attributable to "deindustrialization." At the same time, however, public-sector employees tend to be more unionized than private-sector employees, and so the effects of the growth of services on union density very much depend on the sector in which service employment growth occurs. For the 17 OECD countries for which we have union-density data going back to 1970 (see Table 1.1), there is a very strong correlation between change in union density from 1970 to 1993 and change in public-sector employment as a percentage of total employment ($r = .723$).

The fact that the expansion of service employment between 1970 and 1990 primarily occurred in the public sector goes a long way toward explaining the continued growth of union density in the Nordic countries. Arguably, the existence of separate white-collar unions, and white-collar confederations, also facilitated the unionization of new white-collar strata in these countries. Be that as it may, the existence of separate white-collar unions renders the overall picture still more complicated. As Wallerstein and Golden suggest in their contribution to this volume, the growth of service employment in general, and public-sector employment in particular, has been a source of union fragmentation and, by extension, collective-bargaining fragmentation in the Nordic countries. With increases in the number of relevant actors and a decline in the role of the private blue-collar sector (the traditional domain of centralized wage bargaining) in the wage formation process, the politics of coordinated wage restraint have become considerably more complex (cf. Elvander 1988). Looking across the OECD countries, then, we might say that the shift of employment from industry into services has been associated with either decline of union membership or fragmentation of union organization.

For the contributors to this volume, "postindustrialism" does not represent the end of distributional conflict, as the literature on value shifts tends to imply, but rather the emergence of a new set of distributional trade-offs and potential conflicts. The chapter by Geoffrey Garrett and Christopher Way brings this point out most forcefully. Garrett and Way argue that the logic of wage restraint, as conventionally construed in the corporatism literature, does not apply to public-sector workers and unions. Since the level of employment in the public sector is set by political decisions and is only indirectly related to the level of wages, these workers and unions have less incentive to exercise wage restraint. Based on five-year panel data for 13 OECD countries between 1970 and 1993, Garrett and Way's quantitative analysis shows that the strength of public-sector unions, measured by the size of the public sector and by union density in the public sector relative to the private sector, attenuates the association between labor encompassment, low inflation, and low unemployment.

Focusing on the absence of market discipline, Garrett and Way's account of these results raises the question of whether public-sector unions might recognize the need for wage restraint in order to secure long-term political conditions for public-sector expansion (or the maintenance of an already large public sector). Though Garrett and Way leave this question unanswered, their analysis introduces a new and very interesting twist to the debate on internationalization. At the same time as most OECD countries have become increasingly trade dependent, the segment of the labor force that is sheltered from direct international competition may have increased as a result of the shift of employment into services, and especially public services. Arguably, the conflicts of interest among wage earners created by this dual movement represents one of the most important pressures for change in the corporatist political economies of Northern Europe (cf. Swenson 1992).

The size of the public sector also emerges as an important variable in Pontusson's comparative analysis of wage inequality (this volume). Pontusson notes that the expansion of public-sector employment in the 1960s and especially the 1970s coincided with significant compression of wage differentials in most OECD countries and shows that the size of the public sector is associated with wage compression on a cross-national basis. At least during this particular time period, unions in the public sector appear to have been more egalitarian in their approach to wage formation, while public-sector employers were more likely to accommodate wage compression. In the case of employers, they were less constrained by market forces and, at the same time, more subject to egalitarian political pressures. Pontusson also suggests that wage compression in the public sector is likely to spill over into the private sector since public and private employers compete with each other for unskilled labor. If we accept the commonly held view that wage compression tends to be inflationary and may also dampen employment growth,[16] Pontusson's argument about the distinctively egalitarian logic of public-sector bargaining provides a slightly different explanation of Garrett and Way's empirical results than the one they offer.

NEW PRODUCTION PARADIGMS

Swenson and Pontusson's analysis of the Swedish employer offensive points to the introduction of new technologies, work organization, and production strat-

---

16 For instance, Iversen and Wren (1998) argue that the sluggishness of productivity growth in services makes it more difficult to reconcile employment growth and wage compression as economies become more service oriented. On the inflationary consequences of wage compression, see Martin (1985) for a detailed treatment of the Swedish experience of the 1970s, and Flanagan, Soskice, and Ulman (1983) for a broader discussion.

egies – often conceived, *grosso modo*, in terms of "post-Fordism" – as a source of pressure for change in wage bargaining. Swenson and Pontusson argue that these changes have served to shift relative demand for labor in favor of more skilled workers and that Swedish employers in the 1980s became increasingly frustrated by the failure of the existing wage-bargaining system to accommodate the wage differentiation that such a shift entails. Also, Swedish employers wanted to be able to engage in more local and flexible wage setting, so as to offer incentives to individual workers (or worker teams) to acquire new skills and take on new responsibilities. According to Swenson and Pontusson, these considerations help explain the Swedish employer offensive and also shed light on differences among employer associations in their eagerness to pursue decentralization. Specifically, they explain why it was export-oriented engineering firms that led the campaign to decentralize wage bargaining.

Thelen's discussion of German employers (this volume) suggests that the implications of new production strategies may not be as straightforward as Swenson and Pontusson imply, for Thelen argues that their desire to preserve cooperative industrial relations at the firm-level have constrained German employers in conflicts with unions over the institutional arrangements of wage bargaining. Following Streeck (1992), she suggests that cooperative industrial relations represent a particularly important asset for firms engaged in new, more flexible, and high-quality-oriented production strategies. This line of argument would predict the opposite cross-sectoral variation in employer behavior from those observed by Swenson and Pontusson for Sweden (i.e., engineering employers should be less confrontational than, say, retail employers), but Thelen does not deny that considerations of wage flexibility also play an important role. Her point is rather to emphasize the fundamental ambiguity of employer preferences and, against this backdrop, the importance of the organizational configuration of employer movements in the determination of employer behavior.

The ambiguity of employer preferences has to do with the fact that restructuring wage-bargaining arrangements involves conflict with unions, and hence costs for employers, but Thelen's discussion also suggests a more enduring tension or trade-off. As Richard Freeman and Edward Lazear (1995) argue on theoretical grounds, union–management cooperation through some form of works council system enhances the efficiency of firms, but works councils also empower unions and enable them to claim a larger share of the pie. Wage setting through multiemployer bargaining minimizes the risks that cooperative arrangements pose for employers, and thus facilitate cooperation. Along these lines, the reluctance of German employers to push for formal decentralization of wage bargaining to the plant level might partly be explained in terms of the entrenched power of German works councils. At the same time, it is essential to recognize that the German system of wage bargaining has always been more decentralized and provided for greater interfirm and intrafirm wage differentiation than the Swedish system. Employer demands for greater wage flexibility were more compatible with existing institutional arrangements in the German case (cf. Thelen 1993).

Wallerstein and Golden (this volume) call into question Swenson and Pontusson's argument on the grounds that "post-Fordism" represents an OECD-wide trend, whereas wage-bargaining decentralization can be observed only in some cases, and instead treat the Swedish employer offensive as an attempt to deflate LO's political influence (cf. Martin 1992). As we have seen, decentralization may be a more general trend than Wallerstein and Golden suggest. On the other hand, the extent and nature of production paradigm shifts vary across industrial sectors, and the sectoral composition of industry in turn varies across countries. Our volume raises but does not pursue the question of how much (if any) explanatory leverage on the politics of institutional stability and change these variations provide.

One way to reconcile the different perspectives of our contributors would be to argue that firm size affects the relationship between production paradigms and employers' pursuit of wage flexibility through decentralization. Wallerstein and Golden (this volume) argue that only large firms have the resources to confront strong unions without the support of powerful employers' associations and that the dominant role of large, multinational corporations explains why Swedish employers have pursued more far-reaching decentralization than their Danish counterparts. In a similar vein, Thelen's interpretation of the German case suggests that small and medium-sized firms engaged in "flexible specialization" proved particularly reluctant to engage in militant confrontation with the unions in 1995.

Firm size also constitutes an important variable in Pontusson's comparative analysis of wage inequality (this volume). Despite apparently similar political–institutional arrangements, Austria and Sweden diverge sharply with respect to wage distributive outcomes: By some measures, Austria actually has the most inegalitarian wage structure of any Western European country. Pontusson's explanation of this contrast invokes, among other things, the sharp bifurcation of the Austrian economy between, on one side, a large number of very small firms (including services associated with tourism) and, on the other side, a small number of very large firms (including nationalized firms), as compared to Sweden's more homogeneous, large-firm-dominated industrial structure. The significance of firm size represents another topic for future research that emerges from this volume (cf. also Pontusson 1995b).

INTERESTS, STRATEGIC BEHAVIOR, AND IDEOLOGY

The dominant strand of the comparative political economy literature of the 1970s and 1980s conceived "corporatism" in terms of a compromise between two more or less unified actors, labor and capital. The interests of these actors were assumed to be given, more or less self-evident, and cross-national variations in policy outcomes were attributed to differences in the balance of power between them. Variations in the class balance of power were in turn conceived primarily in terms of variations in labor's mobilizational capacity, as measured by union density and electoral support for labor-affiliated parties.[17]

Relative to this once-conventional view, our volume partakes in several "revisionist movements" in comparative political economy over the last five to ten years. To begin with, the labor-centeredness of the earlier literature has been criticized, and the need to attend to the interests and organizational capacities of employers or, more broadly, capital has been emphasized by Soskice (1990) and many others. A second theme that has emerged in recent years concerns the need to disaggregate "labor" and "capital" and, concomitantly, to problematize their interests, and this has in turn led to a new emphasis on intraclass conflicts of interest and cross-class alliances (cf. Gourevitch 1986; Swenson 1991; Frieden 1995). As indicated in the preceding discussion, our contributors point to the importance of the distinction between trade-exposed and sheltered sectors as cleavage among both wage earners and employers, a distinction which overlaps with that between private and public sectors, and also identify a number of other sources of interest differentiation, such as production strategies and firm size.

Although these themes figure prominently in our volume, several contributions can also be read as a corrective of the revisionist temptation to "bend the stick in the opposite direction." In one "extremist" version of revisionism, issues of power and distribution fade into the background, and comparative political economy comes to revolve entirely around coordination – specifically, the capacity of employers to coordinate among themselves. Alternatively, labor and capital fade into the background as power and distributive conflict are conceived entirely in terms of class factions and cross-class alliances.[18] The contributors to this volume may disagree about the relative importance to be assigned to employer coordination and labor–capital conflict, but we agree that the politics of institutional stability and change in advanced capitalist countries involves both class conflict and class compromise, on the one hand, and intraclass conflict and cross-class alliances, on the other. As a collective effort, our volume seeks to tackle the analytical challenge of bridging these two dimensions.

With respect to cross-class alliances as well as class compromise, it is essential to recognize the distinction between convergence of interests and

---

17 These tenets of the "conventional view" of 15 years ago are developed most explicitly and consistently by Korpi (1978), Stephens (1979), and Esping-Andersen (1985). See Pontusson (1984) for a review and critique of these authors' treatment of the experience of Scandinavian social democracy, and Cameron (1984) for a good example of the conventional view couched more broadly.

18 While some of Soskice's (1990) formulations come close to the first perspective, Swenson (1991) seems to succumb to the latter temptation

strategic behavior. To illustrate in terms of a concrete example, the alliance that export-oriented Swedish engineering employers struck with Metalworkers' Union in 1983 was based on common interests vis-à-vis employers and unions in sheltered sectors, but the confluence of interests between these actors was far from complete. To lure the Metalworkers away from peak-level bargaining, the engineering employers had to offer wage hikes that were higher than what they wanted to pay. And while the union was willing to abandon the principle of LO-wide wage solidarity, it sought to contain wage dispersion among its members and resisted unilateral management control over wage setting. In other words, the alliance was based on compromise and on some calculation by both parties that the net benefits of this particular compromise exceeded those of other possible compromises. Furthermore, the engineering employers allied with other like-minded employer groups in internal SAF politics, and the Metalworkers similarly pursued "within-class alliances" that complemented their "cross-class alliance."

The strategic nature of alliances introduces an element of contingency into the politics of institutional stability and change. Some other alliance is always possible, and there is always some uncertainty about the prospects of success and the actual payoffs of any particular alliance, leaving considerable room for political leadership and even policy mistakes. While most of the chapters in this volume operate at the level of collective actors, with some form of organizational or institutional identity (say, unions, employer associations, or central banks), this is clearly a heuristic simplification, which should not be taken as a denial of the significance of individual actors, be they rank-and-file members or officials of such bodies. The officials of German employer associations emerge as important actors in their own right in Thelen's chapter, and this is even more true for Swedish government officials in Martin's chapter.

To illustrate the range of differences among our contributors, Iversen's and Martin's accounts of the Swedish experience might be contrasted in terms of the importance they assign to contingent political choices. For Iversen, the Swedish experience points to a systemic logic in that changes that occur in one institutional arena (wage bargaining) create pressures for change in other arenas (macroeconomic policy and social policy). By comparison, Martin's account is less deterministic; indeed, Martin repeatedly refers to the macroeconomic policy choices that fueled decentralization of wage bargaining as "mistakes." The question arises, why did powerful people in the Ministry of Finance repeatedly make similar mistakes (err in the same direction)? One might answer this question by invoking Iversen's systemic logic, but one might also answer the question in terms of the rise of academic economists, influenced by new classical thinking, within the social democratic policy elite, and broader ideological currents in Swedish society in the 1980s (Hugenmark 1994).

Recent reforms of the Swedish political economy involve a more or less conscious emulation of the "German model" (Pontusson 1997). As suggested earlier, the core themes of this volume, taken as a whole, are informed by or, at least, consistent with the idea of dual convergence. While the institutional differences between organized and liberal market economies remain as great as they ever were, the range of variation among the organized market economies of Northern Europe appears to have diminished. In particular, the Scandinavian countries have shed some of the social democratic features that have traditionally distinguished them from organized market economies on the continent. Similarly, a case might be made that more welfare-oriented liberal market economies, such as those of New Zealand and the UK, have converged on the America model over the last two decades. This represents the broader comparative framework in which our volume situates recent Northern European developments.

References

Ahrne, Göran and Wallace Clement. 1994. "A new regime?" In Wallace Clement and Rianne Mahon, eds., *Swedish social democracy*. Toronto: Canadian Scholars' Press, 223–244.

Alvarez, Michael, Geoffrey Garrett, and Peter Lange. 1991. "Government partisanship, labor organization and macroeconomic performance," *American Political Science Review*, 85:541–556.

Berger, Suzanne and Ronald Dore, eds. 1996. *National diversity and global capitalism*. Ithaca: Cornell University Press.

Calmfors, Lars. 1993. "Lessons from the macroeconomic experience of Sweden," *European Journal of Political Economy*, 9 (March): 25–72.

Calmfors, Lars and John Driffill. 1988. "Bargaining structure, corporatism, and macroeconomic performance," *Economic Policy*, 6:13–61.

Cameron, David. 1984. "Social democracy, corporatism, labour quiescence, and the representation of economic interest in advanced capitalist society." In John Goldthorpe, ed., *Order and conflict in contemporary capitalism*. Oxford: Clarendon Press, 143–178.

Cargil, Thomas F., Michael M. Hutchison, and Takatoshi Ito. 1997. *Political economy of Japanese monetary policy*. Cambridge, MA: MIT Press.

Clayton, Richard and Jonas Pontusson. 1998. "Welfare state retrenchment revisited," *World Politics*, 51 (October).

Crouch, Colin. 1993. *Industrial relations and European state traditions*. Oxford: Clarendon Press.

Colin. 1995. "Reconstructing corporatism?" In Franz Traxler and Colin Crouch, eds., *Organized industrial relations in Europe*. Aldershot: Avebury, 311–330.

Crouch, Colin and Wolfgang Streeck, eds. 1997. *Political economy of modern capitalism*. London: Sage.

Cukierman, Alex. 1992. *Central bank strategy, credibility, and independence*. Cambridge, MA: MIT Press.

Due, Jesper et al. 1995. "Adjusting the Danish model." In Franz Traxler and Colin, eds., *Organized industrial relations in Europe*. Aldershot: Avebury, 121–150.

Elvander, Nils. 1988. *Den svenska modellen*. Stockholm: Allmänna Förlaget.

Erickson, Christopher and Andrea Ichino. 1995. "Wage differentials in Italy." In Richard Freeman and Lawrence Katz, eds., *Differences and changes in wage structures*. Chicago: University of Chicago Press, 265–306.

Esping-Andersen, Gøsta. 1985. *Politics against markets*. Princeton, NJ: Princeton University Press.

1990. *The three worlds of welfare capitalism*. Princeton, NJ: Princeton University Press.

Flanagan, Robert, David Soskice, and Lloyd Ulman. 1983. *Unionism, economic stabilization, and incomes policies*. Washington, DC: Brookings Institution.

Freeman, Richard and Edward Lazear. 1995. "An economic analysis of works councils." In Joel Rogers and Wolfgang Streeck, eds., *Works councils*. Chicago: University of Chicago Press, 27–50.

Frieden, Jeffry. 1995. "Labor and the politics of exchange rates." In Sanford Jacoby, ed., *The workers of nations*. New York: Oxford University Press, 201–218.

Garrett, Geoffrey. 1998. *Partisan politics in the global economy*. New York: Cambridge University Press.

Glyn, Andrew. 1997. "Low pay and the volume of work." Typescript, Corpus Christi College, Oxford.

Golden, Miriam and Michael Wallerstein. 1996. "Postwar industrial relations in non-corporatist OECD countries." Paper presented at the Tenth International Conference of Europeanists, Chicago, March.

Goodman, John B. 1992. *Monetary sovereignty. The politics of central banking in Western Europe*. Ithaca: Cornell University Press.

Gourevitch, Peter. 1986. *Politics in hard times*. Ithaca: Cornell University Press.

Grilli, Vittorio, Donato Masciandoro, and Guido Tabellini. 1991. "Political and monetary institutions and public financial policies in the industrialized countries." *Economic Policy*, 13:42–92.

Hall, Peter A. 1986. *Governing the economy*. Oxford: Oxford University Press.

1993. "Policy paradigms, social learning, and the state," *Comparative Politics*, 25: 275–296.

1994. "Central bank independence and coordinated wage bargaining: Their interaction in Germany and Europe," *German Politics and Society* 31:1–23.

Hemerijck, Anton. 1995. "Corporatist immobility in the Netherlands." In Franz Traxler and Colin Crouch, eds., *Organized industrial relations in Europe*. Aldershot: Avebury, 183–226.

Hibbs, Douglas and Håkan Locking. 1996. "Wage compression, wage drift, and wage inflation in Sweden," *Labor Economics*, 3 (September): 109–141.

Howell, Chris. 1992. *Regulating labor*. Princeton: NJ: Princeton University Press.

Hugenmark, Agneta. 1994. *Den fängslande marknaden*. Lund: Arkiv.

Hyman, Richard. 1994. "Industrial relations in Western Europe," *Industrial Relations*, 33:1–24.

Inglehart, Ronald. 1977. *The silent revolution.* Princeton, NJ: Princeton University Press.

1990. *Culture shift in advanced industrial society.* Princeton, NJ: Princeton University Press.

Iversen, Torben. 1996. "Power, flexibility and the breakdown of centralized wage bargaining," *Comparative Politics,* 28 (July), 399–436.

1998. "Wage bargaining, central bank independence and the real effects of money," *International Organization,* 52 (Summer): 469–504.

Iversen, Torben and Niels Thygesen. 1998. "Denmark: From external to internal adjustment." In Erik Jones, Jeffry Frieden, and Francisco Torres, eds., *Joining Europe's monetary club: The challenge for smaller member states.* New York: St. Martin's Press.

Iversen, Torben and Anne Wren. 1998. "Equality, employment, and budgetary restraint: The trilemma of the service economy," *World Politics,* 50 (July), 507–546.

Katz, Harry. 1993. "The decentralization of collective bargaining," *Industrial and Labor Relations Review,* 47:3–22.

Katzenstein, Peter. 1985. *Small states in world markets.* Ithaca, NY: Cornell University Press.

Kitschelt, Herbert. 1994. *The transformation of European social democracy.* New York: Cambridge University Press.

Kitschelt et al. In press. "Conclusion: Convergence and divergence in advanced capitalist democracies." In Kitschelt et al., eds., *Continuity and change in contemporary capitalism.* New York: Cambridge University Press.

Korpi, Walter. 1978. *The working class in welfare capitalism.* London: Routledge & Kegan Paul.

Kurzer, Paulette. 1993. *Business and banking.* Ithaca, NY: Cornell University Press.

Lange, Peter, Michael Wallerstein, and Miriam Golden. 1995. "The end of corporatism?" In Sanford Jacoby, ed., *The workers of nations.* New York: Oxford University Press, 76–100.

Layard, Richard, Stephen Nickell, and Richard Jackman. 1991. *Unemployment. Macroeconomic performance and the labour market.* Oxford: Oxford University Press.

Martin, Andrew. 1979. "The dynamics of change in a Keynesian political economy: The Swedish case and its implications." In Colin Crouch, ed., *State and economy in contemporary capitalism.* London: Croom Helm.

1985. "Distributive conflict, inflation and investment." In Leon Lindberg and Charles Maier, eds., *The politics of inflation and stagnation.* Washington, DC: Brookings Institution, 403–466.

1992. "Wage bargaining and Swedish politics." Working paper, Harvard Center for European Studies.

Notermans, Ton. 1993. "The abdication of national policy autonomy," *Politics and Society,* 21:133–168.

OECD. 1991. "Trends in trade union membership," *Employment Outlook,* July, 97–134.

1994. "Collective bargaining," *Employment Outlook,* July, 167–194.

1997. "Economic performance and the structure of collective bargaining," *Employment Outlook*, July, 63–92.

Pempel, T. J. 1982. *Policy and politics in Japan: Creative conservatism.* Philadelphia: Temple University Press.

Pestoff, Victor. 1995. "Towards a new Swedish model of collective bargaining and politics." In Franz Traxler and Colin Crouch, eds., *Organized industrial relations in Europe.* Aldershot: Avebury, 151–182.

Pierson, Paul. 1994. *Dismantling the welfare state: Reagan, Thatcher and the politics of retrenchment.* New York: Cambridge University Press.

1996. "The New Politics of the Welfare State," *World Politics* 48 (2): 143–179.

Pontusson, Jonas. 1984. "Behind and beyond social democracy," *New Left Review,* 143:69–96.

1992. *The limits of social democracy.* Ithaca: Cornell University Press.

1995a. "From comparative public policy to political economy," *Comparative Political Studies,* 28:117–147.

1995b. "Explaining the decline of European social democracy," *World Politics,* 47: 495–533.

1997. "Between neo-liberalism and the German model: Swedish capitalism in transition." In Colin Crouch and Wolfgang Streeck, eds., *Political economy of modern capitalism.* London: Sage, 55–70.

Purcell, John. 1995. "Ideology and the end of institutional industrial relations." In Franz Traxler and Colin Crouch, eds., *Organized industrial relations in Europe.* Aldershot: Avebury, 101–120.

Regini, Marino. 1984. "The conditions for political exchange: How concertation emerged and collapsed in Italy and Great Britain." In John Goldthorpe, ed., *Order and conflict in contemporary capitalism.* Oxford: Clarendon Press, 124–142.

Rhodes, Martin. 1997. "Globalisation, labour markets and welfare states." Working paper (RSC no. 97/36), European University Institute, Florence.

Scharpf, Fritz. 1984. "Economic and institutional constraints on full-employment strategies: Sweden, Austria, and West Germany (1973–1982)." In J. H. Goldthorpe, ed., *Order and conflict in contemporary capitalism.* New York: Oxford University Press, 257–290.

1991. *Crisis and choice in European social democracy.* Ithaca, NY: Cornell University Press.

Schwartz, Herman. 1994. "Small states in big trouble," *World Politics,* 46:527–555.

Soskice, David. 1990. "Wage determination," *Oxford Review of Economic Policy,* 6:36–61.

1992. "The institutional infrastructure for competitiveness." In A. B. Atkinson and R. Brunetta, eds., *The economics of the new Europe.* London: Macmillan.

Soskice, David and Torben Iversen. Forthcoming. "The non-neutrality of monetary policy with large price and wage setters," *Quarterly Journal of Economics.*

Stephens, John. 1979. *The transition from capitalism to socialism.* London: Macmillan.

Streeck, Wolfgang. 1992. *Social institutions and economic performance.* Beverly Hills: Sage.

1993. "The rise and decline of corporatism." In Lloyd Ulman, Barry Eichengreen, and William Dickens, eds., *Labor and an integrated Europe*. Washington, DC: Brookings Institution, 80–99.

Streeck, Wolfgang and Philippe Schmitter. 1991. "From national corporatism to transnational pluralism," *Politics and Society*, June, 133–164.

Swank, Duane. 1998. "Globalization and the welfare state." Paper presented at the Eleventh International Conference of Europeanists, Baltimore, February 26–28.

Swenson, Peter. 1991. "Bringing capital back in, or social democracy reconsidered," *World Politics*, 43:513–544.

1992. "Labor and the limits of the welfare state." In Miriam Golden and Jonas Pontusson, eds, *Bargaining for change*. Ithaca, NY: Cornell University Press.

Thelen, Kathleen. 1991. *Union of parts*. Ithaca, NY: Cornell University Press.

1993. "West European labor in transition," *World Politics*, 46:23–49.

Traxler, Franz. 1992. "Austria." In Anthony Ferner and Richard Hyman, eds., *Industrial relations in the new Europe*. Oxford: Basil Blackwell, 270–297.

1995a. "Farewell to labour market associations?" In Franz Traxler and Colin Crouch, eds., *Organized industrial relations in Europe*. Aldershot: Avebury, 3–19.

1995b. "From demand-side to supply-side corporatism?" In Franz Traxler and Colin Crouch, eds., *Organized industrial relations in Europe*. Aldershot: Avebury, 271–286.

Traxler, Franz and Colin Crouch, eds. 1995. *Organized industrial relations in Europe*. Aldershot: Avebury.

Wallerstein, Michael, Miriam Golden, and Peter Lange. 1996. "Unions, employers and wage-setting institutions in North and Central Europe, 1950–1992." Unpublished paper.

Visser, Jelle. 1997. "Two cheers for corporatism, one for the market," *British Journal of Industrial Relations*, 36(20):269–292.

Werin, Lars (ed.). 1993. *Från räntereglering till inflationsnorm*. Stockholm: SNS Förlag.

2

MACROECONOMIC ANALYSIS AND THE POLITICAL ECONOMY OF UNEMPLOYMENT

David Soskice

This chapter is designed to fill a lacuna in most contemporary work in the comparative political economy of unemployment – that is, that little serious attention is paid to the developments of macroeconomic theory that have taken place over the past two decades. During that period much mainstream (at least Harvard/MIT/London School of Economics [LSE]) macroeconomics has moved toward a broader New Keynesian (NK) position[1] and away from a simplistic neoclassical (NC) approach – if it had ever really been there. New Keynesian models differentiate themselves from the NC model in the attention they pay to three elements: equilibria in which unemployment is involuntary; the role of aggregate demand and of monetary and fiscal policy; and the operation of open economies.

The first goal of the chapter is analytic: It is to provide an understanding of the differences between the NK and NC approaches in ways that will be useful to political economists working on comparative unemployment. In fact the logical structure of NK models parallels that of the neoclassical; indeed the NC model can usefully be seen as a special case of the NK. In important respects the NC model can be identified with the deregulated approach to labor markets, whereas unionized labor markets fit in more easily with NK models. This gives an analytic tool to discuss comparisons between them.

The second goal stems from this: that most quantitative, comparative, political-economic analyses of unemployment have paid attention to only one of the three differentiating elements of NK models mentioned above – namely,

---

1 See the contributions to the *Journal of Economic Perspectives* Keynesian Economics Today Symposium, (Greenwald and Stiglitz 1993; Romer 1993; Mankiw 1993; Tobin 1993); and leading U.S. and UK graduate textbooks (Blanchard and Fischer 1989; Layard, Nickell et al. 1991). An account of the different positions and especially of open economy new Keynesian macroeconomics is in Carlin and Soskice (1990).

involuntary unemployment in equilibrium. Little attention has been directed toward the role of aggregate demand in causing unemployment; and virtually no interest has been shown in the openness and interdependence of advanced economies. Yet much of the unemployment in Northern Europe in the 1990s has been caused by the sharply deflationary policies of the hegemonic economic power of the region, Germany, combined with the interdependence – as a result of the European Monetary System – and openness of the economies of the region. Since these economies have centralized or coordinated systems of wage bargaining, and since the more deregulated Anglo-Saxon economies have pursued expansionary macroeconomic policies over the same period, political economic analyses of unemployment that focus only on the institutions of wage bargaining give potentially misleading results.

The chapter is organized as follows: There are two standard elements in the NC approach: perfectly competitive product and labor markets, which guarantee a unique equilibrium unemployment rate with zero involuntary unemployment; and rational expectations, which guarantees that the actual rate is equal to the equilibrium rate. Most work on the effects of wage bargaining systems on unemployment can be located in the NK approach. Section 2 discusses how different concepts governing wage-bargaining systems (centralization, coordination) should be analyzed in NK closed-economy models. This work differentiates itself from the NC model with respect to the first NC element: introducing imperfect competition in product and labor markets, it shows how different bargaining arrangements affect the equilibrium rate of unemployment. The NK approach in the closed economy implies a unique equilibrium unemployment rate and is quite consistent with rational expectations. Indeed rational expectations and unique equilibrium unemployment rates – though allowing for involuntary unemployment – are either implicitly or explicitly assumed in the work of Calmfors and Driffill (1988), Iversen (1988), and Soskice and Iversen (forthcoming). But the NC approach rules out the possibility that monetary and fiscal policy can affect equilibrium unemployment. Iversen, Franzese–Hall, and Soskice–Iversen by contrast argue that monetary policy can affect equilibrium unemployment by altering the incentive structures in the wage bargaining system (Hall 1994). The Soskice–Iversen argument is spelled out in section 2 to show how it fits into the NK approach even with rational expectations and a unique equilibrium unemployment rate.

Discussion of the role of aggregate demand is delayed until section 3, where the NK model of the open economy is analyzed. There it is shown that a multiplicity of possible equilibrium unemployment rates exist, and that the actual equilibrium unemployment rate depends upon aggregate demand. What is then the effect of different structural characteristics (degree of centralization, coordination, etc.) of the wage-bargaining system on unemployment? It will be argued that high equilibrium unemployment may just reflect deflationary macroeconomic policies. And it is shown that when unemployment is adjusted for aggregate demand factors in the period 1986–94, this raises the statistical effectiveness of coordinated wage bargaining.

In section 4, the interdependence of economies is discussed, first analytically, then in terms of the role of German deflationary policies and the fulfillment of the Maastricht conditions in raising equilibrium unemployment rates throughout Europe in the 1990s. The Dutch and Danish exceptions to this are explained as deriving from a combination of wage restraint and the smallness and openness of their economies.

The conclusion discusses the relative merits of deregulated labor markets and coordinated wage-bargaining systems in the light of the previous sections.

1. THE NEOCLASSICAL MODEL

The neoclassical model of a closed economy has three components: First, it assumes perfect competition in product and labor markets. Second, rational expectations are assumed. And third, it is assumed that the nominal money supply is set exogenously. From these three assumptions follow the central results of the neoclassical model, results which in effect shut down the possibility of a serious science of political economy (or which assign it to explaining how a political system can establish such conditions in the first place).

The first result is that there is *a unique equilibrium level of unemployment.* Throughout this chapter, whether talking of neoclassical or New Keynesian models, we will emphasize how the real wage is determined in two different ways. On the one hand, it stems from business pricing behavior, since prices are a markup on unit costs of production; for an economy as a whole, unit costs reduce to unit labor costs, or the money wage divided by labor productivity (assumed constant in this chapter). Example: the hourly wage is \$10, hourly productivity is 2 units, so that the labor cost per unit is \$5; if the profit markup is 10%, the price is \$5.50; and hence the real wage *implied by business pricing* is \$10/\$5.50 or 1.82 units per hour worked. In other words, the worker gets 91% of the output and the business 9%. In mathematical terms:

$$P = \mu \, W/l \tag{1}$$

where P is the price level, W the money wage, l labour productivity (assumed to be unity in most of what follows), and μ the markup (e.g., 110%). Hence, from the business pricing or product market perspective,

$$w_p = l/\mu \tag{2}$$

where w_p is the price or product-market-determined real wage. Under perfect competition in the product market, price is equal to marginal cost, in this case unit labor costs, so μ is unity and $w_p = l$.

But the real wage is also determined by the labor market. Just as business

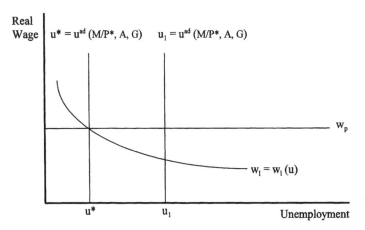

Figure 2.1. *Equilibrium unemployment in the neoclassical model.*

take the money wage as given when setting prices to ensure a particular level of real profits, so participants in the labor market set the money wage on the basis of expected price levels to attain a desired expected real wage. In a perfectly competitive labor market, labor force participants choose how much labor to supply at the going expected real wage. Given the demand for labor in a perfectly competitive labor market, the real wage must be such as to ensure a corresponding supply of labor if the demand is to be met. The higher the expected real wage, the greater the amount of labor supplied to the market. One way of putting this is to say that the lower the rate of unemployment, the higher the expected real wage required by the labor market. So from the labor market side, the real wage, w_1, will be a declining function of unemployment,

$$w_1 = w_1 (u) \tag{3}$$

At any given rate of unemployment, inflation increases when the claims on real wages implied by business pricing are below the claims on real wages resulting from wage setting. (We will see that a similar principle holds, mutatis mutandis, in the New Keynesian world of trade union bargaining.) How does this come about?

Equilibrium unemployment, u^*, equates w_1 with w_p:

$$w_p = 1 = w_1 (u^*) \tag{4}$$

This is shown in Figure 2.1. The concept of equilibrium unemployment used in macroeconomics is: "A particular rate of unemployment is in equilibrium when inflation is stable at that rate." This is the NAIRU (nonaccelerating inflation rate of unemployment) definition. Why does u^* fulfill this condition? Assume price inflation is initially steady at some rate, say 3%, and that this is built into expectations. If $u < u^*$, labor will be willingly only supplied at a real wage above one, that is, with $W > P$; this leads P to rise since businesses will be prepared to produce only if $P = W$; but then workers will need the money wage to rise by the expected rate of inflation of 3% plus what is needed to increase real wages above unity; this then raises the rate of price inflation and eventually the rate of expected price inflation, leading to further increase in wage inflation, and so on. Thus $u < u^*$ is a world of rising inflation rates, just as mutatis mutandis $u > u^*$ implies falling inflation rates. The basic problem is that the real wage required by business pricing is out of line with that required by the supply of labor: only at $u = u^*$ are the requirements of business consistent with those of labor.

The second result is that *actual unemployment is always equal to equilibrium unemployment*. This follows from rational expectations and a unique equilibrium rate of unemployment. Actual real demand in the economy for output is determined by real aggregate demand, and this in turn can be thought of as dependent on the real money supply (M/P), real exogenous components of expenditure (A) – mainly private-sector investment – as well as the influence of fiscal policy (G), and so on. Employment in the economy as a whole depends upon this aggregate real demand; and, hence, given the size of the labor force, aggregate demand also determines the unemployment rate.

This can be summarized as:

$$u = u_{ad} (M/P, A, G) \qquad (5)$$

as shown in the vertical lines in Figure 2.1. Rational expectations assume that there is common knowledge across economic agents of the structure of the economy, that is, (4) and (5), including – critically – the shared assumption that the economy will be in equilibrium. Assuming agents also know the values of M, A, and G, the rational expectation of P, P^*, is such that (4) and (5) both hold, given M, A, and G:

$$u^* = u^{ad} (M/P^*, A, G) \qquad (6)$$

In other words, demand for employment will always be at the equilibrium level if $P = P^*$; moreover, P will equal P^* since businesses will set $P = P^*$ and employees will set $W = P^*$; hence demand and supply of labor will be equated.

The third result is that *all unemployment is voluntary*. If at $u = u^*$ and $w = l$, there was involuntary unemployment, that would imply that w_l intersected w_p to the left of u^*, that is, that some unemployed at u^* would be prepared to work at $w < l$. But w_l intersects w_p at u^*, so no unemployment can be involuntary.

The fourth result is that *the rate of inflation is equal to and determined by the growth of the nominal money supply*. This follows directly from (6). In equilibrium, given A and G, a rise in M must leave the real money supply unchanged, since otherwise the level of unemployment determined by aggregate demand would differ from equilibrium unemployment. Hence, P must rise by the same percentage as M.

Fifth, *neither monetary nor fiscal policy have any effect on equilibrium unemployment*. This follows because equilibrium unemployment is determined by (4). What happens if real government expenditure is permanently decreased – if it has no effect on equilibrium unemployment? If G is permanently reduced, and if A is fixed, then the real money supply will rise to keep aggregate demand constant at the equilibrium unemployment rate. This will come about via rational expectations: namely, because a lower price level will now be needed to maintain equilibrium. The increased real money supply will increase components of private spending, either directly through an increase in wealth or indirectly if the increased money supply lowers interest rates. This is the result that government expenditure "crowds out" private expenditure – hence a reduction in government expenditure leads to private expenditure being crowded in.

2. NEW KEYNESIANISM IN A CLOSED ECONOMY

The neoclassical model has been presented in deliberately stark terms, so as to make the differences with an NK approach as clear as possible. The difference between the two approaches can be divided into the different assumptions underlying the models and differences in their results. As far as assumptions are concerned, the key difference is that of perfect and imperfect competition; in particular, in the NK approach the introduction of price setters in the product market (though that will not be emphasized below) and wage setters in the labor market. The assumption of rational expectations – though often associated with neoclassical economics – is perfectly consistent with the NK approach, though because the latter is more interested in adjustment to equilibrium it is not associated with it. The two central differences as far as results are concerned relate to (i) the possibility of introducing involuntary unemployment in equilibrium – the consequence of dropping the assumption of perfect competition in the labor market; and (ii) the prolonged period of adjustment that may be necessary to restore equilibrium after a disturbance – from dropping the assumption of rational expectations.

INVOLUNTARY EQUILIBRIUM UNEMPLOYMENT

Most political economy work involving union bargaining and its effect on unemployment falls into this area. The argument can be set out in terms similar to those in the last section. Retain the assumption of Figure 2.1 that the price-determined real wage is equal to unity. The critical difference lies in how the real wage is developed in the labor market. In the last section, corresponding to

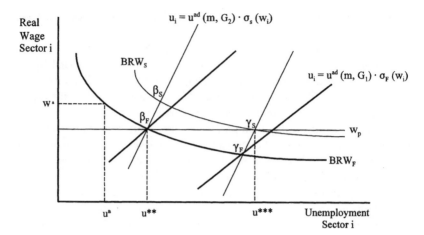

Figure 2.2. *Union bargaining and equilibrium unemployment.*

the assumption of perfect competition in the labor market, this was simply the supply curve of labor showing how many people wanted employment at each real wage. Imperfect competition can take many forms in the labor market (insider–outsider, efficiency wages, etc.), but it will be assumed here that the economy is divided into sectors in each of which trade unions bargain with employers or associations of employers.

(i) Independently Bargaining Unions

We start with the assumption that sectoral unions take no account of their actions outside their own sector. In Figure 2.2, the upward sloping lines, u_i, represent sectoral unemployment rates as depending on two sets of factors: the aggregate demand for labor (and hence inversely unemployment), which is shown in the diagram as a function of the real money supply, m, and government expenditure, G; and the real wage in the industry, w_i. G_1 represents a low level and G_2 a higher level of aggregate demand. Thus shifting the "demand for labor" schedules inward reflects an increase in aggregate demand – hence a reduction in unemployment. The slope of the schedules shows how responsive is demand for labor to industry wages: the flatter the schedule the greater the decrease in unemployment in the industry in response to an industry wage increase.

Assume for the moment that the level of aggregate demand is given at *1*, and employers and unions in each identical sector face u_i. A simple assumption is that the union in each sector is a monopoly union that can decide the point on the u_i schedule that it wants – that is, it can pick the wage and must then accept the employment implications of that choice. Clearly the flatter the demand schedule the more restrained will the union be, since the employment losses of wage increases will be substantial. Thus, at any given level of aggregate demand, the flatter the schedules the lower will be the union's chosen wage. But equally, the higher the level of aggregate demand the greater will be employment at any given real wage: thus if the union maintains some trade-off between the wage and employment, it will choose higher wages as aggregate demand rises, that is, as the union moves from $u_i(G_1)$ to $u_i(G_2)$, and so on. For any given set of demand schedules varying with aggregate demand, a "bargained real wage schedule" can be constructed as shown by BRW_F. The F subscript relates to the flatness of the employment demand schedules. Thus BRW_F is derived from the union's choice of γ_F when $G = G_1$ and β_F when $G = G_2$. BRW_S is analogously derived from the points γ_S and β_S on the steep set of employment demand schedules.[2]

Analogously to the last section, equilibrium unemployment, u^{**}, is determined by the intersection of the relevant BRW – here BRW_F – and the price-determined real wage schedule, here $w_p = 1$. (In fact this assumes that there is complete collective bargaining coverage, so that all employers have to pay union wages.) The argument is straightforward. Suppose $u = u^a < u^{**}$, then unions will set money wage increases so as to bargain a real wage of u^a (say 1.03), while businesses will set price increases so as to restore the real wage to unity. This process leads to ever-rising inflation: if expected inflation is 2%, and the initial real wage is 1, unions will demand 5% nominal wage increases; hence prices will rise by 5%, raising expected inflation eventually to 5% and requiring 8% nominal wage increases in the next bargaining round, and so on. Mutatis mutandis, inflation will continually fall with $u > u^{**}$. Hence u^{**} is the equilibrium unemployment rate with BRW_F. With steeper, more inelastic employment demand schedules, and a higher BRW, BRW_S, the equilibrium unemployment rate is higher at u^{***}.

Both these equilibrium unemployment rates, u^{**} and u^{***}, imply involuntary unemployment. This is because the BRW schedules both lie wholly outside the supply of labor function (see Figure 2.3).[3] Why? Continue the assumption that the union is a monopolist, and assume more specifically that the union's utility function is that of the representative member of the labor force. And imagine that the union is confronted with the employment demand schedule u_i. The union would never choose a wage on the section of u_i to the *left* of the labor supply schedule – for example, at α in Figure 2.3 – since that would be less good for the representative worker than β where the employment demand schedule intersected the labor supply curve: Faced with that real wage the representative worker would choose only to supply at β; moreover, a point

---

2 The assumption that unions are monopolistic can easily be dropped. If unions bargain with employers over wage setting, the more powerful are employers and the less powerful unions, the lower will be the BRW curve, and the lower the equilibrium rate of unemployment. We return shortly to the role employers play in coordinated bargaining.

3 Neglect points a and b and the indifference curves IC for the moment.

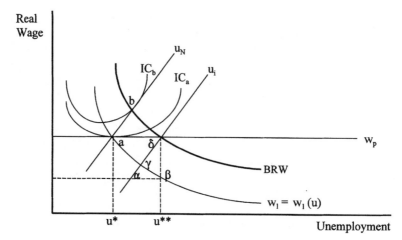

Figure 2.3. *Involuntary equilibrium unemployment.*

higher up the labor supply schedule (e.g., γ) is preferred to one lower down (e.g., β); since γ is preferred to β and β to α, and since it can choose γ, the union will never choose a point to the left and below $w_1(u)$.

We can go further than this and show that the union will always choose a point on u_i above γ, if it is maximizing the interest of the representative worker. The representative worker is confronted with a fixed real wage and faces no trade-off between higher unemployment and a higher real wage. Without such a trade-off she/he chooses γ. But since the representative worker attaches importance to both the real wage and unemployment, the existence of a trade-off implies the worker would choose a point with some increase in the real wage, that is, a point such as δ above and to the right of γ. Hence, the union will do so in the representative worker's interest, and hence the BRW will lie wholly outside and to the right of the supply of labor schedule.

Since the BRW schedules necessarily lie outside the supply curve of labor, it follows that u^* is smaller than u^{**} (or u^{***}). Moreover, at u^* there is no involuntary unemployment. Hence the difference between u^{**} (or u^{***}) and u^* measures involuntary unemployment in equilibrium.

The argument so far implies that the neoclassical model – based on the assumption of perfectly competitive labor markets – produces lower equilibrium unemployment than in the case of more regulated labor markets. This then raises the question: under what circumstances, if any, can labour markets with trade union bargaining produce similar results?

(ii) Coordination, Centralization, and Calmfors–Driffill

Most work in comparative political economy, at least in the corporatist tradition, starts from the view of involuntary unemployment in union-dominated labor markets as the outcome of a Prisoners' Dilemma (PD). In terms of Figure 2.3, two conditions would be necessary for voluntary unemployment in equilibrium: (a) that the BRW passed through the intersection of the labor supply curve and the price-determined real wage horizontal line; and (b) that the vertical line representing the level of aggregate demand passed through the same point. We will return to (b) later in this section, as it is not critical to the PD problem. [In fact, if condition (a) holds, the assumption of rational expectations is sufficient to guarantee (b). In what follows we will assume rational expectations for ease of exposition. It implies that aggregate demand will always be sufficient to produce equilibrium unemployment. Our concern here will be solely with the equilibrium unemployment rate.] The political economist's question is thus: Why are unions insufficiently individually restrained to produce a suitably low BRW, when each union can see that if all unions behaved in such a way, involuntary unemployment would be eliminated?

In terms of the model of the last section, three assumptions need to be underlined. First, unions in different sectors set wages independently of each other – for instance, it is done simultaneously. Second, each union is concerned about the employment and wages only of the labor force in its own sector (imagine the labor force is divided up among sectors); the union maximizes the utility of the representative member of its "own" labor force. And third, wage setting does not affect aggregate demand: The natural assumption here is that aggregate demand is proxied by the real money supply, and the central bank behaves in an accommodating way; thus any price increases are accommodated by a corresponding increase in the nominal money supply, ruling out the possibility that unions might be deterred from wage increases by their knock-on effects on aggregate demand through a reduction in the real money supply.

Given these three assumptions, the Prisoners' Dilemma works as follows. Assume appropriate restraint in $N-1$ sectors, so that their BRWs – which are not shown – cut the horizontal w_p line (representing the price-determined real wage [PRW]) at u^*, a in Figure 2.3. Then the employment demand schedule, U_N, which the Nth union faces, must go through the same point since if the Nth union sets its wage at w_p (i.e., also behaves in an appropriately restrained way), equilibrium unemployment will be at u^* and hence aggregate demand will go through that point. Now consider the indifference curve of the representative labor force member at a, IC_a. It must sit on the PRW at that point by the definition of the labor supply curve: If it sloped upward (downward) at that point, it would pay the individual to supply more (less) labor.[4] Therefore the Nth union will always do better for the representative labor force member by choosing a higher wage on the employment demand schedule, where the highest

---

4 The utility of the representative worker is improved by a vertical move upward, since the real wage is increased while employment remains constant. Hence IC_b represents a higher level of utility than IC_a. The existence of a maximum requires that they be U-shaped upward.

indifference curve just touches it, IC_b at b. All rational unions will reason similarly, so that restraint will not be forthcoming. (This paragraph replays the argument above, as to why the BRW must lie to the right of the labor supply schedule, but using indifference curves.)

Two broad directions have been suggested out of this dilemma. One is labor market deregulation (as has been implicitly suggested above). The other is increased centralization or coordination of wage bargaining. As Calmfors and Driffill pointed out, deregulated labor markets and centralized labor markets are at the opposite ends of the same spectrum (Calmfors and Driffill 1988). In terms of the model used here, the labor market can be said to become more deregulated the greater the number of independent bargaining units. The larger the number of independent bargaining units, the flatter are the employment demand schedules, reflecting the greater elasticity of demand for the output of a sector the smaller the sector is. When a labor market is completely deregulated, the individual employment demand schedules can be assumed to be more or less horizontal; hence an individual union would never have an incentive to sacrifice employment for wages. Therefore, the economy would be in a situation of more or less full employment.

As the number of sectors decreases, so the slope of the employment demand schedules becomes steeper, and ceteris paribus – as we have seen – this produces higher BRWs and higher equilibrium unemployment. According to Calmfors and Driffill, however, this is counteracted by another effect: namely unions will want to take into account their negative externalities as the number of sectors becomes smaller. The argument is as follows: The larger the size of the sector, the greater will be the impact of wage increases on the general price level. Hence, the more will it be in the interest of the union to restrain wage increases to stabilize the general price level. When there is only one sector (which covers the whole economy), the union will have no capacity to influence the real wage but only the price level; it will therefore behave with complete restraint. The upshot of this well-known argument is that a low level of equilibrium unemployment is associated with (i) deregulated labor markets, or very many independent bargaining sectors, and (ii) labor markets with highly centralized bargaining, or very few independent bargaining sectors (Calmfors and Driffill 1988).

There is, however, an important problem with the Calmfors–Driffill argument of an analytic nature. Leaving aside the limiting cases of deregulation or of a completely centralized system, and taking the case of (say) two unions, it is not clear in general why the unions would exercise restraint. The individual union faces an employment demand schedule that defines a trade-off between employment and the real wage. Its interest is in choosing an implicit optimal real wage to maximize its utility subject to the trade-off. The only way in which the aggregate price level might affect the trade-off is via aggregate demand. The trade-off relates employment in a sector positively to the level of aggregate

Table 2.1. *Long-run average unemployment rates for 17 OECD countries, depending on monetary rule and number of unions, 1973–93*

		Number of unions			
		Very small	Intermediate	Very large	Mean
Monetary rule	*Accommodating*	3.9 (3)	7.6 (3)	7.1 (3)	5.0 (9)
	Nonaccommodating	5.6 (2)	3.6 (4)	7.4 (2)	6.2 (8)
	Difference	−1.7	4.0ᵃ	0.3	−1.2

ᵃDifference is significant at .001 level, one-sided test.
Note: Monetary rule refers to central bank independence except for Japan, where a dependent bank has followed a nonaccommodating rule. Number of unions refers to whether wage setting is highly centralized, intermediately centralized, or highly decentralized. Beginning with the top row, the countries in the six boxes of the table are from left to right: Finland, Norway, Sweden; Australia, Belgium, Italy; Britain, France, New Zealand; Austria, Denmark; Germany, Japan, Netherlands, Switzerland; Canada, United States.
Sources: Hutchison, Taketoshi et al. forthcoming: (OECD 1996, 1997): Cukierman et al. 1992.

demand – by assumption here the real money supply, and negatively to the sectoral real wage. A rise in the aggregate price level will reduce the real money supply, and hence lower employment in the sector, *only if* the central bank is pursuing a *non*accommodating monetary rule; this is because the central bank fixes the nominal money supply under such a rule and does not accommodate price increases. The smaller the number of sectors, the bigger is the effect on the aggregate price level of sectoral wage restraint. Hence with a nonaccommodating monetary rule, it will be in the interest of the union to restrain the sectoral money wage more than it otherwise would have done. But, with an accommodating monetary rule, the union has no interest in additional restraint since the real money supply cannot be affected. This counterargument to Calmfors–Driffill was initially proposed by Iversen (1998), and developed further in Soskice and Iversen (1998; forthcoming).

The implication is that, (i) with an accommodating monetary policy, the equilibrium rate of unemployment rises as the number of independently bargaining unions declines until there are only two unions; then unemployment falls with the move from two to a single centralized union; (ii) with a nonaccommodating policy unemployment will be lower when there is a small number of unions than in the accommodating case. The purpose of the Soskice–Iversen paper is analytic rather than empirical, but the data in Table 2.1 – taken from their paper – helps to illustrate the puzzle (the table is literally only illustrative).

The table shows the equilibrium rate of unemployment in 17 OECD countries characterized by different types of unions and monetary rules.[5] With one exception, Cukierman et al.'s index of legal central bank independence is used as a proxy for the monetary rule, dividing the sample into an accommodating and a nonaccommodating category.[6] With regard to the number of unions, centralization of wage bargaining is used as a proxy. Although there is no consensus on the classification of every bargaining system, most industrial relations specialists agree on the ones that are either highly decentralized (Canada, France, New Zealand, the UK and the United States or highly centralized (Austria, Denmark, Finland, Norway, and Sweden). We treat the remainder (Australia, Belgium, Germany, Italy, Japan, Netherlands, and Switzerland) as intermediate cases.[7]

Note that monetary rule appears to be largely unrelated to unemployment when the number of unions is either very large or very small, but that nonaccommodating rules are associated with significantly *lower* unemployment than accommodating rules when the number of unions is intermediate.[8] Although data of this nature can be only suggestive, a number of more detailed empirical studies support the notion that monetary rules matter for unemployment when their interactive effects with the centralization of wage setting are taken into account (Hall 1994; Franzese and Hall, this volume; Iversen forthcoming; Garrett and Way, 1995).

A second criticism of Calmfors–Driffill is that it focuses on centralization of collective bargaining regimes, while coordination may be a more appropriate concept (Soskice 1990). Centralization refers analytically to the number of independent bargaining levels or sectors. But it is normally measured by reference to the number of levels or sectors without consideration of linkages between them. Coordination, by contrast, relates to the linkages between bargaining in formally separate environments. In terms of the Prisoners' Dilemma, a centralized bargaining system "solves" the problem – even when there are several unions involved in the centralized bargain – by in effect creating a

---

5 Equilibrium unemployment rates are proxied by OECD estimates for the nonaccelerating wage rates of unemployment in the period 1973–93 (i.e., post–Bretton Woods), except in the cases of Switzerland and New Zealand, where these are not available (we use national definitions instead) (OECD 1996).

6 The exception is Japan, where the monetary authorities began to adhere to an unambiguously nonaccommodating rule after 1973, even though the central bank remained legally dependent (Hutchison, Taketoshi, et al. forthcoming). This is recognized by Cukiermanm, Webb, and Neyapti, who attribute nonaccommodating monetary policies in Japan to the influence of an exceptionally "conservative" Ministry of Finance (1992:372).

7 The centralization of wage bargaining in different countries is reviewed in a recent OECD study (OECD 1997a). Our classification is consistent with the most frequently used classifications of centralization (Flanagan, Soskice, et al. 1983; Iversen 1998).

8 Any attempt to capture these relationships in a simply additive model would fail, and it is not surprising that past studies employing a simple additive methodology have failed to find any strong employment effects of either central bank independence (Alesina and Summers 1993; Bleaney 1996) or bargaining structure (OECD 1997a).

binding agreement among the parties. When that cannot be done, coordination tries to mimic the same result.

The first point to make about effective coordination is that two institutional elements are necessary for it to work. The first is a system of knowledge transmission, so that different bargaining groups know what outcome is expected of them. This may take the form of consultation across bargaining levels to arrive at agreed figures; or it may take the form of "key" bargains, where one particular sector bargains first, so that other sectors can then follow its lead. In most cases, knowledge transmission includes both consultation and key bargains.

But successful knowledge transmission is insufficient by itself to solve the Prisoners' Dilemma problem. This can be easily seen. Take an economy in which there is a recognized key bargain in a one sector. The other sectors bargain in the knowledge of the outcome of this key bargain. That no more helps the bargainers in the other sectors to exert restraint than it would give an incentive for the second prisoner to remain silent (i.e., cooperate) if he knew that the first prisoner had done so. Or imagine that unions in each sector had reached a nonbinding mutual agreement to restrain wages in individual sector bargaining: They would have no incentive to stick to such an agreement. Hence effective coordination requires more than knowledge transmission.

The second component thus involves some form of potential sanction for those bargainers who do not engage in restraint. If coordination is solely across unions, sanctioning may not be easy. This is because unions are unlikely to be engaged in activities involving cross-sectoral cooperation (apart from the wage bargaining itself). For example, it would be an ineffective sanction for an engineering union to withdraw from vocational training in the hope that this would penalize unrestrained wage bargaining by a public-sector union – since vocational training and most other areas of union activity are conducted on a primarily sectoral basis. Moreover, it is not easy for a key bargainer to sanction inappropriate behavior by followers by its own subsequent wage behavior – as the logic of punishment in repeated games would suggest as a strategy: For if all unions bar one behaved in a restrained way in round 1, the punishment strategy in round 2 of all behaving in an unrestrained way would "not be worth the candle" – it would raise unemployment all round.

Most systems in which coordinated bargaining is important share two characteristics that partly solve the sanctioning requirement. On the one hand, it is usually the case that employers and their organizations play a central role in the coordination. And on the other, it is usually the case that monetary policy is nonaccommodating.

The restraining role of employers operates in two ways. First, the individual sectoral employer interest is in restraint of real wages. Second, it is arguable that there is somewhat greater possibility of cross-sectoral sanctioning among employers than unions. This is because, in those economies in which wage coordination is possible, companies operate within a long-term patient finance background and this is supported by stable cross-shareholding agreements. Cross-shareholdings usually spread across sectors, so that pressure can in principle be brought to bear on the large companies in aberrant sectors. This is probably reinforced by the links between companies via technology transfer.

The second support is that of nonaccommodating monetary policy. This works in broadly similar ways to the analysis of Soskice–Iversen above in the case of independently bargaining unions, but there are some important additions. Assume one union strikes a key bargain and that bargaining in the other sectors follows; unions and perhaps employers in these other sectors are sanctioned if their outcomes are above that of the key bargain; however, the effectiveness of the sanctions diminishes with the unemployment rate – so that close to full employment sanctions are ineffective; hence, restrained only by these potential sanctions, equilibrium unemployment will be above that in the fully centralized bargaining outcome. What additional impact does nonaccommodating monetary policy have? It operates in two ways. As in the independent union bargaining case, each follower union has some incentive to engage in further restraint: as in that case, the degree of this restraint depends inversely on the number of follower unions. In addition, the incentive for the key bargainers to engage in restraint is greatly increased, since – to the extent that their key bargain is followed by the other sectors – a wage cut of $x\%$ in the key sector is equivalent to an economy-wide $x\%$ wage cut. Thus, the sanctioning mechanism and nonaccommodating monetary policy reinforce each other in the coordinating wage-bargaining systems.

Various accounts of the operation of particular coordinated bargaining systems can be found (Hall 1994; Soskice 1990), including a detailed recent statistical discussion (OECD 1997a). Where the concept of coordination is useful is in systems in which there is less than complete centralization. Then it offers a way of looking at the extent to which a functional equivalent to centralization is in existence. Although this functional equivalent may be less effective than complete centralization, its existence may nevertheless sharply modify analyses based purely on measures of centralization. In particular, it leads to an empirical problem with Calmfors–Driffill (see Table 2.2). This concerns two countries, Switzerland and Japan, which play an important statistical role in the Calmfors–Driffill analysis in that they are classified as the 16th and 17th least centralized wage-bargaining systems out of the 19 economies and also have very low unemployment. Thus they strongly reinforce the correlation between decentralized systems and low unemployment. Yet they both score high on the coordinated bargaining index (see also the OECD scores in Table 2.3). Thus it would be more correct to say that they reinforce a quite different correlation, between high coordination and low unemployment.

Table 2.2. *Measures of centralization and employer coordination*

Country	Centralization	Employer coordination
Belgium	8	2 (10)
Denmark	4	3 (5)
France	11	2 (10)
Germany	6	3 (5)
Ireland	12	1 (15)
Italy	13	1 (15)
Netherlands	7	2 (10)
Spain	11	1 (15)
UK	12	1 (15)
Australia	10	1 (15)
New Zealand	9	1 (15)
Canada	17	1 (15)
United States	16	1 (15)
Japan	14	2 (10) *3 (5)*
Austria	1	3 (5)
Finland	5	3 (5)
Norway	2	3 (5)
Sweden	3	3 (5)
Switzerland	15	3 (5)

Sources: Column 2 is the Calmfors–Driffill measure of centralization of wage bargaining systems (Calmfors and Driffill 1988, table 3). Column 3 is the Layard–Nickell–Jackman measure of employer co-ordination in wage bargaining systems (Layard, Nickell et al. 1991, p. 419). Since high coordination is a high number and high central-ization is a low number, and since the spread of coordination goes only from 1 to 3, the numbers in parentheses, $5 = 3$, $10 = 2$, $15 = 1$, are designed to make comparison easier. The LNJ index is similar to that of the author (Soskice 1990), which covers fewer countries; it also argued there that Japanese employer coordination is high – hence the italicized numbers.

3. THE OPEN ECONOMY

In this section we consider the analysis of an open economy within a fixed exchange rate system. This approximates the experience of European economies in the decade from the mid-1980s to the present for members of the Exchange Rate Mechanism (ERM) of the European Monetary System (EMS), and it is close to the experience of most other advanced economies.

The purpose of this and the next section is to show that in open economies aggregate demand can have a profoundly deflationary effect on unemployment for a considerable period of time, and that much of the increase in unemployment in Northern Europe in the 1990s has been the consequence of demand deflation. By contrast the relatively favorable unemployment performance of the United States and the UK has reflected a more benign aggregate-demand management policy. It may, however, be the case (an argument of Iversen will be developed along these lines) that there are structural reasons for these societal differences in aggregate-demand management (Iversen forthcoming).

MULTIPLE UNEMPLOYMENT EQUILIBRIA IN THE OPEN ECONOMY AND THE DETERMINING ROLE OF AGGREGATE DEMAND

The analysis of the open economy is quite different from that of a closed economy. In a closed economy there is a unique level of unemployment at which the price-determined real wage is equal to the bargained real wage, and which is thus consistent with stable inflation. In an open economy there is a range of such unemployment levels. The actual rate of unemployment is determined by the level of aggregate demand. So in the closed economy the unique equilibrium unemployment rate determines the level of aggregate demand necessary to produce stable inflation, whereas in the open economy the level of aggregate demand determines the equilibrium rate of unemployment. Why does the open economy work in such a way?

Put most simply, prices are set in the open economy as a weighted average of domestic unit labor costs and world prices. World prices affect the price level (P) in the open economy as a reflection in part of costs of imported materials and in part of the need to remain competitive against import competition and competition in export markets. Assuming domestic unit labor costs are equal to the nominal wage (W) and a fixed exchange rate of unity, where $P*$ is the world price level, the price-setting equation becomes:

$$P = \alpha W + (1 - \alpha) P* \tag{7}$$

where α is the weight assigned to domestic costs, and this implies, dividing by P and rearranging:

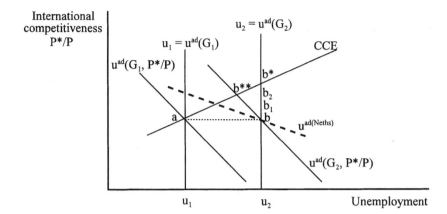

Figure 2.4. *Multiple unemployment equilibrium in the open economy.*

$$w_p = \alpha^{-1} - ((1 - \alpha)/\alpha) \, P^*/P \qquad (8)$$

Thus the price-determined real wage, w_p, varies inversely with P^*/P, the level of international competitiveness, that is, the inverse of the real exchange rate. (Note that a rise in P^*/P, produced by a fall in w, is equivalent to a real devaluation.) Writing the BRW schedule:

$$w_b = w_b \, (u) \qquad (9)$$

it can be seen that the equation of w_b and w_p holds at any level of u, so long as P^*/P is at an appropriate level:

$$w_b \, (u) = w_p = \alpha^{-1} - ((1 - \alpha)/\alpha) \, P^*/P \qquad (10)$$

This relationship, which we can call the Competing Claims Equilibrium (CCE) schedule since it balances the competing claims of business in price setting and labor in wage bargaining, is shown in Figure 2.4 with competitiveness on the vertical axis and u, as before, on the horizontal. It is upward sloping because an increase in unemployment reduces the bargained real wage, implying a fall in w_p and thus permitting an increase in competitiveness (or a real devaluation).

Actual unemployment is determined by aggregate demand, as shown for instance by the vertical line $u_1 = u^{ad} \, (G_1)$. What happens when a reduction in aggregate demand increases unemployment from u_1 to $u_2 = u^{ad} \, (G_2)$, as a result (say) of a cut in government expenditure from G_1 to G_2? Suppose initially price inflation, p, is 3% equal to world price inflation, p^*; and that expected price inflation remains equal to world price inflation of 3% throughout. Assuming that unemployment rises before relative prices change, the economy moves from the initial equilibrium at a to the out of equilibrium position b. At b, the real wage is (say) 1% above the BRW (i.e., competitiveness is below that consistent with this weaker state of the labor market). Hence money wages increase by 2%, 1% less than the expected rate of price inflation of 3%. Prices now increase by a weighted average of money wages and world prices – suppose price inflation is 0.5 of money wage inflation and 0.5 of world price inflation; so price inflation is 2.5%. This implies that real wages fall by 0.5% and competitiveness rises by 0.5%; this moves us halfway up to the CCE to b_1. Now the process continues again, since the real wage is still too high and competitiveness too low; this time real wages fall by a further 0.25% and competitiveness rises by a further 0.25%; we move to b_2. This process continues until the economy reaches b^*. At b^* the economy is again in equilibrium, with price inflation and wage inflation both equal to and stable at 3%.

Given this analysis, there are three reasons why open economies are likely to get stuck at whatever level of unemployment they are at. First, the basis of NAIRU-type approaches to policy-making is that there is a unique unemployment rate that policymakers cannot alter – except perhaps by supply-side structural measures. Monetary or fiscal reflationary action makes sense in this schema only when unemployment is above the equilibrium rate. And this situation is signaled by a continuously falling rate of inflation. As we have seen, such a basis for policy is appropriate to a closed economy, in which there is a unique equilibrium rate of unemployment, but not to an open economy, in which equilibrium unemployment is determined by the level of aggregate demand. In the open economy, an initiating collapse in aggregate demand leads to a temporary fall in inflation below the world inflation rate, but then a subsequent recovery to that rate as a new equilibrium is established at a higher level of unemployment. Thus, *insofar as policymakers are basing policy decisions on a closed economy model with a unique equilibrium unemployment rate*, they will interpret the new equilibrium as an upward shift in the unique equilibrium unemployment rate: Hence they will perceive measures of demand reflation as inappropriate.

There is a second reason why the open economy may get stuck at higher unemployment: the absence of strong automatic mechanisms to bring about reflation. In a closed economy, at least in principle, continuously falling inflation rates lead to an increase in wealth for money holders and lower interest rates, and hence to an increase in aggregate demand. If in addition there are rational expectations, these mechanisms operate instantaneously with a unique equilibrium unemployment rate. Of course, these effects are highly contested in the context of a closed economy (Tobin 1993). In an open economy with quasi-fixed exchange rates no such effect takes place since any level of unemployment is consistent with stable inflation. The only way in which adjustment can take place is via the increase in international competitiveness as a result of lower real wages in the new higher unemployment equilibrium.[9] It is useful to spell out

---

9 Another much longer term mechanism – the gradual accumulation of foreign assets as a result of external surplus – is discussed in section 5.

this possible means of adjustment, since it will be discussed below in relation to the Dutch experience. So far, the u_{ad} schedule has been assumed to be vertical. But exports and imports are components of aggregate demand and depend – positively and negatively, respectively – on the level of competitiveness, P^*/P. With P^*/P as an argument of the schedule, it is now backward sloping as in Figure 2.4. The movement of the economy after an initial cut in G is now from a, the original equilibrium, to b – this movement embodying the (multiplied up) effect of the cut in G before any change in P^*/P; and then from b to b^{**}, in which aggregate demand increases as a result of the effect of the increase in P^*/P on the balance of trade.

It is worth spelling out this argument. With the cut in G to G_2, the economy moves to the new aggregate demand schedule, u^{ad} $(G_2, P^*/P)$. b is below the CCE schedule so that the real wage is higher than it should be, given the weakness of union bargaining power at this higher level of unemployment. As the real wage falls, so international competitiveness increases (see equation (8)). Aggregate demand now rises along $u^{ad}(G_2, P^*/P)$ as the increasing competitiveness stimulates exports and reduces imports. The smaller the economy and the larger the exposed sector, the stronger will this effect be. But it cannot outweigh the initial deflation. That is to say b^{**} will always be at a higher level of unemployment than b.

Let us now return to the political economist's question of the relation between institution and economic performance, in particular that between the degree of coordination in wage bargaining and unemployment. In the closed economy, with its unique equilibrium rate of unemployment, it is reasonable to hypothesize that actual unemployment will roughly measure equilibrium unemployment, at least over a period of time such as a decade. The justification of such an hypothesis is that governments could not face permanently rising inflation – they would be forced to take deflationary action – nor refuse to reflate to reduce unemployment in the face of permanently falling inflation. Thus, actual unemployment would be pushed toward the unique equilibrium rate.

But the analysis in this section implies that the methodology standardly used in comparative political economy to test the relation between coordination and unemployment makes no sense when applied to open economies (except perhaps over very long periods). How, therefore, can the influence of coordinated wage bargaining be assessed? We need first to set out the concept of the lowest sustainable equilibrium rate of unemployment. Returning to Figure 2.4, one might be tempted to say that any level of unemployment was sustainable as an equilibrium. Moving down the equilibrium CCE schedule from right to left, however, the international competitiveness of the economy deteriorates as unemployment falls. This reduces exports and increases imports, thus worsening the external balance; and this is reinforced by the decline in unemployment, which reflects an increase in national income and thus an increase in imports.

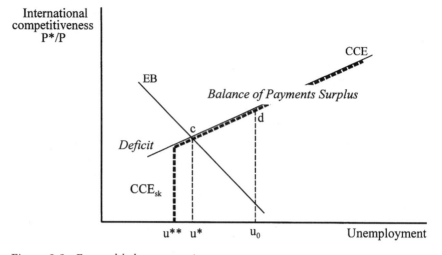

Figure 2.5. *External balance constraint.*

At some point along the CCE, therefore, external balance will be in equilibrium and the economy will be able to remain at a lower level of unemployment only if there are sustainable inflows of capital. Assuming these do not exist, the lowest sustainable equilibrium level of unemployment will be where the CCE hits this external balance constraint.

For subsequent discussion, it will be useful to draw an External Balance schedule that goes through this point (Figure 2.5). Assuming the external balance is zero at c on CCE, the EB schedule will move in a NW direction above the CCE: an increase in competitiveness – which increases exports and reduces imports – allows an increase in unemployment, which increases imports, while still maintaining external balance; and for similar reasons EB will move down and to the right below c. All unemployment levels along CCE to the right of the intersection with EB are sustainable, but the external balance constraint rules out unemployment equilibria to the left of the intersection. Thus the *minimum* sustainable equilibrium rate of unemployment is u^* corresponding to c.

ESTIMATING THE MINIMUM SUSTAINABLE EQUILIBRIUM UNEMPLOYMENT RATE

We now want to test whether there is a relationship between coordinated wage-bargaining systems and the minimum equilibrium unemployment rate. Intuitively we want to subtract some measure of the balance of payments surplus from the actual unemployment rate to get the minimum rate. A good approximation is achieved by simply subtracting a multiple of the external balance as a percentage of GDP from the unemployment rate. The reasoning is explained in Appendix 1. Using this rule, we can compare the actual and adjusted unemployment performance of coordinated and uncoordinated economies over the period 1986–94 (see Table 2.3).

The third column of Table 2.3 shows the approximation to the minimal sustainable equilibrium rate of unemployment. Thus the difference between the second and third columns is the external surplus as a percentage of GDP. What is striking about these (very rough and ready) OECD figures is the difference between the average of the performances of coordinated and uncoordinated economies once the adjustment has been made.

Although there are big within-group variances, for what it is worth, the null hypothesis that the means (11.1 and 5.3) are drawn from the same distribution can be rejected, the sum of the standard deviations of the means being 2.43. Even more striking are the differences between the behavior of the external balances of the two groups of economies (during this period). The mean of the uncoordinated group was a deficit of 3.0% with a standard deviation of 1.056, the standard deviation of the mean being 0.4735; that of the coordinated group

Table 2.3. *Coordination and macroeconomic performance*

	OECD coordination score 1994 (1980 in parenthesis)	Unemployment rate 1986–94	Unemployment rate *minus* current account as % of GDP, 1986–94
Austria	3 (3)	3.6	3.7
Germany (West)	3 (3)	7.0	5.1
Japan	3 (3)	2.5	−0.3
Norway	2.5 (2.5)	4.5	4.5
Italy	2.5 (1.5)	11.5	12.1
Denmark	2+ (2.5)	9.9	9.7
Switzerland	2+ (2+)	1.8	−3.5
Finland	2+ (2+)	8.8	11.5
Sweden	2 (2.5)	3.6	4.7
Netherlands	2 (2)	8.4	5.7
Average (coord)		6.2	5.3
Australia	1.5 (2+)	8.5	13.0
New Zealand	1 (1.5)	7.4	10.2
Canada	1 (1)	9.5	13.1
United Kingdom	1 (1.5)	8.7	10.7
United States	1 (1)	6.3	8.4
Avg (uncoord)		8.0	11.1

−0.84% with a standard deviation of 2.357 and a standard deviation of the mean of 0.736. The null hypothesis of the same population is therefore sharply rejected: a difference between means of 3.84 with the standard deviation of the difference equal to 1.2095. Indeed − leaving aside the Finnish deficit of 2.7%, reflecting the collapse of its main export market rather than domestic demand factors − the maximum deficit of the coordinated group is 1.1% and the minimum deficit of the uncoordinated group is 2.0%.

Thus it can be concluded that aggregate demand policies have been *relatively* much more deflationary in the coordinated economies than in the uncoordinated over this period. This implies that the potential performance of coordinated wage-bargaining systems is underestimated by actual unemployment figures over this period, relative to uncoordinated bargaining systems. Moreover, these figures underestimate the difference since they do not take interdependence of economies into account. This point will be developed in the next section.

EXPLAINING DEFLATIONARY POLICIES

Assuming these differences are systematic for this period, what accounts for them? It is clear that this is an underresearched area, yet one of considerable importance. For it goes sharply against the corporatist literature, which suggested that coordinated bargainers exercised restraint because they were able to conclude full-employment deals with the government (Cameron 1984; Lange and Garrett 1985; Przeworski and Wallerstein 1982). The suggestion here, at least prima facie, is that coordinated bargainers exercise restraint *either because of or in spite of* the inability of government to guarantee full employment levels of aggregate demand. Why does the corporatist argument no longer hold?

Two explanations are developed as to why coordinated economies might be more likely in the period since the late 1980s to pursue a cautious macroeconomic policy. In this section the explanation is based on the move in the 1980s of most coordinated economies to something like a German model. A different − though consistent − explanation based on German hegemony is developed in the next section.

The coordinated economies of Northern Europe could be divided in the early 1980s between the Scandinavian economies with centralized egalitarian bargaining systems and a Keynesian commitment to full employment and those in which there was neither compression of differentials, nor full employment guarantees, nor centralized bargaining. A decade later most of the former (not Norway) had moved to the latter model − which might be called Germanic flexible coordination. The reason behind this convergence on the flexible coordination has been spelled out both by Iversen (1996, this volume) and by Pontusson and Swenson (1996, this volume; see also Soskice 1999). In the Scandinavian social democracies the interest of business and of skilled workers switched from aggregate wage restraint to a concern with the development of skilled committed work forces. This required an end to centralized bargaining, the compression of differentials and full employment for the following reasons: Full employment and narrow differentials meant that companies could not retain employees. Moreover, full employment reinforced the pressure for the compression of differentials, since the bargaining power of the unions representing the lower paid was increased relative to that of skilled workers' unions the closer the economy was to full employment. Under centralized bargaining, the unions representing the lower paid were prepared to engage in real-wage restraint on condition that the skilled unions accepted compression of differentials, and on condition that the government maintained full employment.

By opting out of centralized bargaining, literal full employment was no longer a feasible policy option for government – at least on the assumption that the lower-paid unions could no longer guarantee wage restraint at full employment in the absence of compression of differentials. Thus government was forced to adopt relatively more deflationary policies. To ensure that it was not bounced back into the pursuit of overfull employment policies as a result of political pressures, it was necessary for government to tie its fiscal and monetary hands behind its back. The most obvious choice was then to join or to tie currencies to the European Monetary System. This implied that the monetary authority became nonaccommodating, since its interest rate policy was now dictated by the need to a maintain a fixed exchange rate; and fiscal policy needed to be sufficiently restrained to avoid external pressure on the exchange rate.

How is this consistent with the Soskice–Iversen analysis of an economy, which implies that monetary nonaccommodation leads to a reduction in the equilibrium unemployment rate compared to accommodating monetary policy? There are three parts to the answer.

(i) Given the number of "coordinated" bargaining unions, nonaccommo-dating macropolicies will produce a lower minimum feasible equilibrium unemployment rate. This is because the CCE schedule will be higher with nonaccommodating policies. Why? Any demand schedule that bargainers face (cf. Figure 2.2) will be flatter with nonaccommo-dating policies than in their absence; hence the indifference curve in the nonaccommodating case will be tangential to the demand curve at a lower level of international competitiveness (higher real wage) than in the accommodating case; the CCE traces these points of tangency. Hence the nonaccommodating CCE will intersect the External Balance schedule at a lower unemployment rate than with the accommodating CCE.

(ii) But actual equilibrium unemployment will be determined (at least in the short and medium run) by aggregate demand as well as wage-bargaining behavior. This is the fundamental difference between a closed economy and an open economy. Moreover, as has been pointed out, in the environment of the Exchange Rate Mechanism of the EMS, it is not possible to use monetary or fiscal policy to maintain unemployment at its minimal feasible equilibrium level. Negative aggregate-demand shocks can thus not be corrected. Sweden suffered from three such shocks. First, it had to engage in retrenchment of public expenditure and interest increases to attempt to satisfy foreign exchange markets. Second, there was a sharp rise in the savings ratio as households tried to rebuild their financial position after the rise in interest rates had led to a collapse in property prices and hence put into debt many households who had overborrowed from banks in the late 1980s when bank lending was deregulated. Finally, demand for Swedish exports declined as a result of slow growth in Western Europe from 1992 on, the consequence of German deflationary policies – discussed in the next section.

(iii) It is likely to be the case that the minimum feasible equilibrium unemployment rate will have increased as a result of the move from centralized bargaining to coordinated bargaining. The changes away from centralized full-employment bargaining systems were brought about because neither exporting employers nor skilled-workers unions found the compression of differentials associated with the former acceptable. Hence the preference function of skilled unions is different from that of unions representing low-paid employees: Given the choice, skilled unions will not choose as low levels of unemployment as will low-paid unions, since low unemployment will improve the relative bargaining power of the low-paid unions and thus lead to compression of differentials. Assume that there is a level of unemployment, u^{**}, which skilled unions would be unhappy to go below, then they would cease behaving in a restrained way at around that level of unemployment, so that the shape of the CCE in the coordinated case would be as shown in Figure 2.5 – where it takes the dashed form CCE_{sk}. The minimal feasible equilibrium unemployment rate, u^*, is given by the intersection of the CCE and EB schedules, so that the reduction in equilibrium unemployment would be pronounced only if u^{**} was greater than u^*.

THE SMALL-COUNTRY CASE

There is one partial qualification to the analysis of the last subsection. Wage restraint in a small country is likely to be more successful at reducing unemployment than in a large country. Thus both the Netherlands and Denmark have pursued policies of wage moderation that have brought down unemployment to relatively low levels in the second half of the 1990s, 6.0% in Denmark and 6.3% in the Netherlands in 1996. There are two reasons for this, one stemming from the degree of openness, the other from small size.

(i) The more open an economy, the larger the share of exports and imports in GDP. A given percentage improvement in international competitiveness (brought about by wage moderation) will normally increase exports and decrease imports by a percentage amount that is independent of the share of exports or imports in that economy's GDP. This is because the price elasticity of exports or imports relates to competition in individual world markets, which is normally independent of GDP trade shares. Hence a given degree of wage restraint will have a bigger impact on the GDP of that economy the larger the share of exports and imports in GDP in that economy. In terms of the diagram used above (Figure 2.4), the aggregate demand schedule will be relatively flat in the open-economy case, as shown by the $u^{ad(Neths)}$ schedule. The union will therefore choose a more restrained bargaining policy at b^{***}. It should be noted that this does not depend on whether or not macropolicies are accommodating.

(ii) The smaller the economy pursuing a strategy of wage restraint, the less likely it is that larger economies will respond to that strategy. The case of the Netherlands and Germany is illustrative. The Dutch strategy has been to set Dutch nominal wages in manufacturing 20% below those in German manufacturing. This has led to Dutch exports to Germany rising. But it does not pay German unions to adopt (significantly more) restrained policies because Dutch exports are too small in quantitative terms.

4. INTERDEPENDENCE BETWEEN ECONOMIES AND THE TRANSMISSION OF DEFLATION: THE BUNDESBANK AND MAASTRICHT IN THE 1990S

THE INTERDEPENDENCE OF OPEN ECONOMIES

It has so far been assumed that economies can be analyzed independently – whether open or closed. Almost all work in comparative political economy that looks at the links between wage-setting institutions and unemployment makes this assumption (usually assuming that the economy is closed). But there are powerful direct relationships and feedback mechanisms that bind together those economies with close trade links and/or exchange rate ties. These imply that unemployment in one country may be affected by such factors as monetary and fiscal policy or labor cost developments in related economies. To assess the impact of institutions in country X on X's unemployment, these factors need to be netted out. Since close trading and exchange rate links characterize most of the coordinated economies of Northern Europe, and since the core economy of the region – Germany – was responsible for a series of major deflationary impulses through the 1990s, it is important to understand these propagation mechanisms to appreciate to what extent high unemployment in Northern Europe reflects these demand factors rather than a failure of the underlying institutions. In this subsection these propagation mechanisms are analyzed (there is an additional interest in the analysis since it is equivalent to that governing the interrelationships of member states of the future Single European Currency Area).

There are six effects which need to be distinguished, and which reinforce each other. Two economies will be considered, which can be called G for Germany and S for Sweden.

(i) *Direct aggregate demand effect:* The most basic effect is this: G adopts a deflationary monetary or fiscal policy, which lowers aggregate demand in G, hence G's imports from S, and hence – via the export multiplier – S's aggregate demand, so that unemployment in S rises. But the magnitude of this direct effect is limited. A fall of aggregate demand in G of 1% leads to a similar percentage decline in S's exports to G. But S's exports to G represent only, say, 15% of total exports, and exports are only 40% of S's GDP; hence the percentage fall in S's GDP is the product of the export multiplier (say 2), the percentage fall in S's exports to G (1%) and the share of the latter in S's GDP (of the order of 6%), in total 0.12%.

(ii) *The ERM exchange rate effect:* Suppose G's deflation is induced by monetary policy, as a result of the Bundesbank having raised interest rates by, say, 2%. Then S has to raise interest rates by the same amount if its currency is tied formally or informally to the deutschmark. Thus the effect of G's deflationary policies on S is now of the same order of the magnitude as their effect within G. In other words, German monetary policy changes induces all other members of the ERM to adopt similar monetary policy changes or to leave the ERM, as the UK and Italy did in 1992. The effects of German monetary deflation on Germany are similar to its effects on other members of the ERM.

(iii) *The ERM and Maastricht fiscal effects:* To maintain S's currency in line with the deutschmark in the absence of exchange controls, holders of the currency have to be convinced that S is behaving with fiscal prudence. Interpret this requirement as a condition that S cannot let its public-sector deficit increase. The effect of both (i) and (ii) above is a decline ceteris paribus in S's GDP and hence a decline in tax revenues and an increase in public expenditure as unemployment benefits rise, leading to an increase in the public deficit. To hold the deficit constant,

S has to engage in cuts in public expenditure or increase in taxation. This leads to a cumulative deflationary process, since if expenditure is initially cut by an amount equal to the increase in the deficit, the resulting deflation in economic activity again increases the deficit above its original level.

How should these effects be evaluated? The structure of the argument is that an initial cut in expenditure [for example, a cut in S's exports to G as in (i) above, or a cut in domestic spending as a result of an interest rate increase as in (ii)] leads to a multiplied reduction in GDP. The multiplier will be greater if the government has to engage in further expenditure cuts to prevent the public-sector deficit from rising. In a simple Keynesian model,[10] in which the deficit can increase as income falls, the multiplier is $1/[1 - c(1 - t) + m]$, where c is the marginal propensity to spend out of increased income, t is the average marginal tax take out of increased income, and m the marginal propensity to import; if $c = 0.7$, $t = 0.3$, and $m = 0.4$, the multiplier is small at 1.1. If the deficit has to remain constant, the multiplier changes to $1/[1 - c(1 - t) - t + m]$ and its value rises to 1.66.

(iv) *Cumulative fiscal contraction:* Matters are made worse, however, when a number of related economies are simultaneously behaving in a similar way. So long as a small economy has a high propensity to import, a reduction in expenditure falls only partially on domestic demand since some part of the cut will fall on imports. In the multiplier formulas above, the greater is m the smaller the multiplier. In effect, deflation is being in part dumped on the economies with which S has the strongest trading links. But that is possible only if those economies are not under a public-sector deficit constraint. Both under ERM and under the Maastricht conditions, the ERM members and (a closely related set) the potential members of the single currency area are all operating under the requirement that deficits are steadily falling.

The effect is substantially to increase the multiplier. The reasoning is as follows: Assume there is no trade outside the group; it is in fact quite small, the total import propensity of the EU being around 10%, compared to the average propensity to import of the individual member countries of around 30% for the big economies and 50% for the smaller ones. Suppose, in fact, that there are just two economies, who trade uniquely with each other. Then the cushion provided by imports ceases to exist. For if expenditure is reduced in S, some portion of which – via reduction in imports from G – reduces expenditure in G, the government of both economies will have to take action to prevent deficits from rising as a result of reduced tax revenues. In the formula

10 The formulas are derived in Appendix 2.

for the multiplier, m now disappears (or is reduced to 0.1); the multiplier rises to around 3.

(v) *Wage propagation:* The above four mechanisms operate directly via demand shifts. They are reinforced by cost or price effects. When G adopts deflationary policies, real-wage inflation in G is held back on account of rising unemployment. Independently of any demand-side effect, this reduces the level of S's international competitiveness, since the real wage in S remains constant. Wage bargainers in S may at once respond to this situation by moderating wages to restore international competitiveness. If they do not, the S government may see this as a further reason for deflating to reduce domestic inflationary pressures.

(vi) *Unemployment equilibrium and shifting external balance constraints:* In all of the above, deflation moves economies from one equilibrium level of unemployment to a higher equilibrium level (as explained in the previous section). In addition, deflation in one country can raise the minimum sustainable equilibrium unemployment rate in others: When G deflates, it creates an external surplus (assuming it was previously in equilibrium) since its exports remain constant while its imports decrease. This implies that a counterpart deficit is created in those economies from which it imports. Thus S sees G's deflation in the form of an outward shift of its EB schedule. Since S's minimum equilibrium unemployment is determined by the intersection of the EB schedule and the CCE schedule, this outward shift of the EB schedule raises minimum equilibrium unemployment in S.

The implication of this is that the analysis of the previous section – in which it was argued that actual equilibrium unemployment might be above minimum equilibrium unemployment on account of domestic deflationary policies – may have taken insufficient account of the effect of deflation on minimum sustainable equilibrium unemployment. This is because domestic deflationary policies cannot shift the external balance schedule, but deflationary policies of trading partners can. In fact it can be seen in Table 2.3 that Germany – the major deflator in the Coordinated Economies group – has a balance of payments surplus (corrected unemployment below actual unemployment), while Sweden has a deficit and Denmark, Austria, and Norway are just in external balance.

By way of conclusion to this subsection, it will be noted that a number of mechanisms jointly reinforce the idea of an *asymmetric deflationary bias*. That is to say, governments have to respond to fiscal deficit and external deficit by deflation, but markets are nervous about reflationary fiscal packages even under conditions of fiscal surplus and external surplus. Moreover, monetary policy, for economies within the ERM, has to follow German monetary policy – interest rate reductions independently of the Bundesbank risk currencies falling below the ERM floor. These asymmetric deflationary conditions follow from two factors: membership of the Exchange Rate Mechanisms, and the leading role of the Bundesbank within the mechanism. Membership of the mechanism implies that markets are continuously testing those members who are seen as potentially candidates for leaving the mechanism. Thus Sweden in particular (and the UK in the early 1980s) was seen as being under political pressure to ease fiscal policy. Hence any sign of fiscal "weakness" was punished by the markets. And the leading role of the Bundesbank, with deflationary preferences, meant that there was no leadership available for coordinated reflation even under conditions of high unemployment and low inflation. We now turn to discuss the deflationary bias in German policy in more detail.

THE SOURCES OF DEFLATION: THE BUNDESBANK AND MAASTRICHT

The Exchange Rate Mechanism of the EMS works under German, specifically Bundesbank, hegemony. When the Bundesbank raises interest rates, other members of the ERM are forced to follow to maintain exchange-rate parities. The Bundesbank's concern is with the German inflation rate, not the European or ERM one. Its policies take no account of unemployment elsewhere in the ERM region. It can therefore adopt a tougher nonaccommodating stance than other ERM central banks, since other currencies have to adjust to the deutschmark rather than the other way round. It chooses to do so because it faces powerful actors in the German inflation-setting system who are large and coordinated enough to respond to its implicit threat strategy. That strategy is to use interest rate increases in response to what it perceives as inflationary pressures – whether those pressures come from wage bargainers, government, or import cost or tax increases uncompensated by wage moderation. Interest rate hikes dampen the labor market and specifically "punish" government by producing a slowdown in growth and export-sector unions by pushing up the exchange rate.

Moreover, the punishment is likely to be prolonged: If inflationary wage increases occur, as they did between 1990 and 1992 (or, another example, if the government imposes a parity exchange rate between ostmarks and deutschmarks against the Bundesbank's advice, as it did in 1990), the Bundesbank's antiinflationary reputation is damaged. The Bundesbank has both to punish the breach of the implicit understanding and to rebuild its damaged reputation – requiring a longer punishment phase. It is therefore unwilling to respond to the deflation it produces by symmetric cuts in interest rates. By contrast to the Federal Reserve Board, a fall in inflation to some target level is not the signal for the Bundesbank to pull down nominal interest rates sufficiently fast to cut real rates and hence stimulate domestic demand growth (Carlin and Soskice 1997). This is a consequence of the need of the Bundesbank to punish powerful unions; the Fed has no such need.

Two conditions are therefore necessary for the Bundesbank to maintain low inflation without putting unemployment at risk in Germany: first, that domestic actors – wage bargainers and governments – respond to the threat strategy of the Bundesbank with suitably noninflationary behavior; and/or second, that the improvement in German competitiveness that results – or exogenous factors – bring about a sufficient revival of foreign demand. The first condition broke down in the difficult period accompanying reunification of 1990 to 1992 (Carlin and Soskice 1997; Tullio, Steinherr et al. 1996). The second condition has become progressively less attainable since the development of a quasi-fixed exchange rate system in Western Europe, because the bulk of Germany's exports go to members of the system: for the greater the extent to which Germany's main trading partners follow German deflation, the less competitive advantage that deflation can gain for Germany. The consequence has been that the Bundesbank unleashed a savage deflation: In 1993 German GDP fell by 2%, the deutschmark appreciated by 15% between 1991 and 1995, and relative unit labor costs rose by 20%. For the reasons spelled out in the last subsection similar effects – only somewhat muted – were felt throughout the ERM member states. Only the UK, opting out of the ERM in 1992 and not returning, has been able to pursue a loose monetary policy and escape most of the rising unemployment.

To the monetary deflation across the ERM caused by the Bundesbank was added the fiscal deflation resulting from the concerns of those member states who aimed to join EMU to meet the Maastricht conditions. These required inter alia that public sector deficits be reduced to 3% by 1997. Of the countries listed in Table 2.3, the potential candidates for membership of EMU are all coordinated economies. Progressive fulfillment of the Maastricht public-sector deficit conditions has been strongly deflationary because the reductions in government expenditure have been multiplied by the constant deficit multiplier with limited ability to offload on other economies via import reductions; this is spelled out in (iv) in the previous subsection.

To conclude, it is misleading to argue that coordinated wage bargaining has become progressively more ineffective during the late 1980s and 1990s using standard arguments appropriate to a closed economy (section 2). Even if adjustments are made for open economies (section 3), the impact of aggregate demand on minimum equilibrium unemployment is only partially accounted for. A full analysis requires taking account of the interdependencies between economies. None of these adjustments would matter a great deal if one of three conditions held: (i) that the analysis concerned the long period, say 20 years or so, rather than a shorter period in which aggregate demand can play an important distorting role;[11] (ii) that trading links were roughly equally distributed

---

11 The arguments in this and the last section have concerned medium-run equilibria. If all economies were identical, these would not be stable inflation equilibria, since each economy cannot have a level of international competitiveness greater than unity. Hence the only long-run equilibrium for identical economies is where the CCE schedule cuts a horizontal line with unit international competitiveness.

across advanced economies, so that Western European economies traded as much with the United States as within Western Europe; and (iii) that deflationary policies were adopted randomly across economies, and did not affect coordinated more than uncoordinated economies. The problem for the analysis of the effectiveness of coordinated bargaining – as a viable alternative or superior option to deregulated labor markets – is that none of these three conditions apply: First, the interest in showing the ineffectiveness of coordinated bargaining stems from the weak unemployment performance of coordinated economies in the 1990s – in which it is claimed that a changing environment now favors deregulated labor markets; thus analysis of the longer term is ruled out. Second, most coordinated wage setting takes place in economies linked by close trading ties. Third, the ERM of the EMS and its domination by the Bundesbank has imposed deflationary policies in the 1990s on the largely coordinated economies who are its members.

6. BY WAY OF CONCLUSION: COMPARING DEREGULATED AND COORDINATED ECONOMIES

Where does this leave the comparison of deregulated and coordinated economies? If the analysis of the first and second sections of the chapter are taken seriously, the implication is that in a closed economy equilibrium unemployment in the deregulated economies will always be lower than in the coordinated economies – unless coordination is perfectly effective, in which case equilibrium unemployment will be the same. This analysis can be taken over to the open-economy case at least where the external balance schedule is the same for a deregulated and a coordinated economy.

As we have suggested, however, coordinated economies have performed on average relatively well compared to deregulated economies as far as unemployment is concerned (Table 2.3) over the period 1986–94, when demand factors are taken into account. The comparison is sharper when Finland and Italy are removed from the comparison – both having suffered from exceptional factors.

Although this evidence is no more than suggestive, it points to the existence of other factors than those discussed. Three possible factors are the following, though there is no satisfactory evidence yet:

(i) Education and training systems. Deregulated economies have difficulty in equipping the least able or privileged children with basic employability skills. Part of the reason for this is that employers are unprepared to engage in serious initial training, because the wage-setting system exposes them to poaching. Instead, at the bottom end of the labor market, they offer only unskilled employment possibilities and these give children who believe it unlikely that they will be able to get better jobs little incentive for taking school seriously. Thus both education and training elude them. By contrast, employers are more engaged in coordinated economies, both in apprenticeship systems and in maintaining close contact with public vocational training.

Why should this difference in skills at the bottom affect unemployment in the 1980s and 1990s? One position is that technological change has reduced the demand for unskilled workers relative to skilled; and there is strong evidence that "in all [OECD] countries, unemployment rates for the unskilled are several times higher than for the skilled," (OECD 1997c): 93. In all economies, unemployment rates for the unskilled are high because unskilled jobs tend to be more insecure (OECD 1997b: table 5.9), and hence the probability of unemployment spells is higher. In addition, the lower the productivity and hence potential earnings of an individual, the greater the chance that unemployment benefits will exceed potential earnings, thus increasing the likelihood of unemployment. Against this, the more deregulated the economy the lower unemployment benefits are likely to be and the more flexible are wages downward.

Thus if the weakness of training in deregulated economies is to help explain possible weaknesses in their unemployment performance relative to coordinated economies, it needs to be seen empirically whether or not their training failure at the bottom end of the labor market is or is not compensated by low unemployment benefits and downward flexibility in wages.

(ii) Another aspect of coordinated economies is greater job tenure (OECD 1997b: table 5.5, table 5A.1). This is not an absolutely clear-cut relation, since Denmark and the Netherlands have low job tenure – probably due to small firm size. To the extent to which the relation holds, the degree of frictional unemployment will be lower.

(iii) The fact that the UK, the United States, New Zealand, Australia, and Ireland have relatively deregulated labor markets does not mean that unions are nonexistent. We assumed in the discussion in sections 1 and 2 of market imperfections in the new Keynesian approach and their absence in the neoclassical that deregulation of labor markets would produce perfect competition. The continued existence of unions in the deregulated economies will be consistent with neoclassical results (in terms of no involuntary unemployment in equilibrium) only if the unions face more or less horizontal demand for labor schedules in their sectors. But if unions did face horizontal demand schedules, they would have no bargaining power, and hence it would be difficult to understand why they existed. But to the extent to which they do face nonhorizontal labor demand schedules, and given that they do not coordinate their bargaining, the result is to push up the bargained real-wage schedule above the supply-of-labor schedule and hence raise equilibrium unemployment.

We may conclude then that there are a number of factors that differentiate coordinated and deregulated economies that may explain unemployment differences. These seem to suggest, together with the integration of the demand side into the analysis, an important agenda for the future.

Appendix 1:

ADJUSTMENT TO TAKE ACCOUNT OF AGGREGATE-DEMAND EFFECTS ON UNEMPLOYMENT IN AN OPEN ECONOMY

The actual unemployment rate, $u = 1 - e$, where e is the employment rate, E/LF, employment (E) divided by the labor force (LF). Assuming constant labor productivity (LP), $E = Y/LP$, so that $u = 1 - Y/(LF \cdot LP)$, where Y is GDP. And so

$$u = u_{min} + (Y_{min} - Y)/(LF \cdot LP) \tag{A1.1}$$

where u and Y are the actual rates of unemployment and GDP and u_{min} and Y_{min} the minimum sustainable rates. Let B be the external balance, $B = X(\theta) - m(\theta)Y$, where $\theta = P*/P$, X is the level of real exports, and m is the propensity to import. Noting that $B_{min} = 0 = X(\theta_{min}) - m(\theta_{min})Y_{min}$,

$$B - B_{min} = B = X(\theta) - X(\theta_{min}) - m(\theta)Y + m(\theta_{min})Y_{min}$$

or to a first-order approximation,

$$B = X'(\theta)(\theta - \theta_{min}) - m'(\theta)(\theta - \theta_{min})Y_{min} - m(\theta)(Y - Y_{min})$$

and so long as θ is not too much greater than θ_{min},

$$B \approx - m(\theta)(Y - Y_{min}) \tag{A1.2}$$

Substituting (A1.1) into (A1.2) gives:

$$u - (m \cdot LF \cdot LP)^{-1} \cdot B = u - m^{-1}eb \approx u_{min} \tag{A1.3}$$

using $b = B/Y$, $LP = Y/E$, and $e = E/LF$. Since e, the employment rate $1 - u$, is close to 1, we can approximate u_{min} by subtracting $m^{-1}b$, i.e., a multiple of the external balance as a proportion of GDP from u. m varies from about 0.15 for the United States or Japan to around 0.5 for small economies. Therefore a potentially conservative adjustment is $m^{-1}e = 1$.[12]

---

12 If the CCE schedule were horizontal and the EB vertical, the adjustment in (A1.3) would be correct. To the extent that the CCE slopes up and the EB slopes down, the adjustment biases the minimum equilibrium rate down. Assuming $m^{-1} = 1$ compensates for this.

Appendix 2:

DERIVING MULTIPLIER FORMULAS
FOR INTERDEPENDENT ECONOMIES

Y is real GDP, A is autonomous private expenditure (mainly investment), G is real government expenditure, X is real exports, c is the propensity to consume, t is the percentage tax take, and m is the propensity to import out of real income (which is equal by national accounting to GDP).

$$Y = c(1 - t)Y + A + G + X - mY \tag{A2.1}$$

Δ is the first difference operator. For a given change in exports, ΔX, the equilibrium multiplied up change in GDP, ΔY is calculated as follows:

(i) Standard multiplier formula, with no requirement to maintain budget balance:

$$\Delta Y = c(1 - t)\Delta Y + \Delta X - m\Delta Y \tag{A2.2}$$

since $\Delta A = \Delta G = 0$; hence

$$\Delta Y = (1 - c(1 - t) + m)^{-1} \Delta X \tag{A2.3}$$

(ii) Multiplier formula with requirement that the government deficit be held constant – i.e., not permitted to increase when GDP declines:

ΔG can no longer be held at zero, since it has to equal changes in tax revenue as a result of changing GDP. This means we now have to satisfy two equations:

$$\Delta G = t\Delta Y \tag{A2.4}$$

$$\Delta Y = c(1 - t)\Delta Y + \Delta G + \Delta X - m\Delta Y \tag{A2.5}$$

Substituting (A2.4) into (A2.5) produces the multiplier:

$$\Delta Y = (1 - c(1 - t) - t + m)^{-1}\Delta X \tag{A2.6}$$

(iii) Multiplier formula, when all economies in the region are acting identically, and when regional trade with the outside world is low (we assume zero here): Return to (A2.5), and assume that there are only two identical economies in the region. Then $\Delta X = m\Delta Y$, so that m in (A2.6) is zero, giving:

$$\Delta Y = (1 - c(1 - t) - t)^{-1}\Delta A \tag{A2.7}$$

Note that exports are now endogenous, so we cannot talk of an export multiplier. What the multiplier in (A2.7) represents is the effect of a common monetary shock, in which each country in the region has to raise its interest rate by the same amount as a result of ERM membership. The change in autonomous expenditure, ΔA, is then the consequence of this monetary tightening.

References

Alesina, A., and L. Summers. "Bank Independence and Macroeconomic Performance: Some Comparative Evidence," *Journal of Money, Credit and Banking.* CCLVI, 151–162.

Bleaney, M. (1996). "Central Bank Independence, Wage-Bargaining Structure, and Macroeconomic Performance in OECD Countries," *Oxford Economic Papers*, XLVIII, 20–38.

Blanchard, O. and S. Fischer (1989). *Lectures on Macroeconomics.* Cambridge, MA: MIT Press.

Calmfors, L. and J. Driffill (1988). "Bargaining Structure, Corporatism and Macroeconomic Performance." *Economic Policy* 6: 13–61.

Cameron, D. R. (1984). Social Democracy, Corporatism, Labour Quiescence, and the Representation of Economic Interest in Advanced Capitalist Society. *Order and Conflict in Contemporary Capitalism. Studies in the Political Economy of Western European Nations.* J. H. Goldthorpe, ed. New York: Oxford University Press: 143–178.

Carlin, W. and D. Soskice (1990). *Macroeconomics and the Wage Bargain. A Modern Approach to Employment, Inflation and the Exchange Rate.* Oxford: Oxford University Press.

(1997). "Shocks to the System: The German Political Economy under Stress." *National Institute Economic Review* (January), 57–76.

Cukierman, Alex, Steven B. Webb, and Bilin Neyapti 1992. "Measuring the Independence of Central Banks." *The World Bank Economic Review* 6(3): 353–98.

Flanagan, R. J., D. W. Soskice, and L. Ulman. (1983). *Unionism, Economic Stabilization, and Incomes Policies. European Experience.* Washington DC: Brookings Institution.

Garrett, G., and C. Wang (1995). "Unions, Governments and Central Banks in Strategic Interaction." Paper presented at the annual meeting of the American Political Science Association.

Greenwald, B. and J. Stiglitz (1993). "New and Old Keynesians." *Journal of Economic Perspectives* 7(1): 23–44.

Hall, P. (1994). "Central Bank Independence and Coordinated Wage Bargaining: Their Interaction in Germany and Europe." *German Politics and Society* 31: 1–23.

Hutchison, M. M., I. Taketoshi, et al. (forthcoming). *Political Economy of Japanese Monetary Policy.* Cambridge MA: MIT Press.

Iversen, T. (1996). "Power, Flexibility and the Breakdown of Centralised Wage Bargaining." *Comparative Politics* (July): 399–436.

(1998). "Wage Bargaining, Central Bank Independence and the Real Effects of Money." *International Organization* (Summer).

(Forthcoming). *Contested Economic Institutions: The Politics of Wage Bargaining and Macroeconomics.* New York: Cambridge University Press.

Lange, P. and G. Garrett (1985). "The Politics of Growth: Strategic Interaction and Economic Performance in the Advanced Industrial Democracies, 1974– 1980." *Journal of Politics* 47: 792–827.

Layard, R., S. Nickell, et al. (1991). *Unemployment: Macroeconomic Performance and the Labour Market.* Oxford: Oxford University Press.

Mankiw, N. G. (1993). "Symposium on Keynesian Economics Today." *Journal of Economic Perspectives* 7(1): 3–4.

OECD (1996). *The Fiscal Position and Business Cycles Data Base.* Paris: OECD.

(1997a). "Economic Performance and the Structure of Collective Bargaining." *Employment Outlook* (July): 63–92.

(1997b). "Is Job Insecurity on the Increase in OECD Countries?" *Employment Outlook* (July): 129–60.

(1997c). "Trade, Earnings and Employment." *Employment Outlook* (July): 93–128.

Pontusson, J. and P. Swenson (1996). "Labor Markets, Production Strategies and Wage Bargaining Institutions: The Swedish Employers' Offensive in Comparative Perspective." *Comparative Political Studies* 29(2): 223–50.

Przeworski, A. and M. Wallerstein (1982). "The Structure of Class Conflict in Democratic Capitalist Systems." *American Political Science Review* 76(2): 215–40.

Romer, D. (1993). "The New Keynesian Synthesis." *Journal of Economic Perspectives* 7(1): 5–24.

Soskice, D. (1990). "Wage Determination: The Changing Role of Institutions in Advanced Industrialised Countries." *Oxford Review of Economic Policy* 6(4): 1–23.

(1999). Divergent Production Regimes. Coordinated and Uncoordinated Market Economies in the 1980s and 1990s. *Continuity and Change in Contemporary Capitalism.* H. Kitschelt, P. Lange, G. Marks, and J. D. Stephens, eds., New York: Cambridge University Press: 101–134.

Soskice, D. and T. Iversen (1998) "Multiple Wage-Bargaining Systems in the Single European Economy area." Oxford Review of Economic Policy 14(3).

(Forthcoming). "The Non-Neutrality of Monetary Policy with Large Wage or Price Quotes." Quarterly Journal of Economics.

Tobin, J. (1993). "Price Flexibility and Output Stability: An Old Keynesian View." *Journal of Economic Perspectives* 7(1): 45–66.

Tullio, G., A. Steinherr, et al. (1996). German Wage and Price Inflation before and after Unification. *Inflation and Wage Behaviour in Europe.* P. d. Grauwe, S. Micossi, and G. Tullio, eds. Oxford: Clarendon Press.

PART I

WAGE
BARGAINING

3

THE SWEDISH EMPLOYER OFFENSIVE AGAINST CENTRALIZED WAGE BARGAINING

Peter Swenson and Jonas Pontusson

Recent developments have brought the question of institutional change to the forefront of the research agenda of comparative political economists. In Western Europe, as elsewhere, dramatic changes in domestic politics have accompanied equally dramatic shifts in internationally determined parameters of economic performance and policy-making. It has become commonplace for students of West European political economy to speak of the decline of corporatism, that is, the decline of institutional arrangements for collaborative or "tripartite" governance of labor markets by representatives of capital, labor, and the state. Along with the profound transformations underway in the national and international governance of capital, product, and service markets, this development would appear to mark a major turning point.

This chapter treats the decentralization of wage bargaining in Sweden as a case study of institutional change. In the comparative political economy literature, Sweden has stood out as a paragon of institutionalized class compromise, and the system of centralized, economy-wide wage bargaining was, quite rightly, identified as the keystone of the Swedish system of corporatist market governance. However, this characterization of the Swedish case is no longer valid.

As we shall document, Sweden's powerful engineering employers began to push for decentralization of wage setting in the early 1980s and achieved what they wanted, in a fitful and conflictual process, by the early 1990s. At their

This chapter is an extension of two earlier articles, published in *Arkiv för studier i arbetarrörelsens historia*, no. 53–54 (1993) and *Comparative Political Studies* 29:2:223–50 (1996). We thank Sage Publications for permission to excerpt from the latter article. We also wish to thank Geoffrey Garrett, Peter Hall, Torben Iversen, Andrew Martin, David Soskice, Kathleen Thelen, Lowell Turner, and Michael Wallerstein for their encouragement and critical feedback.

insistence, the Swedish Employers' Confederation (Svenska Arbetsgivareförenin-gen; henceforth SAF) simply closed down its own bargaining and statistics departments in the Spring of 1990. Because wage bargaining has been so important in the postwar Swedish political economy, its decentralization has altered the overall configuration of political-economic institutions (cf. Iversen this volume). Decentralization has undermined the authority and political influ-ence of the peak organizations of labor and capital, in turn changing the politics of economic policy-making and of electoral mobilization. The campaign to decentralize wage bargaining in fact forms part of a broader business challenge to Sweden's "negotiated economy," where all important markets are interac-tively regulated in a centralized, institutionalized process of bargaining among private organizations and state agencies. Advocating structural reforms – priva-tization, deregulation, and EC membership – leading Swedish businessmen have thus renounced their old role in co-managing the Social Democratic welfare state in the 1980s. In a dramatic act of rebellion against corporatism, for example, SAF withdrew its representatives from the boards of state agencies in 1991 (see Ahrne and Clement 1994; Pestoff 1995).

Swedish employers have been able to play different union interests against each other in their efforts to reorganize wage bargaining, just as opponents of change have attempted to exploit divisions among employers. Although a com-prehensive account of the decentralization of wage bargaining would have to deal with the motives and calculations of different union actors in cross-class alliance politics, in this chapter we focus on employers because they have held the initiative and clearly have been the principal agents of institutional change.[1] This in itself is nothing new. Indeed, the system of peak-level bargaining that distinguished the Swedish model of the postwar era was, in large measure, created by SAF as a means to organize wage restraint and to control the interfirm and intersectoral wage structure (Swenson 1989, 1997).

The future structure of Swedish wage bargaining remains contested and uncertain, but it is clear that the institutional preferences of the most powerful among Swedish employers have changed. In what follows, we advance two explanations of the change in the institutional preferences of employers. Briefly stated, our first explanation is that long-term changes in the structure of em-ployment altered the dynamics of centralized wage bargaining from the late 1960s onward by increasing the influence of actors sheltered from international competition – in particular, public sector employers and unions. Export-oriented engineering employers perceived the resulting distributional outcomes of wage bargaining as rigid and heavy burdens that violated the centralized system's foundational and consensual norms of labor market governance. From this

---

1 See Lash (1985) and Iversen (1996) for accounts of the decentralization of Swedish wage bargaining that assign a more prominent role to union actors. In previous work, we have challenged the conventional image of Sweden as the land where labor rules (Pontusson 1984, 1992a; Swenson 1991a).

perspective, the engineering employers did not abandon the model of wage bargaining that they had helped create in the 1950s; rather, they abandoned a new model that had emerged, over their objections, in the 1970s.

Our second explanation treats the campaign to decentralize wage bargaining as part of a broader effort by engineering employers to reorganize production in response to changes in technology and market pressures. New production strategies led these employers to assign greater value to wage flexibility than they had in the past. The wage rigidities inherent in centralized bargaining as it had evolved in Sweden thus became increasingly unacceptable to engineering employers.

Whereas the first argument suggests that old interests struggled against new rigidities, the second suggests that new interests clashed with old rigidities. At the same time, the two arguments share certain analytical premises. In contrast to the recent emphasis on the institutional determinants of preferences among students of comparative political economy, both of the arguments that we advance invoke socioeconomic and political changes, exogenous to the institutions of wage bargaining, to explain employer preferences and institutional change. Furthermore, both arguments hold that exogenous conditions influenced events by changing material (economic) constraints on the actors involved rather than their cultural or ideological motivations. In particular, we reject the idea that the growth of "postmaterialist" values constitutes a significant force behind the breakup of corporatist bargaining arrangements. Finally, the two arguments share a rejection of simplistic class models of conflict and emphasize conflicts of interest within "labor" and "capital." The first argument derives the impetus behind institutional change from a change in power relations – not between capital and labor, but rather between cross-class coalitions intersecting both classes. The second treats the change in institutional preferences as a consequence of changing and diverging interests – again, within a heterogeneous class of employers.

We put each of these arguments to work in an attempt to explain distinct elements in the timing and evolution of the Swedish employer offensive. The argument about alliances and resulting distribution of power within centralized wage bargaining provides the most compelling explanation of the origins and initial phases of the employer offensive, but the "production profile" argument (cf. Gourevitch 1986) explains better why the engineering sector's offensive has continued into the 1990s. Both arguments shed light on variations among employers in their institutional preferences and strategic behavior.

We organize our analysis as follows. First, we sketch the relevant features of the system of centralized bargaining before it was dismantled. Second, we describe the shift in power relations within centralized bargaining that resulted in new policies violating the distributional terms of centralization that engineering employers had endorsed in the 1950s. In the third section, we analyze how engineering's new production strategies and corporate pay practices at the company level evolved against the grain of distributional rigidities imposed from above. In our fourth and fifth sections we delve in detail into the character of the cross-class alliance behind recent institutional restructuring, and then place it in the context of the politics of changing macroeconomic policy and Swedish membership in the European Union. Finally, in our conclusion, we consider the implications of our analysis of the decentralization of wage bargaining in Sweden for general theories of the decline of corporatism, and we show how our analytical approach might be extended to account for cross-national variations in the extent and nature of change in the institutional arrangements of labor-market governance.

THE SWEDISH SYSTEM OF CENTRALIZED WAGE BARGAINING

The concept of centralization captures what we might call the procedural dimension of the Swedish model of wage bargaining. The model always had a substantive dimension as well, with two major components: wage restraint and wage solidarity. Whereas wage restraint refers to the distribution of income between wage earners and employers, wage solidarity refers to the distribution of income among wage earners (and thereby the distribution of labor supply and wage costs among employers). The meanings of wage solidarity have changed over time, but they always implied boosting the relative position of low-wage workers. The well-known logic of the "Rehn–Meidner model," elaborated by two labor union economists in the early 1950s and approved of by leading employers, stipulated that this wage-policy orientation would help to promote not only income equality but also productivity growth (see Martin 1984).

A mutually recognized purpose of restraint in centralized wage bargaining was to help maintain the competitiveness of Swedish exports. Wage solidarity helped too, for example by holding back wages in engineering and, for complex reasons, the construction sector (Swenson 1997). Accordingly, bargaining in the 1950s implicitly and later explicitly took account of the "room for wage increases" (*löneutrymmet*), which was in principle determined by objective criteria that unions and employers, both concerned about international competition, could jointly agree upon.[2] A more or less egalitarian allocation of allowable aggregate wage increases among different sectors would follow in accordance with the employers' interests in regulating competition over labor and maintaining competitiveness, as well as union leaders' objectives in legitimating central-

---

2 This understanding of the external parameters of wage bargaining was formalized in the so-called EFO model, developed by union and employer economists in the late 1960s (Edgren, Faxén, and Odhner 1970).

ized control. The unions could sell restraint to impatient members by claiming credit for solidaristic redistribution, while the employers' organizations could justify redistribution by pointing to the overall restraint achieved, though there was practically no opposition and indeed even considerable employer support for the limited redistributive character of the peak agreements before the 1970s.[3] On occasion, government pressure and inducements, and non-wage concessions by employers, were necessary to purchase union restraint.

The centralization distinguishing the Swedish model refers to peak-level bargaining, that is, wage negotiations between encompassing multiindustry confederations of unions and employers. In the private sector, SAF and its blue-collar union counterpart, Landsorganisationen (LO), first became directly involved in wage bargaining during the Second World War. After a few years' hiatus, LO and SAF resumed their role in wage bargaining in the 1950s. From 1956 to 1983, contracts signed by individual LO unions and SAF affiliates followed in time and content the overall settlement between LO and SAF. In the 1970s, "bargaining cartels" of public-sector unions and private-sector white-collar unions formed to create new arenas of peak-level bargaining for the rest of the economy. At each bargaining round, the two or more separate peak-level settlements tended to be closely patterned on each other (Elvander 1988).

In contrast to industry-level *contracts,* peak-level *agreements* were not legally binding, but decisive nevertheless, for they indicated which demands LO and SAF would back up with their considerable resources in case of conflict at the industry level. Subsequent local bargaining at individual workplaces, required for implementation of the industry contracts, controlled actual earnings. Indeed, average increases determined at this tertiary level usually exceeded contractual provisions. This extracontractual "wage drift" typically counteracted both the redistributive and the restraining effects of centralization. It also provided a safety valve for distributive conflicts within the unions, as well as for recruitment needs of companies short on manpower.

THE EMPLOYER OFFENSIVE

The substantive and procedural elements of centralized wage bargaining in Sweden were inextricably linked. Hence, when leaders of SAF's most powerful affiliate, the Association of Engineering Employers (Verkstadsföreningen; henceforth VF), decided to exorcize solidaristic wage policy, they gradually discovered they had to destroy the policy's host, centralization.[4] VF's discontent can be

3 See Swenson (1992, 1997) for an historical analysis of employers and wage solidarity in Sweden. Pontusson (this volume) questions some aspects of Swenson's employer-centered account of wage compression. The formulations in this chapter represent our common ground.
4 The following, highly abbreviated account of wage-bargaining developments draws on Lash (1985), Elvander (1988), Ahlén (1989), Martin (1991), De Geer (1992), and Kjellberg (1992). It should be

traced at least as far back as the LO–SAF agreement of 1969, which stretched the norms of solidaristic redistribution beyond those that VF had originally affirmed. The wage explosion of 1974–76 added fuel to employer discontent when peak-level bargaining failed even to deliver restraint and led SAF to adopt a much tougher but ultimately ineffectual bargaining stance in the late 1970s.

The first breakthrough for employer advocates of institutional change came in 1983, when VF successfully enticed the Metalworkers' Union (Svenska Metallindustriarbetareförbundet; Metall for short) to defect from peak-level bargaining. In exchange for concessions, VF offered Metall more than LO was asking for. SAF proceeded to negotiate with LO when its other unions insisted on peak-level negotiations. Two separate settlements for blue-collar workers in engineering and the other industries resulted. The next year, SAF joined VF, insisting that there be no peak-level bargaining. High industry-level settlements in 1984 fueled domestic inflation, however, and in 1985 the government intervened to orchestrate a peak-level incomes agreement capping industry-level and public-sector contracts. The following year SAF once more agreed to peak-level bargaining in the aftermath of Olof Palme's assassination, having advocated decentralization beforehand. But in 1988 SAF again insisted on industry-level negotiations only. The 1989 round looked like 1983 when VF and Metall negotiated separately, while rump-SAF and the corresponding LO unions struck their own agreement. As in 1983–85, these settlements proved quite inflationary, and the government intervened with a new incomes policy initiative in 1991.

In the early 1990s, critics of centralization became even more ambitious. They increasingly questioned centralized industry-level (multiemployer) bargaining, having now eliminated peak-level (multiindustry) bargaining. In 1993, SAF began advocating "coordinated decentralization": Working time and other general terms of employment would be regulated at the industry level, while wage bargaining would occur at the firm level.[5] Major engineering firms, most notably Asea-Brown Boveri (ABB), whose CEO was chairman of VF, also began making "partnership contracts" (*medarbetaravtal*) at the firm level in 1991, encompassing white-collar as well as blue-collar employees, and wage as well as non-wage issues (Kjellberg 1992:132–6; Mahon 1994). Since partnership contracts at the firm level would tend to clash with centralized contracts negotiated separately with blue- and white-collar organizations, employer interest in this innovation created incentives to drop centralized multiemployer contracts altogether.

Modest in their wage demands, the LO unions threatened to strike in 1993

noted that VF merged with its sister association, Mekanförbundet, to form Sveriges Verkstadsindustrier (VI) in 1992. For the sake of clarity, we stick with the old acronym.

5 Commonly cited as a model by employer advocates of decentralization, a "wageless" industry agreement was signed by SAF's General Employer Group (Almega) and the Foremen's Union (SALF) in 1992.

if the employers insisted on company-level negotiations. The engineering employers' continuing campaign to decentralize wage bargaining was also resisted by forces within SAF and the government. In particular, employer associations representing small and medium-sized businesses, but even larger employers in some sectors, expressed their deep concern that decentralization would intensify wage rivalries, disrupt production and trade, and fuel inflation. In the end, the engineering employers chose to avoid a confrontation and settled for an industry-level wage agreement with the lowest wage increases in more than 40 years.

From the early 1980s to the early 1990s, wage bargaining see-sawed between peak-level and industry-level negotiations, but an apparently decisive shift occurred in the first half of the 1990s. Since 1993, peak-level bargaining has no longer been at issue; rather, the question of whether – or to what extent – industry-level negotiations will determine wage setting has emerged as the issue of contention between employers and unions. A realignment of forces within SAF precipitated this shift. The new SAF chairman, Ulf Laurin, an engineering employer himself, was appointed in 1989 to be a strong advocate of change. In 1990, SAF simply shut down its bargaining and statistics units and in 1991, the organization withdrew its representatives from most corporatist bodies. While rejecting corporatism, SAF adopted a new role as public policy advocate. In a program adopted in 1990, entitled "Markets and Diversity" (SAF 1990a), SAF paid no attention to issues of collective bargaining, shifting emphasis to broad political and ideological concerns. SAF's new mandate emphasized the formation of public opinion and lobbying rather than negotiation with government officials and other interest groups in tripartite arenas.[6]

The abruptness of the shift in the first half of the 1990s should not be exaggerated. The peak-level wage bargaining that occurred in the mid-1980s, and again in 1991, was procedurally and substantively different from that of 1956–83. For one thing, it was orchestrated by the government; indeed, there was no bargaining at all between LO and SAF leading up to the settlement proposed by a government-appointed commission in 1991. Second, the peak-level settlements of 1985–86 and 1991 focused on aggregate wage increases, omitting customary details about the distribution of wage increases within sectors and firms, and the parties to industry-level bargaining abandoned their customary no-strike/lockout commitments even after the peak-level agreements were signed. Industry-level agreements also became significantly less restrictive after 1983, leaving more flexibility in the allocation of increases at the local level. Already in the period 1983–88, these developments were accompanied by a significant widening of wage differentials among blue-collar workers (see Hibbs 1990).

While the future structure of Swedish wage bargaining remains contested,

6 This reorientation began during the wage-earner funds debate of 1978–82: see De Geer (1992:ch. 16).

the institutional preferences of the most influential Swedish employers have clearly changed, and their new posture precludes a return to past practices. The change is most obvious in the case of the large, export-oriented engineering employers dominating VF, SAF's largest affiliate. There is a genuine puzzle here, for these same employers actively contributed to the building of central-ized wage bargaining institutions. For them, the original centralization of bar-gaining institutions represented a means to contain militancy and wage pres-sures in sectors of the economy that were sheltered against international competition, and therefore to prevent them from spilling over into the traded goods sectors. In the 1950s and 1960s, engineering employers and even SAF affiliates from low-pay sectors favored centralization and some aspects of solida-ristic wage policy as a means to manage union whipsawing and interfirm and intersectoral competition for labor in tight labor markets.

Clearly, labor market conditions alone cannot provide an adequate expla-nation of the engineering employers' decentralization campaign, for it spans two very different business-cycle phases. The slackening of labor markets during the recession of the early 1980s might have meant that the engineering employers no longer needed LO's help to achieve wage restraint. However, their campaign continued unabated – indeed, became more aggressive – during the boom in the second half of the 1980s, when labor scarcity returned with a vengeance. Having responded to tight labor markets and inflationary pressures by imposing peak-level bargaining on the unions in the 1950s, they responded to similar conditions by advocating more decentralized forms of wage bargaining in the 1980s.

By their own account, employer advocates of decentralization wanted to achieve two basic things (see SAF 1987, 1990b; VF n.d.). First, they wanted wage differentials between export-oriented and sheltered (including public) sectors to rise in order to secure an adequate supply of motivated labor to export-oriented sectors. Second, they wanted employers to be able to use wages as a means to stimulate employee commitment within firms, and thereby stimulate quality improvements and productivity growth. Our puzzle reappears in new form: Why did these arguments become so compelling to engineering employers at this particular time? In other words, why didn't such considera-tions lead engineering employers to oppose peak-level bargaining all along, regardless of labor market conditions?

SHIFTS IN POWER AND POLICY WITHIN FIXED INSTITUTIONS

Our first explanation of the campaign to decentralize wage bargaining charac-terizes it as the engineering employers' response to evolving pay-distribution practices within the unchanging structural shell of centralized bargaining. The three-tiered system of wage bargaining established in the 1950s initially provided engineering employers with a mechanism to achieve both wage restraint and wage flexibility. Through the 1960s, LO–SAF agreements did little to disturb wage distributional patterns within private-sector firms. As Hibbs and Locking (1996) demonstrate, however, a remarkably even pay structure across firms and industries was achieved during this first phase of redistributive peak-level bargaining. The leveling of wages across firms and sectors in fact harmonized well with employers' broadly consensual notions of fair and rational competition in labor markets over manpower made scarce by the institutionally administered pricing of labor at levels low enough, given macroeconomic conditions, that labor markets could not clear (Swenson 1997).

During the next phase, however, from 1969 onward, peak-level bargaining became increasingly invasive in intrafirm pay setting, creating entirely different distributional results. In short, as Hibbs and Locking show, the peak bargaining brought a dramatic compression of pay within firms, across occupations and skill levels. Solidaristic wage policy had evolved in ways that violated the distributional principles that employers had originally endorsed. As such the engineering employers' revolt in the 1980s was in part one of old interests against new rigidities. In other words, the engineering employers did not abandon the Swedish model they had helped set up in the 1950s; rather, they abandoned a newer model that had been imposed upon them by a new alignment of forces in the 1970s.

The new invasiveness of peak-level bargaining imposed two major nuisances according to engineering employers: interoccupational leveling and wage-drift compensation clauses. Pressure for interoccupational wage compression within firms came mostly from Metall's leadership in response to pressure from low-pay members and their militant advocates. Intersectoral leveling, they argued, gave them nothing, for it only held metalworkers' wages back and did not reduce inequalities among them. Meanwhile, interoccupational compression was gathering steam in the public sector, whose unions gained the right to strike in 1965. Against a pliant Social Democratic employer front, and supported by a severe shortage of labor, especially of women, public-sector unions forced through a more radical solidaristic wage policy in the wage round of 1971. Extra boosts negotiated routinely outside the private-sector bargaining system for low-pay government workers powerfully aided low-pay workers in Metall in the coming years (cf. Pontusson this volume).

Against VF's better judgement, the SAF leadership in the 1970s caved in to demands for intrafirm, interoccupational leveling, hoping to avoid strikes and lockouts. Provisions for interoccupational leveling, first introduced in 1969, in fact hit the engineering employers hardest. More militant and facing a comparatively wide wage spread in their sector, Metall was more inclined to pursue interoccupational leveling than other private-sector LO unions. In the 1970s, other unions routinely chose not to push the matter as far, for the peak-level provision was formulated as a default option to come into effect only when unions and employers failed to agree on other distributional principles in their subsequent industry-level negotiations. That other employers were able to escape much peak-level invasion into intrafirm pay distribution effectively isolated and neutralized VF in SAF's internal politics. VF leaders' impassioned pleas for relief from this "wage policy lunacy" (*lönepolitiskt vansinne*) fell on the apparently indifferent ears of other employer groups, which had been given more slack by their respective unions.[7]

While interoccupational wage leveling was imposed on the engineering employers in 1969, VF leaders themselves initiated the thinking behind wage-drift compensation, or so-called earnings development guarantees, their other major irritant. In 1966, VF proposed that anticipated wage drift (extracontractual increases over the contract period) should be calculated as part of the costs of wage agreements, so that those who expected wage drift (especially in engineering, where piecework and related drift were common) would accept lower raises. At the same time, those who got little or no drift (many workers outside engineering) would accept comparable agreements, resting assured that they would be compensated retroactively for some portion of the drifting groups' improvements.

The idea was to lower overall negotiated agreements by conceding in principle and in advance the right of groups outside engineering to parity in wage developments, so that they did not insist on high agreements in anticipation of others' wage drift. Other groups within SAF resisted the idea of wage-drift guarantees, but government mediators were at once smitten by the idea and for years to come pushed wage-drift guarantees on labor and employer negotiators to hasten agreement. Whether or not wage-drift guarantees worked as intended, VF turned against them when they spread to the growing white-collar and public-sector bargaining units outside the LO–SAF arena. Manual workers in engineering resented white-collar groups riding on their wage drift, which they regarded as a result of increased productivity, especially due to incentive pay systems. Consequently, they insisted on higher negotiated increases relative to what was negotiated for white-collar unions, a demand already legitimated by solidaristic wage policy. Public-sector workers, especially at the low end of the pay scale, were also becoming what a private sector union leader called "pay parasites," and because solidaristic wage policy was accepted by Social Democratic government employers, they were also getting extra-high increases for the sake of approaching parity with the private sector (Swenson 1991b). Intended to neutralize one source of inflationary wage rivalry within the private, blue-collar sector, wage-drift guarantees unintentionally unleashed other, more powerful wage rivalries across sectors.

---

7 Quote from VF's Åke Nordlander from the minutes of SAF's board meeting, 15 August 1977. See also Larsson (1985: 378).

Interoccupational leveling and wage drift guarantees within and outside the LO–SAF arena combined to produce disaster, according to engineering employers (Treslow 1986:59–60). Compression of wages from below – imposed from above – forced individual employers to stretch out the pay scale at the top in firm-level negotiations or allow piecework earnings to drift upward to compensate high-pay workers for loss in relative pay. When skilled workers pushed for these compensatory differential-maintaining increases in local bargaining, employers, wishing to preserve the managerial and recruitment advantages of wider pay scales, frequently conceded. Compliance, in other words, with the centralized system's efforts to restrain wages suffered. Collusion and defection at this level would then register as wage drift and set in motion another round of demands for compensation outside the engineering sector. Interoccupational leveling imposed from above thus produced extra wage drift and launched the inflationary wage–wage spiral boosted by the wage-drift guarantees. Now engineering employers were painfully wedged between increasing pay-related rigidities on management at the microlevel and high inflation at the macrolevel.

In sum, the original solidaristic wage policy of centrally negotiated *interindustry* wage leveling (extra increases from below, restraint above) within the private sector helped legitimate centralized union confederation control and restraint of the bargaining process, something engineering employers favored. Chronically scarce labor in Sweden during World War II and after, generated in part by the institutionally restrained pricing of labor, had helped give rise to norms of fair competition over manpower among employers that were well served by centralized bargaining and leveling across and within sectors. Class relations stabilized on the basis of centralized bargaining and a largely consensual solidaristic wage policy caused employers to demobilize politically, thereby strengthening the Social Democrats' hold on political power. Their hold on power allowed them to expand the welfare state and foster strong public-sector unions. These unions, in turn, together with growing white-collar unions in the private sector, extended the principles of solidaristic wage policy in ways that ultimately generated new inflexibilities and inflation. Unfortunately for engineering employers, the egalitarianism of intersectoral leveling that they endorsed inspired and legitimated strong pressures for *intrafirm* and *intersectoral* leveling, bringing intolerable rigidifying and inflationary consequences.

Isolated against an alliance of unions ready to drag all employers in SAF into a conflict in support of the new peak-level policies, and government mediators and employers pressuring VF to accept what Metall and LO were prepared to strike for, VF caved in begrudgingly for over a decade of wage rounds. In internal SAF debate, VF leaders expressed increasing indignation and outrage at the turn of events. But other employers in SAF were relatively unhurt by the new policies, and government employers endorsed them. Neither wanted to assume the costs of conflict that a return to the old norms would entail. Seeing the initial distributional terms of centralization violated by this alliance, engineering employers finally sought decentralization to dismantle the institutions that housed the alliance.

NEW PRODUCTION STRATEGIES AND CORPORATE PAY PRACTICES

Changes in the sphere of production also help explain the employer offensive against centralized wage bargaining and solidaristic wage policy. Like engineering employers elsewhere in the advanced industrial countries (Piore and Sabel 1984; Streeck 1987, 1991), and unlike Swedish employers in some other sectors, Swedish engineering employers felt compelled to pursue "diversified quality production" or "flexible specialization" in the manufacture of high value-added, internationally tradable consumer durables and producer goods. This applies especially to Fordist mass producers like Volvo, Saab-Scania, and Electrolux, but also to smaller-batch manufacturers of electrical, telecommunication, and mechanical engineering products like Asea-Brown Boveri (ABB), LM Ericsson, and Alfa-Laval. To improve productivity, flexibility, and quality, and therefore competitiveness in international markets, both of these groups discovered a need for more discretion in the use of wage incentives than the centralized bargaining system allowed.

As capital costs increased after the mid-1970s, firms also became increasingly concerned with efficient and flexible use of machinery and in reducing the amounts of money tied up in inventories and unfinished products, which in their view required new strategies for managing and rewarding labor. Teamwork became one such strategy, requiring pay policies flexibly tailored to the worksite. No hard data exist, but many examples cited in the literature suggest that such innovations spread rapidly throughout Swedish manufacturing industry and especially engineering after the mid-1970s. Volvo's innovation strategy, for one, relied largely on worker skills and initiative in group settings (see Berggren 1992; Pontusson 1992b).

The decline of traditional incentive pay practices, which dovetailed with centrally negotiated contracts, substantiates the association between technological and managerial changes and Swedish engineering employers' institutional preferences regarding wage-bargaining structures. International comparisons of the postwar period up to about 1970 put Sweden at the top in terms of the use of payment-by-results systems (ILO 1951:81–8; OECD 1970:42–3). In the 1970s, however, incentive pay began to lose favor among employers, and a drastic decline of piece work schemes took place. According to a SAF survey, piece work covered 12 percent of working hours of manual labor in 1985, as compared to 33 percent in 1970 (SAF 1986). In the 1980s, while traditional piece work continued to decline, new forms of incentive pay spread rapidly.

According to a 1991 survey, 55 percent of Metall's membership received some form of payment by results, usually comprised of a basic fixed component, with a personal supplement and bonuses determined by the performance of work teams or larger corporate units (Svenska Metallindustriarbetareförbundet 1992). Also, all the leading engineering firms, and others, introduced various profit-sharing and convertible-debenture (loan *cum* stock option) schemes for blue-collar as well as white-collar employees in the 1980s (see Kjellberg 1992:108–9; Elvander 1992:48–54; Sköldebrand 1989, 1990).

In Sweden, traditional incentive pay forms served three purposes. First, they reduced monitoring costs, especially for a country where foremen are heavily unionized and therefore less loyal to management and where tight labor markets have made the costs of "shirking" low. Second, they reduced Swedish workers' resistance to rationalization from above, for they provided at least an illusory sense to the workers affected that they could, through wage drift, reap the returns of productivity increases (and not share them with others via redistributive wage policy). Finally, drift resulting from incentive pay allowed engineering employers to pay a premium to metalworkers in a kind of "efficiency wage" strategy for maintaining commitment and reducing turnover. Wage drift kept many engineering workers perpetually one step ahead of where they would be if contracts alone determined earnings.

In part, engineering employers moved to more fixed hourly wages and even monthly wages in the 1970s because centrally negotiated wage-drift clauses accelerated the spillover of wage growth from the engineering sector to low-productivity growth sectors. This spillover both was inflationary and undermined engineering employers' efficiency wage advantages. The incentive effect on output was possibly also reduced for individual workers on piecerates, for they would benefit from wage-drift guarantees even if their piece work earnings did not grow.

Equally important, while traditional incentive pay had been designed to buy acceptance of unpleasant working conditions and production changes imposed from above, they did little to encourage long-term and spontaneous commitment, flexibility, and innovation rising from below. These qualities in workers, after all, were needed for diversified quality production, which requires active participation in generating new production techniques for new products, not just passive acceptance of new production techniques for old products.

Some of the new incentive schemes of the 1980s, such as profit sharing, probably represented evasive action against interoccupational leveling and wage-drift compensation in central wage agreements and against payroll and income taxation. The benefits that employees derive from such schemes are not included in official wage statistics and cannot be used to justify solidaristic adjustments and drift compensation. In this regard, centralized bargaining provided an incentive, not a problem for such practices. On the other hand, to the extent that centrally negotiated wages, even at the industry level, absorbed a large share of available company income, less would be available for the new incentives. The same would hold true for other innovations in company pay practices.

Technological changes blurring the old lines between blue-collar and white-collar labor in engineering also weakened engineering employers' support for centralized bargaining. Increasingly, skilled workers began programming as well as monitoring computerized machinery, thereby invading white-collar territory (cf. Nilsson 1988). The number of CNC machine tools per 100,000 employees in the engineering industry increased from 80 in 1968 to 761 in 1976, and 2,218 in 1984; the number of robots in the engineering industry increased from 430 in 1984 to 677 in 1987 (Edquist and Glimmel 1989). This new technology created the opportunity and imperative to use in-house training, pay increases, and job enlargement to create "career pathways" (job ladders reaching into traditional white-collar strata) to reduce the turnover of skilled employees who knew their company's facilities and needs.[8] Employers also responded with firm-level "partnership" agreements (see above) for both blue-collar and white-collar employees. Centralized bargaining for the entire private sector, carried out separately with LO and the bargaining cartel of private-sector white-collar unions (Privattjänstemannakartellen; PTK for short), were difficult to reconcile with firm-based pay schemes harmonizing manual and nonmanual remuneration with training and promotion schemes tailored to the workplace.

New technology-related problems in coping with high labor turnover among skilled workers pushed Swedish engineering employers toward decentralized bargaining in other ways as well. Increasing corporate investment in human capital led to an intensified search for solutions to Swedish industry's chronic turnover problem. Their efforts in the 1970s to improve the quality of industrial work were in part a response to the problem of turnover and absenteeism within the constraints of centralized solidaristic wage bargaining – to reduce turnover without increasing wages and therefore wage drift (Pontusson 1992b).[9] Later efforts included exploration of the usual "efficiency wage" (high-wage) and "deferred payment" (e.g., seniority-based) schemes common in segmented, dualistic labor markets. The system of centralized bargaining proved hostile to such things – even the employers' own confederation had suppressed them in the past.

Furthermore, engineering employers claimed that carefully designed wage

8 The need for career pathways was repeatedly stressed at the SAF congress of 1987, which resolved that employment conditions for blue-collar and white-collar employees should be the same and that "the outmoded concepts of worker (*arbetare*) and employee (*tjänsteman*) be abandoned in favor of the concept of coworker (*medarbetare*)" (SAF 1988: 96).

9 Unions played a relatively small role here: Ideas about "work humanization" implemented as part of the new production strategies of the 1980s were, in large measure, articulated by SAF's campaign to promote "new factories" in the 1970s, a campaign that SAF also conceived in part as a means to preempt or deflect the labor movement's codetermination offensive. See Schiller (1988:ch.10).

incentives were necessary to elicit active worker participation in company-based training in skills required by the new technology. While employers' Fordist tendencies had to some extent reduced their need to invest in worker skills, and therefore rendered them relatively immune to turnover, now their sophisticated fixed and human-capital investments increased their sensitivity to turnover. According to surveys carried out by the Central Bureau of Statistics, the proportion of the entire labor force that had participated in some form of training during working hours in the previous year increased from 27 percent in 1975 to 36 percent in 1979, and 46 percent in 1986. The proportion participating in employer-paid training increased from 23 percent in 1986 to 32 percent in 1989 for the labor force as a whole, and from 21 percent in 1986 to 27 percent in 1989 for the engineering industry (SCB 1990).

In short, for a host of reasons, new production strategies mandated greater flexibility in wage setting than the old centralized system allowed. Engineering employers had begun, however, to call into question the system of centralized wage bargaining early in the 1970s, when they would only have dimly perceived the new production strategies on the horizon. Therefore the argument set out in the previous section about new rigidities, imposed by a centralized system they once favored, provides a better explanation of the origins of their offensive against centralization.

The continuation and radicalization of the employers' decentralization campaign through the late 1980s and into the 1990s, on the other hand, calls for an additional and complementary explanation focusing on new production strategies. In the course of the 1980s, the locus of wage bargaining shifted to industry-level and firm-level negotiations, and the provisions for interoccupational leveling and wage-drift compensation against which the engineering employers initially rebelled were in large part dismantled. If the engineering employers had wanted only to do away with these provisions, their offensive should not have continued as it did. In short, an adequate account of the lengthy employer offensive requires us to employ both arguments emphasizing, first, increasing rigidities imposed on constant demands for flexibility and, later, increasing demands for flexibility that outstripped what had once been accepted as sufficient before the new rigidities had been introduced.

INSTITUTIONAL RESTRUCTURING AND CROSS-CLASS REALIGNMENT

In their desire to turn back the clock on wage leveling, engineering employers had mixed and evolving but clear motives for decentralizing wage bargaining. Their success remains to be explained, for other employers in SAF blocked their efforts against a labor confederation still broadly committed to centralization and solidaristic wage policy. Just as in other phases in the history of Swedish collective bargaining, institutional change was marked by divisions within classes and alliances across classes.

In effect, VF engineered the shifting of cross-class alliances to secure a more decentralized regime of labor-market governance. As we shall show, VF applied pressure against other employers with threats of leaving SAF, persuading them to accept restrictions on the confederation's powers to bargain centrally and therefore to submit to external (government) pressure to accept solidaristic agreements. The association also offered inducements instead of pressure to workers employed in engineering to defect from centralization, thus exploiting distributional divisions within the labor movement to help dismantle the system. The labor component of this cross-class alliance, as we will see, also joined forces in declaring support for stringent fiscal and monetary policies that could substitute for centralization as a means of maintaining wage restraint outside the engineering sector, while allowing it increasing freedom to introduce more wage flexibility within the sector.

A certain level of indifference if not outright opposition on the part of other SAF employer groups to decentralization can partly be explained by the default or escape clause described earlier, which other employers, together with their respective unions, exploited to avoid interoccupational leveling. There were other, more industry-specific reasons as well, for example in the commercial and retail service sector organized by the Commercial Employers' Association (Handelns Arbetsgivareorganisation; henceforth HAO). HAO was the most persistent opponent of decentralization and the second largest SAF affiliate after VF, employing 14 percent of SAF members' entire labor force in 1980, compared to VF's 25 percent (Kuuse 1986:151).

Tensions between VF and HAO date from 1965, when VF leaders expressed anxiety about HAO's admission to SAF, which had been prompted by the desire of larger department stores and grocery chains to be included in centralized bargaining. Confirming their fears, VF subsequently concluded that HAO's growth and representation in SAF meant that "it became increasingly difficult for the engineering industry to gain a hearing within SAF for its arguments that it be the pacesetter in pay increases" (Treslow 1988). In other words, by the mid- and late-1970s, HAO had proved to be, along with representatives of other important home-market sectors like construction, the most averse to frontal collisions with LO over the wage issues pinching engineering employers' feet.[10] It was hard, for example, to convince HAO members on VF's behalf of the need to lock out workers and customers, because both could simply cross the street to Konsum and PUB, competitors in the huge cooperative movement organized outside of SAF and friendly to the Social Democrats (Ehrenkrona 1991:273). Peak-level bargaining had become a source of security for big retail

---

10 HAO's long-standing commitment to centralized bargaining is noted by De Geer (1989:271) and documented by De Geer and Zetterberg (1987:81).

employers afraid of standing alone against unions in decentralized negotiations. Instead, they simply hitched a free ride on VF's struggle to impose overall restraint in centralized negotiations, which ensured practically strike-free relations at the sectoral level.[11]

In addition to fearing conflict over solidaristic wage policy, HAO employers had relatively little reason to fight the policy itself. For one thing, they were forced to compete for low-pay labor with the sheltered public sector, where upward compression of wages was already being forced by militant public-sector unions. As SAF's soft underbelly, HAO therefore sometimes became the target of LO's limited and selective strikes (often overtime strikes), as in 1977 when the outcome of LO–SAF negotiations hung on settlements in the public sector (De Geer 1989:213–16, 232–3; Andersson 1977:97). Also, HAO had less reason to object to solidaristic wage policy because, in the words of SAF chairman Laurin, "HAO and other so-called home-market associations [have] completely different opportunities for compensating themselves with price increases for rising wages" (Olivecrona 1991:19–20). Cartel arrangements, legal and legion in the sector, facilitated shifting costs to consumers. Labor and capital colluded at the political level in this affair: Between 1974 and 1980, clauses in LO–SAF agreements committed both unions and employers in home-market sectors to joint lobbying for relaxation of government price controls to accommodate their concessions to solidaristic wage policy. Naturally, VF leaders objected to this cross-class collusion (De Geer 1989:186, 192, 243).

The contrast between VF's views and those of SAF's fifth-largest affiliate, the Forest Products Association (Skogsindustriförbundet) is also instructive. Like engineering, the forest-product sector (lumber, pulp, and paper) is highly export-dependent – indeed, more so than many engineering firms. Dependence on export markets and the importance of prices in these markets severely restricted the ability of forest-product employers to pass on wage increases to consumers. Despite these shared concerns with VF, however, the Forest Products Association advocated "strong central negotiations and restrictions on local freedom of action" through the 1980s (De Geer 1989:131).

Compared to engineering, the forest-product industry worried less about wages as a management tool and as a cost of production. First, the costs to managerial control of interoccupational leveling was less than in engineering, because employers in this quintessential process industry, generating mass quantities of highly standardized products, did not require new production strategies requiring wage flexibility to the same degree.[12] Second, the forest-product industries were from the beginning more capital intensive, and became even more so after the 1960s. Therefore wages as a share of production costs have

11 Interview with Olof Ljunggren (SAF's executive director 1978–89), 28 June 1991.
12 Even the LO union in the sector did not, at least early on, use the leverage made available in the LO–SAF agreements to force interoccupational leveling – as did Metall.

declined, and the industry has been able to afford premium wages to unskilled as well as skilled employees. The imposition of wage solidarity was a matter of indifference or even of immediate advantage for forest-product employers, because lower- pay workers, of whom there were relatively few, got the higher increases, and the higher- pay workers were held back.

Also, capital intensity rendered forest products more vulnerable to industrial conflict than engineering. The costs of shutting down the flow of pulp and paper in a sympathy lockout with VF would have been great, the more so because SAF's compensation to firms for lockout losses are determined according to the number of workers employed, not fixed capital costs. Buyers, moreover, of the industry's standardized products could quickly find new suppliers. Overall, then, forest-product employers felt more protected from industrial conflict within existing arrangements than within a more decentralized system, and they used their influence to block VF's attempts to mobilize SAF for action against solidaristic wage policy.

The significance of opposition from sectors like these revealed itself as VF engaged in strategic maneuvering, first within and then against the institutions of centralized industrial relations. First, in the 1970s, VF attempted to use its weight in SAF to mobilize the confederation against interoccupational leveling and wage-drift compensation – within the framework of peak-level bargaining. Failing in this, VF shifted to a strategy of opting out of peak-level bargaining by entering into separate negotiations with Metall in the early 1980s. The results, however, were disappointing again. VF discovered that multisectoral bargaining between LO and SAF, even if it excluded engineering, had spillover problems for engineering. So in the late 1980s, VF embarked on a successful strategy of preventing SAF from engaging in peak-level bargaining altogether. Finally, VF entered a final and inconclusive phase, pushing for further decentralization of bargaining to the company or plant level.

VF entered each of these phases, described below, both in response to the increasingly felt urgency of removing rigidities in wage setting across and within firms and in response to the failures of previous phases. Frustrated by the indifference of other employer groups about interoccupational leveling and wage-drift guarantees, the engineering employers initially contemplated withdrawing from the system of peak-level bargaining in 1976. But fearful of going it alone without SAF's help against Metall, which would be backed by LO, they instead opted to push SAF toward a greater militancy against wage increases in general, and intrafirm wage compression and wage-drift guarantees in particular.

Two developments led VF to believe – mistakenly – that SAF might be brought around to its position in 1976. First, VF won the appointment of Curt Nicolin of ASEA (now Asea-Brown Boveri) as new SAF - chairman and, under Nicolin's leadership, SAF agreed to VF's demand for special representation on SAF's "little delegation" in LO–SAF negotiations. Second, the recent replacement of the Social Democrats after 44 years in power by a bourgeois coalition, they thought, would create political and economic conditions favorable to employer demands (De Geer 1989:342–4). The bourgeois governments of the late 1970s let the employers down, however, as they failed to undertake any significant cuts in payroll and income taxes and relied on deficit spending and public-sector expansion to maintain full employment. At the same time, VF again discovered that while other SAF affiliates paid lip service to the distributional principles behind its opposition to contractual provisions for interoccupational leveling, they were unwilling to engage in industrial conflict on VF's behalf. Confronted with pressure from government mediators to accept business as usual, an ambivalent SAF board, backed by an ambivalent membership, repeatedly caved in on the by-now standard distributional formulas and clauses that VF had come to hate. The results of the jumbo strike and lockout of 1980, during which the government leaned on SAF to accommodate union demands, proved the point (De Geer 1989:263–6).

After the 1980 debacle VF began preparations for withdrawal from peak-level bargaining, including creation of a strike fund of its own in 1981 and driving through SAF rule changes weakening its authority vis-à-vis its sectoral associations. Henceforth a three-quarter majority would be required for the SAF board to enjoin associations to cancel agreements deemed to be in conflict with general employer interests, and a two-third majority would be needed to prevent an association from proclaiming a lockout. With virtually all other groups in opposition, VF forced these changes through with threats of secession (Elvander 1988:84–5; De Geer 1992:142–3).

In the 1983 wage round, VF did not, however, seek a separate confrontation with Metall. Instead, in a surprise move, the engineering sector simply offered overall pay increases higher than those demanded by LO, and thereby enticed Metall, under new leadership more responsive to skilled workers, to drop the interoccupational leveling and wage-drift compensation clauses and to accept an increase in wage differentials.[13] The separate peace amounted to an alliance of engineering employers with the increasingly discontented higher-pay groups in Metall against low-pay groups favored by the former leadership. On the employer side, VF's go-it-alone strategy clearly angered other SAF affiliates; within labor, Metall antagonized other LO unions by stepping out of the arrangement and then formally renouncing solidaristic wage policy in 1985–86 (Ahlén 1989: 338).

Experiences during the latter half of the 1980s, however, persuaded VF leaders that separate negotiations with Metall could not fully solve their prob-

---

13 Interview with Karl-Olof Faxén, SAF, June 1983. While LO had demanded an average wage increase of 2.1 percent before and throughout its negotiations with SAF, the settlement with VF gave the Metalworkers 2.2 percent (*Dagens Nyheter* 11 November 1982 and 6 March 1983). An extra tier in the standard three-tier minimum-rate structure was added at the top of the VF–Metalworkers contract. The engineering agreement also contained no rules for distribution of allowable increases within firms.

lems. Although VF could formally disconnect itself from peak-level bargaining, its member firms could not isolate themselves from labor-market mechanisms (intersectoral competition over labor) and moral pressure (intersectoral wage comparisons and equity demands) emanating from rump-SAF negotiations with rump-LO unions. In those negotiations, low-pay unions in LO would sometimes target SAF's weakest link, the commercial sector organized by HAO, which in turn was inclined toward concessions because of wage trends in the labor market shared with the public sector. According to De Geer (1992:148), the mixed bargaining arrangement had "combined all the worst disadvantages of central and association-level negotiations," for LO could still "control events" with its leverage in the rump SAF–LO agreement.

In 1989, for example, wage increases and employment expansion in the public sector and home market effectively forced SAF into an inflationary wage settlement that was especially costly at the low end of the pay scale. Union leaders in Metall and engineering employers were forced by the exigencies of demand for scarce labor, especially at entry level, to follow suit (VF 1990a:4; VF 1990b:1–2). Doing so, however, made it expensive to continue increasing interoccupational wage differentials, which was favored both by the dominant Metall faction and VF. Exasperated with the wage round of 1989, VF forced through radical organizational changes in SAF, effectively dismantling SAF's capacity to coordinate wage bargaining outside the engineering sector. As with the changes introduced in 1982, these changes followed VF's threats to leave SAF.

Other SAF groups, handed a choice between a disabled and a dismembered SAF, elected a reduction of its authority. Under the new leadership of Ulf Laurin, the SAF board shut down its negotiation and statistics units, formally declaring in February 1990 that SAF would no longer negotiate over wages or general working conditions with LO. SAF affiliates now acquired greater freedom to engage in lockouts. SAF retained the right to decide about compensation payments from the strike fund, but the board subsequently decided that this fund would not be increased further, thus in effect inducing the sectoral associations to begin establishing their own funds (De Geer 1992:148–50).

For VF, disabling SAF represented a way to attenuate, if not to eliminate, the indirect influence that public-sector and home-market employers had over wage settlements in the internationally exposed engineering sector. If the public and service sectors continued to set the pace, especially at the low end of the pay structure, then at least decentralized, fragmented negotiations in the rest of the private sector might mute the market pressures and wage rivalries penetrating into engineering. If bakeries, newspaper publishers, or retail establishments alone settled too high, other employer groups would not have to follow.

In the early 1990s, Metall leaders remained ambivalent about the breakdown of peak-level bargaining, but not because they mourned solidaristic wage policy's passing. Indeed, they shared the view that VF should be free to pay higher wages to metalworkers, while public- and service-sector wages would be held back. They also pronounced a new affirmation of the principle of occupational wage differentiation instead of compression (Ahlén 1989:343).

On the other hand, they did not entirely give up the idea of centralization or multiindustry coordination of wage bargaining by LO, alone or jointly with SAF. Their purpose was to rein in public-sector wage militancy, not reintroduce solidaristic wage policy as other unions wished. At the 1991 LO congress, Metall moved that the LO secretariat should "coordinate new national agreements between LO's member associations," even if SAF refused to do likewise, in a resolution that forcefully and repeatedly asserted the interests of workers in the traded-goods sector: "Wage relations in the Swedish labor market must to a greater degree derive from and be marked by the exposed sector's ever greater significance for the country's economic development and therefore the possibilities of defending the welfare of all of us." In the name of both distributional justice and national economic performance, Metall asserted, "the exposed sector must be the wage leader" (LO 1991b:179–83).

Metall and VF, therefore, were not far apart on the basics of wage distribution across sectors, though disagreement prevailed about the structure of bargaining relations for achieving the shared goals. In any event, Metall rejected the idea of centralization for traditional solidaristic wage policy, as did VF. Metall in fact proved perfectly pliable on the question of wage distribution within sectors, as VF continued pushing for increased flexibility into the 1990s. In 1993, Metall signed an agreement with VF that meant "a large step toward company based wage formation" and that "company autonomy is now greater than ever before in wage matters" (VI 1993:5–6). The distribution of allowable wage increases was to be left entirely up to local negotiations.

The 1993 agreement was also the first in the sector to incorporate "common wage principles for both manual and white collar workers." That Metall went along with this decentralizing trend, while maintaining hopes of some broad coordination at the peak level, was manifested in earlier cooperation in fashioning and implementing a new job-evaluation system, which VF saw as the basis upon which to "construct a company-tailored, individual, and differentiated wage setting process" (VF 1990c:6). Metall also cooperated in and supported the 1991 LO policy report calling for wage justice through career and pay development (*befattningsutveckling*), or job ladders reaching up out of traditional manual work into white collar positions – a possibility facilitated by the new, more decentralized and flexible arrangements (see LO 1991a:151–223). Above all, these things favored skilled workers in Metall, a key group in the new cross-class alliance.

WAGE BARGAINING AND MACROECONOMIC POLICY

Turbulent developments in Swedish macroeconomic performance and policy, resulting in part from profound changes in Sweden's position in the international political economy, have made a return to centralization unlikely. This holds even for centralization for purposes limited to enforcement of the wage leadership of the internationally traded–goods sector over the sheltered public and service sectors – a distributional objective both VF and Metall explicitly agree on.

If anything, Metall seems to have signaled its endorsement of an emerging macroeconomic and regulatory regime that will impose intersectoral control without centralized bargaining. This shift toward policies heartily supported by engineering employers followed upon experiences during the 1980s with the failures of the "Third Way," the recovery strategy adopted by the Social Democrats when they returned to power in 1982. As Andrew Martin (this volume) explains, the new government relied on a massive devaluation to restore corporate profits and thereby stimulate the expansion of output and employment in the private sector (cf. also Pontusson 1992c). The extraordinary levels of corporate profitability that resulted rendered LO's efforts to organize wage restraint exceedingly difficult by fueling interfirm competition for scarce labor, especially skilled labor, and weakening employer resistance to local wage demands. The government also deregulated credit markets, which triggered a building boom and wage explosion in construction, adding to the inflationary force of the devaluation.

Sweden's high rate of inflation in the second half of the decade (significantly above the OECD average) eventually forced the government to reverse its macroeconomic stance. Though the effort to peg the krona to the ecu could not be sustained in the face of currency speculation, Sweden clearly shifted to a less accommodating macroeconomic regime as the bourgeois government that replaced the Social Democrats in 1991 allowed unemployment to rise to unprecedented levels (Iversen, this volume). The employment crisis of the first half of the 1990s probably sealed the fate of peak-level bargaining as far as Swedish employers were concerned by weakening residual interest, based on historical experience, in recentralization as an instrument to control the inflationary spread of wage increases across sectoral lines.

In light of these experiences, too, Metall emerged as a critic of the macroeconomic policies of the Third Way and joined forces with employers calling for restrictive monetary policy and EU membership. At the 1991 LO congress, for example, Metall officially called for "a stringent economic policy aimed at reducing demand and price increases in the shelted sectors" and "increased competition through a continued deregulation in the sheltered sector of the economy." (LO 1991b:183). Important locals in Metall, but not other unions, also came out strongly for Sweden's entry into the European Union, suggesting that this union was the one with the deepest internal basis of support for integration (LO 1991c:481–6).

The broad consensus that has since emerged in Swedish party politics (though not in public opinion) behind entry into the European Union and behind its ambitions to create the basis for stable fixed currencies may also make Metall's residual interests in centralization for intersectoral control superfluous. Stringent fiscal policy will impose discipline on high wage settlements in the public sector. Central bank policies devoted to reducing inflation and stabilizing the value of the krona relative to harder currencies will concentrate downward pressure on wages in the sheltered construction industry through high interest rates and high unemployment, with their direct, immediate, and powerful effect on construction.[14] Finally, tougher EU rules regarding cartel and other anticompetitive practices will serve Metall's and also engineering employers' interests in suppressing prices and hence wages in the sheltered sectors – especially in the retail sector – without centralized bargaining or wage coordination.

In short, recent macro- and microregulatory changes associated with European integration, favored strongly by Metall as well as VF, should help cement and stabilize the new cross-class alliance behind wage-bargaining decentralized at least as far as the industry level. From the standpoint of labor-market governance, Sweden may look a lot more like Germany, where the strong Bundesbank ensured that construction and the public sector could not play a wage leadership role and, for much of the postwar period, even joined conservative forces in criticizing IG Metall's militancy (cf. Swenson 1989, 1991b; Pontusson 1997; Franzese and Hall this volume).

THEORETICAL IMPLICATIONS AND CROSS-NATIONAL COMPARISONS

The Swedish case of institutional change in the governance of labor markets speaks directly to the literature on corporatism and its decline. The best thinking on the matter can be found in recent articles by Wolfgang Streeck and Philippe Schmitter, who provide a cogent package of explanations for the phenomenon (Schmitter 1989; Streeck and Schmitter 1991; Streeck 1993). They identify three sets of corrosive developments wearing away at corporatism gen-

---

14 The building sector is of course highly sensitive to interest rates. Also labor surplus associated with unemployment means high-wage workers can easily be dropped and then rehired at lower rates (as long as they do not go below negotiated or statutory minima). In other words, because of labor-intensive operations based on short-term, project-related employment relations without routinized internal labor-market practices (long-term employment guarantees, downwardly inflexible wages), wages in the building sector are especially sensitive to surpluses and shortages in external labor markets.

erally and, by strong implication, centralized wage bargaining. First, Streeck and Schmitter attribute the decline of corporatism to a transformation in the "political capacities of European nation-states." Fiscal crises, monetary instability, and economic interdependence have "severely limited the ability of national governments, acting individually, to maintain full employment by Keynesian methods and deliver their part of the neocorporatist social contract." Also, "budget constraints combined with the fiscal crisis of the welfare state sharply curtailed the government's ability to offer unions compensation for restraint in collective bargaining" (Streeck 1993:83; cf. Streeck and Schmitter 1991:145).

Second, Streeck and Schmitter invoke changes in social structure and culture, such as the shift of employment to the service sector, the growth of white-collar and female employment, increasing ethnic heterogeneity, and "growing individualization of lifestyles and normative orientations." As the social cohesion of the working class eroded, Streeck argues, unions found it difficult to transform special member interests into general demands and policies. During the 1970s and 1980s, "the substantive content of interest conflicts and the focus of policy attention shifted away from class-based lines of cleavage toward a panoply of discrete issues focusing on consumer protection, quality of life, gender, environmental, ethical, and other problems . . ." (Streeck 1993:84).

Finally, Streeck and Schmitter link, as we do, the decline of corporatism to changes in the organization of production associated with the decline of Fordism, suggesting that "both unions and employer associations are today finding themselves increasingly shut out of an expanding range of workplace-specific deliberations and bargaining between their local constituents." Meanwhile, "fragmentation of demand and flexible technology offered firms and their managements a range of choice unknown in the worlds of Fordism and Taylorism, not least of which was the choice between relatively low-wage, low-price mass production and high-skilled, high-wage, more or less customized, quality production" (Streeck and Schmitter 1991:147).

To the extent that they bear on centralized governance of labor markets, the first two of these arguments are problematic on several counts. To begin with, their diffuse, general emphasis on changing structural conditions tends partially to obscure the interests and strategic calculations of the decisive collective actors involved in corporatist bargaining. To the extent that they nevertheless implicitly recognize the importance of strategic actors and instrumental motivations, the explanation for the decline of corporatism strikes us as too labor centered. In Streeck and Schmitter's framework, governments must deliver Keynesian and other policies as their part of the bargain to purchase cooperation of the social partners. By implication, unions, not employers, are the spoilers. They, after all, are the ones seeking such rewards for cooperation in centralized arrangements. In other words, cooperation breaks down when governments fail to "gain concessions from labor" with policy inducements. But this scenario departs radically from the Swedish events described above, suggesting that attention and analysis should be refocused to explain others as well.

Divisions among Swedish employers on centralization also cast considerable doubt on Streeck and Schmitter's idea that changes in social structure and attendant political culture bear much responsibility for the breakdown of corporatism, at least in Sweden. Individualistic, environmental, gender, or other nonclass or postmaterial issues did not pit members against unions, union against union, union against state, or union against employers in any way that brought decentralization. Metalworkers' motives were good old-fashioned material ones for joining engineering employers as, together, they left the centralized arrangement in 1983. Initially, employers' desire for decentralization had to do with increasing rigidities imposed in the centralized pay-setting process. Later, new technology and market pressure for yet more flexibility and productivity added to the pressure. Workers' changed mind-sets regarding work or hierarchical authority had little to do with it. The fact that opposition to decentralization came from HAO, whose members comprised a far higher proportion of white-collar and service personnel than manufacturing – the host of more class-oriented values – also casts doubt on the sociological explanation tracing the decline of corporatism to the decline of the blue-collar manufacturing work force. Moreover, opponents of decentralization in SAF held out against it longest in the white-collar sector generally, even in manufacturing and not just in retail and other service sectors.

By contrast, the arguments advanced by Streeck and Schmitter about the need for diversity and flexibility in production are consistent with our interpretation of the Swedish experience. Ironically, though, the strength of the argument appears to be undermined by recent research showing that perhaps the Swedish experience is unique. According to Peter Lange, Michael Wallerstein, and Miriam Golden (1995), there is little evidence of a generalized trend toward more decentralized wage bargaining in Western Europe (see also Wallerstein and Golden this volume). Their analysis suggests that the need for flexibility, which we along with Streeck and Schmitter argue is a general, international phenomenon, cannot explain decentralization in Sweden because it has not had the same effect elsewhere. In other words, some of the explanations of Swedish employer behavior that we have advanced might be misguided because they rely on independent variables that are not sufficiently idiosyncratic (Sweden-specific). Why hasn't the apparently universal shift to more flexible production strategies led to employer-initiated wage-bargaining decentralization throughout the OECD countries?

As Iversen and Pontusson (this volume) argue, Lange, Wallerstein, and Golden's quantitative measures of wage-bargaining centralization are limited by their focus on procedural issues and the role of peak organizations in wage bargaining. From a broader perspective, the Swedish case may be less unique than Lange, Wallerstein, and Golden suggest. At the same time, we believe that the analysis presented above is fully consistent with the cross-national variations in the evolution of wage-bargaining arrangements captured by their quantitative measures. For example, we would argue that new production strategies have led German as well as Swedish engineering employers to introduce new pay systems and, generally speaking, upgrade the value assigned to wage flexibility relative to wage restraint. The German system of collective bargaining was more decentralized to begin with and could more readily accommodate new employer interests. In other words, German employers did not have to challenge the existing procedural framework to achieve the substantive changes they wanted (Thelen 1993).

The contrast between Sweden and Austria may be more interesting than the one between Sweden and Germany, since the Austrian system of wage bargaining has involved a more centralized form of coordination than the German system. The conventional view of the Austrian case in the corporatism literature exaggerates, however, the degree to which the peak organizations of labor and capital have been involved in the wage-bargaining process. In fact, there has never been a Swedish-style peak-level wage settlement in Austria (cf. Traxler forthcoming; Iversen 1996; and Pontusson this volume). And, most importantly for our present purposes, Austrian unions never made any sustained effort to compress wage differentials. Indeed, the wage gap between poorly and highly paid blue-collar workers is greater in Austria than in any other European OECD country (Rowthorn 1992:91–2; Pontusson this volume). Wage compression, then, has not been a serious problem for Austrian employers.

For these reasons, similar changes in the social and economic context may produce different institutional outcomes in different countries. Cross-national variation in the politics of institutional change may also be related to variations in the extent and nature of institutionally exogenous material changes. In some countries, most notably Sweden, public employment grew much more rapidly than in other countries in the 1960s and 1970s, and public policies helped empower public-sector unions (cf. Swenson 1991b). It stands to reason that the shifts in bargaining outcomes associated with these developments was more pronounced in Sweden than in most other countries, placing unique levels of strain on institutionalized bargaining relations in the private sector.

The same type of argument can be made with respect to new production strategies and changing employer interests. As the Swedish case suggests, the imperatives and chances to reorganize production on a more flexible basis are particularly strong in engineering industries. Employers in more capital-intensive process industries have had less incentive to challenge centralized wage bargaining. The fact that the latter sectors (energy and forest products) represent a larger component of organized capital might explain why Wallerstein and Golden (this volume) find that Norway and Finland have not experienced sustained employer campaigns to decentralize wage bargaining to the same extent as Sweden and Denmark. Such considerations also bear on the contrast between Sweden and Austria, for the kind of export-oriented engineering firms that spearheaded the Swedish employer offensive are far less prominent in the Austrian case.[15] The Austrian case thus represents a mirror image of the Swedish case: On the one hand, centralized bargaining has not produced the same wage rigidities in Austria and, additionally, Austrian employers have not been under the same pressure to reorganize production.

CONCLUSION

Viewing the Swedish case through comparative lenses suggests that material changes exogenous to the institutions of wage bargaining are a major source of employer preferences for change in those institutions. However, it also shows that these forces, though partly international, do not work their way evenly across countries, bringing a uniform demise of corporatism and centralized bargaining. The industrial structure varies across countries, and different sectors, including the public sector, respond differently to changing external market and technological forces. Therefore, change in the structure of national bargaining systems, built and maintained by distinct cross-class and cross-sectoral coalitions, are also likely to vary.

From a comparative perspective, Sweden is distinguished, on the one hand, by its large, export-oriented engineering sector in manufacturing and, on the other, by its large public sector. Until recently, it has also been distinguished by a particular kind of centralization, defended by a distinct coalition of interests and by government mediation, that imposed unusually invasive demands on engineering. The engineering sector was therefore the key agent in bringing about change.

Engineering employers' institutional preferences for decentralization derived from material preferences for flexibility. These primary needs were being ignored or violated by centralization's coalition of interests and forces, including those emanating from the public sector, even as engineering manufacturers' perceived need for flexibility increased through the 1970s and 1980s. The institutions manifestly failed to shape and therefore adapt engineering's preferences to the rigidities they imposed. Likewise, the institutions failed to adjust themselves adequately to the urgent, exogeneously determined preferences of engineering employers. Failing to regain flexibility within the framework of centralization, a logical if not politically feasible strategy according to our analysis, engineering employers ultimately set about dismantling the system instead.

---

15 The distinctive characteristic of Austrian industrial structure is its bifurcation into a sector of small firms producing light consumer goods and a sector of large (often state-owned) firms engaged in capital-intensive production. See Katzenstein (1984) and Pontusson (this volume).

104 UNIONS, EMPLOYERS, AND CENTRAL BANKS

References

Ahlén, Kristina. 1989. "Swedish collective bargaining under pressure," *British Journal of Industrial Relations*, 23:215–240.

Ahrne, Göran and Wallace Clement. 1994. "A new regime? Class representation within the Swedish state." In Wallace Clement and Rianne Mahon, eds., *Swedish social democracy*. Toronto: Canadian Scholars' Press, 223–244.

Andersson, Karl-Olof. 1977. *Spelet om lönerna*. Stockholm: Pogo Press.

Berggren, Christian. 1992. *Alternatives to lean production*. Ithaca, NY: ILR Press.

De Geer, Hans. 1989. *I vänstervind och högervåg*. Stockholm: Allmänna Förlaget.

1992. *The rise and fall of the Swedish Model*. Chichester: Carden Publications.

De Geer, Hans and Hans Zetterberg. 1987. *Mål, motiv och verksamhet: En SIFO-undersökning*. Stockholm: SAF.

Edgren, Gösta, Karl-Olof Faxén, and Clas-Erik Odhner. 1970. *Lönebildning och samhällsekonomi*. Stockholm: Rabén & Sjögren.

Edquist, Charles and Hans Glimmel. 1989. "Swedish frontiers of change." Department of Technology and Social Change, Linköping University.

Ehrenkrona, Olof. 1991. *Nicolin*. Stockholm: Timbro.

Elvander, Nils. 1988. *Den svenska modellen*. Stockholm: Allmänna Förlaget.

1992. *Lokal lönemarknad*. Stockholm: SNS Förlag.

Gourevitch, Peter. 1986. *Politics in hard times*. Ithaca, NY: Cornell University Press.

Hibbs, Douglas. 1990. "Wage compression under solidarity bargaining in Sweden." Working paper, Trade Union Institute for Economic Research, Stockholm.

Hibbs, Douglas and Håkan Locking. 1996. "Wage dispersion and productive efficiency." Working paper, Trade Union Institute for Economic Research, Stockholm.

ILO. 1951. *Payment by results*. Geneva.

Iversen, Torben. 1996. "Power, flexibility, and the breakdown of centralized wage bargaining," *Comparative Politics*, 28:399–437.

Katzenstein, Peter. 1984. *Corporatism and change*. Ithaca, NY: Cornell University Press.

Kjellberg, Anders. 1992. "Sweden: Can the model survive?" In Anthony Ferner and Richard Hyman, eds., *Industrial relations in the New Europe*. Oxford: Basil Blackwell, 88–142.

Kuuse, Jan. 1986. *Strukturomvandlingen och arbetsmarknadens organisering*. Stockholm: SAF.

Lange, Peter, Michael Wallerstein, and Miriam Golden. 1995. "The end of corporatism?" In Sanford Jacoby, ed., *The workers of nations*. New York: Oxford University Press, 76–100.

Larsson, Matts Bergom. 1985. "Den svenska modellen ur branschperspektiv." In Bertil Kugelberg et al., eds., *Fred eller fejd*. Stockholm: SAF, 357–419.

Lash, Scott. 1985. "The end of neo-corporatism," *British Journal of Industrial Relations*, 23:215–240.

LO. 1991a. *Det utvecklande arbetet – En rapport till LO-kongressen*. Stockholm: Landsorganisationen.

LO. 1991b. *LO-kongressen. Motioner Del 1*. Stockholm: Landsorganisationen.

LO. 1991c. *LO-kongressen. Motioner Del 2*. Stockholm: Landsorganisationen.

Mahon, Rianne. 1994. "Wage-earners and/or co-workers?" *Economic and Industrial Democracy*, 15:355–384.

Martin, Andrew. 1984. "Trade unions in Sweden." In Peter Gourevitch et al., eds., *Unions and economic crisis*. London: George Allen & Unwin, 189–359.

1991. "Wage bargaining and Swedish politics." Center for European Studies, Harvard University.

Nilsson, Tommy. 1988. *Arbetare eller tjänstemän?* Lund: Arkiv.

OECD. 1970. *Forms of wage and salary payment for high productivity*. Paris.

Olivecrona, Gustav. 1991. *Samtal med Ulf Laurin*. Stockholm: T. Fischer & Co.

Pestoff, Victor. 1995. "Towards a new Swedish model of collective bargaining and politics." In Colin Crouch and Franz Traxler, eds., *Organized industrial relations in Europe*. Aldershot: Avebury, 151–82.

Piore, Michael and Charles Sabel. 1984. *The second industrial divide*. New York: Basic Books.

Pontusson, Jonas. 1984. "Behind and beyond social democracy in Sweden," *New Left Review*, 143: 69–96.

1992a. *The limits of social democracy*. Ithaca, NY: Cornell University Press.

1992b. "Unions, new technology and job redesign at Volvo and British Leyland." In Jonas Pontusson and Miriam Golden, eds., *Bargaining for change*. Ithaca NY: Cornell University Press, 277–306.

1992c. "At the end of the Third Road: Swedish social democracy in crisis," *Politics and Society*, 20:305–332.

1997. "Between neo-liberalism and the German Model: Swedish capitalism in transition." In Colin Crouch and Wolfgang Streeck, eds., *Political economy of modern capitalism*. London: Sage, 55–70.

Rowthorn, Bob. 1992. "Corporatism and labor market performance." In Jukka Pekkarinen, Matti Pohjola, and Bob Rowthorn, eds., *Social corporatism*. Oxford: Clarendon Press, 82–131.

SAF. 1986. *Löneformsundersökning 1985*. Stockholm.

SAF. 1987. *Lönen – ett medel för tillväxt*. Stockholm.

SAF. 1988. *Framtiden finns i företagen*. Stockholm.

SAF. 1990a. *Marknad och mångfald*. Stockholm.

SAF. 1990b. *Produktivitet och arbete*. Stockholm.

SCB. 1990. *Bakgrundsmaterial om vuxenutbildning*, no. 2.

Schiller, Bernt. 1988. *"Det förödande 70-talet"*. Stockholm: Arbetsmiljöfonden.

Schmitter, Philippe. 1989. "Corporatism is dead! Long live corporatism!" *Government and Opposition*, 24:54–73.

Sköldebrand, Barbro. 1989. "Anställd och ägare: konvertibler." Swedish Center for Working Life, Stockholm.

1990. "Anställd och ägare: företagsanknutna stiftelser och fonder." Swedish Center for Working Life, Stockholm.

Streeck, Wolfgang. 1987. "Industrial relations and industrial change," *Economic and Industrial Democracy*, 8:437–62.

1991. "On the institutional conditions of diversified quality production." In Egon Matzner and Wolfgang Streeck, eds., *Beyond Keynesianism*. Aldershot: Edward Elgar, 21–61.

106   UNIONS, EMPLOYERS, AND CENTRAL BANKS

1993. "The rise and decline of neocorporatism." In Lloyd Ulman, Barry Eichen-green, and William Dickens, eds., *Labor and an integrated Europe*. Washing-ton, DC: Brookings Institution, 80–99.

Streeck, Wolfgang and Philippe Schmitter. 1991. "From national corporatism to transnational pluralism," *Politics and Society*, 19:133–64.

Svenska Metallindustriarbetareförbundet. 1992. *En rapport om lönesystem inom Metall*. Stockholm.

Swenson, Peter. 1989. *Fair shares: Unions, pay and politics in Sweden and West Germany*. Ithaca, NY: Cornell University Press.

1991a. "Bringing capital back in, or social democracy reconsidered," *World Politics*, 43:69–96.

1991b. "Labor and the limits of the welfare state," *Comparative Politics*, 23:379–99.

1992. "Managing the managers," *Scandinavian Journal of History*, 16:335–56.

1997. "Employers unite: Labor market governance and the welfare state in Sweden and the United States." Manuscript, Department of Political Science, Northwestern University.

Thelen, Kathleen. 1993. "West European labor in transition," *World Politics*, 46:23–49.

Traxler, Franz. Forthcoming. "European transformation and institution-building in East and West." In Randall W. Kindley and David Good, eds., *The challenge of globalization and institution building: Lessons from small European states*. Boulder, CO: Westview Press, 1997.

Treslow, Kjell. 1986. *Verkstadsföreningen under 90 år*. Stockholm: VF.

1988. "The Swedish Model." Paper presented at the New Sweden conference, Indiana University, September.

VF. n.d. *Arbete, lön, effektivitet*. Stockholm.

VF. 1990a. *Årsberättelse*. Stockholm. Verkstadsföreningen.

VF. 1990b. "Sanningen om löneglidningen." *VF-journalen* No. 3.

VF 1990c. "VF och Metall underlättar för lokala lönesystem." *VF-journalen* No. 3.

VI. 1993. *Årsberättelse*. Stockholm. Verkstadsindustrier.

4

POSTWAR WAGE SETTING IN THE NORDIC COUNTRIES

Michael Wallerstein and Miriam Golden

The Nordic countries have commonly been considered models of highly central-ized systems of wage bargaining. In the American literature, they are known as exemplars of corporatism, the polar opposite of such decentralized systems of wage setting as the United States. Yet, as the editors to this volume suggest in their introductory essay, a decentralization of wage setting is generally believed to characterize the corporatist countries of Northern Europe in the 1980s and 1990s. In this chapter, we investigate whether such a decentralization has been underway in Denmark, Finland, Norway, and Sweden.

Why should the level of wage setting matter? One reason is that it is believed to affect economic efficiency and macroeconomic performance. This has been a controversial issue, one that has generated wildly divergent views on the merits (or conversely the deficiencies) of bargaining centralization. On one side are those who believe that centralized negotiations improve economic perfor-mance by allowing wage setters to incorporate various externalities into their decisions that would otherwise be ignored by actors who have only local respon-sibilities. On the other side are those who believe that any centralized system of

This is a substantially revised version of "The Fragmentation of the Bargaining Society: Wage setting in the Nordic Countries, 1950–1992," Comparative Political Studies, 1997, 30: 699–731. The data reported here was collected as part of a project funded by National Science Foundation grants SES-9309391 and SES-9108485 to UCLA and SES-9110228, and SBR-9309414 to Duke University with Miriam Golden, Peter Lange and Michael Wallerstein as principal investigators. Additional support came from UCLA's Institute of Industrial Relations and the Committee on Research of the Academic Senate. We thank Jonathan Moses, David Ellison and David Yamanishi for their help in preparing this paper. We thank Lowell Turner, Peter Swenson, John Stephens and the editors of this volume for helpful discussions of the paper.

wage determination is likely to suffer many of the same informational and incentive failures as central planning.[1]

Recently, however, many scholars have assumed a more qualified and historically contingent stance, proposing that centralized bargaining, while not in principle inefficient, has become less efficient or less feasible over time. According to this line of argument, centralized wage-setting institutions worked well during Europe's "golden age," or the first three decades after the Second World War. However, in the years since the first oil shock of 1973–74, so the argument goes, European economies have changed in ways that have reduced the efficiency of centralized wage determination. As a result, it is argued, wage setting, where it was not already decentralized, is undergoing a general tendency toward decentralization.

The alleged causes of such changes are said to be multiple. They include changes in production techniques, changes in occupational structures, and the increased integration of world markets. Domestic and international factors are both believed to be at work in shifting the preferences of employers away from centralized bargaining arrangements. As a result, actors whose support was crucial for the implementation and continuation of centralized bargaining – above all, employers – are now forcing a fundamental shift in the locus of wage bargaining. Everywhere, it is asserted, wages are increasingly being set at the industry or plant level rather than through peak-level agreements.

Before we can begin to assess the relative importance of different possible causes of decentralization and fragmentation, however, we need better and more systematic information on what has really changed in industrial relations in the past two decades. As the editors to this volume note in their introductory essay, there is a plethora of views about the simple facts, and even more confusion about how to interpret them. While some scholars see a universal trend toward decentralization (Katz 1993), others have been more impressed with the divergence of national experiences and the absence of a general pattern (Hyman 1994). So far, however, the literature has been largely anecdotal. The purpose of this paper is to present systematic data on the extent to which bargaining has indeed become more decentralized in the Nordic countries in recent years and to discuss the inferences that can be made regarding the causes of decentralization, where decentralization has in fact occurred.[2] We focus specifically on the Nordic countries because wage setting in these countries was highly centralized for a longer period of time than anywhere else in Western Europe.[3] Thus, these

---

1 See Karl Moene, Michael Wallerstein, and Michael Hoel (1993) with comments by Lars Calmfors (1993) and Assar Lindbeck (1993) for a survey of the debate.

2 This chapter updates and corrects data first published in Lange, Wallerstein, and Golden (1995).

3 In all of the Nordic countries, unions and employers either negotiated a single wage agreement or adopted a unified contract ratification procedure for all blue-collar workers in the private sector for most of the postwar period. The only other European country with equally centralized bargaining was the Netherlands before 1968. In Austria, the union confederation has extensive authority over its

are the countries where any general tendency toward decentralization should be especially visible.

To anticipate our findings, our data show that a substantial decentralization of wage setting had occurred in Sweden but not in the other three Nordic countries we analyzed, at least not as of 1992, when our data set ends. The decentralization that occurred in Denmark in the 1980s was followed by the establishment of new, centralized bargaining institutions in the 1990s, at least in comparison with wage-setting institutions in non-Nordic countries. Norway became more, not less, centralized between the early 1980s and the early 1990s. The pattern of bargaining in Finland remained stable from 1968 through 1992. None of the existing accounts of the decline in centralized wage setting can easily explain these cross-national differences, precisely because such accounts focus on explaining purported uniformities across countries, uniformities that our analysis fails to substantiate. We offer one possible interpretation for what we would label "Swedish exceptionalism" in the concluding section to this essay.

In the next section, we describe our measures of the centralization of private-sector wage setting. Subsequent sections detail the various kinds of changes in the centralization of wage setting that have occurred in each of the four Nordic countries from 1950 through 1992. We then analyze the findings with a discussion of the extent to which there has or has not been a common trend away from centralized bargaining in Northern Europe. Since our results are controversial, we next discuss why other observers sometimes argue that decentralization has been more common in the Nordic countries than we believe is the case and examine other kinds of data to see if they corroborate our findings. In our conclusions, we discuss special features of the Swedish case that may explain why a significant decentralization of wage setting has occurred in Sweden but not elsewhere in northern Europe.

1. MEASURES OF THE CENTRALIZATION OF WAGE SETTING

There are many aspects of trade unions and of employer organizations that might plausibly affect their ability to coordinate wage setting on a national or sectoral level. In another paper (Wallerstein, Golden, and Lange 1997), we present extensive data on union density and the coverage of collective contracts, union concentration (including the number of union confederations, the number of affiliated unions in each, and the concentration of membership within partic-

affiliates, but bargaining occurs largely at the industry level. See Wallerstein, Golden, and Lange (1997) for a comparison of collective bargaining institutions in the Nordic countries with those found in Germany, Austria, Belgium, and the Netherlands.

ular unions), and the statutory authority of union and employers' organizations over their affiliates for the Nordic countries, among others. In this chapter we concentrate on the extent of centralization of private-sector wage bargaining and how it has changed over time.

As the editors to this volume note, the centralization of wage bargaining is difficult to measure. First, bargaining done at different levels can, and sometimes does, vary from bargaining round to bargaining round because the practice of bargaining is normally not clearly predetermined according to formal rules. In the Nordic countries, union confederations do not have statutory authority to bargain on behalf of their affiliates. They do so only with the consent of the affiliated unions and employers' associations, consent that must in principle be renegotiated at each bargaining round. To accommodate change over time, we have coded the level of bargaining for each bargaining round separately.[4]

Second, exclusively centralized bargaining hardly ever occurs. Multitiered bargaining is, in fact, a more accurate depiction than centralized bargaining, even (if not especially) in the Nordic countries. In these countries, central agreements are typically negotiated by the peak associations but are subsequently implemented via negotiations at the industry level, which are in turn generally followed by negotiations at the plant level. While the bargaining process is hierarchically ordered (unlike the decentralized and atomized bargaining situations that characterize the United States and the UK), determining the relative weights of different levels in setting overall wages is a difficult theoretical and empirical task. We describe the constraints imposed on plant-level bargaining, but our coding attempts systematically to measure only changes in the relative roles of the peak associations, the industry-level unions, and employer associations in the wage setting process. Thus, as Iversen and Pontusson rightly note in their introductory essay, our coding effectively misses much of the changing relationship between industry-level and firm-level bargaining, mainly because systematic data over time on the relationship between industry and local-level bargaining do not exist.

Third, all the Nordic countries house separate confederations for blue-collar and white-collar workers, as well as for workers with university degrees and, in the case of Finland, foremen and technicians. Each different confederation may play a different role in bargaining. In Norway and Sweden, the white-collar and professional confederations do not participate in collective bargaining for the private sector. In Denmark, white-collar and professional confederations do not bargain on behalf of their affiliates, but representatives of all three union confed-

---

4 For information regarding confederal and government involvement in each bargaining round, we used both secondary sources and, starting in the mid-1970s, reports in the *European Industrial Relations Review*. We found the following sources particularly useful. Sweden: Swenson (1989), Kjellberg (1992), Calmfors and Forslund (1990), De Geer (1992); Norway: Rødseth and Holden (1990), Strøm, Stølen, and Torp (1988), Frøland (1993); Finland: Knoellinger (1960), Tyrväinen (1989), Eriksson, Suvanto, and Vartia (1990); Denmark: Due et al (1994).

erations participate in the mediation procedure. In Finland, wage setting for white-collar workers in manufacturing is even more centralized than for blue-collar workers, with all white-collar workers in manufacturing covered by a single contract. Our coding is confined only to the process of wage negotiations between the main blue-collar confederation in each country and the main employer association. Coding for other types of confederations presented intractable data problems. Historically, blue-collar confederations and their affiliates have set the pattern for wage negotiations in the private sector and, in that sense, they dominate private-sector wage setting. We thus contend that we have coded for the most important organizations in the private-sector wage-setting process.

Fourth, there are many forms of participation in bargaining that are hard to capture, such as the informal influence exerted by higher-level officials over lower-level negotiators and the implicit threats and promises that may be made by government officials. These factors may well affect the outcome of wage negotiations. For obvious reasons, we record only interventions in wage setting that are observable to outsiders. We have no way of knowing how our coding would have been affected had we been able to include information on informal bargaining interactions. It is possible that such interactions serve by and large to reinforce existing formal arrangements, and that therefore our coding would not have been much different.

Fifth, our coding is heavily procedural, as the editors to this volume note, and focuses on the extent of confederal involvement in wage setting. We do incorporate the crucial distinction between central agreements that contain an industrial peace clause (discussed below) and central agreements that do not. We do not, however, code the substance of the wage agreements that are negotiated. Central agreements may specify every workers' wage increase or the central agreement may specify only a few parameters of the wage distribution, such as the mean or the minimum, with the rest to be determined in lower-level bargaining. The enormous variety of ways in which clauses in the central agreement impose constraints on the wage distribution as well as the problem of interpreting whether the constraints in the central agreement are effective precludes coding substantive controls by central wage setters over lower-level bargaining.

Finally, wage setting can be centralized through different institutional mechanisms. We have used three separate scales of bargaining centralization to capture the diverse arenas in which it can originate. The first, an 11-fold index, measures the involvement of the major blue-collar union confederations in private-sector wage setting, as is reported in Table 4.1. The second, a 15-fold index, measures government involvement in private-sector wage setting, on the premise that even if organized labor fails to act at a central level, the government can impose centralization on the wage-setting process. That index is reported in Table 4.2. The third comprises a four-fold index of bargaining centralization,

Table 4.1. *Index of confederal involvement in private-sector wage setting*

Level	Description
1	Confederation(s) uninvolved in wage setting in any of the subsequent ways
2	Confederation(s) participates in talks or in formulation of demands for some affiliates
3	Confederation(s) participates in talks or in formulation of demands for all affiliates
4	Confederation(s) negotiates non-wage benefits
5	Confederation(s) negotiates a part of the wage agreement, such as the cost-of-living adjustment
6	Confederation(s) represents affiliates in mediation with centralized ratification
7	Confederation(s) represents affiliates in arbitration
8	Confederation(s) bargains for affiliates in industry-level negotiations
9	Confederation(s) negotiates national wage agreement without peace obligation
10	Confederation(s) negotiates national wage agreement with peace obligation
11	Confederation(s) negotiates national wage agreement with limits on supplementary bargaining

an index which in part summarizes the first two measures but which also contains additional information. Reported in Table 4.3, the index of bargaining centralization measures the highest level at which wage setting occurs.

We measure confederal involvement for every bargaining round, usually every two years, with intervening years coded identically to the year in which bargaining occurred. Government involvement and bargaining centralization are measured annually. The hierarchy of categories in all three indices reflects both the role of the central confederation (or the government) and the degree to which central agreements constrain and dominate wage negotiations at lower levels. We consider bargaining more centralized both as higher-level actors – confederations or governments – exhibit greater involvement in the process and as their activities more strictly preclude independent bargaining by lower-level actors. Our scale of bargaining level measures authoritative bargaining centralization regardless of whether it originates with a confederation, the government, or, as we detail below, occasionally through agreements among industry-level unions. Because of this final feature, the scale contains information not found in the scales of confederal or government involvement in bargaining. These three scales allow us to compare the centralization of wage setting cross-nationally and longitudinally in the four Nordic countries.

Table 4.2. *Index of government involvement in private-sector wage setting*

Level	Description
1	Government uninvolved in wage setting
2	Government establishes minimum wage(s)
3	Government extends collective agreements
4	Government provides economic forecasts to bargaining partners
5	Government recommends wage guidelines or norms
6	Government and unions negotiate wage guidelines
7	Government imposes wage controls in selected industries
8	Government imposes cost-of-living adjustment
9	Formal tripartite agreement for national wage schedule without sanctions
10	Formal tripartite agreement for national wage schedule with sanctions
11	Government arbitrator imposes wage schedules without sanctions on unions
12	Government arbitrator imposes national wage schedule with sanctions
13	Government imposes national wage schedule with sanctions
14	Formal tripartite agreement for national wage schedule with supplementary local bargaining prohibited
15	Government imposes wage freeze and prohibits supplementary local bargaining

Table 4.3. *Index of bargaining level*

Level	Description
1	Plant-level wage setting
2	Industry-level wage setting
3	Central wage setting without sanctions
4	Central wage setting with sanctions

The scales can also be used effectively to cover other OECD countries (as in Golden and Wallerstein 1996).

The ordering of categories reflects our judgments about the extent and nature of central control over the wage-setting process. Central agreements always impose a floor on wages, thereby effectively setting minimum wages. In the absence of an industrial peace clause, industry and local-level negotiators are free to bargain and to strike for additional wage increases above those specified in the central agreement. With an industrial peace clause, bargaining at lower levels may be permitted but strikes and lockouts are prohibited for the life of the central agreement. In these situations, central agreements come closer to setting actual (not minimum) wages. Although other forms of industrial action, such as go-slow or work-to-rule actions, are not prohibited and no clause in a contract can prevent a wildcat strike, the existence of an industrial peace clause significantly increases the ability of the central officials to control the wage increases obtained at lower levels in multilevel bargaining (Moene, Wallerstein, and Hoel 1993:ch. 12). Thus, as the scales presented in Tables 4.1 and 4.3 show, we consider agreements with peace clauses to be more centralized then those without them.

The scale for government involvement, presented in Table 4.2, measures various types of both parliamentary and governmental involvement in the private-sector wage-setting process. We judge wage setting by parliament to be more centralized than wage setting by a government-appointed mediator. A mediator's mandate is to craft an agreement that is acceptable to both unions and employers, thereby avoiding industrial conflict. For parliament, in contrast, the government's economic goals may be the primary consideration. Parliamentary involvement is thus typically more restrictive on subsequent wage setting than that of a mediator. Our scale also distinguishes a government-imposed wage contract, government participation in tripartite talks in which a wage contract is negotiated as part of a broader package including policy changes, and government attempts to influence the wage agreement without formally participating in negotiations.

The scale of bargaining centralization measures a concept distinct from those captured by our first two indices. Bargaining can be highly centralized even if neither government involvement nor confederal involvement is high. For example, in Denmark prior to the mid- 1970s, industry-level wage agreements for private-sector workers were typically concatenated by the government mediator. That is to say, the mediator submitted a linked set of industry-level wage agreements to be voted on by the union membership under the condition that all agreements would be considered ratified if a majority of LO members voted positively, regardless of whether or not a majority in any particular LO affiliate voted positively. Since the contracts imposed a peace obligation once ratified, we consider this system to be one of centralized wage setting with sanctions.[5]

---

5 The categories for the bargaining-level scale can be derived from the indices of government and confederal involvement in wage setting using the following algorithm. If government involvement is scored 10, 12, 13, 14, or 15 or if confederal involvement is scored 6, 10, or 11, then the bargaining level is category 4. If government involvement is 8, 9, or 11 or if confederal involvement is 7, 8, or 9, the country year is coded as category 3. In all other cases but one, the category is 2 for the Nordic countries. The one exception is Denmark in 1992. For reasons we discuss in the text, we coded this bargaining round as category 4.

2. COUNTRY DISCUSSIONS OF CONFEDERAL AND GOVERNMENT INVOLVEMENT IN WAGE SETTING

In this section, we describe the main features of the process of private-sector wage setting and the major changes that have occurred in each of the Nordic countries between 1950 and 1992. Our main focus is on the changing relationship between industry-level unions, employers' associations, national peak associations, and governments.

SWEDEN

Sweden is often upheld as the exemplar of a highly centralized bargaining system that functioned smoothly in the early postwar period but collapsed decisively and dramatically in the 1980s. In fact, the history of the Swedish system of wage setting from the end of the war to 1992 can be divided into three periods. In the first period, 1946–55, the primary wage negotiations in most bargaining rounds occurred at the industry not the confederal level.[6] The second period of centralized bargaining begins in 1956. In every bargaining round from 1956 through 1982, the main blue-collar union confederation, the Landsorganisationen (LO), and the main employers' organization, the Svenska Arbetsgivareföreningen (SAF), negotiated a frame agreement that covered most of the blue-collar work force in the private sector. The third period begins with the collapse of central negotiations in 1983. From 1983 through 1992, the level of confederal involvement has oscillated from one bargaining round to the next and government involvement in wage setting has increased. In spite of attempts to restore centralized bargaining in the mid-1980s and again in the early 1990s, wage setting had been decisively decentralized to the industry level by the end of our study in 1992. The involvement of LO and SAF in private-sector wage setting from 1950 through 1992 is illustrated in Figure 4.1.

The central agreements negotiated by LO and SAF from 1956 through 1982 were always followed by industry-level talks, which were followed in turn by bargaining at the plant level. In principle, the central agreements were merely advisory, and the legally binding contracts were signed at the industry level. In practice, the central agreements determined the content of the subsequent industry-level contracts, since both sides imposed an industrial peace obligation on their members once the central agreement was signed.

---

6 Though most bargaining rounds were conducted industry by industry in the initial postwar period, the centralized bargaining that began in 1956 was not unprecedented. In 1952, LO acceded to a government request to freeze real wages, but insisted on receiving compensation for inflation. SAF refused to allow any of its members to negotiate a cost-of-living index on its own. In response, most of LO's unions agreed to allow LO to negotiate on their behalf. The result was the first central agreement signed between LO and SAF.

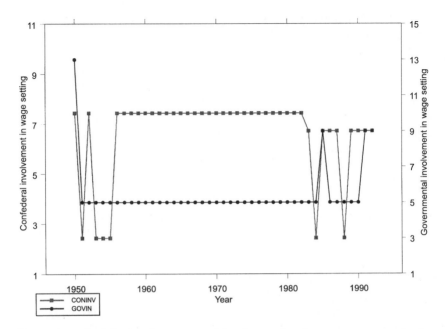

Figure 4.1. *Confederal and governmental involvement in private-sector wage setting in Sweden, 1950–92.*

Plant-level bargaining was restricted to implementing what had not been fully specified in the industry-level wage agreement, at least in principle. Thus, plant-level demands typically had to be approved by the national union and counterproposals made by employers had to be reported to the national union. Strikes were prohibited at the local level, and any prolonged conflict using alternate but legal means, such as work-to-rule actions, provoked intervention by the national union. In practice, local bargaining often proceeded with substantial autonomy as long as no dispute occurred.

In the years from 1956 to 1965, the central agreements between LO and SAF dominated private-sector wage setting. Although the union of industrial white-collar workers, the Svenska Industritjänstemannaförbundet (SIF), bargained centrally with SAF independently of LO, the agreement that emerged followed the pattern set by the LO–SAF agreement. Both LO and SAF followed an informal rule of insisting that the terms of the LO–SAF contract be applied in all other wage agreements signed by SAF (Olsson 1991:28).

Beginning in 1966, however, the weight of the LO–SAF agreement in the Swedish labor market began to decline. In 1966, public-sector workers obtained the right to strike. Public-sector unions grew rapidly and soon rivaled private-sector unions in size and influence. The year 1966 was also the first year that white-collar private-sector workers won a wage increase significantly above that obtained by LO as compensation for the wage-drift received by blue-collar workers. In 1969, three large white-collar unions concluded a five-year agreement in advance of LO–SAF negotiations. In 1973, white-collar and professional unions in the private sector established a bargaining cartel, the Privattjänste-mannakartellen (PTK), to negotiate on their behalf, thereby creating a new, important actor in Swedish collective bargaining. The PTK negotiated central agreements for private-sector white-collar and professional workers (who comprised between 25 and 30 percent of the private-sector work force) from 1974 through 1982. In the late 1970s, PTK and LO engaged in coordinated bargaining with SAF, but coordination broke down in 1980 over the policy of solidaristic bargaining (Kjellberg 1992:104).

The third period for confederal involvement in Swedish wage setting in which the role of the confederations in wage bargaining was severely reduced begins in 1983. In 1982, the statutes of SAF were changed, reducing the peak association's authority over its members.[7] Previously, a simple majority on the SAF board could deny permission to an affiliated association to sign a wage agreement that was deemed contrary to employers' common interest. Subsequently, a three-fourths majority was required. In addition, a two-thirds majority rather than a simple majority was now required to prevent a member organization from initiating a lockout. Finally, SAF stopped adding to its strike funds in the 1980s. As SAF ceased to hold sufficient funds to cover a major dispute, the industry-level employers' associations began building strike funds of their own.

In 1983, SAF initially refused to bargain centrally with LO. Employers in metalworking, the Verkstadsföreningen (VF), took the lead in negotiating a separate agreement with Svenska Metall. Outside of the metalworking sector, an impasse was declared at the industry level and a central agreement between LO and SAF was reached through mediation. The three biggest members of PTK also broke away from centralized bargaining in 1983 to negotiate separate agreements with VF (Ahlén 1989:334). The 1983 PTK–SAF agreement, like the 1983 LO–SAF agreement, excluded the metalworking sector.

Since 1983, the initial level of bargaining has oscillated between the confederations and the industrial unions. In 1984, wage agreements for LO unions were negotiated exclusively at the industry level. Central agreements between the LO and SAF were signed in 1985 and 1986, but no attempt was made to negotiate a central agreement in the 1988 bargaining round. A central agreement was negotiated in 1989 without the participation of the metalworking industry, although the separate agreement in metalworking was almost identical to the one negotiated by SAF and LO. In contrast to the central agreements in

---

7 In contrast, the substantial statutory authority of LO has not changed significantly since 1941. See Wallerstein, Golden, and Lange (1997) for details regarding the statutory authority of the main blue-collar and employers' confederations in the four Nordic countries.

the period 1956–82, none of the central agreements negotiated by the LO after 1982 included an industrial peace obligation. Finally, in 1990, the SAF board announced the discontinuation of its bargaining department, thereby eliminating SAF's capacity to engage in confederal-level negotiations. Although SAF relented in its drive to decentralize bargaining to the extent of participating in the Rehnberg Commission in 1991 (described below), direct confederal participation in wage bargaining had ended.[8]

Government involvement in private-sector Swedish wage setting is typically low. Sweden is the only Nordic country in which the government almost never directly participated in private-sector wage setting, although informal consultations between the government and the central labor market actors occurred continually. In the Haga discussions of 1974 and 1975, the government tried to tie an income tax reduction to wage restraint, but the government guidelines were ignored in the subsequent wage negotiations (Ahlén 1989:338). Not until the Rosenbad meetings prior to the 1985 bargaining round was the government successful in forcing the unions to comply with government guidelines in exchange for tax rebates and a freeze on distributed company earnings. This occurred only under the threat of government countermeasures if the wage guideline was exceeded.

The most extensive government intervention in private-sector wage setting since the end of the war occurred in 1991–92. When it became apparent that the unions wanted to exercise their right to renegotiate compensation for inflation during the second year of the 1989–90 contract, the government introduced a two-year wage freeze coupled with a ban on strikes and a ceiling on price increases. The measure was defeated in parliament, forcing the Social Democratic government to resign. A new Social Democratic government then appointed a national body, the Rehnberg Commission, comprised of a government mediator and one representative from each of the peak associations, SAF, LO, TCO, and SACO. The Rehnberg Commission was given the mandate to negotiate a two-year wage agreement for the entire labor market, an agreement subsequently implemented in industry-level bargaining. By the next bargaining round in 1993, the Social Democrats had been replaced by a government of the so-called bourgeois parties that was uninterested in sustaining centralized bargaining, however, and the Commission was not reappointed (Martin 1995).

---

8 PTK continued to bargain with SAF outside the metalworking sector until 1988. In 1986, LO and PTK were able to reestablish coordinated bargaining for the first time since 1980. In 1988, however, PTK collapsed as each member bargained separately with SAF. PTK did negotiate a two-year central agreement with SAF in 1989. The Rehnberg Commission that negotiated the two-year stabilization plan of 1991, however, included representatives from the white-collar and professional confederations, not PTK.

NORWAY

As in Sweden, the centralization of wage setting in Norway has fluctuated over the course of the postwar era. For much of the period, the pattern was similar: a phase of initially less centralized wage setting followed by a long period of confederal control over the process. More recently, the extent of confederal involvement in wage setting has diverged between Sweden and Norway. Whereas in both countries, wage setting became less centralized in the early 1980s, in Norway highly centralized wage setting was restored by the end of the decade (Kahn 1995). Finally, the Norwegian government has been more often and more deeply involved in private-sector wage setting than its Swedish counterpart, especially in periods of high confederal control.

As in the other Nordic countries, bargaining in Norway can occur at three levels: for the private sector as a whole, at the industry level, and at the plant level. The principal peak associations in the private sector are the Landsorganisasjonen i Norge (LO), which represents mostly blue-collar workers, and the Næringslivets Hovedorganisasjon (NHO), formerly the Norsk Arbeidsgiverforening (NAF), which represents employers. Bargains struck at the confederal level always include an industrial peace obligation once they have been ratified. The LO's ratification procedure consists of a vote by the entire membership. Even in bargaining rounds where the confederations do not bargain directly, the confederations "coordinate behind the scenes, and have to approve agreements before they become final" (Rødseth and Holden 1990:239). No strikes or lockouts can occur without the approval of the peak associations.

Plant bargaining is allowed in some industries but not others.[9] The metalworkers, until recently the largest LO union, have always had the right to bargain at the plant level. For such workers, the centrally negotiated wage serves as a minimum. Although strikes in pursuit of local wage increases are prohibited by the industrial peace clause, other forms of conflict, such as work-to-rule or go-slows, are common. The extent of national control by industry unions over enterprise bargaining varies. Some unions have the right to bargain on behalf of their locals, others to veto local demands that are viewed as excessive. All unions, however, have the right to intervene in and to take over plant-level negotiations if an agreement cannot be reached.

Figure 4.2 presents changes in confederal and government involvement in private-sector wage setting in Norway since 1950. The level of bargaining for each round is decided by LO and NAF prior to the expiration of the old contract. Industry-level bargaining predominated in the early 1950s and again in the early 1980s. From 1958 until 1982, as well as 1988–92, the primary negotiations have with few exceptions been conducted at the confederal level.

9 Over the postwar period, the number of unions allowing supplementary local bargaining has increased. Today, almost all workers in manufacturing have local bargaining rights.

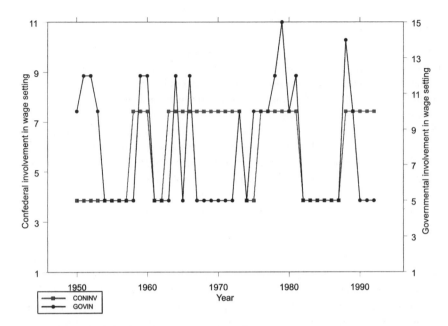

Figure 4.2. *Confederal and governmental involvement in private-sector wage setting in Norway, 1950–92.*

Prior to 1976, compensation for inflation was either automatic or took the form of renegotiations if the price index exceeded some threshold. Since 1976, negotiations over compensation for inflation in the second year of the contract have become standard. These negotiations are always conducted at the confederal level.

Government involvement in private-sector wage setting in Norway has taken several different forms. In the late 1940s, the Norwegian government established the Economic Cooperation Council to forge a consensus over wages, prices, and subsidies. The Council was composed of representatives of all major interest groups, including LO and NAF. In 1962, the Economic Cooperation Council was replaced by the Contact Committee. In 1966, the government appointed a Technical Estimates Committee, which included both LO and NAF officials, to provide impartial macroeconomic data and projections of the impact of different wage settlements. Government involvement in wage negotiations in the form of consulting with the bargaining partners in the Contact Committee, providing projections of the "room" for wage increases in the Technical Estimates Committee, and using price subsidies or other policy changes to encourage "responsible" wage settlements have occurred continually throughout the postwar period.

At times, the government has intervened more forcefully. Parliament has periodically interposed itself in wage disputes by passing a "wage law" forcing the parties into compulsory arbitration. Until 1953, most important bargaining rounds were determined through arbitration (Frøland 1993).[10] Since the early 1950s, governments have mandated compulsory arbitration less often, although they have occasionally done so both during main contract talks and during intermediate negotiations regarding the cost-of-living adjustment. Only the arbitration of disputes involving LO unions is included in Figure 4.2. In the 1980s, there was frequent use of arbitration in the oil sector, in the public sector, and for unions outside LO, none of which is reflected in our data (Strøm, Stølen, and Torp 1988).

In 1973 and from 1975 until 1980, wage negotiations took the form of "combined settlements" in which the government participated in the bargaining process along with LO, NAF, and representatives of the farming and fishing associations. The outcome in most of these years was an explicit agreement that included both wages and public policies designed to guarantee a specific increase in real, disposable income for virtually every Norwegian household. In 1978 the tripartite talks broke down and parliament sent LO and NAF into compulsory arbitration. From the fall of 1978 through 1979, the government proclaimed a wage and price freeze, suspended renegotiations over a cost-of-living adjustment and, for the first time, prohibited plant-level bargaining.

The experiment with tripartite bargaining came to an end in the early 1980s. During the oil boom of the early 1980s, wage bargaining was conducted at the industry level. With the collapse of the price of oil in the mid-1980s, however, both government and confederal involvement in wage setting increased. In 1988, LO and NAF negotiated a contract conditional on the enactment of a law prohibiting wage increases for workers outside LO from being greater than those received by LO members. In addition, plant bargaining was prohibited during the first year of the contract. In 1989, the LO–NAF cost-of-living negotiations were again extended by parliament to cover non-LO members, but plant bargaining was allowed. From 1989 through 1992 when our study ends, collective bargaining resumed at the confederal level without direct government involvement. The reestablishment of centralized bargaining in Norway in the late 1980s contrasts sharply with the extensive decentralization that occurred across the border in Sweden.

FINLAND

The trajectory of Finnish wage setting has differed from either the Swedish or the Norwegian pattern. In the early 1950s, wages were largely set by the government in consultation with the national peak associations of unions and employers. After the wartime wage and price controls expired in 1955, govern-

10 Postwar price and profit controls remained in place until 1954.

ment involvement waned and wage agreements were concluded at the industry or confederal level. Government involvement assumed greater importance in the late 1960s, when a period of national-level tripartite bargaining began that has endured to the present.

Throughout the postwar period, the main blue-collar confederation, the Suomen Ammattilittojen Keskusjärjestö (SAK), has been divided between a strong Communist minority and a Social Democratic majority. A schism in the Social Democratic Party in 1957, related in part to conflicts over cooperation with the Communist Party, was followed by a split in SAK and the formation of a rival confederation, the Suomen Ammattijärjestö (SAJ), in 1960. Many of Finland's national industrial unions split into two, while others preserved their unity by declining to be affiliated with either confederation. A period of political cooperation between the Social Democrats and the Communists that began in 1966 (and lasted until 1971) led to a reunification of the main confederations in 1969.

As a condition of the dissolution of SAJ and the reentry of SAJ unions into SAK, the authority of SAK was reduced in 1971. According to the new rules, affiliates have the right to opt out of any central agreement signed by SAK and the main employers' confederation, the Suomen Työnantajain Keskusliitto (STK), within two weeks of the signing of the agreement. In addition, affiliates are no longer required to seek approval of SAK before initiating wage negotiations or calling a strike, as had been the case before. In contrast to the blue-collar unions in Norway and Sweden, strike funds are held exclusively by the affiliated unions, not SAK.

Plant-level bargaining occurs under the strict supervision of industry unions and employers' associations, at least on paper. Enterprise demands have to be approved by the executive board of the national union before they can be presented to the employer. If demands are rejected by the employer, strike action also requires approval by the national union. Although the national union is usually empowered to end local strikes as well, wildcats are endemic in Finland. An OECD study reported that of the many hundreds of strikes occurring in the five-year period from 1971 to 1976, only 10 were conducted according to union rules (OECD 1979:14). Thus, the high degree of de jure authority that the national unions have vis-à-vis union locals may be a misleading indicator of the de facto authority the national unions exercise.

Figure 4.3 presents changes in confederal (SAK and STK) and government involvement in private-sector wage setting in the postwar period. The history of collective bargaining in Finland since the Second World War can be divided into three periods. The first, which lasted from the end of the war through the end of 1955, was characterized by widespread government regulation of wages and prices. Although wages and prices were subject to government control for most of the decade after the end of the Second World War, the central labor market organizations were not without influence. Their representatives sat on

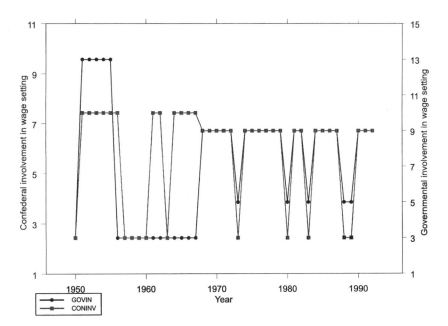

Figure 4.3. *Confederal and governmental involvement in private-sector wage setting in Finland, 1950–92.*

the board that administered the wage and price controls. Moreover, as Knoellinger noted, ". . . government regulation has not been forced on the labor market organizations against their will. Neither has it continued longer than they themselves desired" (1960:8). Indeed, relaxation of wage controls in 1950 was opposed by the central organizations.

The government's wartime authority to set wages and prices and to prohibit industrial conflict expired at the end of 1955. The second period of collective bargaining began with a general strike in 1956 as prices jumped and unions demanded compensation. The general strike ended with a one-year agreement between SAK and STK, followed by three years of bargaining at the industry level. In the 1960s, bargaining between central organizations became more common, even though this was the period when the union movement was split. Two-year agreements between SAK and STK were signed in 1961 and 1964. In 1966, the central organizations agreed to a three-year contract.

The third period of collective bargaining began in 1968 when the government, in talks with the central organizations, obtained the suspension of the three-year agreement following a large devaluation in 1967. A one-year stabilization package was accepted, which included the abolition of the cost-of-living adjustment in wage contracts. The agreement of 1968, followed by the merger in 1969 of rival union confederations, initiated a period of comprehensive incomes policy agreements that lasted through 1992. Since 1968, wage negotiations have always begun with talks between the central organizations in the labor market, the association of farmers, and the government. In 1973, 1980, 1983, and 1988 the central organizations were unable to come to an agreement and negotiations continued at the industry level without a framework agreement. The usual pattern since 1968, however, has been for industry-level negotiations to take place within a framework negotiated by the central organizations.

Formally, the framework agreement is not binding. In particular, affiliated unions have two weeks after the central agreement is signed to announce their intention to exit the central wage settlement and bargain independently. Since the mid-1970s, it has become customary for one or two SAK affiliates to attempt to win higher wage increases than allowed under the central agreement. For blue-collar workers, the legally binding agreements are those signed by the industrial unions. Only industry-level agreements impose an industrial peace obligation.

Although the government does not sign the central wage agreement, it has been intimately involved in central negotiations since 1968. In 1967, the government appointed a special Incomes Policy Official, whose role is to represent the government in negotiations with the central labor market organizations. This official often acts as a mediator when talks between the central organizations reach an impasse. On other occasions, the President or the Prime Minister has mediated disputes. It is typical for the final package to consist of an agreement on wage increases, price subsidies, changes in tax or welfare programs, and income support for farmers. In addition, there is a group of experts composed of representatives from the government and the central labor market organizations called the Incomes Policy Research Committee that provides the bargaining partners with economic statistics and forecasts.

DENMARK

Danish wage setting superficially exhibits a pattern similar to the Swedish: a lengthy period of centralized wage setting starting in the 1950s and lasting until the early 1980s, followed by a period of declining confederal participation in wage setting. In contrast to Sweden, however, in Denmark government mediation or direct wage setting by parliament occurred continually throughout the postwar period until the early 1980s. Moreover, the decentralization of wage setting that occurred in Denmark in the 1980s was reversed in manufacturing by the early 1990s. While the role of the peak associations declined, new bargaining organizations were established to negotiate a centralized agreement that encompasses the manufacturing sector, but not the private sector as a whole.

The authority of the main union confederation in Denmark, the Landsorganisationen i Danmark (LO), has been a constant source of contention since the

LO was founded in 1898. Traditionally, the main proponent of centralization was the Dansk Metallarbejderforbund (Metall), the union of skilled workers in metalworking. The main opponent to centralized authority was traditionally the Specialarbejderborbundet i Danmark (SiD), the national union of unskilled and semiskilled workers, and the country's largest union. In the 1980s, both Metall and SiD reversed their positions, with Metall favoring decentralization and SiD supporting greater centralization.

Within the Scandinavian context, the decentralizers have always won. The Danish LO has weaker statutory authority than that exercised by the LO in Sweden or Norway. All strike funds are held by Danish national unions, for example. In the event of a strike approved by LO, the confederation collects contributions from nonstriking unions on an ad hoc basis to subsidize the unions on strike. Affiliates need not obtain LO's approval in formulating their wage demands. Nor does LO have the authority to conclude agreements on behalf of its affiliates, except in matters of general scope such as the maximum length of the working day, vacations, and cost-of-living adjustments.

The weak statutory authority of LO, however, understates its role in wage bargaining. For much of the postwar period, affiliates allowed the confederation to bargain on their behalf on matters of general interest, including average wage increases, even though LO lacked the formal authority to conclude such agreements. Moreover, LO has sole authority to represent affiliates in mediation. The role of LO in the mediation process has been very important, since almost all settlements in the postwar period that were not imposed by Parliament have been drafted by a State Mediator in consultation with LO and the employers' confederation. In addition, the mediator has the authority to concatenate wage agreements – that is, to tie wage agreements together and define the bargaining unit to include the entire LO for purposes of the ratification vote – only with the approval of LO and employers (Due et al. 1994:130). Moreover, while the Danish LO has less authority than its counterparts in the other Nordic countries, the Danish employers' confederation, the Dansk Arbejdsgiverforening (DA), is second to none in its authority over the collective agreements signed by its affiliates.

Whether or not plant bargaining is allowed varies by industry. Until recently, the Danish labor market was divided between sectors with standard-wage contracts and sectors with minimum-wage contracts. With a standard-wage contract, plant bargaining is, in principle, prohibited. In the minimum-wage sector, which includes the metalworking industry, locals have traditionally exercised substantial independence in negotiating wage supplements. As in Britain, there has been a tendency for locals of different crafts within the same plant to form joint bargaining units at the plant level. In metalworking, which is the most important industry in the minimum-wage sector, the independence of shop stewards is backed by a clause in the contract forbidding Metall from participating in plant-level wage bargaining. Whether plant unions have the

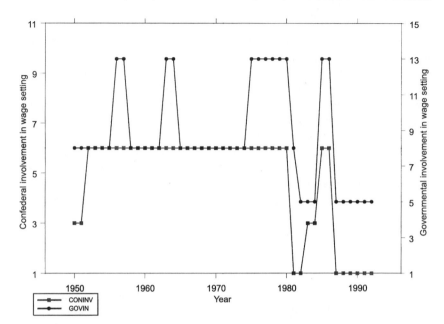

Figure 4.4. *Confederal and governmental involvement in private-sector wage setting in Denmark, 1950–92.*

right to bargain over wages or not, stewards never have the right to initiate a strike. Once a contract is signed at the industry level, a peace obligation is imposed. Shop stewards can be sued for negligence if they fail to maintain industrial peace.

In the 1980s, employers took the initiative in increasing controls on plant bargaining. The "wage regulation mechanism" that was introduced in the 1983 bargaining round restricted plant bargaining rights in the minimum-wage sector in two ways (Scheuer 1992:192). First, a cap was placed on the number of times plant bargaining could occur. Second, industry-level employers' organizations were allowed to set a ceiling on the wage increases granted at the plant level. The wage regulatory mechanism was extended and tightened in the central agreements of 1985, 1987 (which was for four years), and 1991. The ceiling on plant-level increases was allowed to expire in 1993, but not the limits on the number of plant pay negotiations during the year (Due et al 1994:226–7).

The changing pattern of confederal and government involvement in private-sector wage setting is displayed in Figure 4.4. Throughout the postwar period, collective bargaining in Denmark followed a sequence and a timetable that had been originally negotiated by LO and DA in 1936 and subsequently amended in 1951. The negotiation rules distinguished specific issues from general issues. Specific issues were to be negotiated at the industry level, while general issues, including general wage increases, were immediately passed on to the confederal level. The first stage of bargaining consisted of direct negotiations between the individual national unions and industry employers' associations. In the event that unions and employers in an industry were unable to agree, the dispute went to LO and DA, who negotiated on their affiliates' behalf. If no agreement was reached by LO and DA, the dispute went to the State Mediator. The State Mediator had a minimum of three weeks to resolve outstanding differences before a strike or lockout could begin. During the critical stage of mediation, negotiations were conducted between three persons: the State Mediator, the chair (or vice-chair) of LO, and the chair (or vice-chair) of DA. The mediator was empowered to submit a proposed settlement for a ratification vote. In addition, the mediator was empowered to concatenate agreements. Even if a majority from one or more unions voted against, all agreements were considered ratified if a majority of workers in the LO as a whole voted in favor.[11]

In practice, every bargaining round from 1952 through 1979 ended up in mediation. When mediation was unsuccessful, the government generally intervened. In 1956, 1975, and 1977, the mediator's draft proposal was enacted into law by parliament after the proposal was rejected by one or both of the two sides. In 1963 and again in 1979, parliament extended the previous contracts by law when mediation failed. In addition to direct wage controls, governments repeatedly influenced wage growth through various types of price and profit controls until 1982, when a Social Democratic government was replaced by a center-right coalition and the cost-of-living index was initially suspended and then revoked.

From 1951 through 1974, most bargaining rounds ended with ratification of the mediator's proposal. In the second half of the 1970s, by contrast, every bargaining round ended with parliamentary intervention. In 1981, the bargaining partners broke the pattern of political intervention. Agreements covering 80 percent of the LO–DA area were settled at the industry level without the involvement of either the confederations or the mediator and without concatenation.

The confederations played a reduced role in most of the subsequent bargaining rounds. In 1983, some industries – shops and offices, textiles, slaughterhouses, tobacco, newspapers, and shipping – settled on their own. In other industries, no agreement was reached and the negotiations were referred by DA and LO to the State Mediator. In 1985, there were neither agreements at the industry level nor in mediation. After DA rejected a tentative mediation proposal, the government intervened to end the conflict and impose a wage settle-

11 In fact, since different unions have different ratification procedures, the voting procedure is quite a bit more complicated than simply adding all votes together. Roughly speaking, however, all concatenated contracts are ratified if there is an overall majority in favor. See Due et al (1994: ch. 5), for details.

ment. In 1987, agreements were reached at the industry level in most cases. The metalworking sector set the pattern. Unusually, the agreement was for four years, but with renegotiations after two. The renegotiations in 1989 occurred at the local and industry levels.

Further significant change in the bargaining system occurred in the period 1989–91, when a series of mergers among employers' organizations resulted in the establishment of a single association for all industrial employers, called Dansk Industri (DI). On one hand, the formation of DI represented a significant centralization of bargaining in that DI was committed to the twin goals of "one firm, one organization" and "one firm, one labor agreement." On the other hand, the formation of DI, encompassing roughly half of the wage bill of the entire DA, represented an implicit reduction of the authority of the employers' confederation.

A proposal within LO to respond by merging LO's affiliates into five bargaining cartels – industry, construction, transport and services, municipal employees, and state employees – was adopted in 1990 and revoked in 1991. Despite the formal defeat of the reorganization plan, unions representing both skilled and unskilled industrial workers proceeded on their own to join the cartel in the metalworking sector in 1992, thus forming a bargaining organization that mirrored the structure of DI. By 1992, the earlier centralized system of wage setting in which industry-level agreements covering the private sector were negotiated and concatenated by LO, DA, and the State Mediator had been replaced by another centralized system in which all workers in manufacturing are covered by a single agreement negotiated by newly formed bargaining organizations (Scheuer 1992).

3. BARGAINING CENTRALIZATION IN THE FOUR COUNTRIES

Our coding of bargaining centralization for all four countries is presented in Figure 4.5. With the exception of Denmark, the figure presents coding that parallels and summarizes the country coding presented above of confederal and government involvement in wage setting.

In Sweden, we observe the well-known, dramatic decline in bargaining centralization that was the result of the cessation of central agreements and the diminution of the roles of SAF and LO. Between 1956 and 1982, the Swedish LO and SAF never failed to negotiate a central agreement that covered all bargaining by LO affiliates and imposed an industrial peace obligation. Since 1983, there have been bargaining rounds in which the central agreement excluded the metalworking sector (1983, 1989) and bargaining rounds without central negotiations at all (1984, 1988). Moreover, even when a central agree-

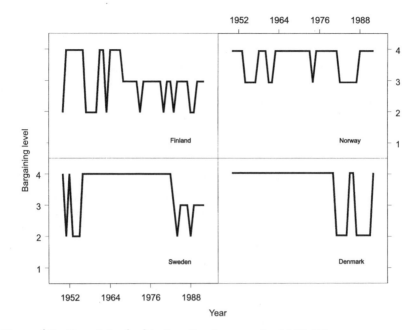

Figure 4.5. *Bargaining level in Scandinavian countries, 1950–92.*

ment has been signed, since 1983 none has included an industrial peace clause. In various ways, therefore, Swedish bargaining has been decentralized. The SAF's decision in 1990 to dismantle its collective-bargaining unit is an indication of the strength of employer opposition to a resumption of bargaining at the confederal level.

In Norway, the 1980s saw the restoration of a system of centralized bargaining that had existed from 1958 through 1973. Government participation in wage setting increased significantly in the late 1970s as the country struggled with adjusting to declining export markets.[12] Government intervention took the form of tripartite negotiations of grand settlements covering the entire economically active population. Increased government involvement was followed by a period of industry-level bargaining in the early 1980s. Unlike Sweden, however, centralized bargaining was reestablished in the late 1980s in response to the decline in the price of oil and the perception, shared by both employers and union leaders, that wage growth needed to be curtailed.

In Finland, little change in collective bargaining institutions occurred after the reunification of the blue-collar unions in 1968. Although SAK accepted a diminution of its authority in collective bargaining as the price of unification,

12 Norway did not become a major oil producer until the 1980s.

the unification itself together with the regular government involvement in tripartite negotiations since 1968 has produced, on balance, a more centralized system of wage setting than existed in the prior decade.

Only in the Danish case is the coding of bargaining level obviously different than the coding of confederal and government involvement because of the formation of supraindustry bargaining cartels that have replaced the peak associations as central actors in the wage-setting process. The Danish LO never had the authority over wage setting exercised by the main union confederations in Norway or Sweden. As the sole representative of its affiliates before the State Mediator, however, the Danish LO negotiated a centralized collective agreement covering all its affiliates in almost every year from 1952 through 1974. In 1975, mediated wage contracts gave way to six consecutive years of direct wage setting by parliament as unions and firms struggled to adjust to a sharply harsher economic environment. In the early 1980s, both unions and employers sought decentralized wage-negotiations to restore collective bargaining without government interference. Since 1987, wage negotiations in Denmark have been conducted without confederal participation.

Yet an exclusive focus on the confederal level in the Danish case conveys a misleading impression of the extent of decentralization. While the peak associations have clearly declined in importance, Danish unions and employers' associations have partially reorganized into highly concentrated units. The role of the LO unions in wage bargaining in the manufacturing sector has been superseded by the formation of a bargaining cartel that encompasses approximately half the private-sector membership of LO (Scheuer 1992). Similar bargaining cartels exist in construction and in the public sector. Moreover, the Danish Employers' Confederation, unlike its Swedish counterpart, has continued to be actively involved in reviewing and, on occasion, vetoing the wage contracts signed by its members.

4. HOW OTHER ANALYSES COMPARE

How do the results of our coding compare with other studies of bargaining centralization in the Nordic countries? We can compare our coding with two other types of studies. The first are studies that also seek to assess and code systematically the level of bargaining centralization in the four countries considered here. The second kind of studies is less obvious. Measures of wage compression are indirect ways of measuring the same phenomena we seek to measure, namely, the overall level of bargaining centralization. Examining the results of studies of compression can provide indirect, additional information to help us assess the accuracy of our coding.

The only other study of which we are aware that codes bargaining centralization in the Nordic countries for the postwar era is by Torben Iversen (1996).

Iversen's coding, although using somewhat different scales, is essentially identical to ours with the exception of the case of Denmark in the 1990s (see Figure 1 in Iversen 1996). Iversen argues that Denmark, like Sweden, has witnessed a substantial decentralization of bargaining. Though we agree with regard to the declining importance of LO in wage setting, we disagree with his inference that wage setting in Denmark has become much less centralized. The reason, to repeat, is because of the emergence of supraindustrial bargaining cartels that group very large numbers of workers into bargaining units that are only a small step below the central level.

One way to judge whether or not Danish wage setting has become as decentralized as in Sweden is to look at economic outcomes that we know are closely connected to bargaining centralization. Various studies have shown that the extent of wage compression is very closely and directly linked to the degree of bargaining centralization; indeed, a recent OECD study argues that this is probably the only robust finding in the literature regarding the impact of centralization on economic performance (OECD 1997; see also Wallerstein 1999 Rueda and Pontusson 1998). If bargaining has become decentralized in both Sweden and Denmark, as Iversen argues, we would expect substantial increases in wage differentials to have occurred in both countries from the 1980s to the present. In fact, wage inequality among blue-collar workers has increased significantly in Sweden since the mid-1980s (Hibbs and Locking 1996; Iversen forthcoming). Although wage inequality also widened in Denmark since 1985 (unlike Norway, where wage inequality declined throughout the 1980s), Iversen's data show that the increase in blue-collar wage inequality in Denmark is slight, much less than in Sweden.[13] Thus, the evidence on wage compression corroborates a significant decentralization of bargaining in Sweden but not in Denmark.

5. CONCLUSION: EXPLANATIONS OF SWEDISH EXCEPTIONALISM

The striking feature of the data we have collected on changes in collective bargaining institutions in the postwar period in the four Nordic countries is the

---

13 Although Iversen's (forthcoming: ch. 6) measures of wage dispersion in Sweden and Denmark are not directly comparable, the difference in the magnitude of the increase of wage inequality between Sweden and Denmark is sufficiently large such that it is unlikely the contrast reflects only differences in how wage dispersion is measured. Between 1982, the last year of centralized bargaining, and 1990, the last year of data, wage dispersion among manual private-sector workers in Sweden (as measured by the difference between the wage of the worker at the 75th percentile and the 25th percentile divided by the median wage) increased by 50 percent. During roughly the same time period, wage dispersion among manual private-sector workers in Denmark (as measured by the difference between the mean wage of skilled workers and the mean wage of unskilled women, divided by the mean wage of unskilled men) increased by only 3 or 4 percent.

diversity of national experiences and the absence of strong evidence of a common trend, at least up to 1992. Only the Swedish case offers clear and unequivocal support to scholars who see a movement toward greater discretion over wages at the industry level. The new Danish system of large bargaining cartels is hardly evidence of a move toward industry-level bargaining, at least not as industry-level bargaining is usually understood. Bargaining in Norway was recentralized in the late 1980s, while events in Finland reveal no significant change in the level of centralization.

Our conclusion regarding the absence of a general trend in the Nordic countries is subject to several qualifications. First, it may be too early to tell. Sweden may have started down a path that will eventually be followed by the other countries we study here. Since the future is unknowable, this objection is unanswerable. Second, our measures may be too coarse or too formalistic to capture some forms of the decentralization of wage setting that may have occurred in our four countries. We have suggested how such concerns can be tested with data on wage compression. At least in the comparison of Sweden and Denmark, the data on wage inequality appear to confirm that our coding accurately captures real bargaining processes. There may be other measures that could be used to verify the importance of the formal aspects of wage setting that we have coded.[14] Nevertheless, using our measures of centralization, it is clear that Sweden is unique among the Nordic countries in the nature and degree of decentralization that has occurred.

The lack of a uniform pattern of decentralization of wage setting casts doubt on explanations of decentralization that are cast in terms of universal changes said to have affected all countries in Europe, such as changes in production, changes in occupational structure, or increased economic openness. It is difficult to think of a reason why "flexible-specialization" or "holistic" methods of production should be more important in Sweden than in Denmark, Norway, or Finland. Nor do measures of economic integration in world markets distinguish Sweden from the other Nordic countries. In 1991–92, exports plus imports as a share of GDP averaged 49 percent in Finland, 54 percent in Sweden, 67 percent in Denmark, and 75 percent in Norway (OECD 1994, 1995). The

---

14 The common practice of using the share of the total wage increase that is obtained at the plant level as a measure of the importance of local bargaining can be very misleading. The key question is not what share of the wage increase comes from wage-drift, but which level of wage setting determines overall wage growth. If central negotiators anticipate the drift that will occur over the life of the agreement, and if changes in drift do not fully offset changes in the centrally negotiated increase, the central agreement can be the main determinant of the variation in wage growth even when the share of the wage increase received as drift is high. Instead of using the share of drift in the total wage increase, a better measure of centralization would be the extent to which the central wage agreement explains wage growth over the contract period in a statistical model. For theoretical and empirical discussions of the relative influence of central and local bargains in multitiered systems of wage setting, see Moene (1988), Moene, Wallerstein, and Hoel (1993), Holden (1989, 1998), and Hibbs and Locking (1996).

liberalization of financial markets occurred almost simultaneously in Sweden, Norway, and Finland in the mid-1980s, thereby casting doubt on explanations that stress heightened capital mobility (Garrett and Way 1995). Likewise, occupational structures have undergone similar transformations across the Nordic countries, resulting in similar rearrangements of union structures. As we document elsewhere, union movements have become much more fragmented in all four countries as rival white-collar and professional confederations have gradually stripped the main blue-collar confederations of their traditional union monopoly and as public-sector unions and white-collar unions have displaced metalworkers as the largest affiliates of the main blue-collar confederations (Wallerstein, Golden, and Lange 1997). On these measures, Sweden does not exhibit a distinct profile. Hence, Swedish exceptionalism seems unrelated to the increasing fragmentation of organized labor per se.[15]

One possibility, suggested by Pontusson and Swenson's (1996) description of Swedish employers' opposition to wage leveling as well as by Hibbs and Locking's (1995) finding that the equalization of wages across occupations (but not across plants or industries) reduced productive efficiency in Sweden in the 1970s, is that an egalitarian wage policy was pursued with greater vigor in Sweden than elsewhere. Yet some form of "solidaristic bargaining" was adopted in all four countries. In particular, the three Scandinavian countries all have remarkably compressed wage scales in comparison to other OECD countries. In the early 1980s, when Swedish wages were most compressed, wage differentials in Denmark and Norway were not much higher (OECD 1996). The implementation of an egalitarian wage policy may have been particularly detrimental to productivity or profitability in Sweden, but the Swedish wage scale does not appear to be uniquely egalitarian according to broad measures of wage inequality, such as the ratio of wages of workers at the 90th and 10th percentiles in the wage distribution, that are collected by the OECD.

We believe that the most compelling explanation for why a lasting decentralization of wage bargaining to the industry level occurred only in Sweden among the Nordic countries starts with the observable difference between the political goals of Swedish employers compared with their counterparts in Denmark, Finland, and Norway. Sweden stands out among the Nordic countries for the depth of the political antagonism between the leaders of the employers' confederation and the unions. In the early 1970s, Swedish unions obtained new

15 We have not discussed Iversen's (1996) argument that Norwegian employers are uniquely unable to control wage costs without centralized bargaining because of the destabilizing influence of high wages in the oil-producing sector. Since workers in the oil sector in Norway are not covered by the central agreement, however, it is not clear how centralized bargaining keeps the wages of oil-sector workers in line. Moreover, the implied premise that Swedish employers are able to control wage costs under conditions of full employment without centralized bargaining is questionable. In fact, Swedish wages increased in the latter half of the 1980s at an unsustainable rate and were brought under control only when open unemployment quadrupled in 1990–92.

legal rights concerning local union officials, representation on company boards, employment security, and workplace health and safety. From the employers' perspective, this labor legislation broke a longstanding implicit agreement to respect employers' "right to manage" inside the plant and to refrain from using political influence to obtain what the unions could not obtain through collective bargaining. Even worse, from the employers' point of view, was the proposal to create wage-earner funds that would enable the unions to become majority owners of large Swedish firms. Although Swedish employers succeeded in altering the wage-earner fund proposal in such a way as to preclude union control over management, employers had no desire to return to the status quo ante that had generated such threats (Elster 1989).[16]

In response, the Swedish employers' confederation transformed itself from an organization devoted to negotiating and administering collective agreements to a political body dedicated to reducing the unions' political strength (Martin 1995; Huber and Stephens 1998). Many union officials in Sweden believe that the employers' drive to decentralize bargaining in the 1980s was part of the larger political offensive aimed at weakening the Swedish LO, both in politics and in the labor market (Martin 1991:82, 84). Officials of the employers' association, perhaps predictably, deny that they were attempting to reduce the political power of organized labor. In archival research, Peter Swenson failed to find any discussion of the political effects of decentralization in the minutes of the board meetings of the Swedish employers' confederation, thereby lending credence to employers' claims that they were primarily motivated by a desire to reduce LO's influence over the distribution of wages (Pontusson and Swenson 1996). At the same time, however, employers generally conceded that the decentralization of bargaining would have the political consequence of diminishing the influence of LO, and that such an effect was welcome (Martin 1991:91). Even if political goals were not their main aim in decentralizing bargaining to the industry level, Swedish employers have applauded the political consequences of the change in bargaining institutions.

Any lasting system of wage setting must be responsive to changes in the economic environment. Adjustments in the distribution of wages and benefits, however, do not necessarily require abandoning centralized bargaining. Whether or not employers and unions are willing to cooperate in modifying central agreements to accommodate changes in technology and in market conditions depends on the political relationships that exist within and between the unions

---

16 The combination of sufficient wage restraint to maintain full employment and wage compression generated large profits for Swedish firms, creating a difficult political problem for the union leadership in maintaining rank-and-file support. The wage-earner fund proposal was the leadership's attempt to find something to offer the rank and file in exchange for their continual wage moderation that would not come at the expense of employment. See Moene and Wallerstein (1995, 1997) for an examination of the economics of wage compression amidst wage restraint. For a description in English of the proposed wage-earner funds, see Heclo and Madsen (1987: ch. 6).

and employers' confederations. In Sweden, it is not surprising that a satisfactory compromise that would have preserved centralized bargaining was not achieved in the midst of an employers' offensive aimed at reducing the influence of the labor confederation in national politics as well as in the labor market.

References

Ahlén, Kristina. 1989. Swedish Collective Bargaining Under Pressure: Inter-Union Rivalry and Incomes Policy. *British Journal of Industrial Relations*, 27: 330–46.

Calmfors, Lars. 1993. Comment on Moene, Wallerstein and Hoel. In Robert Flanagan, Karl Ove Moene, and Michael Wallerstein, *Trade Union Behavior, Pay Bargaining and Economic Performance*. Oxford: Oxford University Press.

Calmfors, Lars and Anders Forslund. 1990. Wage Formation in Sweden. In Lars Calmfors, ed., *Wage Formation and Macroeconomic Policy in the Nordic Countries*. Oxford: Oxford University Press.

De Geer, Hans. 1992. *The Rise and Fall of the Swedish Model*. Stockholm: SAF.

Due, Jesper, Jorgen Steen Madsen, Carsten Stroby Jensen, and Lars Kjerulff Petersen. 1994. *The Survival of the Danish Model*. Copenhagen: DJOF Publishers.

Elster, Jon. 1989. *The Cement of Society*. Cambridge: Cambridge University Press.

Eriksson, Tor, Antti Suvanto, and Pentti Vartia. 1990. Wage Formation in Finland. In Lars Calmfors, ed., *Wage Formation and Macroeconomic Policy in the Nordic Countries*. Oxford: Oxford University Press.

Frøland, Hans Otto. 1993. Corporatism within Organized Capitalism: Norwegian Incomes Policy 1935–1965. *Jahrbuch für Wirtschafts Geschichte*, 1993/2: 191–218.

Garrett, Geoffrey and Christopher Way. 1995. The Sectoral Composition of Trade Unions, Corporatism and Economic Performance. In Barry Eichengreen, Jeffry Frieden, and Jürgen von Hagen, eds., *Monetary and Fiscal Policy in an Integrated Europe*. Berlin: Springer.

Golden, Miriam and Michael Wallerstein. 1996. Reinterpreting Postwar Industrial Relations: Comparative Data on Advanced Industrial Societies. University of California at Los Angeles and Northwestern University: unpublished manuscript.

Heclo, Hugh and Henrik Madsen. 1987. *Policy and Politics in Sweden: Principled Pragmatism*. Philadelphia: Temple University Press.

Hibbs, Douglas A. Jr. and Håkan Locking. 1995. Wage Dispersion and Productive Efficiency: Evidence from Sweden. Stockholm: FIEF Working Paper No. 128.

1996. Wage Compression, Wage Drift and Wage Inflation in Sweden. *Labour Economics*, 3: 109–41.

Holden, Steinar. 1989. Wage Drift and Bargaining: Evidence from Norway. *Economica*, 56: 419–32.

1998. Wage Drift and the Relevance of Centralised Wage Setting. *Scandinavian Journal of Economics*, 100: 711–731.

Huber, Evelyne and John D. Stephens. 1998. Internationalization and the Social

Democratic Welfare State: Crisis and Future Prospects. *Comparative Political Studies*, 31:353–97.

Hyman, Richard. 1994. Industrial Relations in Western Europe: An Era of Ambiguity? *Industrial Relations*, 33: 1–24.

Iversen, Torben. 1996. Power, Flexibility and the Breakdown of Centralized Wage Bargaining: The Cases of Denmark and Sweden in Comparative Perspective. *Comparative Politics*, 28:399–436.

——— Forthcoming. Contested Economic Institutions: The Politics of Macroeconomics and Wage Bargaining in Advanced Democracies. Cambridge: Cambridge University Press.

Kahn, Lawrence. 1995. Against the Wind: Bargaining Decentralization and Wage Inequality in Norway 1982–89. Cornell University: unpublished manuscript.

Katz, Harry C. 1993. The Decentralization of Collective Bargaining: A Literature Review and Comparative Analysis. *Industrial and Labor Relations Review*, 47:3–22.

Kjellberg, Anders. 1992. Sweden: Can the Model Survive? In Anthony Ferner and Richard Hyman, eds., *Industrial Relations in the New Europe*. Oxford: Blackwell.

Knoellinger, Carl Erik. 1960. *Labor in Finland*. Cambridge, MA: Harvard University Press.

Lange, Peter, Michael Wallerstein, and Miriam Golden. 1995. The End of Corporatism? Wage Setting in the Nordic and Germanic Countries. In Sanford Jacoby, ed., *Workers of Nations: Industrial Relations in a Global Economy*. Oxford: Oxford University Press.

Lindbeck, Assar. 1993. Comment on Moene, Wallerstein, and Hoel. In Robert Flanagan, Karl Ove Moene, and Michael Wallerstein, *Trade Union Behavior, Pay Bargaining and Economic Performance*. Oxford: Oxford University Press.

Martin, Andrew. 1991. Wage Bargaining and Swedish Politics: The Political Implications of the End of Central Negotiations. Working Paper No. 6. Cambridge, MA: Center for European Studies, Harvard University.

——— 1995. The Swedish Model: Demise or Reconfiguration? In Thomas Kochan, Richard Locke, and Michael Piore, eds., *Employment Relations in a Changing World Economy*. Cambridge, MA: MIT Press.

Moene, Karl Ove. 1988. Union Threats and Wage Determination. *Economic Journal*, 98:471–543.

Moene, Karl Ove and Michael Wallerstein. 1995. How Social Democracy Worked: Labor Market Institutions. *Politics and Society*, 23: 185–211.

——— 1997. Pay Inequality. *Journal of Labor Economics*, 15:403–30.

Moene, Karl Ove, Michael Wallerstein, and Michael Hoel. 1993. Bargaining Structure and Economic Performance. In Robert Flanagan, Karl Ove Moene, and Michael Wallerstein, *Trade Union Behavior, Pay Bargaining and Economic Performance*. Oxford: Oxford University Press.

Olsson, Anders S. 1991. *The Swedish Wage Negotiation System*. Aldershot: Dartmouth.

Organization for Economic Cooperation and Development. 1979. *Wage Policies and Collective Bargaining Developments in Finland, Ireland and Norway*. Paris: OECD.

Organization for Economic Cooperation and Development. 1994. *Employment Outlook*, July. Paris: OECD.

Organization for Economic Cooperation and Development. 1995. *Employment Outlook*, July. Paris: OECD.

Organization for Economic Cooperation and Development. 1996. *Employment Outlook*, July. Paris: OECD.

Organization for Economic Cooperation and Development. 1997. *Employment Outlook*, July. Paris: OECD.

Pontusson, Jonas and Peter Swenson. 1996. Labor Markets, Production Strategies and Wage-Bargaining Institutions: The Swedish Employer Offensive in Comparative Perspective. *Comparative Political Studies*, 29 (Spring): 223–50.

Rødseth, Asbjørn and Steinar Holden. 1990. Wage Formation in Norway. In Lars Calmfors, ed., *Wage Formation and Macroeconomic Policy in the Nordic Countries*. Oxford: Oxford University Press.

Rueda, David and Jonas Pontusson. 1998. Wage Inequality and Varieties of Capitalism. Cornell University: Institute for European Studies Working Paper No. 97.6.

Scheuer, Steen. 1992. Denmark: Return to Decentralization. In Anthony Ferner and Richard Hyman, eds., *Industrial Relations in the New Europe*. Oxford: Basil Blackwell.

Strøm, Steinar, Nils Martin Stølen, and Hege Torp. 1988. *Inntektsdannelsen i Norge*. Oslo: NOU (Norges Offentlige Utredninger).

Swenson, Peter. 1989. *Fair Shares: Unions, Pay and Politics in Sweden and West Germany*. Ithaca, NY: Cornell University Press.

Tyrväinen, Timo. 1989. A Guide to the Finnish Labour Market. *Finnish Economic Papers*, 2: 160–75.

Wallerstein, Michael. 1999. Wage Setting Institutions and Pay Inequality in Advanced Industrial Societies. *American Journal of Political Science*, 43: 649–680.

Wallerstein, Michael, Miriam Golden, and Peter Lange. 1997. Unions, Employer Associations, and Wage-Setting Institutions in Northern and Central Europe, 1950–1992. *Industrial Relations and Labor Review*, 50: 379–401.

5

WHY GERMAN EMPLOYERS CANNOT BRING THEMSELVES TO DISMANTLE THE GERMAN MODEL

Kathleen Thelen

Intensified competition in international markets, increased capital mobility, and changing production technologies are creating new and serious problems for labor movements in the advanced industrial countries (e.g., Streeck 1987, 1993; Locke and Thelen 1995). A large and growing literature has been devoted to assessing the impact of these developments on industrial-relations institutions and practices cross-nationally. While some authors emphasize a common trend toward bargaining decentralization (e.g., Katz 1993), others see continued national diversity (Boyer 1996; Hyman 1994). Previous concerns that current international trends would produce a convergence of industrial-relations systems through competitive deregulation have been partly allayed by empirical studies that point instead to a high degree of *stability* in bargaining institutions across most of the advanced industrial countries (e.g., Wallerstein and Golden, this volume).

Much attention has been devoted to explaining cases such as Denmark and Sweden that *have* in fact experienced significant institutional change.[1] But we know that bargaining institutions in cases typically coded as "stable" – such as Germany – have been under tremendous strain lately as well (Turner 1998; Silvia 1996). Institutional resiliency is often chalked up rather unsatisfyingly to institutional "stickiness," or it is attributed vaguely to the "continuing interests" of various actors in existing arrangements – but without tracing precisely

Thanks to Michael Fichter, Bob Hancké, Rainer Hank, Torben Iversen, Jutta Kneißel, Andrew Martin, Cathie Jo Martin, Sofia Perez, Jonas Pontusson, Wolfgang Streeck, Peter Swenson, Lowell Turner, Michael Wallerstein, and Nicholas Ziegler for comments on this chapter. And special thanks to Andreas Drinkuth for sending the press clippings without which this article could not have been written. All translations are by the author, unless otherwise noted.
1 For example, in this volume alone, Swenson and Pontusson, Wallerstein and Golden, and Martin.

which actors and what interests.[2] As a result, we are left with a continuing overabundance of ("globalization") theories that tell us why these systems should be breaking down when in fact what we need is a more robust explanation for why – despite these strains – many of these systems are holding together at all.

Germany is a good case to mine for insights and hypotheses into these questions because here the deep *ambivalence* of employers toward traditional bargaining institutions has been very much on public display. Germany has been invoked as a case in point *both* for those analysts wishing to draw attention to new strains and pressures in collective-bargaining institutions (Streeck 1995; Mahnkopf 1991), *and* by those who stress the resiliency of these arrangements in spite of such pressures (Lange, Wallerstein, and Golden, 1995; Turner 1998). In emphasizing one dimension, however, each side has a tendency simply to downplay or ignore the other.

An analysis of Germany can also help advance the theoretical debate on contemporary labor politics because in fact this case appears quite anomalous in light of conventional theory. The received wisdom holds that high unemployment (as has prevailed in Germany since the 1980s) threatens centralized bargaining by weakening unions and undermining labor solidarity. According to these theories, employers were willing to engage in centralized negotiations with national unions in the 1970s because they needed to enlist labor's support in fighting inflation in the context of near full employment. In the 1980s and 1990s, by contrast, employers no longer need these arrangements because they can count on the discipline of the market both to hold back wages and to ensure labor peace. Moreover, employers' new demands for flexibility are best served by a broad deregulation of markets, including especially labor-market deregulation. In this view, then, contemporary strains on centralized bargaining emanate first and foremost from employer pressures. In the context of high unemployment, these pressures are in fact exacerbated by internal strains, as local work forces attempt to opt out of national agreements to save their own jobs [a phenomenon that Wolfgang Streeck (1984) aptly termed "wildcat cooperation"]. By the logic of this argument, national labor associations are left virtually alone defending traditional (centralized) bargaining arrangements – both against aggressive employers and against growing "plant egoism" at the local level.

Recent events in Germany do not bear out the conventional wisdom. Against predictions of labor fragmentation, we find instead that German *employers* and not unions are suffering the greatest strategic and organizational disarray. Despite record unemployment, German unions have scored some rather impres-

---

2 One reason for this is that some of the most important studies documenting stability (e.g., the various studies by Wallerstein, Golden, and Lange) are pitched at a high level of aggregation, and as such need to be augmented by analyses that get close enough to the actors and their interests to provide the necessary "micro-foundational" explanation for that stability.

sive victories over disorganized employers – most notably in eastern Germany in 1993 (see Turner 1998), in Bavaria in 1995 (see below), and in Lower Saxony in 1996. The Bavarian strike is particularly interesting; it did not at all play out in a way that conventional theories would have predicted, because employers, not unions, were the ones who felt the effects of wildcat cooperation. The firms that were meant to lead the charge against the metalworkers' union (IG Metall) instead resisted locking their workers out because they did not want to upset the cooperative relations they had built up with their work forces and their works councils. Instead, these firms pressed the employers' association to settle the conflict, on terms that in the end were rather generous to the union.

The Bavarian case is by no means an aberration.[3] A subsequent conflict in the following year (over sick pay) followed a similar trajectory, with the employers' association – full of bluster – staking out a hard-line position at the beginning, only to retreat in the face of widespread defections among member firms. In the aftermath of this second conflict, the head of the employers' association for the metalworking industry was publicly bemoaning the fact that his organization could no longer hold its own in conflicts with the union, against the threat of a strike – all this in the context of record unemployment![4]

Finally, and again at odds with the received wisdom, the German case demonstrates dramatically that employer weakness and fragmentation does not translate automatically – if at all – into labor "strength" (Pontusson 1987; Katzenstein 1985; Swenson 1989). In fact, paradoxically, the union victories mentioned above have only deepened the crisis of centralized bargaining by precipitating the "flight" of a number of firms out of the employers' associations altogether, thus destabilizing traditional bargaining institutions further (Silvia, 1996:56). In fact, it has come to a point in Germany where leading unions such as the IG Metall now view *employers'* lack of solidarity as *their* number one problem.[5]

The German experience contrasts rather sharply with developments in Sweden as laid out by Swenson and Pontusson in Chapter 3. Whereas in Sweden we have a case of employers self-consciously and systematically abandoning traditional bargaining institutions that they perceived as no longer serving their

---

3 It is perhaps important to point out that the Bavarian strike was in fact a national event because of pattern bargaining in the metalworking industry and the pacesetting role played by IG Metall within the economy as a whole. That is, in 1995 IG Metall singled out Bavaria to set the pattern for the entire metalworking industry, and this in turn became a benchmark for other sectors as well.

4 In fact he went so far as to suggest changes in Germany's strike laws, a suggestion that even conservative Chancellor Kohl dismissed as "misguided." See *Handelsblatt*, December 10, 1996; *Die Tageszeitung*, December 10, 1996; *Wirtschaftswoche*, December 13, 1996.

5 See especially, the article by IG Metall President Klaus Zwickel in *Frankfurter Allgemeine Zeitung*, April 6, 1995, and the interview with (then) IG Metall Vice President Walter Riester, in *Augsburger Allgemeine*, April 1, 1996; also Schroeder (1995: passim, but especially pp. 44 and 60). Silvia provides further evidence, citing an IG Metall campaign in Saxony to recruit members for its employer counterpart, Gesamtmetall (1996:46).

interests, in Germany the leading employers' association has become increasingly disoriented and fractious, unable to forge a consensus on how to proceed. And whereas in Sweden, the association of metalworking employers (Verkstadsföreningen or VF; since then renamed Verkstadsindustrier or VI) played a central role in precipitating the breakdown of traditional bargaining arrangements, its German counterpart (Gesamtmetall) is currently consumed with internal conflict over whether and how to reform traditional bargaining structures, leaving the organization in an unprecedented state of disarray and near paralysis. In short, in Sweden we have a case of employers mobilizing against "the system," while in Germany employers are also mobilized but as much against themselves as anything else.

There is a genuine puzzle here: German employers are clearly chafing within the traditional institutions, but they cannot bring themselves to dismantle them. Why not? The answer I propose in this essay is that German employers are ambivalent about abandoning traditional bargaining institutions both in the sense that they *disagree among themselves* on this issue and in the sense that they are in some ways *quite unsure* of whether the alternatives to the current system would unequivocally serve their best interests.

First, German employers disagree among themselves on the question of how urgent and indeed how desirable are changes in existing bargaining institutions. As Swenson and Pontusson point out, conflicts of interest also existed in Sweden; however, in that case, it was confederal bargaining that was at stake. The differential impact of centralized solidaristic wage bargaining on different sectors there meant that opposition and support for existing arrangements was organized along industry lines, so that proponents of decentralization had in their industry associations a ready-made organizational vehicle for pursuing their interests. Such sector-based politics play a role in Germany too, but bargaining is already conducted at the industry level and thus to a large extent already accommodates different sectoral conditions. In Germany, conflicts over decentralization focus much more on the balance between industry and local bargaining, and as such, they cut through the industry-based employers' associations. In the case that is the focus of this study – the Metalworking Employers, Association (Gesamtmetall) – one important line of cleavage is between small and medium-sized firms on one hand and large firms on the other. The small and medium-sized firms that are most critical of the current structure lack a separate organizational vehicle for bringing these changes about.

This leads to the second source of ambivalence among employers in Germany, namely, that even the critics are themselves frequently conflicted about the *desirability* of dismantling the system. Again the contrast to Sweden can help clarify the point. In Sweden the opponents had in their industry-based associations not only a vehicle through which to organize the fight; they also had in these associations a ready-made *alternative* to confederal bargaining (i.e., industry-level regulation). Critics of the German system do not have a similar alternative, and indeed, many of them recognize that they would be the first to lose out in a wage free-for-all if industry bargaining were eliminated altogether.

Moreover, if these employers are unsure what full decentralization might mean for competition among firms in the labor market, they also have reason to worry about what it would mean for relations with labor representatives within their own plants. Arguments about the virtues of plant-oriented bargaining are laced with invidious comparisons of "rigid" rules imposed by "external" unions, versus more "flexible" locally negotiated arrangements. In general, German employers enjoy more cooperative (if not conflict-free) relations with their own works councils than with the national unions. But the fact of the matter is that employers could not simply delegate ever more bargaining responsibilities to the plant level without fundamentally altering their relations with works councils. This goes especially for a radical decentralization of wage bargaining, for as Sadowski, Backes-Gellner, and Frick (1995) have argued, one of the main reasons that employers get along with their works councils so well in the joint regulation of *production* issues is precisely because works councils are by law unable to use their substantial legal rights to force a redistribution of the surplus generated by that cooperation (see also Streeck 1996).

In short, critics of existing bargaining arrangements in Germany are less effective than they were in Sweden partly because of institutional–organizational factors (problems of organizing the opposition) but also because they have good reasons to be less sure that abandoning traditional bargaining institutions would yield unequivocally positive results. Full decentralization would both squander the benefits of wage coordination and also blur the lines between union representation (outside the plant) and works councils (inside the plant) in ways that would introduce new conflicts and dynamics at the plant level that employers have every interest in avoiding.

The rest of this chapter proceeds in four steps. The first section provides a sketch of industrial relations in Germany over the past decade and discusses how recent trends have been interpreted in the literature. The second section analyzes a major (national) industrial dispute between unions and employers, set in Bavaria in 1995. This episode reveals the limitations of the received wisdom on the German case and highlights the role of employers' own interests in shoring up traditional bargaining institutions. The third section lays out the logic of German employers' reticence to abandon traditional bargaining arrangements in light of the considerations noted above. Where relevant, I contrast the German situation with that in Sweden. A final section draws out the broader theoretical implications of this analysis for the study of labor in advanced capitalism more generally. In particular, the analysis here suggests that two central concepts in the contemporary labor literature – employer coordination and globalization – need to be fundamentally recast.

A SKETCH OF RECENT DEVELOPMENTS IN GERMAN INDUSTRIAL RELATIONS

As Stephen Silvia (1997) points out, pressures on Germany's collective-bargaining system, while exacerbated substantially by the strains of unification, began well before 1989. Issues of bargaining decentralization, or the balance between industry-level and plant-level bargaining, came up very explicitly in the outcome of a major struggle in 1984 in the metalworking industry over working-time reduction (see Thelen 1991:ch. 7). That conflict ended when employers and the union reached a compromise that exchanged working-time reduction (to 38½ hours) for flexibility in implementing the reduction at the plant level. The central contract laid down parameters for a second round of bargaining in which plant works councils and managers would negotiate over how to distribute the reductions both over time and across the work force. The 1984 compromise on "negotiated decentralization" set the pattern for peaceful compromise in two subsequent bargaining rounds – in 1987 and 1990 – over further reductions in working time. These later contracts adopted virtually the same formula as in 1984 – reduction of working hours within centrally defined parameters – though they specified somewhat more flexible parameters for the local implementation of the new terms.

Beneath the surface, however, considerable conflict was brewing within the employers' association. It turns out that small and medium-sized firms often had a harder time taking advantage of the "flexibility" clauses in the contracts than large firms, which might, for example, make up for lost working times by expanding shift work (Silvia 1996:38–40). Large firms in the automobile industry have developed extremely complicated working-time arrangements that take full advantage of the options available in existing contracts.[6] But smaller companies – often lacking a personnel department – cannot so easily exploit the potential for flexible working times.[7] For these reasons, working-time reduction "raised costs for small firms disproportionately higher than for larger ones, and thereby permanently upset the fragile balance between large and small firms from the same sector around a single minimum compensation-package" (Silvia 1996:37). Increasingly, voices of disgruntlement could be heard expressing concern over the dominant role played by large firms within the employers association. These big producers, often enjoying cozier relations with unions, appeared unwilling to hold a hard line against IG Metall and fully represent the interests of the small and medium-sized enterprises (Silvia 1996: esp. 38–40).

Before this conflict reached any kind of resolution, the Wall came down and collective bargaining was swept up in the vortex of a rather different –

---

6 See *Handelsblatt*, September 4, 1995, for a description of various working-time models – which sometimes involve over 100 different working-time arrangements – in large automobile firms.
7 See, e.g., *Handelsblatt*, April 3, 1995.

though in many ways intersecting – set of problems. In 1991, the employers' association for the metalworking industry and IG Metall negotiated a plan for the speedy step-by-step increase in Eastern wages to bring these in line with wage levels in the West. In light of the collapse of Eastern markets and the gaping chasm between productivity in the East and West, however, many eastern firms – particularly smaller firms – opted to stay out of the employers' association and thus outside the bargain altogether. The resulting organizational problems – along with increasing voices of discontent from among the organization's membership – brought calls for change within Gesamtmetall. This led to the resignation of the organization's president, Werner Stumpfe, who had led Gesamtmetall from 1985 to 1991 and thus was deeply implicated in both the working-time agreements of the 1980s and the 1991 agreement for the East. Stumpfe's successor, Hans-Joachim Gottschol was drawn from the ranks of Germany's *Mittelstand* (small and medium-sized firm sector) in an explicit concession to criticism by these firms of Stumpfe's excessive "social partnership" with the union.

Gottschol came in like a lion, initiating a major conflict with IG Metall in the East in 1993 over the pace at which wages there would be raised to match levels in the West. In an unprecedented and probably illegal move, Gesamtmetall unilaterally revoked the existing contract (negotiated by Stumpfe in 1991). Amid fears that high unemployment would make it impossible for the union to mobilize workers in the East, the IG Metall readied for a strike. In fact the strike was quite successful, as the union succeeded in rallying the support of its inexperienced Eastern members under extremely adverse economic and political conditions.[8] In the end, the union was able to force employers to reinstate the existing bargain (though with a two-year delay) and also to declare that its midterm contract cancellation would not set a precedent. The employers did win a new contractual provision allowing firms in particularly dire economic straits to apply for a temporary exemption from the wage contract under the so-called hardship clause. But whereas Gesamtmetall had sought to put works councils (which cannot strike) in charge of negotiating such hardship clauses, the union succeeded in reserving this role for the union (which can).

All indications are that Gesamtmetall was led to embrace a more bellicose stance in part by its own internal problems. Silvia notes that Gesamtmetall's membership has been declining since the mid-1980s: "In 1980, 56 percent of all work places in the western German metalworking industry employing 73 percent of all employees belonged to a Gesamtmetall affiliate; density in terms of employment peaked in 1984 at 75 percent. Yet by 1994, these measures of association density had slipped to 43 and 65 percent, respectively [in the West]" (Silvia 1996:38). The problems in the East are even greater. After the Wall

---

8 The best treatment of the strike, including an analysis of why the union was as successful as it was, is in Turner (1998: prologue). On the effects of the strike on employers, see especially Silvia (1996).

came down, firms held by the agency charged with privatizing East German industry (*Treuhandanstalt*), were also members of the employers' association. But as soon as these firms were privatized, the new ("refounded") companies often opted not to join (Silvia 1996:46). The result in metalworking was a decline in Gesamtmetall-affiliated membership in the East, from 57.4 percent (in terms of employment) in 1992 to 35 percent in 1994 and "[b]y mid decade, two-thirds of all manufacturing firms were not members of an employers' association" (Silvia 1996:46). Overall, and nation-wide, this organizational hemorrhaging appears to be most pronounced among small and, especially, medium-sized firms.[9]

A separate but related problem is a growing tendency on the part of some firms to ignore the terms of the central bargain. Here what happens is that a works council either explicitly (though informally and indeed illegally) agrees to subcontractual wages or simply closes one eye when management violates the contract. This practice, while not unknown in the West, is particularly widespread in the East, where firms teeter on bankruptcy. A survey of firms in one Eastern state (Mecklenburg-Vorpommern) revealed that 60 percent of workers in the firms surveyed were paid below the collectively bargained rate (*Ostsee-Zeitung*, October 25, 1996). In a similar vein, Silvia cites the head of the metal industry association in Saxony as saying that only two-fifths of the firms in his organization respect all of the terms in the collective-bargaining agreement (1996:47).

INTERPRETATIONS

These features represent the familiar face of the crisis of German industrial relations – aggressive employers, widespread defections from the system, unions fighting for their organizational lives under adverse economic and political conditions. The literature on German labor is replete with analyses of the centrifugal forces at work, before unification and certainly intensified after the Wall came down, though scholars differ on how to interpret these trends. Some "optimists" (for lack of a better term) have been impressed with the relative stability of formal bargaining institutions in the face of these substantial, indeed unprecedented, pressures (Turner 1998, Wallerstein, Golden, and Lange, 1997; Lange et al., 1995), while other observers have emphasized more ominous trends (Mahnkopf 1991; Silvia 1996, 1997).

Lowell Turner's analysis (1998) anchors the optimist position. In his view

---

9 On this subject, see especially Schroeder and Ruppert (1996), whose analysis is based on a survey of 161 metalworking firms in four bargaining districts (three in the West, one in the East) that left the employers' association between 1990 and 1995. The results of this study show that, in the East, the problem of "association-flight" is most acute among small firms (20–99 employees); whereas in the West, the problem is most prevalent among medium-sized firms (100–499 employees). See especially pp. 12–14.

the system has proved very resilient to recent strains, and the reason is that employers who have gone on the offensive against traditional bargaining institutions have been thwarted by German unions that have been strong enough to defend those institutions by fighting back – and prevailing – in crucial battles such as in the East in 1993. Turner's analysis stays very close to the conventional wisdom sketched out above in that it characterizes employers as the aggressors and unions as the main defenders of traditional bargaining institutions.

Stephen Silvia (1996) stakes out the more pessimistic position, which stresses the weakness of labor in the context of high unemployment but also, especially, draws attention to the centrifugal forces at work within the employer associations themselves. In this view, collective-bargaining institutions are seriously threatened as defections (formal and informal) from the employers' associations and from collective bargains undermine the whole system of encompassing collective contracts (*Flächentarifverträge*) on which the German system is premised.

Both perspectives have substantial merit and yet neither one of them really tells the whole story. Turner's analysis, by casting the problem as one of unions versus employers (and emphasizing union strength as the key to institutional resiliency) misses the deep ambivalence within the employers' associations that is more fully captured by Silvia's analysis. But in Silvia's work the breakdown of the German model is if anything overdetermined, and he has no explanation for its observed resilience to hold against Turner's "labor strength" hypothesis. Silvia's analysis emphasizes (and richly documents) the problems with the system, including employers' deep *discontent* with traditional bargaining arrangements. However, he does not fully reconcile this with the conclusion that "most employers have also continued to support the postwar German industrial order" (Silvia 1996:109). In short, whereas Turner has misspecified the sources of resiliency in German industrial relations, Silvia does not really provide any sustained explanation for this resiliency at all; indeed, most of his evidence appears to point in the other direction.

To understand this apparent paradox, we need to delve more deeply into employers' interests in the German industrial-relations system as it now stands. All the literature cited above acknowledges the problems within the employers' camp and the pressures this creates for German unions – with optimists and pessimists disagreeing mostly on the magnitude of the problem, for example, the number of defections or the extent of subcontractual working conditions. But there is in fact *another face* to Gesamtmetall's crisis as well, one that has been almost completely neglected in the existing literature. This alternative face of the crisis of the employers' association was dramatically on display in the 1995 strike in Bavaria. This event merits a detailed treatment since it illustrates vividly the complexity of employers' interests and the centrifugal but also centripetal forces that are at work in terms of bargaining institutions in Germany.

Recall that traditional theories predict that high unemployment would unleash powerful forces eroding solidarity on the labor side, in the form of "wildcat cooperation" by works councils willing to make concessions to their employers in order to save jobs in the firm. We saw above that there is evidence to support such claims, for example as Eastern works councils actively or passively support subcontractual wages. But the 1995 strike reveals that wildcat cooperation and firm-level defections from central authority are as much a problem for employers as for unions. IG Metall resoundingly won the 1995 strike, and it was able to do so in large part because the employers who were meant to lead the charge against the national union refused to rally behind Gesamtmetall's call to arms and instead prevailed upon the employers' association to find a solution that would spare them the conflict.

THE 1995 STRIKE IN BAVARIA

The 1995 strike was fought against the backdrop of overall very high unemployment in Germany [9.4 % nationally; 14% (officially) in the East, somewhat lower in the West: 8.3 %].[10] IG Metall was looking for a real-wage increase, having exercised wage moderation in the previous two rounds, resulting in real-wage cuts for workers. The early stages of negotiations were remarkable for the hard-line position that employers staked out. Most controversially, Gesamtmetall refused to respond to IG Metall's demand for a 6 percent wage increase with its own counteroffer, insisting that the union needed to make concessions allowing more flexibility in the contracts before wage increases could even be discussed.[11] The association floated various proposals involving union concessions on existing benefits, all of which were rejected by IG Metall.[12] When warning strikes failed to move Gesamtmetall to make a counteroffer, the union mobilized for a strike.

IG Metall's strike strategy was radically different from that in the 1984 conflict over working-time reduction, the last major confrontation with employers in the West. In 1984, the union had pursued a "mini-max" strategy, which meant the union called out only a very few firms but specifically selected production sites which, when struck, would have a maximum impact in the economy. By targeting key auto-supplier firms, the union was able to bring production to a halt in the large automobile companies as well. The mini-max strategy took advantage of provisions in the German legal code that guaranteed unemployment compensation to workers who were laid off due to strikes *in other*

---

10 Figures from German Embassy Press Department, "A Comparative Economic Review," German Embassy, Washington DC, December 1996, p. 3.
11 *Stuttgarter Nachrichten*, February 11, 1995.
12 See, e.g., *Frankfurter Allgemeine Zeitung*, February 4, 1995; *Handelsblatt*, February 6, 1995.

(nonstriking) bargaining districts, which for the IG Metall meant that fewer workers had to be supported with union strike funds. In 1984, Gesamtmetall had responded to the union's mini-max strategy by locking workers out on a wide scale (the so-called cold lockout), while also contesting the right of workers outside the striking district to receive unemployment benefits. The unions won the court battle over benefits to "cold" locked-out workers in that year, but employers pursued the issue through legislative channels after the strike was over. In 1986, the conservative government changed the law to restrict the rights of workers who were indirectly idled by strikes elsewhere to claim compensation (Silvia 1988).

Although the constitutionality of the changes made in 1986 was still contested at the time of the 1995 conflict in Bavaria, the uncertain legal climate led the union to pursue a very different (indeed, the opposite) strategy. The union in the meantime had created a "strike information system" (*Arbeitskampf-informationssystem*, or *Akis*) which, based on information gathered from works councils and local union offices, provides a "map" of linkages (especially supplier chains) among firms across the country.[13] In the Bavarian strike, IG Metall used this system to target a relatively small number of firms in which the effects of the strike would be limited to Bavaria. This move was designed to preclude Gesamtmetall from taking advantage of the new 1986 law to expand the strike by locking out workers on a wide scale.[14]

Moreover, whereas the union frequently calls out workers in its best organized and most powerful district (Baden-Württemberg, home to a large number of machine tool companies as well as industrial giants such as Daimler Benz) in strike situations, IG Metall instead turned to Bavaria to set the national pattern for the industry as a whole. This was somewhat surprising, given that Bavaria is one of the least well-organized districts overall (though it has some union strongholds such as Nürnberg) and had not led a bargaining round since 1954 (which, by the way, had also been a disastrous defeat for the union). What nonetheless made Bavaria attractive as the pacesetter in 1995 were the economic conditions there, including the lowest unemployment rate of any German state at the time (7%) in the context of a mild recovery after the deep recession of the early 1990s. On February 21, Bavarian workers voted overwhelmingly to strike.[15]

One expected a classic confrontation. As noted above, the employers' association for years had been under intense pressure from its members – especially but not exclusively small and medium-sized companies – both to hold the line on wage increases and also, more importantly, to force IG Metall to accept greater flexibility in central contracts. And what better place to fight this battle

13 Interview with Wolfgang Schroeder, collective bargaining department of IG Metall, June 1997.
14 *Nürnberger Nachrichten*, February 23, 1995.
15 88% in favor. Metall Pressedienst, IG Metall Pressestelle, Frankfurt/Main, February 22, 1995.

than in Bavaria, where the union is weaker than in other districts and where the regional employers' association contains a large number of small and medium-sized enterprises of just the sort that had been railing at Gesamtmetall in previous rounds for being "too soft" on the union?[16] As it turned out, however, the conflict followed a radically different script, one that the union might well have written. What was truly remarkable – and by all accounts unexpected – was the unwillingness of Bavarian employers to defend the hard-line position that Gesamtmetall staked out early in the conflict.

The discord on the employer side was palpable from the start. In particular, Gesamtmetall's refusal to make a counteroffer, a public-relations disaster, was also not well received among the organization's members. Firms on the union's strike list were particularly critical. A representative of AEG-Nürnberg (house-hold appliances), for example, called Gesamtmetall's stonewalling strategy "an ice-cold provocation and an affront to the union, not to make any kind of concrete offer while demanding negotiations; it is like extending an invitation without giving the guest a chair."[17] The head of the company, Carlhanns Damm, mused openly about leaving the employers' association to negotiate a separate agreement with the union.[18] Nor was AEG alone. A few days later the heads of several firms in the machine and electrical industry got together to discuss a compromise.[19] The grumbling was sufficient to prompt Gesamtme-tall's president, Hans-Joachim Gottschol, to circulate a letter to all member firms explaining the association's reasoning[20] – apparently to no effect, however, as individual firm managers and even associations, including a prominent rep-resentative of the *Mittelstand* (the CDU-Mittelstandsvereinigung) continued to call on Gesamtmetall to make an offer.[21]

Firms that had once pressed Gesamtmetall to pursue a more aggressive bargaining strategy suddenly appeared to be losing heart. Why? In the face of a looming conflict with the union, employers worried openly about the effects of a strike on the cooperative relations they had developed within their own plants, which they saw as crucial to their competitive success. One prominent critic of Gesamtmetall's hard line was the firm FAUN (produces trash-removal equip-

---

16 The Association of Bavarian Metalworking Employers (Verband Bayerischen Metallarbeitgeber, VBM) has a membership of around 600 firms with about 750 plants and is one of the most hawkish regional associations in Gesamtmetall. Some large firms such as Siemens, M.A.N., and BMW dominate the regional economy, but not the regional association. Fully 3/4 of the VBM's members are small- to medium-sized firms (fewer than 500 employees) and a quarter of them in fact employ fewer than 50 workers (*Frankfurter Allgemeine Zeitung*, March 2, 1995).
17 *Nürnberger Nachrichten*, February 25, 1995.
18 *Süddeutsche Zeitung* and *Arbeiter Zeitung*, February 25, 1995, and *Nürnberger Nachrichten*, February 25/26, 1995.
19 *Frankfurter Allgemeine Zeitung*, February 28, 1995.
20 *Frankfurter Allgemeine Zeitung*, February 27, 1995. The letter cited the heavy costs of concessions made by the employers in previous years, the costs of the 35-hour work week, and so on.
21 *Frankfurter Allgemeine Sonntagszeitung*, February 26, 1995.

ment for municipal governments). On February 23, 1995, the head of the company wrote a letter to the president of the IG Metall's local office, Gerd Lobodda, which is worth quoting at length: "We assure you that, despite the strike, we will not abandon our course of dialogue and cooperation, and we ask that you too continue on the course of dialogue and consensus in Mittelfranken [the region]. . . . Let us do everything we can so that at the end of this conflict the door is still open for new solutions. . . . Of course we need more flexible and plant-oriented collective contracts for the future. But these concepts do not come overnight and they cannot be achieved through strikes. These concepts demand dialogue and discussion and the building up of mutual trust." FAUN management sent a copy of this letter as well to the head of the regional employers' association, pleading for a consensual solution to the conflict and exhorting the association to "Take care that no new walls are put up in our country."[22]

The day before the strike began, employers' "line of defense [was] crumbling," as the headline of the major business newspaper declared.[23] One employer (airplane maker Burkhart Grob) reacted to the announcement of the strike by giving his 1,646 workers a day and a half paid vacation. Still another is reported to have offered the IG Metall a 3 percent wage increase if it would spare the firm from being targeted in the strike.[24] In another bargaining district, a firm (Danfoss in Flensburg) offered its workers a 4 percent increase through a plant agreement, a rather dramatic move, given that the head of the company is also the head of the regional employers' association (Nordmetall).[25]

The strike itself had a surreal quality to it, as employers engaged in extremely public displays of solidarity with their *own workers* rather than with each other. Thus, for example, on February 25, Nuremberg local newspapers featured pictures of the manager of the local Siemens plant (transformers) alongside the pickets singing worker solidarity songs with his employees. The heads of both the union local and the national IG Metall were also in the chorus.[26] FAUN manager Tralau (co-signatory to the letter quoted above) invited his striking workers to breakfast in the company cantine, where he gave a speech denouncing the hard-line position of his employers' association: "If they cannot talk to each other 'up there' [in bargaining at higher levels], then at least we can talk here in Neunkirchen." Referring to the recent turnaround in the company's economic position (a result of restructuring), Tralau declared: "You know better than anyone what damned hard times we have behind us. In the past eight years [in which the company recorded losses every year], you have done your best to get us

22 Both letters are dated February 23, 1995, and were included in "Pressespiegel zum Streik: 25. Februar 1995," distributed by the union local in Nürnberg.
23 *Handelsblatt,* February 24, 1995.
24 The last two examples are from *Handelsblatt,* February 24, 1995.
25 *Stuttgarter Zeitung,* March 3, 1995.
26 *Nürnberger Nachrichten,* February 25/26, 1995; *Nürnberger Zeitung,* February 25, 1995.

out of that. It is unthinkable now not even to make an offer to those of you who helped. . . . *With or without the employers' association*, we will find a solution" (italics mine).[27] And to the press: "My workers have earned a wage offer. After all, they have had three years of sacrifice [referring to real-wage losses in previous bargaining rounds] but still helped to turn the firm around."[28]

The unrest on the employers' side only intensified when Gesamtmetall began making plans to answer the strike with a lockout. At this point the scattered voices of those already affected by the strike merged with those of a much larger number of employers who would be drawn into it through an escalation of the conflict. Large firms such as BMW were against the lockout which, in the context of the recovery, would redound to the advantage of their competitors (such as Daimler Benz) in other bargaining districts who were unaffected by the strike. But more importantly, many of the small and medium-sized firms that dominated the Bavarian branch of the employers' association opposed the lockout as well.[29] And thus "emerged in Bavaria a paradoxical situation in which – after originally pushing for a hard line – some small and medium-sized firms [*Mittelständler*] turned around to prevail upon Gesamtmetall to become more conciliatory toward the union."[30]

The managing director of Gesamtmetall, Dieter Kirchner, rejected the criticisms of Gesamtmetall's strategy, criticisms which he said came at the wrong time and only made it harder to reach an agreement with the union.[31] To initiate a lockout, Gesamtmetall needed to gain a majority in favor within the regional branch association of the struck district. When the vote for a lockout came in Bavaria, Gesamtmetall carried the day in the employers' assembly, but not without considerable controversy and open opposition.[32] As Germany's business daily noted, "The 'notables' (*Honoratioren*) in the Bavarian employers' association were always as hard as 'Krupp-steel' when an agreement was being sought in some other region. But they are as pliable as can be (*beweglich wie die Windhunde*) when it is their necks that are on the line and the strike is in their region."[33]

In fact it never came to a lockout. Fourteen days into the strike, Gesamtmetall faced two alternatives – accept the deal on the table or escalate the conflict.[34] Given the reluctance of Bavarian employers to lock out, Gesamtmetall bowed to internal pressures and settled. Circumventing the Bavarian district leadership, a deal was worked out in negotiations between representatives of the national associations (Dieter Hundt, then Vice-President of Gesamtmetall, and Walter Riester, then IG Metall Vice-President). The resulting two-year agree-

27 *Pegnitz Zeitung*, February 25/26, 1995. 28 *Nürnberger Nachrichten*, February 25, 1995.
29 *Stuttgarter Zeitung*, March 3, 1995; *Welt am Sonntag*, November 3, 1996; and *Süddeutsche Zeitung*, March 1, 1995.
30 *Stuttgarter Zeitung*, March 3, 1995. 31 *Süddeutsche Zeitung*, March 1, 1995.
32 *Handelsblatt*, March 3, 1995. 33 *Handelsblatt*, March 3/4, 1995.
34 *Manager Magazine*, June 1995.

ment called for a lump sum payment of DM 152.50 per month for the first four months (January–April 1995), followed by a 3.4 percent increase for May to October 1995, and then a further 3.6 percent increase for the next year. The deal reaffirmed a previously negotiated step in working-time reduction, from 36 hours to 35 hours, effective October 1995.[35] Though employers won a long-term contract (two years rather than the usual one-year wage agreement), they made no progress on their goal of "flexibilizing" central agreements. The settlement was widely viewed as a major victory for the union, which had insisted on making this a wage round and on securing a real-wage increase. Even Gesamtmetall representatives could not put a positive spin on it and acknowledged that the whole episode had been a catastrophe from the perspective of employers.[36] As the German Press Service summarized: "The hard-line strategy of Gesamtmetall President Hans-Joachim Gottschol and his managing director Dieter Kirchner did not take off in the end".[37]

The fallout continued long after the strike was over. The wage settlement only fueled the fires of criticism. As the head of the CDU-CSU Association of Small and Medium-Sized Firms, Klaus Bregger, groused, "We could have gotten this expensive an agreement without a strike."[38] Many firms announced their intention to leave the employers' association,[39] though the actual number of departures was smaller.[40] The terms of the Bavarian deal were adopted in other bargaining districts but by narrow margins.[41]

The events of 1995 contributed directly to a leadership shake-up at Gesamtmetall headquarters. The organization's long-time managing director (and one of the organization's most prominent "hawks"), Dieter Kirchner, stepped down in a gale of criticism. The president Hans-Joachim Gottschol – who, as pointed out above, was himself a *Mittelständler* and had explicitly been brought in to pursue a harder line against the union in response to the criticisms leveled at Gesamtmetall by the country's small and medium-sized business sector – came under intense fire and declined to run for a second term.[42] The positions of managing director and president were merged and things came full circle as the organization's *previous* president and well known "social partner" Werner Stumpfe was brought back to lead Gesamtmetall.[43]

---

35 *Metall Pressedienst*, March 7, 1995; also *Nürnberger Nachrichten*, March 8, 1995.

36 See, eg., *Frankfurter Allgemeine Zeitung*, April 4, 1995, where Gottschol blames IG Metall for imposing too costly a settlement on Gesamtmetall. Elsewhere, Gottschol called the agreement "a big step backward" (*Frankfurter Allgemeine Zeitung*, May 26, 1995). See also the discussion of the outcome in Gesamtmetall's biannual report for 1994–95.

37 *DPA-Basisdienst*, March 7, 1995.   38 *Frankfurter Rundschau*, March 13, 1995.

39 *Handelsblatt*, March 28, 1995.

40 *Augsburger Allgemeine*, July 25, 1995; *Offenbach Post*, July 26, 1995.

41 *Handelsblatt*, March 23, 1995.   42 *Handelsblatt*, June 23, 1995.

43 On the leadership change and on Stumpfe in particular, see *Kölner Stadt-Anzeiger*, November 15, 1995; *Süddeutsche Zeitung*, November 9 and 16, 1995; *Die Welt*, November 9, 1995; *Handelsblatt* December 15, 1995.

GERMAN EMPLOYERS AGAINST THEMSELVES

In Sweden, metalworking employers went on the offensive against traditional bargaining institutions that they perceived no longer served their interests. Against LO's resistance, they used the carrots and sticks available to them to force important changes in the unions' solidaristic wage policy by severing the link between public- and private-sector wages and eliminating interoccupational leveling clauses that compensated unskilled workers for skilled workers' wage-drift.[44] The image is one of an employers' association that knew exactly what it wanted and then systematically went after it.

This could not be further from the image projected by Gesamtmetall in recent years. Responding to criticisms of previous bargaining outcomes, Gesamtmetall went on the offensive in 1995, only to provoke a backlash of internal opposition and then to beat an ungraceful retreat. IG Metall's victory over disorganized employers, in turn, only heightened the crisis within Gesamtmetall, which found itself under a barrage of criticism and in worse organizational disarray than ever. And in a final ironic twist, the organization regrouped by reinstalling as its leader a well-known advocate of "social partnership" who had played a leading role in collective-bargaining agreements in the 1980s and early 1990s that had provoked the criticism in the first place. If Swedish employers project an image of self-conscious strategists, German employers appear positively schizophrenic.

The Bavarian strike gives us an angle on German industrial relations that existing accounts do not provide. This is not a case – as Turner would have it – of unions defending traditional bargaining institutions by beating back employer demands for flexibility; if anything, it is a case of employers defeating themselves.[45] The strike did feature employer defections from the central association that figure prominently in the analysis of "pessimists" like Silvia. But Silvia only deals with defectors of the sort who wish to opt out of (or radically flexibilize) existing bargaining arrangements. In Bavaria, as we have seen, defections by employers were of a very different ("wildcat cooperation") variety, and if anything they abetted the union mightily in resisting demands for a more flexible contract.

The 1995 strike is not an isolated incident; in fact, the next year a conflict over sick pay followed a very similar trajectory. In 1996 the conservative government passed a law making it possible for firms to reduce sick-pay compensation from 100 percent of a worker's wage to 80 percent. This was at odds with existing collective bargains in the metalworking industry (which provided full compensation) but Gesamtmetall encouraged its member firms to go ahead and implement the reductions (arguing that the legislation superseded the

44 Swenson and Pontusson, this volume.
45 There was even some surprise on the union side at how quickly the employers caved in.

collective contract). Daimler Benz was among the first to try to do so, but management backed down in the face of shop-floor unrest and the widespread refusal of other companies (including rival BMW) to follow suit.[46] A high-ranking representative of the employers' association for Berlin/Brandenburg confirmed the general pattern that emerged, in which most firms resisted the association's calls to implement the law, and those that went ahead with the change found themselves abandoned when other firms failed to follow their lead.[47] Top officials in the employers' associations stepped into this debacle in the belief that firms (which, after all, say they prefer "flexible" plant-level deals over rigid, uniform rules) would welcome the chance to bargain locally over this issue.[48] In the event, however, companies absolutely ran away from the prospect of handling this very hot issue individually and instead clamored for a *industry-level* solution on sick pay. The 1996 collective-bargaining round was moved forward to deal with this situation; the outcome reinstated full sick-pay compensation.[49]

Why can't German employers bring themselves to abandon the German model? The next sections propose two sorts of answers and explain the ambivalence of German employers by exploring how the situation they face is in fact quite different from that faced by Swedish employers in the 1980s.

HANGING TOGETHER MAY BE PREFERABLE TO THE ALTERNATIVE

German business is *collectively* ambivalent in the sense that there are vast differences among employers in the intensity of their dissatisfaction with traditional bargaining institutions. One reason that these institutions have held up as well as they have is that the strongest proponents of decentralization are organizationally not well positioned to contest existing arrangements. In Sweden, employer discontent with the system was concentrated within the VF, which both provided an *organizational vehicle* for mobilizing the opposition to the status quo and posed a viable *alternative institutional foundation* for the reconstitution of coordinated bargaining on less centralized terms.[50] As Swenson and Pontusson's

---

46 *Offenbach Post*, December 10, 1996. According to Klaus Zwickel (IG Metall president) only 12 of some 700 firms in the machine tool industry tried to cut sick pay, while the vast majority stuck to the terms of the existing collective bargain (*Leipziger Volkszeitung*, October 28, 1996).

47 Interview with a member of the collective bargaining department of the Verband der Metall- und Elektroindustrie in Berlin and Brandenburg, June 19, 1997. The companies that took the lead on this issue had the worst of both worlds, having incurred the wrath of their employees (and the union) but often being then forced to retreat and so with nothing to show for it.

48 *Frankfurter Rundschau*, December 10, 1996.

49 However, the union did agree to very modest wage increases in that year, as well as the exclusion of extras such as Christmas and overtime pay from the base wage on which sick pay is calculated.

50 The argument developed in this section owes a great debt to conversations with my colleague Peter Swenson.

analysis shows, the metalworking sector was particularly – and in certain respects even uniquely – disadvantaged by LO's solidaristic wage policy (this volume). This situation fostered unity within that industry association by highlighting how their collective interests differed from those of employers in other sectors, and thus how metalworking firms specifically would benefit from a renegotiation of existing bargaining arrangements.

The structure of the situation in Germany is quite different. Most obviously, Germany already has industry-level bargaining, and critics and supporters of traditional bargaining institutions coexist *within* the employers' associations at that level. The sectoral approach adopted by Swenson and Pontusson captures the decisive "fault lines" for Sweden in the 1980s but not for Germany today, where the most serious pressures for decentralization emanate from conflicts of interest *within* the sectoral employers' associations. As pointed out above, one of the most important cleavages within the employers' camp runs along lines of firm size. Thus, unlike in Sweden, those with an ax to grind do not have a ready-made organizational vehicle to set against Gesamtmetall.

This does not mean that critics are completely unorganized. Two organizations – the Arbeitsgemeinschaft Selbständiger Unternehmer (Working Group of Independent Entrepreneurs, or ASU) and the Verband Mittelständiger Unternehmer (Association for Small and Medium-Sized Enterprises, or VMU) have given voice to the concerns of Germany's *Mittelstand* (small and medium-sized firms) (Silvia 1996:41). They have proposed a number of changes in existing bargaining arrangements, all of them in one way or another aimed at allowing more flexibility for local bargaining on wages and benefits.[51] The BDI (Association of German Industry) has also emerged as a strong critic of recent collective-bargaining outcomes and has repeatedly called for more plant-based wage bargaining. However, unlike in Sweden, the associational "centers" of the opposition have no formal role to play in collective bargaining.[52]

In addition, in Sweden the VF provided more than just an organizational vehicle through which to mount a challenge to traditional (confederal) bargaining; it could also present itself as a viable *alternative* to it. In other words, the breakdown of confederal bargaining did not mean an end to wage coordination, though it did of course affect the level at which such coordination would occur. In Ger-

---

51 Proposals have ranged from a separate clause in central agreements specifically tailored for small- and medium-sized firms (*Mittelstandsklausel*), to central contracts that set only the parameters for wage increases (e.g., 1–5%) and/or establish a "menu" of benefits that works councils would then negotiate locally, to the insertion in all contracts of an opening clause allowing firms in "hardship cases" to negotiate subcontractual rates (Silvia 1996:41–2; see also *Süddeutsche Zeitung*, February 25/26, 1995 for the VMU concept; interview with Manfred Muster, Bremen IG Metall, 1994).

52 The BDI (and especially its president Hans-Olaf Henkel) is responsible for some of the most radical rhetoric, but other organizations – those that actually have to negotiate with the unions – do not necessarily see this as helpful. In fact, Fritz-Heinz Himmelreich (a leader in the BDA, recently retired) denounced BDI criticism and demands as "interference" (*Wirtschaftswoche*, October 24, 1996).

many, where industry bargaining is already the norm, the decentralization debate has centered much more on the balance between industry- and firm-level bargaining. The structure of the situation is thus such that employers in Germany are by and large stuck with reforming the current system rather than abandoning it altogether if they wish to continue to reap the benefits of coordination.[53]

To understand why the more radical alternatives have not carried the day in Germany, we need only invoke some of the standard explanations of the benefits of coordination for employers as a whole. One of the most prominent of these is to control competition among firms for workers, especially skilled workers. Soskice (1990), for example, has emphasized this point in arguing that employers' interest in continued wage coordination is if anything stronger now than ever, because the new terms of competition since the 1980s (emphasizing innovation and rapid adaptation) have only increased firms' dependence on skilled workers and social peace. High unemployment is no substitute for coordinated union restraint because skilled workers cannot be replaced by the less skilled workers who comprise the bulk of the unemployed.

The structure of bargaining in Germany facilitates such "negotiated restraint" and differs from the Swedish system of the 1980s where, as Swenson and Pontusson point out, skilled workers' wage-drift became a source of great strain on the system as a whole. Beyond the obvious difference of the Swedish unions' more aggressive solidaristic wage policy, there are also more subtle differences between the two systems, having to do with the linkages among bargaining levels. In Sweden, locally negotiated wage-drift becomes part of the base wage on which subsequent percent increases (negotiated at higher levels) are calculated, which means that negotiators at higher levels have to anticipate, and adjust their demands to accommodate, expected drift at the plant level. In Germany, by contrast, the plant-level bargaining that produces wage-drift is not officially permitted, though there is sufficient ambiguity and, often, opportunity, for works councils to improve on the industrial contract through *informal* local bargaining. However, because bargaining at this level is informal, the resulting increases do not feed back into the next bargaining round as they do in Sweden (see Thelen 1993:42). In Germany, then, wage increases at different levels are not cumulative; locally bargained wage-drift in effect *disappears* with each new bargaining round in the sense that increases won at the industry level are added only to the worker's previous formal contractual rate.[54]

53 There has been some talk of more branch-specific bargaining. For example, the trade association for the machine-building industry, the VDMA, has at various points called for a greater role in collective bargaining policy (*Stuttgarter Zeitung*, April 4, 1995). Analysts such as Hans Mundorf endorse this idea, though he also notes that this alternative is blocked by the present organizational structure, which distinguishes between trade associations (like the VDMA) and employer associations (like Gesamtmetall and its regional affiliates), with the latter jealously guarding their right to negotiate contracts with unions (*Handelsblatt*, December 2, 1996).

54 The downward pressure on skilled workers' wages in Germany may if anything have increased in the 1980s when labor frequently made working-time reduction the priority (over wage increases) in

Coordinated wage bargaining also imposes a uniform timetable for negotiations across firms and protects individual companies from disruptive, isolated, wage disputes. As many authors have emphasized, recent innovations such as just-in-time production and total quality control have made production regimes if anything even more vulnerable to industrial strife. As a representative of the metal employers' association put it, "firms are deathly afraid [*haben höllische Angst*] of conflict" for fear of losing orders and customers.[55] Importantly for the present argument, this may be even more true for small firms, which often compete among themselves (as suppliers to larger firms) on the basis of the quality of their products and their ability to guarantee on-time delivery.[56] Where such firms compete less on the basis of price than on their "reliability," disruptions in production can result in the permanent loss of a customer or market share. It is this heightened vulnerability to industrial strife that explains why – despite record unemployment levels – the head of Gesamtmetall complains about a "lack of parity" (in *labor's* favor) in collective bargaining today; as he puts it, "interruptions in production now cause damage that cannot be made up" (*Süddeutsche Zeitung*, December 10, 1996).[57]

In short, coordinated bargaining traditionally has tempered disruptive competition among employers in the labor market and contributed to peace on the shop floor. And so when Gesamtmetall's managing director Kirchner threatened to disband Gesamtmetall entirely, representatives even of dissident associations rushed to distance themselves from Kirchner's remarks.[58] German employers are

central bargaining. While (percent) wage increases by definition do nothing to reduce the gap between the wages of skilled and unskilled workers, reduced working hours are shared by all. Indeed, if anything, skilled workers were more likely to be excluded from the benefits of shorter working times because of provisions in the contracts that allowed employers and works councils to negotiate *longer* regular working hours for workers who were considered particularly indispensable to production. Other features of the German political economy also strongly encouraged wage restraint on the part of IG Metall (see especially Hall, 1994; Franzese and Hall this volume, on the interaction of collective bargaining and central bank autonomy).

55 Interview with a member of the collective bargaining department of the Metal Employers Association for Berlin/Brandenburg, June 1997. On how production relations have heightened employers' vulnerability to and fear of strikes, see also *Handelsblatt*, September 16, 1997; December 10, 1996; and August 26, 1997.

56 In fact, this was strongly implied by the employers' association representative cited earlier. He reports that when a conflict with the union is looming, he is inundated with calls from worried employers wondering if they will be drawn into the fray. And companies that are subsidiaries or suppliers to foreign firms "are the first to call."

57 It should also be noted that IG Metall's strike strategy in 1995 directly invoked employers' competition *against each other in the market* as a lever. In the previous mini-max strategy, the idea was to "take out" the whole industry (while minimizing costs to the union), and this strategy of course generates solidarity among firms, against the union. In the new strategy, the union struck only a few firms, which as we have seen were then quite isolated and – under pressure of losing ground to their competitors – therefore led the drive for a speedy (if also costly) settlement with the union.

58 Specifically, Kirchner said that there were two options: either reform existing institutions or, failing that, disband the association. See *Focus*, July 24, 1995. For responses, see *Handelsblatt* July 25, 1995, and *Offenbach Post*, July 26, 1995. As an employers' representative argued, in the absence of broad-

well aware of the dangers of destroying the organization and in so doing, as they say, "sawing off the branch on which we are all sitting."[59] An editorial in the *Frankfurter Allgemeine Zeitung* (a leading business-oriented newspaper) called Kirchner's statement a "cry for help" rather than a "statement of intent" (July 26, 1995). In the other major business newspaper (*Handelsblatt*), the verdict was much the same and the prediction was that employers would find the alternatives to coordinated bargaining even worse.[60] All of these observations go back to a still rather broadly shared sentiment, namely, that abandoning industry-wide bargaining institutions altogether would unleash a wage free-for-all that even Gesamtmetall's most strident critics are loathe to contemplate.[61] In sum, and as industry analyst Hans Mundorf put it, the critics of existing institutions need to ask themselves how collective bargaining would look without the associations and "for that they have no answer" (*Handelsblatt*, June 7, 1995).

THE DISCREET CHARM OF THE GERMAN MODEL[62]

The previous section discussed the decentralization debate from the perspective of relations among firms in the labor market. But a radical decentralization of bargaining in Germany would also affect relations within plants in ways that employers have every reason to worry about.

Here in fact proponents of decentralization confront an interesting dilemma. The attraction of more decentralized bargaining for many employers is that they have a long history of constructive (if not conflict-free) relations with their works councils. Works councils possess strong codetermination rights that constrain managers in important ways, but they are also more sensitive to the interests of the firm and willing to accommodate, if frequently for a price. Thus, while employers denounce the "overweening power" of unions, they over-

based collective agreements, "it could quickly lead to chaos in collective bargaining" (*Offenbach Post*, July 26, 1995).

59 An outgoing leader of the BDA (Fritz-Heinz Himmelreich), responding to the idea of letting works councils negotiate wage agreements, argued: "Bringing wage bargaining into the plant calls the works council's peace obligation into question. . . . I fear that the consequences would hardly be better than with collective negotiations. . . . There is a world of difference between a collective bargain that sets framework conditions within which firms can operate versus a situation in which the individual firm is exposed to a complete wage competition. Neither employees nor employers can be expected to cope with such a system" (*Wirtschaftswoche*, October 24, 1996).

60 *Handelsblatt*, August 2, 1995; also April 18, 1995.

61 As a member of the ASU argued, most employers do not want collective bargaining for their own plants because "this endangers labor peace in the plant" (*Hamburger Abendblatt*, June 17, 1995). There is also the worry that the government would step into the vacuum left by the demise of coordinated collective bargaining (see, e.g., the interview with Himmelreich, outgoing leader of BDA; *Wirtschaftswoche*, October 24, 1996).

62 An adaptation of Jonah Levy's (1999) adaptation of this classic phrase.

whelmingly embrace the works council system as a valued institution (Wever 1995).[63] The conservative *Handelsblatt* recently called codetermination a "great blessing" (*hohes Gut*) that contributes decisively to the social peace that is a distinct "*Standortvorteil*" (asset for Germany as an industrial location).[64] In short, German employers would generally much prefer to deal with their own "responsible" works councils than with "rigid" external unions.

The problem with this is that if works councils were actually to take on more of the bargaining responsibilities traditionally reserved for unions, this would in fact very likely undermine the foundations on which employers' constructive relations with their works councils are premised. The reason has to do with the structure of Germany's "dual" system of industrial relations as a whole and the behaviors it encourages on the part of unions, works councils, and employers. Streeck noted years ago that the formal autonomy of works councils (and the legal prohibition against their engaging in wage bargaining) stabilizes the system to the extent that it prevents works councils from interfering with unions' representational monopoly in that area (Streeck 1979). These observations point to the benefits to *unions* of the dual system.

But employers too benefit from the legal prohibitions against formal, independent wage bargaining at the plant level, as Streeck himself has recently noted (Streeck 1996). Studies show that the constructive, efficiency-enhancing effects of codetermination are premised on the way in which this institution is embedded within the dual system as a whole, and specifically the fact that a works council's *strong rights* to codetermine production and personnel issues are combined with *severe restrictions* on their ability to negotiate wages (see especially Sadowski et al. 1995 and Freeman and Lazear 1995).[65] In other words, the positive role that works councils play in production issues is underwritten by strict limitations on their ability to negotiate distributional issues (Streeck

---

63 As Kotthoff puts it, "If anything may be called 'robust' these days, it is first of all the system and culture of co-determination in German firms" (cited in Sadowski et al. 1995:505).

64 *Handelsblatt*, September 4, 1995.

65 Sadowski et al. cite some of the productivity-enhancing effects of German codetermination. They argue: "Mandated participation increases workers' stake in the firm and transforms them into 'specific human capitalists' – partners on a more or less equal footing with financial capitalists and management. Yet the potential of co-determination to enhance the level of the joint surplus will not be realized in all cases: employers will resist co-determination if works councils can be expected to affect the distribution of the surplus strongly in favour of the workers. . . . The separation of wage bargaining from works councils' powers in the German model of worker representation, the so-called 'duality of worker representation', seems to meet this condition for institutional efficiency" (1995:494). Freeman and Lazear (1995) arrive at the same conclusion via a different, more formal route (see especially pp. 31–2). They argue that "works councils are most likely to improve enterprise surplus when they have limited but definite power in the enterprise" (1995:49). Like Sadowski et al., they emphasize especially restrictions on local wage bargaining: "By setting the bulk of pay packages at the industry level, leaving only modest potential increments for bargaining by firms, and by forbidding councils from using labor's main weapon, the strike, European labor relations systems limit councils' ability to increase labor's rents at the expense of the total surplus" (1995:49).

1996:36). The demise of industry-wide bargaining and full decentralization of wage negotiations to the plant level would certainly blur the legal distinction between works councils and unions, and would open possibilities for plant labor representatives to use works councils' rather substantial *legal* rights (e.g., on personnel matters) to extract concessions from employers over wages.[66] This prospect, as Mundorf has noted, cannot look very appealing to employers who have long benefited from the exclusion of formal wage bargaining from plant negotiations.[67]

A radical decentralization of wage bargaining within Germany's "dual system" of industrial relations would require changes in the Works Constitution Act that governs plant-level industrial relations, and this has also given employers pause.[68] An internal document of the Central Confederation of German Employers (BDA) explicitly defended the traditional separation of industry-wide collective bargaining from plant-level codetermination with the argument that this separation is one of the foundations on which "good working relations" between works councils and management rest.[69] Employers are especially concerned about what would happen to the works council's famous "peace obligation" were works councilors to become the central actors in wage bargaining. The longtime head of Gesamtmetall's collective-bargaining department (recently retired) argues strongly for staying with a "strict separation" of the two levels, because changing the Works Constitution Act would raise an uncomfortable choice between submitting conflicts to compulsory conciliation or granting works councils the right to strike.[70]

Thus, despite the sometimes very dramatic public rhetoric (see, e.g., *Handelsblatt*, June 16, 1997, p. 5), internal documents suggest that employers are in fact approaching the issue of bargaining decentralization quite gingerly. The

---

66 Also, and as Sadowski et al. point out, the recent decline in union membership in Germany has not been matched by a decline in union dominance within works councils, which has instead been steady throughout. "With a voter turnout constant at 77%, the member-unions of the DGB gained two-thirds of all council seats [in 1995], a percentage comparable to 1990 and even higher than in the elections between 1978 and 1987. The non-unionized candidates have continued to acquire a constant share of one-fourth of the seats since 1978" (1995:505).

67 *Handelsblatt*, August 2, 1995.

68 Paragraph 77,3 of the Works Constitution Act prohibits works councils from bargaining over issues that have been dealt with, or are typically dealt with, in collective bargaining (unless the contract explicitly allows for supplementary plant agreements). Recognizing the divisiveness of any initiative to change the Works Constitution Act, a joint BDI/BDA working group on collective bargaining reform recently recommended deferring all discussion of such changes for the time being [letter from BDA leadership (signed by Himmelreich and Wisskirchen) to all member associations, July 3, 1996, p. 2]. That this remains an issue at all is probably attributable to the extremely hard-line position of the BDI leadership.

69 BDA, *"Reform von Tarifpolitik und Tarifrecht,"* document dated July 3, 1996, p. 3.

70 Friedrich Siebel, *"Der Flächentarif als Zukunftsmodell"* (mimeo), especially pp. 4–6. And for another ringing defense of the current system (from the employers' side), see the interview with Karl Molitor in *Handelsblatt*, February 25, 1997, p. 6.

BDA document cited above, for example, recommends all sorts of changes to make existing contracts more flexible, but it also cites a litany of dangers that would follow from any major structural shift in wage-bargaining competencies to the plant level (either through legislated "opening clauses" or through a change in Works Constitution Act paragraph 77,3 – see footnote 68 above). These include the threat of an expansion of works councils' codetermination rights to wages and all other material conditions of work; the threat of greater legislative interference (since there is no constitutional guarantee of "plant autonomy" analogous to Germany's hallowed principle of "collective bargaining autonomy"); the threat of even higher wage settlements (especially in economic good times); threats to cooperative relations with works councils; the disadvantage of having conflicts over wages settled by "outsiders" in conciliation procedures; the likelihood that the prohibition against strikes by works councils would become untenable; the threat that drawn-out legal battles would interfere with a firm's capacity for long-term strategic planning; the threat of enhanced union influence in the plant; and a weakening of solidarity among employers, which could contribute as well to higher wage deals with the proliferation of individual company agreements.[71]

Some of these same concerns are also echoed in the report of a working group on "Codetermination and Collective Bargaining," which was chaired by the former managing director of the employers association for the chemical industry, and included representatives of both employers and unions.[72] The report acknowledges the growing interaction and points of contact (*Berührungspunkte*) between collective bargaining and plant-based codetermination, and indeed it argues that the latter can be a useful tool for easing current strains on encompassing collective contracts by serving as a vehicle for "controlled flexibility" (p. 3). But the report also maintains that the positive interaction between these two systems depends on maintaining (rather than erasing) the traditional division of labor between them. Among other things, the working group concluded that the "differentiated implementation" of collective contracts depends on a functioning system of plant-level codetermination and that, conversely, "without the 'relief' afforded by the collective bargaining contract, cooperative relations between works councils and employers would be difficult to achieve" (p. 2). Thus, the conclusion that emerges is that "the ability of codetermination to function depends crucially on preserving the division of tasks between it and collective bargaining autonomy," and the report specifically mentions that retaining paragraph 77,3 of the Works Constitution Act is "of fundamental importance" in this regard (p. 2).

The 1996 conflict over sick pay (sketched out above) is sometimes cited as

---

71 BDA, *"Reform von Tarifpolitik und Tarifrecht,"* July 3, 1996, pp. 3–4.

72 Arbeitsausschuß, *"Mitbestimmung und Tarifwesen,"* Bericht für die Mitbestimmungskommission, presented at a meeting of the Mitbestimmungskommission, Gütersloh, October 15, 1997.

a warning of what the demise of industry-level bargaining might bring. The former president of the BDA argues that this conflict "showed how dangerous it can be to bring wage conflicts into the firm. Employers who previously had spoken out in favor of more plant-based wage policy were the ones calling most loudly for a solution through collective bargaining."[73] These observations were echoed as well in remarks by Klaus Zwickel, the head of the IG Metall, who noted that the conflict brought out how strong an interest employers – and especially those in small and medium-sized companies – have in comprehensive collective bargaining. "Precisely in these small and medium-sized enterprises, where employers and workers still know each other personally, the bosses wanted to avoid conflict in their 'own house.' The comprehensive collective contract in most cases removes such conflicts from the factory floor and shifts them to the hotel conference room (*von der Werkshalle in die Hotelhalle*)." Moreover, he continued, the comprehensive contract "blesses firms with a peace obligation . . . [which] sensible employers know the value of" (*Leipziger Volkszeitung*, October 28, 1996).

Over the years, German employers have dealt with strong works councils not by fighting with them but by adapting to them and indeed incorporating them into their strategies in the market. Employers' success in this has in a very real sense resulted in a situation in which they are now quite dependent on continued cooperation and peace at the plant level.[74] In light of this, and as Wolfgang Streeck points out, contemplating all of the changes that would be involved in a radical decentralization of wage negotiations "raises the question of whether there might also be interests worth considering that would speak instead to preserving the distinction and established forms of coordination between collective contract and plant agreement, union and works council, and collective bargaining autonomy and codetermination" (Streeck 1996:35). Among other things, "shifting wage policy away from the plant and to the sectoral level has, in the past, relieved plants of conflicts and allowed labor representatives at that level to concentrate on issues that have less to do with distributional conflicts and more with the modalities of productive cooperation. Opening the codetermination system to wage negotiations would very probably cancel this 'relief-effect' " (Streeck 1996:36).

There is a saying in Germany that "you cannot dance at two weddings" and this seems to be the problem that employers there face. Avoiding "rigid" union regulations by delegating more issues (up to and including wage bargaining) to their more "responsible" works councils is possible only to a limited extent under the existing legal framework. And it is a good thing, too, because as this section has pointed out, full decentralization would undermine the traditional distinction between distributional conflicts (largely fought outside the plant) and production issues (regulated within the plant) and in doing so

73 *Wirtschaftswoche*, October 24, 1996.   74 Thanks to Bob Hancké for emphasizing this point.

might well eliminate the very basis upon which cooperative relations on the shop floor are premised in the first place.

CONCLUSION

At a time when most of the literature on labor in the advanced capitalist countries points to problems of "union weakness" and an "employer offensive" against labor, and when the collapse of the once formidable German model seems if anything overdetermined, what we in fact need is a more robust explanation for why German employers have had such a hard time abandoning traditional bargaining institutions. What is well known and indisputable is that the German system is under tremendous strain, partly but not entirely as a result of the economic and social dislocations since unification. But what is not fully appreciated in the existing literature is that the kind of crisis German unions are experiencing is quite different from the one that conventional theories predicted, for despite record unemployment levels, German employers and not unions are the ones whose solidarity is most tenuous.

Unions have in fact been relatively successful in recent bargaining rounds, despite high unemployment. Most notably, IG Metall did very well against a fragmented and internally divided Gesamtmetall in the last two strikes in 1993 and 1995, as well as in the 1996 conflict over sick pay. Far from shoring up the system, however, these victories only heightened the crisis by further fragmenting the employers' association and in some cases encouraging firms to opt out of the system altogether (Silvia 1996:56). The head of IG Metall acknowledged this in a very telling statement in the wake of the Bavarian strike. He argued that though the union gained members as a result of the victory while Gesamtmetall lost members, this was no cause for rejoicing. "For me the [current] situation is not cause for . . . *Schadenfreude* [taking pleasure in another's misfortune] but rather for worry," and he emphasized that "collective bargaining autonomy requires strong bargaining partners" (*Frankfurter Allgemeine Zeitung*, April 6, 1995).

We know from previous work that employer "strength" need not imply labor weakness (Pontusson 1987; Katzenstein 1985; Swenson 1989). This analysis demonstrates that the reverse is also true, since current developments in Germany underscore decisively that employer "weakness" does not translate into union "strength" (Silvia 1996:56). This chapter has also suggested some of the reasons why German employers find it hard to abandon the German model. These reasons go back in part to the structural difficulties that opponents of the system have in articulating a viable alternative within the context of existing structures; but more importantly perhaps, to the possibly quite negative consequences – for employers themselves – of radical decentralization. In contrast to Turner, then, my analysis emphasizes how German employers' own *ambivalence* and indeed employers' own *interests*, as much as German unions' continued strength, accounts for the survival of traditional institutions in Germany.

German employers are thus not likely to dismantle traditional bargaining institutions in a dramatic collective move as in Sweden. But if the German model is unlikely to end with a bang, the more serious danger is that it will erode gradually and fade with a whimper. This is because, lacking an *organized* vehicle for exercising voice within the existing structures, individual firms have increasingly taken to exercising their exit options. Individual exit has all the advantages and virtually none of the disadvantages of radical (formal institutional) decentralization. So long as enough employers stay in the system, defectors can in fact dance at both weddings, since informal, isolated (and sometimes illegal) forms of decentralization still operate under the formal "protections" of the existing system – wage coordination at the industry level and the works council's peace obligation at the plant level.[75] At some point, of course, the whole system tips, as industry-wide bargaining would no longer generate the collective benefits on which defectors could free-ride.

The other possibility is that employers and unions – both of course intensely aware of the current corrosion of the formal institutions – undertake reforms that can shore up comprehensive collective bargaining, in all likelihood, by making contracts more flexible still. In the metalworking sector, the two sides are still far apart on what steps might be necessary, but there are reformers in positions of power within both associations.[76] Moreover, the 1997 industry contract (negotiated with the assistance of a state-appointed mediator) has been interpreted as involving just the kind of flexibility that can serve as the basis for future reform (*Frankfurter Allgemeine Zeitung*, September 29, 1997, p. 17; *Handelsblatt*, October 1, 1997, p. 2).[77] In that bargaining round, IG Metall

75 Gesamtmetall has in fact become an accomplice in this type of free-riding strategy; some of its regional offices have founded new organizations that "breakaway" firms can join. These new organizations offer benefits similar to the traditional employers' association (e.g., legal assistance), but the members are not bound by the collective agreements that the regional associations conclude with the union. Although aware that the availability of such an option might itself encourage firms to defect from the collective bargain, advocates see such organizations as a way of maintaining contact with firms that would otherwise simply go it alone (interview with a representative of the Metalworking Employers' Association for Berlin/Brandenburg, 1994; also *Frankfurter Allgemeine Zeitung*, September 22, 1997, p. 15).

76 Before being named Labor Minister in the new SPD-Green government, IG Metall vice-president Walter Riester emerged as a vocal proponent of stability through controlled flexibilization. See the interviews and statements in *Wochenzeitung 'Freitag'*, September 5, 1997; *Neue Ruhr-Zeitung*, August 28, 1997; and *Die Woche*, August 29, 1997. The chemical industry, which was always characterized by strong social partnership, has already taken more dramatic steps toward "bargained flexibilization." A recent agreement in that sector includes an opening clause that allows works councils and managers in troubled firms to negotiate up to a 10% reduction in wages in exchange for employment guarantees (*Der Spiegel* 24/1997: 93–94; *Frankfurter Allgemeine Zeitung*, June 5, 1997:15; *Die Zeit*, June 13, 1997:26).

77 The 1997 bargaining round revolved around the issue of "senior part-time work" (*Altersteilzeit*) and aimed at building on legislation that provides incentives for employers to ease older workers out of

made strategic concessions on an issue that was of special significance for small and medium-sized firms and, in so doing, also helped Gesamtmetall bridge the growing chasm within its ranks.[78] Also important from the perspective of employers, the settlement extended the existing working-time agreement until the end of the year 2000 (thus tabling for the time being demands by IG Metall president Klaus Zwickel to move toward a 32-hour work week). And finally, the agreement called for talks between the union and the employers' association over the reform of encompassing collective bargaining. All this prompted Gesamtmetall's president to conclude that, with this agreement, "collective bargaining in the metalworking and electrical engineering industry had passed a crucial test" (press release, September 28, 1997).[79]

THEORETICAL CONCLUSIONS

The analysis above leads to two general theoretical points. First, in a very well-known theoretical contribution, David Soskice (1990, 1991, 1999) has drawn attention to the importance of employer coordination in the political economy of advanced industrial societies. Looking across a wide range of countries, Soskice draws a broad distinction between those economies where employers have a strong capacity for coordination and those where they lack such capacity (in his terms, "coordinated" versus "non-coordinated" market economies). As an economist, Soskice is especially interested in how institutional arrangements can ameliorate or exacerbate collective-action problems that can result in suboptimal economic outcomes. His analysis of the coordinated market economies thus

employment to make room for younger workers and the unemployed. According to the 1997 contract for the metalworking industry, a quite generous package of wages and benefits awaits workers who reduce their working times through *Altersteilzeit*; however, these more generous conditions kick in only when the works council and management agree (*Handelsblatt*, September 29, 1997: 1, 3; *Frankfurter Allgemeine Zeitung*, September 29, 1997: 17; *Die Zeit*, October 3, 1997: 38).

78 Large firms were especially interested in an agreement with the union on *Altersteilzeit*, for they were eager to use this measure as a way of rejuvenating their work forces (*Handelsblatt*, September 16, 1997). The sticking point in the negotiations was over the question of whether elderly workers would themselves be able to claim *Altersteilzeit* as an individual right (the union's demand) or whether this would have to be negotiated with management. Small and medium-sized firms were adamant that management retain control, and by requiring agreement between the works council and management, the contract accommodated their demands. This is what allowed Gesamtmetall president Stumpfe to hail this deal as a "solution for small and large firms" alike (press release, September 28, 1997)

79 It is worth noting that in this conflict, too, Gesamtmetall showed absolutely no willingness to engage the union in industrial conflict. When IG Metall threatened to strike, the response of the employers' association was not, as in the past, to threaten a lockout. The veiled but ultimately more plausible (and also more effective) threat that hung in the air was, rather, that a settlement on the union's terms would result in further defections from the employers' association (see, e.g., the interview with Gesamtmetall president Stumpfe in *Kölner Stadt-Anzeiger*, September 20, 1997; see also *Wirtschaftswoche*, August 1997: 28; *Handelsblatt*, August 26, 1997). Thanks to Rainer Hank for pointing this out to me.

emphasizes the contribution of employer coordination to economic success, for example by reducing transaction costs and/or facilitating collective action in the market.

The present analysis confirms (and, indeed, is informed by) Soskice's basic insights about the role of employers and employer organizations in shaping industrial relations and political-economic outcomes generally. At the same time, however, this chapter embraces a somewhat different view of employer coordination. Whereas Soskice tends to depict coordination as a static *attribute*, in other words, a characteristic of some, though not all, national models, my analysis of Germany (including comparative glances toward Sweden) suggests that it may be more appropriate to think of coordination as a *process* and indeed an outcome that has to be actively sustained and nurtured, produced and reproduced. In other words, where Soskice stresses the economic benefits of *having* coordination, my analysis emphasizes the dynamics of *sustaining* it.

Moreover, and related to this, where Soskice's heuristic tends to emphasize the *functional contribution* of coordination to economic success in the coordinated market economies, the vantage point adopted in this chapter draws attention to the *political* dimension. Coordination – conceived as a political process – involves reconciling conflicts of interest among employers, as well as the exercise of power by some groups over others (e.g., in Gesamtmetall, traditionally, large firms over small and medium-sized firms). From this alternative perspective, we can see that – far from being a static, or even a self-sustaining, feature of particular systems – employer coordination involves a *political settlement*, and indeed, one that may have to be renegotiated periodically. Against a more functionalist view, it also seems clear that there is absolutely nothing to guarantee that employers will succeed in reconstituting their organizations on the basis of a new coalition or internal balance of power, despite the fact that their failure to do so might well be against their own individual and collective interests. The unions will be crucial actors in this, but in a way unanticipated by most conventional theories, because it is clear that the continued stability of bargaining institutions in Germany depends as much on union's strategic flexibility as it does on union strength.

Second, this analysis suggests that the contemporary labor literature has embraced an overly one-sided view of globalization and its effects on labor. The conventional wisdom is that globalization – understood mostly as capital mobility or the threat of exit – has shifted the balance of power in industrial relations decisively toward capital. The idea is that globalization involves the search by firms for the most congenial investment locations, and thus drives competitive deregulation (or "Delawarization") as countries try to attract or maintain investment. This conceptualization may apply quite well to multinational firms that can shop around for the ideal production location, but it is not at all clear that it fits for a large number of small and medium-sized (and often family-owned) firms in countries like Germany, for many of these firms do not really have exit options, nor even a credible exit threat.

This is not to say that such firms do not participate in globalization, only that for them it may mean something quite different. For many of them, globalization has to be understood more in terms of the new linkages that it creates among firms, often across national borders. Zysman, Doherty, and Schwartz (1996), for example, write of sprawling "cross-national production networks" in which different parts of a product are produced in different countries, with decisions on where to locate particular aspects of production being based on distinctive cross-national institutional strengths. In this conception, firms in "high everything" economies like Germany can survive and indeed thrive if they occupy some specialized niche within the production chain. Such firms compete with potential alternative producers above all on the basis of quality and reliability.

Emphasizing this aspect of globalization, however, leads to rather different conclusions regarding labor relations than the "globalization as capital mobility" thesis. Where relations among companies are increasingly tightly coupled and where firms compete on the basis of quality and reliability in the context of just-in-time production, employers become much more dependent on the active (not passive) cooperation of their workers and extremely vulnerable to overt labor conflict. Much of the literature glosses over this aspect of contemporary labor relations. And yet, as we have seen, it is crucial to understanding the strategic dilemmas that German employers currently face. Without it, it would be very difficult to explain why – despite all the advantages that high unemployment and capital mobility presumably confer on them – German employers, not unions, are the ones who worry openly about their ability to win a strike.

The point is not to embrace one view of globalization over the other. Rather, the argument is that this phenomenon is more complex than is typically recognized. Globalization combines contradictory logics, and which logic prevails in particular cases will depend in part on the strategies that specific firms are pursuing in the market. The analysis presented here gives us a glimpse of the alternative face of globalization and corrects the one-sided view (as capital mobility) that pervades the contemporary labor literature. As such, it provides important insights into the sources of institutional *resiliency*, as well as change, in Germany and beyond.

References

Boyer, Robert. 1996. "The Convergence Hypothesis Revisited: Globalization but Still the Century of Nations?" in Suzanne Berger and Ronald Dore, eds., *National Diversity and Global Capitalism*. Ithaca, NY: Cornell University Press.

Freeman, Richard B. and Edward P. Lazear. 1995. "An Economic Analysis of Works Councils," in Joel Rogers and Wolfgang Streeck, eds., *Works Councils: Consultation, Representation and Cooperation in Industrial Relations*. Chicago: University of Chicago Press, 27–50.

Hall, Peter A. 1994. "Central Bank Independence and Coordinated Wage Bargain-

168   UNIONS, EMPLOYERS, AND CENTRAL BANKS

ing: Their Interaction in Germany and Europe." *German Politics and Society* 31 (Spring), 1–23.

Hyman, Richard. 1994. "Industrial Relations in Western Europe: An Era of Ambiguity?" *Industrial Relations* 33:1 (January), 1–24.

Katz, Harry. 1993. "The Decentralization of Collective Bargaining: A Literature Review and Comparative Analysis." *Industrial and Labor Relations Review* 47:1 (October), 3–22.

Katzenstein, Peter J. 1985. *Small States in World Markets: Industrial Policy in Europe.* Ithaca, NY: Cornell University Press.

Lange, Peter, Michael Wallerstein, and Miriam Golden. 1995. "The End of Corporatism? Wage Setting in the Nordic and Germanic Countries," in Sanford Jacoby, ed., *Workers of Nations: Industrial Relations in a Global Economy.* Oxford: Oxford University Press.

Levy, Jonas. 1999. *Tocqueville's Revenge: State, Society, and Economy in Contemporary France.* Cambridge, MA: Harvard University Press.

Locke, Richard M. and Kathleen Thelen. 1995. "Apples and Oranges Revisited: Contextualized Comparisons and the Study of Comparative Labor Politics. *Politics and Society* 23:3 (September), 337–67.

Mahnkopf, Birgit. 1991. *"Vorwärts in die Vergangenheit? Pessimistische Spekulationen Über die Zukunft der Gewerkschaften in der neuen Bundesrepublik,"* in Ulrich Busch, Michael Heine, Hansjörg Herr, and Andreas Westphal, eds., *Wirtschaftspolitische Konsequenzen der deutschen Vereinigung.* Frankfurt/Main: Campus Verlag.

Pontusson, Jonas. 1987. "Radicalization and Retreat in Swedish Social Democracy." *New Left Review* 165 (September/October), 5–32.

Reder, Melvin and Lloyd Ulman. 1993. "Unionism and Unification," in Lloyd Ulman, Barry Eichengreen, and William T. Dickens, eds., *Labor and an Integrated Europe.* Washington, DC: Brookings Institution.

Sadowski, Dieter, Uschi Backes-Gellner, and Bernd Frick. 1995. "Works Councils: Barriers or Boosts for the Competitiveness of German Firms?" *British Journal of Industrial Relations* 33:3 (September), 493–513.

Schroeder, Wolfgang. 1995. *"Arbeitgeberverbände in der Klemme: Motivations- und Verpflichtungskrisen,"* in Reinhard Bispinck, ed., *Tarifpolitik der Zukunft: Was wird aus dem Flächentarifvertrag?* Hamburg: VSA Verlag, 44–64.

Schroeder, Wolfgang and Burkard Ruppert. 1996. *Austritte aus Arbeitgeberverbänden: Eine Gefahr für das deutsche Modell?* Marburg: Schüren.

Silvia, Stephen J. 1988. "The West German Labor Law Controversy: A Struggle for the Factory of the Future." *Comparative Politics* 20:2 (January).

Silvia, Stephen J. 1996. "Globalization and the German Economy: Labor Unions," Paper presented at the APSA meetings, San Francisco, August 29–September 1, 1996.

1997. "German Unification and Emerging Divisions within German Employers' Associations: Cause or Catalyst?" *Comparative Politics* 29:2 (January), 187–208.

Soskice, David. 1990. "Reinterpreting Corporatism and Explaining Unemployment: Co-ordinated and Non-co-ordinated Market Economies," in Renata Brunetta and Carlo Dell'Aringa, eds., *Labour Relations and Economic Performance.* London: Macmillan.

1991. "The Institutional Infrastructure for International Competitiveness: A Comparative Analysis of the UK and Germany," in A. B. Atkinson and R. Brunetta, eds., *The Economics of the New Europe*. International Economic Association Conference Volume Series. London: Macmillan.

1999. "Divergent Production Regimes: Coordinated and Uncoordinated Market Economies in the 1980s and 1990s," in Herbert Kitschelt, Peter Lange, Gary Marks, and John D. Stephens, eds., *Continuity and Change in Contemporary Capitalism*. New York: Cambridge University Press.

Streeck, Wolfgang. 1979. *"Gewerkschaftsorganisation und industrielle Beziehungen: Einige Stabilitätsprobleme industriegewerkschaftlicher Interessenvertretung und ihre Lösung im System der industriellen Beziehungen der Bundesrepublik Deutschland."* IIM Discussion Paper 79–30. Berlin: Wissenschaftszentrum Berlin für Sozialforschung.

Streeck, Wolfgang. 1984. "Neo-Corporatist Industrial Relations and the Economic Crisis in Western Germany," in John H. Goldthorpe, ed., *Order and Conflict in Contemporary Capitalism*. Oxford: Oxford University Press.

1987. "The Uncertainties of Management in the Management of Uncertainty: Employers, Labor Relations and Industrial Adjustment in the 1980s." *Work, Employment and Society* 1:3 (September), 281–308.

1993. "The Rise and Decline of Neo-Corporatism," in Lloyd Ulman, Barry Eichengreen, and William T. Dickens, eds., *Labor and an Integrated Europe*. Washington, DC: Brookings Institution.

1995. "German Capitalism: Does It Exist? Can It Survive?" in Colin Crouch and Wolfgang Streeck, eds., *Modern Capitalism or Modern Capitalisms?* London: Francis Pinter.

1996. *Mitbestimmung: Offene Fragen*. Gütersloh: Verlag Bertelsmann Stiftung.

Swenson, Peter. 1989. *Fair Shares: Unions, Pay and Politics in Sweden and West Germany*. Ithaca, NY: Cornell University Press.

Thelen, Kathleen. 1991. *Union of Parts: Labor Politics in Postwar Germany*. Ithaca, NY: Cornell University Press.

1993. "European Labor in Transition: Sweden and Germany Compared." *World Politics* 46: 1 (October), 23–49.

Turner, Lowell. 1998. *Defending the High Road: Labor and Politics in Unified Germany*. Ithaca, NY: Cornell University Press.

Wallerstein, Michael, Miriam Golden, and Peter Lange. 1997. "Unions, Employers' Associations and Wage-Setting Institutions in Northern and Central Europe, 1950–1992." *Industrial and Labor Relations Review* 50:3 (April), 379–401.

Wever, Kirsten S. 1995. *Negotiating Competitiveness: Employment Relations and Organizational Innovation in Germany and the United States*. Boston: Harvard Business School Press.

Zysman, John, Eileen Doherty, and Andrew Schwartz. 1996. "Tales from the 'Global Economy': Cross-National Production Networks and the Reorganization of the European Economy," BRIE Working Paper #83. University of California, Berkeley: BRIE, September.

PART II

MACROECONOMIC REGIMES

6

INSTITUTIONAL DIMENSIONS OF COORDINATING WAGE BARGAINING AND MONETARY POLICY

Robert J. Franzese, Jr., and Peter A. Hall

Few propositions are more widely accepted today among policymakers and economists than the assertion that, by making its central bank more independent from the national government, a nation can secure better levels of economic performance. The financial press has concluded that "the argument for central bank independence . . . appears overwhelming," and many nations have made their central banks more independent during the 1990's.[1] Even the new monetary union now being established in Europe is organized around a central bank designed to be highly independent of political control (Goodhart 1995; de la Dehesa et al. 1993; Fratianni and von Hagen 1992; Gros and Thygesen 1992).

The argument for central bank independence rests on three pillars. First, a body of economic theory has been developed to explain why the independence of the central bank enhances economic performance (Persson and Tabellini 1994; Cukierman 1992). Second, several national cases are cited to support this view, of which the most prominent is the Federal Republic of Germany whose Bundesbank also provides the model for the new European Central Bank (Canzoneri, Grilli, and Masson 1993; Fratianni, von Hagen, and Waller 1992). Third, an influential set of empirical studies seems to confirm that, by making the central

In the course of our research on this topic, which dates back to 1992–93, we have accumulated far more debts than we can enumerate here, notably to those who provided us with comments on various papers stemming from this research. We want to thank them and to acknowledge, in particular, Torben Iversen and David Soskice for many stimulating discussions in recent years. Finally, the reader should note that earlier versions of this paper appeared in the working paper series of the Berkeley Center for German and European Studies and the Wissenschaftszentrum Berlin and that some passages in this paper draw on Hall and Franzese 1998 where a more extended data analysis is presented.

1 *The Financial Times* 12 November 1992:20.

bank more independent, a nation can secure lower rates of inflation without any adverse economic effects (Alesina and Summers 1993; Grilli, Masciandaro, and Tabellini 1991).

The object of this chapter is to question the current consensus in favor of central bank independence. We proceed by examining each of the pillars on which the case for it rests, beginning with the theoretical rationale, following with a reconsideration of the German case, and concluding with the reanalysis of cross-national data. We close by discussing the implications for economic performance under the European Monetary Union.

Our analysis begins from the contention that monetary policy-making involves a signaling process between the central bank and economic actors. We argue (a) that the advantages of independence turn on the effectiveness of this signaling process and (b) that the effectiveness of the signaling process is conditioned, in turn, by the organization of the broader political economy and, most notably, the extent of coordination in wage bargaining. Although increasing the independence of the central bank will lower the rate of inflation, it will not always do so without adverse economic consequences. Instead, the character of a nation's wage-bargaining system will affect the efficiency of the signaling mechanism and therefore the unemployment cost of the inflation gains secured via central bank independence.

With this argument, the chapter integrates two well-developed bodies of literature that have long been separated from each other: the literature on central bank independence and the literature on the coordination of wage bargaining (Soskice 1990; Calmfors and Driffill 1988; Lange and Garrett 1985; Cameron 1984; Bruno and Sachs 1984) There is strong evidence that the key variables highlighted in both literatures independently affect economic performance, but we show that they also interact with each other in the determination of performance.

I. THE THEORY OF CENTRAL BANK INDEPENDENCE

Underpinning the literature on central bank independence is a standard neoclassical model, which assumes that the rate of inflation is determined primarily by the rate of growth of the money supply, which is controlled by the central bank, while the rate of unemployment is affected by unanticipated changes in policy and the level of real wages.[2] Within this framework, several advantages can be adduced for central bank independence. A central bank independent of political control may be better placed to stimulate the economy because economic actors

---

2 Although some of these postulates may be contentious, we do not take issue with them here as our own arguments hold under a variety of economic assumptions including those of the standard neoclassical framework.

are less likely to anticipate that it will engage in monetary expansion (Cukierman 1992). Similarly, there may be more muted political business-cycles where control over monetary policy rests with an independent central bank (Clark, Reichert, Lomas, and Parker 1998; Alesina 1988; Beck 1982).

We focus here on the claim most frequently cited in favor of central bank independence, which turns on the time-inconsistency problems that occur when nominal wage and price contracts of some duration must be fixed before the trajectory of monetary policy is known with certainty. In such contexts, which are common in the industrialized world, wage and price contractors will agree on nominal wages and prices higher than the real levels they seek in order to allow for the possibility that future inflation will lower their real wages and returns. As a consequence, wage and price settlements will be more inflationary than they might otherwise be.

The central bank can reduce the "inflation increment" that wage and price bargainers build into their contracts by promising to pursue antiinflationary policies, but these assurances may not be credible if the bank is known to be responsive to politicians for whom expansionary policy is often more electorally attractive. Thus, making the central bank more independent of political control will enhance the credibility of its assurances about the future course of monetary policy, thereby allowing wage and price contractors to agree on less-inflationary settlements. In this way, increasing the independence of the central bank may lead to a lower rate of inflation without any other adverse economic consequences (Cukierman 1992; Lohmann 1992; Rogoff 1985; Barro and Gordon 1983; Kydland and Prescott 1977).

This is a powerful theory, now widely accepted in economics, whose basic logic we also accept (cf. Posen 1995a, 1995b). Notice that, at its heart, this is a theory about signaling and coordination. The premise is that, by signaling its intentions with regard to the future course of monetary policy, the central bank can lead wage and price contractors to alter their behavior and, notably, to coordinate on lower nominal wage and price contracts. The independence of the bank can affect this process in two ways. First, since more independent central banks are likely to pursue more restrictive monetary policies, independence can depress wage and price settlements via what might be termed a "conservatism effect." Second, because greater independence confers greater credibility on the signals the bank sends, it can reduce wage and price contracts by rendering the bank's assurances about the course of monetary policy more believable. How well this "credibility effect" operates depends on the propensity of wage and price contractors to respond to signals from the bank relative to other pressures upon them and on their ability to coordinate on appropriate behavior.

It is with regard to this last set of issues that the conventional theory of central bank independence is deficient. As a theory, it has the great advantage of drawing our attention to the importance of signaling to monetary policy-making, to the importance of the credibility of the signals sent from the central bank, and to the significance of independence for such credibility. Conventional analyses of central bank independence, however, pay little attention to the broader complexities of the signaling process itself. In general, they adopt a rational-expectations perspective that assumes all the relevant economic actors will have very high levels of information and, more critically, high levels of confidence about the behavior of other actors. In brief, it is assumed that each wage and price contractor can predict not only the effects of an announced monetary policy on the economy but also the behavior of all other relevant actors in the face of such an announcement and the effects of that behavior. Under these assumptions, rationality alone should lead the actors to coordinate on optimal forms of behavior.

There are good reasons for thinking that such assumptions may not be adequate to the real world. First, the precise effects of monetary policy can rarely be predicted with complete confidence, even by experts (Eichengreen 1996). Second, and of greater theoretical significance, even if some actors can make accurate predictions, the presence of others with a capacity to affect the economy who may be operating from different predictions interferes with the ability of all to coordinate on an equilibrium specified by the monetary announcement. Given the large number of wage and price bargainers in the economy, it is unlikely that all will be able to predict the effects of monetary policy with precision, let alone predict the predictions and behavior of others. The conventional theory of central bank independence is one which assumes that full information and rationality alone will produce effective coordination but, in most settings to which it is applied, information is not full enough to induce such coordination.

Indeed, the settings associated with wage bargaining are widely recognized to be ones afflicted by collective action problems that arise when the actors have some bargaining power and so must condition their wage and price settlements on expected settlements elsewhere but enjoy less-than-complete information about what other actors are likely to do (Calmfors 1993; Layard, Nickell, and Jackman 1991; Carlin and Soskice 1990). In such instances, effective coordination requires the presence of the kind of institutional arrangements to which the "new political economy" draws our attention, namely institutions that provide the actors with a basis for monitoring behavior, deliberating with each other, and making credible commitments (Milgrom and Roberts 1992; Alt and Shepsle 1990).

These considerations suggest that the effectiveness of the signaling and coordination process between the central bank and economic actors will depend on the presence of institutions for resolving the collective action problems that wage bargainers face. The limitation of most theories of central bank independence is that, by focusing on the characteristics of the central bank, they neglect the contribution that other institutions may make to the overall signaling and coordination process on which many of the advantages of central bank independence depend. Conversely, theories of coordinated wage bargaining often neglect the contribution that monetary policy and central bank independence may make to the achievement of effective wage coordination. In what follows, we seek to rectify these problems by constructing an analysis that appreciates the interactive effects between the institutions of central bank independence and those associated with wage-bargaining coordination.[3]

II. THE COORDINATION OF WAGE BARGAINING

We focus here on "the coordination of wage bargaining," a term that refers to the degree to which the determination of wage settlements is actively coordinated across the economy by trade union and employer organizations. That, in turn, depends heavily on the organizational structures for wage bargaining which can vary from country to country.

The full set of institutional arrangements required for coordinated wage bargaining is complex because they must support cooperative outcomes in five nested sets of strategic interactions (Thelen 1991; Scharpf 1988, 1991; Tsebelis 1990). The first is the interaction that takes place inside each dyad of bargainers between the organizations representing workers and those representing employers. A second takes place between the leaders of bargaining organizations and the rank and file members whose support they must retain. We focus here on the third interaction between the bargainers in each dyad and their counterparts in other dyads and on a fourth interaction between wage bargainers as a group and the authorities controlling economic policy. A fifth interaction occurs between the authorities controlling monetary policy and those controlling fiscal policy.

With regard to the interactions examined here, an early literature associated wage coordination entirely with highly centralized trade union movements bargaining with employer confederations at the peak level. In recent years, two amendments have been made to this view. First, it has been shown that employers' organizations can play a role in the coordination of wage bargaining as important as that of trade unions (Thelen 1994; Soskice 1990; Swenson 1989).

---

3 For an early formulation, see Hall (1994). Franzese (1994, 1996, 1999) expands the analysis, considering also the impact of the sectoral-structural position of the bargainers in a model similar to the more informal framework presented here. Iversen (1994, 1996) considers the role of labor's goals with regard to wage equalization in a somewhat different model. Iversen and Soskice (1997) demonstrate that real effects of monetary conservatism can stem from market power even given rational expectations, complete information, perfect credibility, and no nominal rigidities. Cukierman (1997) adds unions with a direct distaste for inflation to an otherwise neoclassical model and now holds several conclusions in common with those derived by Hall, Franzese, Iversen, and Soskice.

Second, it has been noted that effective coordination can take place within either of two organizational structures. In one, the principal locus of bargaining is at the economy-wide or peak level, where negotiations occur among highly centralized trade union and employers' confederations. In the other, wage negotiation takes place primarily among trade unions and employer organizations highly concentrated at the sectoral level but equipped with sufficient economy-wide linkages to transmit the settlement reached in a leading sector across the economy (Iversen 1994; Golden 1993).

The impact of variation in the level of wage coordination on the economy as a whole, and on the effectiveness of the signaling process between wage bargainers and the central bank in particular, can best be appreciated by comparing two polar cases.

Consider, first, the case in which wage bargaining is largely uncoordinated. Here, each bargaining unit, generally a dyad of employer and union, must reach a settlement in the context of considerable uncertainty about what the settlements reached by other bargaining units will be. Three effects follow from this structural context.

First, the union in each dyad will be tempted to seek a nominal wage settlement that exceeds its real-wage target in order to offset the real-wage losses it will suffer if other settlements are more inflationary than its own, and employers may well accede, anticipating that inflation will erode some of their nominal wage concessions. Where inflation-expectations are high, these "inflation increments" are likely to be correspondingly high.

Second, in such settings, the actors in any one bargaining unit are unlikely to let considerations about the effect of their settlement on the overall economy influence their decision making, because any one bargaining unit is normally too small for its settlement to have a large impact on the economy. This posture will be reinforced by the fact that other bargaining units can be expected to take a similar view; hence, if one union moderates its nominal-wage settlement in the interest of the national economy, it may suffer real-wage losses from the failure of other units to do so.

Third, when the economy-wide level of wage settlements proves inflationary, the fiscal or monetary authorities may respond with deflationary policies. In an uncoordinated setting, however, the actors in any one of the many bargaining units are unlikely to let the prospect of such a policy-response influence their own settlement much because they know that the government will be producing a policy in response not to it but to settlements across the economy, which they cannot control. Again, if any one bargaining unit moderates its nominal wage settlement with this in mind, it may suffer from the failure of other units to do so. Thus, in uncoordinated settings, wage bargainers are unlikely to be highly responsive to threats from the fiscal or monetary authorities to respond to inflationary settlements with deflation.

Compare now the case in which wage bargaining is coordinated. In such settings, a central or lead bargain has great influence over the level of wage settlements in the economy as a whole and subsequent bargains generally follow the pattern it sets with small adjustments for local conditions. Several implications follow from this.

First, since the members of each bargaining unit, and especially the one negotiating the lead settlement, know what the level of subsequent wage settlements is likely to be once they have settled on their own, they need not build an increment for anticipated inflation arising from other settlements into their own agreement.

Second, because the lead bargaining unit knows that its settlement is likely to be generalized to the whole economy, the actors within it have strong incentives to take the impact of their settlement on the overall economy into account when negotiating it. After all, they can predict that impact because their settlement is likely to produce similar settlements elsewhere; and the aggregate economic effects will fall on their own members. For this reason, we can expect concerns about the aggregate levels of inflation, unemployment, and competitiveness in the national economy to influence individual wage settlements more strongly in coordinated systems of wage bargaining. This suggests that, where wage bargaining is more coordinated, we should see lower rates of inflation, whether or not the central bank is independent.

Most central to our argument, however, is the way in which the coordination of wage bargaining can lend force to the signals sent from the central bank. Because the lead settlement is likely to be copied with clear effects for the whole economy, those negotiating it know that the central bank is likely to respond directly to it. This renders the principal wage bargainers highly sensitive to signals sent from the central bank about the appropriateness of pending wage settlements and the likely stance of monetary policy in the face of them. In short, the signals sent from the central bank are more likely to affect the level of wage settlements in settings where wage bargaining is coordinated than in settings where it is not.

The important implication of this is that, where wage bargaining is coordinated, the central bank may be able to induce wage moderation and reduce the rate of inflation by signaling its policy intentions to wage bargainers, without any need to resort to policies that raise the level of unemployment. Where wage bargaining is uncoordinated so that the many small bargaining units are not especially sensitive to signals sent from the central bank, the latter may be able to reduce the rate of inflation only by pursuing restrictive monetary policies that encourage wage and price moderation by dampening the level of economic activity and raising the level of unemployment.

In sum, we have argued that the system of wage bargaining is a key component of the overall signaling mechanism that links the central bank to economic actors and that this mechanism will be more effective where wage bargaining is coordinated than where it is not. Although increasing the independence of the central bank is likely to reduce the rate of inflation in any setting, through a combination of "conservatism" and "credibility" effects, its ability to do so without corresponding increases in unemployment is likely to depend on whether wage bargaining is coordinated. Conversely, although a higher level of wage coordination may lower the rate of unemployment in any setting, by facilitating coordination on wage levels appropriate to prevailing monetary policy, its effects are likely to increase with the independence of the central bank for two reasons. First, where the central bank is highly independent, the greater likelihood that it will be firmly committed to a strict monetary target means that any failure of wage bargainers to coordinate on appropriate wage levels is more likely to result in higher levels of unemployment than it would if the bank were subject to greater political control and less committed to tight monetary policy.[4] Second, in at least some cases, the presence of a highly independent central bank may improve the effectiveness of a wage coordination system because its more credible promises/threats about the course of monetary policy will help to push subsequent wage bargains into line with the lead bargain.

In the next section, we explore the applicability of this theory to the case most often adduced in support of central bank independence, that of Germany.

III. THE GERMAN MODEL

The German Bundesbank is the most independent central bank in the world and, for most of the postwar period, the Germany economy achieved low rates of inflation at relatively low rates of unemployment (Lohmann 1994). Thus, many advocates of central bank independence invoke the German case as a model, most recently for the design of the new European Central Bank (Alesina and Grilli 1993; Eichengreen 1992). A closer examination of Germany, however, reveals that its economic performance benefits not only from an independent central bank but also from a highly coordinated system of wage

---

4 The reasoning here is that failures in wage coordination commonly lead to higher nominal wage levels. Where the central bank pursues policies that are nonaccommodating, these are likely to translate into higher real wage levels and higher levels of unemployment. Where the central bank is more accommodating, the results may vary. In some cases, the results may be higher levels of unemployment. In others, however, higher levels of inflation may offset nominal-wage gains to limit real-wage increases and the unemployment associated with them and/or currency devaluation may be used to offset the impact of higher nominal wages. The institutional assumption, as noted above, is that more independent central banks tend to pursue firmer commitments to monetary and exchange-rate targets or, loosely speaking, more rigorous monetary policy.

bargaining.[5] In fact, the German case exemplifies how coordinated wage bargaining can enhance the effects of central bank independence and vice versa.[6]

Consider first the institutions that underpin wage bargaining in Germany. The German work force is organized into 17 large unions, often covering entire industries, which also belong to an overarching union confederation, the Deutschegewirkschaftsbund (DGB).[7] These unions bargain with employers' associations, also organized by industrial sector, representing 80 percent of German employers. Thus, collective bargaining is relatively centralized at the industry level. Both the unions and the employers' associations are strongly positioned vis-à-vis their rank and file by virtue of the control they exercise over a range of resources important to their members, such as skill certification and vocational training schemes.

The system is supported by a legal framework that regulates many aspects of the bargaining process, specifies that only legally recognized unions can conclude collective wage agreements, and allows industry settlements to be extended to cover all companies in a sector by agreement between the union, the employers' association, and the regional governments. At the plant level, the system is underpinned by a system of elected works councils on which the unions are generally influential, which can negotiate local working conditions and, less formally, local pay structures (Thelen 1992; Berghahn and Karsten 1987; Katzenstein 1987; Markovits 1986; Streeck 1984a).

Equally central to the operation of the system is the less-formal arrangement whereby the settlements of most industries follow the precedent set by the bargain reached in a leading sector each year. For most of the postwar period, these leading bargains have been concluded between IG Metall, the massive metalworkers union which organizes a range of industries including automobiles, engineering, and steel, and the corresponding employers' federation, Gesamptmetall.[8] A variety of factors converge to give IG Metall this role and to ensure that other industries will follow its lead. Since it is the largest and one of the strongest

---

5 Although the focus of this analysis is on the organization of the political economy, other factors may also have contributed to Germany's inflation performance, including perhaps a cultural aversion to inflation born of the hyperinflation experience in the 1920s. We are inclined to see the latter as a minor contributor to the outcome, but others accord it a more prominent role. See Hirsch and Goldthorpe (1978) and Lindberg and Maier (1985).

6 For analyses that explore the German case more fully than we can here, see Soskice (1990), Scharpf (1991), Streeck (1984a, b). See also Hall (1986:ch. 9) for an early formulation of similar arguments.

7 Two smaller union confederations, the DAG and DBB, are not in a position to have much influence on the overall outcomes. The former is very small, and the DBB represents civil servants whose pay is set by legislation (but cf. Franzese 1994, 1996, 1997 and Garrett and Way 1995b on the public sector in this context).

8 The notable exception occurred in 1974 when ÖTV, the public-sector union, took the lead in a negotiating round with less than ideal results. For a description of the events, see Goodman (1992: 71); for a discussion of the implications, see Garrett and Way (1995b) and Franzese (1994, 1996, 1997).

German unions, the others can follow its lead knowing they would be unlikely to improve on its settlement, and both the DGB and centralized employers' associations act as a powerful coordinators of sectoral agreements (Thelen 1991; Markovits 1986; Flanagan, Soskice, and Ulman: ch. 5).

It is clear that this system tends to promote low rates of inflation. Since the lead bargainers in the metalworking industries know that their settlement is likely to be generalized to the whole economy, IG Metall need not seek an additional increment to guard against unanticipated levels of inflation that might follow from subsequent settlements. Both IG Metall and the corresponding employers' federation also have strong incentives to take the overall economic impact of any potential settlement into account when determining it. Thus, the system of wage coordination itself tends to reduce rates of inflation.

In addition, we also find a particular kind of interaction between wage bargainers and the central bank in Germany. The highly-public *pas de deux* between the Bundesbank and the principal wage bargainers, which occurs at the time of every wage round in Germany, is a prominent feature of politics. The bank often issues pointed comments on the initial wage demands made by the union involved in the leading settlement, accompanied by detailed commentary about the state of the economy and warnings about the policy consequences of overly inflationary wage settlements. Because bargaining is relatively centralized, the principal negotiators are not left in much doubt about whether the bank intends to respond to their particular settlement; and it is not uncommon for them to issue counter statements about the likely effect of their demands on the state of the economy (Scharpf 1988, 1991: ch. 7; Berghahn and Karsten 1987; Streeck 1984a, b). Notice that this kind of dialogue between wage bargainers and the central bank is completely absent from U.S. economic politics. From our theoretical perspective this difference in political discourse is entirely understandable: the Federal Reserve and the Bundesbank speak differently because they have audiences with different institutional structures.

In sum, the coordination of German wage bargaining renders the process of signaling that takes place between the central bank and wage bargainers highly effective. The bank can respond directly to a leading settlement; and it behooves those negotiating it to take seriously the bank's threats to do so. The system does not work perfectly: At times, wage bargainers defy the bank, whether to test its resolve or to satisfy their rank and file; but there can be no doubt that over the long run they have paid careful attention to its threats. Those pressures that have arisen from time to time for wage bargainers to defect from relative restraint have usually been defused because the likely strong response of the Bundesbank was known to the wage bargainers who in turn had the institutionally determined capacity to respond. It is clear that, as a result, the Bundesbank has been able to use this signaling mechanism on many occasions to induce more moderate wage settlements without having to resort to draconian monetary policies or sharply higher levels of unemployment.

The independence of the Bundesbank also enhances the effectiveness of this signaling process, as conventional theory suggests, by rendering the threats that the bank issues more credible than they might be if monetary policy were controlled by elected politicians. Indeed, as Iversen (1994, 1996; Iversen and Soskice 1997) has suggested, central bank independence may have special importance for enhancing the effectiveness of wage coordination in systems, like the German, where bargaining is coordinated but the locus of bargaining is at the industry level. Here, effective coordination depends on other industry bargains following the lead settlement, and the added credibility that independence confers on the threats emanating from the central bank may help to ensure that they do so.

The German case also suggests that the effectiveness of such signaling mechanisms may be enhanced when the export sector is large and plays a pivotal role in wage bargaining (Franzese 1994, 1996, 1997). The metalworking sector, which produces the lead bargain in most years, has a high export concentration. In itself, this induces lower settlements because wage bargainers in export sectors are especially concerned to maintain unit labor costs at internationally competitive levels. Actors in such sectors are also especially sensitive to signals from the central bank, however, because the restrictive monetary policies that the bank wields not only depress the level of economic activity but also tend to appreciate the exchange rate, thereby threatening export sectors especially severely by rendering their products more expensive in world markets.

In sum, there are good reasons for thinking that the capacity of postwar Germany to secure low rates of inflation at low rates of unemployment is not attributable solely to the independence of the Bundesbank. Germany also has a highly coordinated system of wage bargaining that is itself conducive to lower rates of inflation and that renders the signaling mechanism between the bank and wage bargainers highly effective. It is the *combination* of central bank independence and coordinated wage bargaining that is so conducive to effective economic performance in Germany.

IV. CROSS-NATIONAL EMPIRICAL ANALYSIS

Much of the current enthusiasm for central bank independence stems from a set of influential empirical studies, based on cross-national comparison of average rates of inflation and unemployment, which conclude that, when the independence of the central bank is increased, the rate of inflation will fall without any adverse economic consequences. One such article concludes "having an independent central bank is almost like having a free lunch; there are benefits but no apparent costs in terms of macroeconomic performance" (Grilli et al. 1991: 375).

If our theoretical argument is correct, however, most of these studies suffer from a serious specification problem. In keeping with a neoclassical model that portrays the economy as largely homogenous across nations, virtually the only institutional variable included in such analyses is one reflecting the degree of independence of the central bank.[9] We propose including a further institutional variable representing the degree to which wage bargaining is coordinated. Once it is added, two new possibilities arise: We may find that some of the inflation effects hitherto attributed to the central bank are actually attributable to the wage bargaining system and/or it may be that the precise impact of increasing the independence of the central bank depends on the character of wage bargaining. Three specific hypotheses follow from the theory developed in preceding sections.

First, nothing in our account contradicts the conventional proposition that an increase in the independence of the central bank will lower the rate of inflation experienced by a nation. Thus, we expect to see a negative relationship between central bank independence and the rate of inflation in cross-national data.

Second, for the reasons adduced in Section II, individual bargaining units face more institutional incentives to avoid inflationary wage settlements in settings where wage bargaining is coordinated. Accordingly, we expect increases in the level of wage coordination to have an independent effect that lowers the rate of inflation.

Finally, our theoretical perspective suggests that there should be interaction effects between the level of central bank independence and the level of wage coordination, most notably with respect to unemployment. In nations where wage bargaining is highly coordinated, increasing the independence of the central bank should reduce the rate of inflation without substantially increasing unemployment because the signaling system linking the bank to economic actors will be highly effective there. By contrast, in nations where wage bargaining is less coordinated, increasing the independence of the central bank may lower the rate of inflation only at the cost of higher levels of unemployment because the signaling system in such settings is not efficient enough to allow the bank to reduce the rate of inflation without implementing real monetary policies that increase the rate of unemployment. Thus, we expect the unemployment cost of central bank independence to increase as the coordination of wage bargaining decreases. The corollary is that the unemployment benefit of coordinated wage bargaining should increase with the independence of the central bank. As noted above, the reasoning behind the corollary is that, where the central bank is more independent, it can reinforce the level of coordination secured by institutions for wage coordination and, in the context of a highly independent central bank dedicated to monetary rigor, slippages in wage coor-

9 For notable exceptions, see Havrilesky and Granato (1993), Bleaney (1996), and Al-Marhubi and Willett (n.d.). For a useful survey, see Eijffinger and De Haan (1996).

dination are more likely produce higher levels of unemployment than they will where the central bank is more accommodating.

We test these hypotheses with a data set covering all the OECD nations for which comparable data could be secured for the period from 1955 to 1990.[10] To measure central bank independence, we use an average of five indices, which assess both the legal status of the central bank and its reputation for independence.[11] To measure the degree to which wage bargaining is coordinated, we construct an index based on the one devised by Soskice (1990), extrapolated to a wider range of cases using the assessments Layard et al. (1991) make of trade union and employer coordination and standard accounts of industrial relations systems.[12] This index codes each nation at one of five points (0, .25, .50, .75, 1.0) based on the degree to which wage bargaining has been coordinated by trade unions or employer associations over the course of the 1955–90 period. Our dependent variables are the average rates of inflation and unemployment for this period as portrayed by (internationally comparable) OECD measures.

We have deliberately taken a cross-sectional approach to the data analysis. Although this limits the degrees of freedom, we think it especially appropriate for assessing the impact of structural variables, such as central bank independence and the coordination of wage bargaining, which are long-lived and do not change dramatically over the period.[13] Our premise is that the effects of

10 These 18 cases represent all the major developed democracies from which Greece, Spain, and Portugal are excluded because they had nondemocratic regimes for substantial portions of the period and it is difficult to assess a central bank's "independence" from an authoritarian regime. Obviously, the credibility of any nominal/legal degree of central bank independence ought to be discounted in authoritarian regimes relative to democracies, but it is not clear by how much. Similar considerations plague the coding of wage-bargaining systems comparably across authoritarian and democratic regimes.

11 The five indices are those most commonly employed in the literature: LVAU, an unweighted average of several legal characteristics, and QVAU, an unweighted average of survey results for CBI, from Cukierman (1992); EC, the rating of the economic independence of the central bank, and POL, the rating for political independence from Grilli et al. (1991); and the original index from Bade and Parkin (1982).

12 For example, Soskice (1990:55), Layard et al. (1991:52), Flanagan et al. (1983), Ferner and Hyman (1992), Baglioni and Crouch (1990), and Crouch (1993). Some scholars prefer an index based on union organization but this violates the important observation of Soskice (1990), Swenson (1989), and others that employers' associations also contribute to wage coordination.

13 Alesina and Summers (1993) employ a similar approach and offer a similar defense. Close inspection of such time-sensitive indices of central bank independence and trade-union characteristics as do exist suggests that these variables did not shift substantially in the 1955–1990 period. (The recent widespread movement toward more independent central banks came after our sample ends in 1990.) For example, 96.6% of the country-decade variance in Cukierman's (1992) LVAU index (the only time-variant index available) is solely cross-sectional (cross-country). Since time-variant measures of wage–price bargaining coordination do not exist, we can look only at rough proxies such as Golden and Wallerstein's (1999) annual-level data for union confederation involvement in wage bargaining in six high-coordination countries. Only 33% of the variation in this index is unique to country-year. Variation in the effective coordination of wage bargaining over this period is likely to be lower

such variables show up most clearly when assessed over a long period of time and that greater confidence can be placed in any relationships that are revealed if they persist over a variety of different economic contexts, extending from the years of postwar growth when inflation and unemployment were generally low, through the high-inflation period of the 1970s, to the high-unemployment decade of the 1980s.

Moreover, the empirical analyses from which the central bank independence literature has drawn its most influential support have been based almost entirely on this kind of cross-sectional analysis of the average postwar experience of the 15 to 21 developed democracies examined here. We adopt the same approach in order to ensure comparability with such analyses. In recognition of the limited degrees of freedom, we apply a variety of tests assessing the robustness of our findings.[14]

We begin with some simple cross-tabulations that display the basic patterns in the data. Because the presence of country-specific factors beyond the present theory may affect the precise levels of inflation and unemployment in any one nation, we should not expect the hypothesized relationships to show up in every pairwise comparison of cases. If operative, however, they should be more likely to appear, ceteris paribus, when the cases are broadly aggregated, as they are in Table 6.1, where we divide the OECD nations into four groups according to whether they have a low or high level of central bank independence and low or high levels of coordination in wage bargaining, reporting the average rates of inflation and unemployment for the countries in each cell.

As our first hypothesis and conventional analysis predicts, Table 6.1 indicates that countries with more independent central banks tend to have lower rates of inflation. In addition, as our second hypothesis predicts, increases in the level of wage coordination are also associated with lower rates of inflation. Note that the effect of coordination (independence) on inflation is greater in nations with low levels of central bank independence (coordination). This stands to reason. If increases in wage-bargaining coordination and central bank independence both lower the rate of inflation, the independent impact on inflation of each of them is likely to be somewhat greater where the other is not operative.

Most important from the perspective of our analysis are the results for

than variation in union–confederal involvement and far lower in low-coordination countries than in these six. Thus, 33% might serve as a very generous estimate of the upper bound on the share of total variation of coordination in wage–price bargaining that is country–time unique.

14 These included sequential deletion of cases and reestimation, checks of robustness to alternative measures of bargaining coordination and/or central bank independence, cross-validation of model selection by out-of-sample predictive power (Beck and Katz 1995), checks of robustness against alternative (to OLS plus White's standard errors) means of estimating the regression, running the regressions without any control variables (to maximize degrees of freedom), etc. The results are quite robust to these sorts of perturbations; details available from the authors on request.

Table 6.1. *Average inflation and unemployment rates secured in OECD countries under alternative institutional arrangements, 1955–90*

		Inflation rates				Unemployment rates	
		Central Bank Independence				Central Bank Independence	
Coor-dinated		Low	High	Coor-dinated		Low	High
Wage	Low	7.5 (6)	4.8 (2)	Wage	Low	4.7 (6)	6.1 (2)
Barg.	High	6.2 (4)	4.8 (4)	Barg.	High	2.3 (4)	2.8 (4)

Notes: Cases were coded as follows: CWB: low = 0 and 0.25, high = 0.75 and 1; CBI: low = below 0.50, high = above 0.50. Cases where CWB = medium (0.5) are omitted here but retained elsewhere. The number of countries in each category is given in parentheses after the postwar-average inflation or unemployment.

unemployment displayed on the right-hand side of the table, which provide some evidence in support of our third hypothesis. In nations where the level of wage coordination is high, an increase in the independence of the central bank is associated with a relatively small increase in unemployment (0.5 points). In nations where the coordination of wage bargaining is low and the signaling mechanism between the central bank and economic actors correspondingly less effective, however, an increase in the independence of the central bank is associated with substantially higher levels of unemployment (1.4 points or nearly three times as much). Conversely, where central bank independence is high, coordination lowers unemployment by more (3.3 points) than where central bank independence is low (2.4 points).

To examine the empirical record regarding these hypotheses in a more systematic and thorough way, we also apply multiple-regression analysis, which can assess the effects of these structural variables (CBI and CWB) while controlling for a number of other economic and political variables that might be expected to influence the level of inflation or unemployment. Specifically, we control for (a) the economic openness of the economy, on the premise that more open economies may experience greater pressure to moderate the level of inflation and more unemployment induced by fluctuations in the international economy; (b) the level of real per capita gross domestic product, on the premise that less-developed nations may be more tempted to rely on seignorage for revenue and more susceptible to high levels of unemployment; (c) the representation of left parties in the cabinet to reflect the widely accepted view that social democratic governments are more likely to tolerate inflation than their conservative counterparts; and (d) union density to reflect the common argument that the collective-bargaining power of labor, controlling for (net of) its coordination, has a deleterious effect on wage restraint and therefore inflation and unemployment.[15]

The basic format of the regressions to be reported here is:

$$\pi = C'\alpha^{\pi} + \beta^{\pi}_{cbi}CBI + \beta^{\pi}_{cwb}CWB + \beta^{\pi}_{cc}CBI \cdot CWB + \varepsilon^{\pi}$$

$$U = C'\alpha^{u} + \beta^{u}_{cbi}CBI + \beta^{u}_{cwb}CWB + \beta^{u}_{cc}CBI \cdot CWB + \varepsilon^{u}$$

where π is inflation and U is unemployment, C is a vector of controls (described above) plus the constant, α is a vector of coefficients on those controls and constant, and CWB and CBI are our measures of coordinated wage bargaining and central bank independence respectively. It should be noted that in regressions with an interaction term like this, the *effects* of CBI and CWB on the dependent variable are given, *not* by the *coefficients* on each of those terms alone, but by $b_{cwb} + b_{cc}CBI$ and $b_{cbi} + b_{cc}CWB$, respectively. Likewise the statistical significance of these *effects* must be assessed, *not* with regard to the standard error of the individual *coefficients*, but according to the standard error of the *effect* which is different for each level that the other variable assumes.

The principal results, displayed in Table 6.2, provide strong confirmation for our first and second hypotheses.[16] The level of central bank independence and the level of wage coordination both display an independent and statistically significant negative relationship to the average rate of inflation experienced by nations over the 1955–90 period.[17] For example, holding CWB fixed at 0.5 (the level of the Netherlands and Belgium), an increase in central bank independence of 0.25 points (roughly the distance between Norway and the United States) reduces inflation by about 0.75 percentage points. Likewise, holding CBI fixed at 0.5 (about the level of Finland, Denmark, and Australia), an increase in the coordination of wage bargaining of 0.25 points (one interval on our 5-point scale) reduces inflation by about 0.66 percentage points.[18]

Similarly, our third hypothesis – that the unemployment costs of central

15 Economic openness is measured by exports plus imports as a percentage of gross domestic product (data from IMF, International Financial Statistics). The representation of the left in the cabinet is based on data from Lane, McKay, and Newton (1991) and Woldendorp Keman, and Budge (1994) and classification of left parties as in Swank (1989). Per capita GDP is from the Penn World Tables version 5.6. Union density is taken from Golden and Wallerstein (forthcoming) who, in turn, are working from Visser (1992). Unemployment and inflation are the internationally comparable figures compiled from OECD sources by Layard et al. (1991).

16 Dropping insignificant variables and reestimating reduced models, as is often done, is inadvisable as such a procedure tends to overestimate significance levels. If we did so here, our results would be strengthened further.

17 The effects of CBI and of CWB on inflation are both estimated to be negative over the entire range of the other variable, and both are statistically significantly so (.10 level or better) over around three-fourths of that range.

18 At these points, the effect of CWB is significant at the .05 level while that of CBI is significant at the .07 level.

Table 6.2. *Cross-sectional estimates of the inflation and unemployment effects of central bank independence, coordinated wage bargaining, and their interaction*

Independent variables (range of values)	Dependent variables	
	Inflation	Unemployment
Intercept	+27.13	+43.25
(1)	$(13.6)^{.07}$	$(12.9)^{.01}$
Union density	+3.156	+.8553
(.183–.726)	$(2.75)^{.28}$	$(3.11)^{.79}$
Left cabinet strength	+1.875	+2.296
(0–.833)	$(2.72)^{.51}$	$(1.35)^{.12}$
Trade openness	−1.790	+2.036
(.112–.952)	$(1.38)^{.23}$	$(.971)^{.06}$
In real GDP (per capita)	−2.045	−4.846
(8.60–9.52)	$(1.47)^{.19}$	$(1.44)^{.01}$
Coordination of wage bargaining (CWB)	−4.238	+1.004
(0–1)	$(1.73)^{.03}$	$(1.53)^{.53}$
Central bank independence (CBI)	−4.635	+11.53
(.146–.931)	$(2.28)^{.07}$	$(2.75)^{.002}$
Interaction (CWB x CBI)	+3.224	−13.05
(0–.699)	$(2.65)^{.25}$	$(3.25)^{.003}$
Number of observations (° freedom)	18 (10)	18 (10)
Adjusted R^2 (S.E. of regression)	.548 (1.06)	.806 (.896)

Notes: Coefficient estimates in bold; coefficient standard-errors in italics; approximate p-level at which the null hypothesis that the coefficient is zero can be rejected superscripted to that. Equations estimated by OLS with White's robust standard errors. Sample range of the independent variables in parentheses below their names.

bank independence depend negatively on the degree of coordination of wage bargaining and that the unemployment benefits of coordinated wage bargaining depend positively on the independence of the central bank – receives strong support here: The coefficient on the interaction term is large, negative, and statistically significant.

The net effects of central bank independence can be seen most clearly in Table 6.3 which reports contingent coefficients, displaying the impact of a unit increase in the level of central bank independence in settings characterized by different levels of wage coordination. The effect of an increase in central bank independence on inflation is negative at all levels of wage coordination but strongest in systems where wage coordination is too low to have a major impact of its own on inflation. Even more important, the effect of an increase in central bank independence on the rate of unemployment is relatively small and even

Table 6.3. *The estimated impact of a unit increase in central bank independence at various degrees of coordination in the wage-bargaining system*

Level of wage bargaining coordination	Conditional parameter estimates for the effect of a unit increase in central bank independence on . . .	
	Inflation	Unemployment
0.00 (United States, UK, Ireland)	**−4.63** (2.28)^{03}	**+11.5** (2.75)^{00}
0.25 (France, Italy, New Zealand)	**−3.83** (1.82)^{03}	**+8.26** (2.04)^{00}
0.50 (Belgium, Netherlands)	**−3.02** (1.51)^{04}	**+5.00** (1.44)^{00}
0.75 (Japan, Germany, Denmark, Finland, Switzerland)	**−2.22** (1.45)^{04}	**+1.74** (1.15)^{08}
1.00 (Austria, Norway, Sweden)	**−1.41** (1.69)^{21}	**−1.52** (1.37)^{15}

Notes: Estimated effect of a unit increase in CBI at that level of CWB (b_{cbi} + b_{cc}CWB) in bold; conditional standard-errors of the effects at that level of CWB in parentheses; p-level of one-sided t-test at that point superscripted in italics.

marginally negative in settings where wage bargaining is coordinated but large and positive in settings where wage bargaining is relatively uncoordinated. We interpret this as following from the "conservatism effect" noted above: more independent central banks attach greater weight to securing low levels of inflation relative to low levels of unemployment but, when wage bargaining is uncoordinated, are unable to do so via "credibility effects" alone, that is, without monetary policies that, in combination with the level of wage and price contracts, tend to raise the level of unemployment.

Table 6.4 provides the analogous information regarding the estimated effects of coordination in wage bargaining on inflation and unemployment in settings characterized by different levels of independence of the central bank. The impact of coordination on inflation is, as we have argued, generally negative; in fact, when central bank independence is low, coordination in wage bargaining can itself lower inflation by a significant amount. The impact of wage coordination on inflation is smaller and the effect less statistically significant, however, when central bank independence is high, presumably because the latter has already achieved much of the feasible reduction in inflation. Finally, Table 6.4 confirms that increases in the coordination of wage bargaining tend to reduce the rate of unemployment and do so more strongly as central bank independence increases.

Finally, Table 6.5 summarizes these results by reporting the estimated rates of inflation and unemployment that can be expected to occur at different levels of central bank independence and wage coordination and at the sample means

Table 6.4. *The estimated impact of a unit increase in coordination of wage bargaining at various degrees of independence of the central bank*

Level of central bank independence	Conditional parameter estimates for the effect of a unit increase in coordinated wage bargaining on . . .	
	Inflation	Unemployment
0.14 (New Zealand)	-3.79 $(1.48)^{.01}$	$-.822$ $(1.12)^{.24}$
0.37 (Italy)	-3.04 $(1.20)^{.01}$	-3.82 $(.620)^{.00}$
0.56 (Netherlands)	-2.43 $(1.18)^{.03}$	-6.30 $(.714)^{.00}$
0.75 (United States)	-1.82 $(1.37)^{.11}$	-8.78 $(1.18)^{.00}$
0.93 (Germany)	-1.24 $(1.67)^{.24}$	-11.1 $(1.72)^{.00}$

Notes: Estimated effect of a unit increase in CWB at that level of CBI (b_{cwb} + b_{cc}CBI) in bold; conditional standard-errors of the effects at that level of CBI in parentheses; p-level of one-sided t-test at that point superscripted in italics.

Table 6.5. *Estimated inflation and unemployment rates at different levels of central bank independence and wage coordination (at means of other variables)*

Central bank independence	Level of coordinated wage-bargaining					
	0.00		0.50		1.00	
	Infl	Unem	Infl	Unem	Infl	Unem
0.00	9.55	.948	7.43	1.45	5.31	1.95
0.25	8.39	3.83	6.67	2.70	4.96	1.57
0.50	7.23	6.71	5.92	3.95	4.60	1.19
0.75	6.07	9.59	5.16	5.20	4.25	.811
1.00	4.91	12.5	4.40	6.45	3.90	.431

of the other variables. The first columns in the table indicate that, when wage bargaining is entirely uncoordinated, a 0.25 increase in central bank independence (about the gap from Australia to the United States) reduces the rate of inflation by about 1.16 points but at the cost of increasing the rate of unemployment by about 2.88 points. By contrast, as the last two columns indicate, in settings where wage bargaining is highly coordinated, a similar increase in the independence of the central bank brings smaller marginal reductions in the rate of inflation ($-.36$) but does so without increasing the rate of unemployment (in fact it may lower unemployment a little: $-.38$).

V. IMPLICATIONS FOR COMPARATIVE POLITICAL ECONOMY

These findings have important implications for our understanding of the political economy. First, they lend strong support to the contention, long prominent in comparative political economy, that economic performance is deeply affected by the institutional organization of the political economy. It may be difficult at best, and misleading at worst, to explain economic performance without reference to cross-national variation in the institutional structures of the political economy.

Second, this analysis speaks to the problem of how coordination is secured in the economy. Many neoclassical models assume that the behavior of economic actors will be coordinated by competitive market mechanisms and that nonmarket institutions should be seen primarily as factors that interfere with effective coordination. However, our analysis suggests that, in many contexts, nonmarket institutions make an important, and sometimes indispensable, contribution to the coordination of economic behavior. That is precisely what institutional frameworks for coordinating wage bargaining do in the context of the signaling process between central banks and economic actors. In many settings, it may be unrealistic to assume that economic coordination will be secured solely via rational action in competitive markets in the context of full information. More attention must be devoted to the way in which diverse institutional arrangements resolve the coordination problems of the economy.

Third, our analysis also suggests that, when exploring the impact of institutional variables, we should be especially attentive to the presence of interaction effects among them (cf. Beck et al. 1993; Alvarez et al. 1991; Soskice 1991). The impact of central bank independence, for instance, seems to depend heavily on the character of a nation's wage bargaining system.

It is on these grounds that we challenge the influential claim that, by increasing the independence of its central bank, a nation can improve its rate of inflation without any adverse economic effects. Once the character of the wage-bargaining system is incorporated into the analysis, we find that this proposition holds true only for nations with relatively coordinated wage-bargaining systems. In nations where wage bargaining is not coordinated, increasing the independence of the central bank may lower the rate of inflation only at the cost of significant increases in unemployment. In support of this contention, we provide a theoretical rationale, evidence from close inspection of the critical German case, and results from an analysis of cross-national data.

In this context, it should be noted that our analysis departs to some extent from an older literature in comparative political economy that saw the presence of an independent central bank as an impediment to the achievement of effective economic performance (cf. Scharpf 1991). In some measure, that is because these studies defined economic performance largely in terms of the rate of unemployment while ours considers both unemployment and inflation.

There are more important respects in which our analysis differs from these antecedents, however. The latter were driven primarily by a Keynesian reasoning that saw demand stimulus as an effective way to lower rates of unemployment and independent central banks as an obstacle to such stimuli. By contrast, we begin from "new" classical assumptions which dictate more skepticism about the likelihood that a demand stimulus will reduce unemployment and more attention to strategic interactions in the whole economy. On this basis, we have developed a multifaceted rationale for why increases in central bank independence may generate higher levels of unemployment in some settings while enhancing inflation performance without substantial unemployment effects in others.

In general, the movement from these older lines of analysis to ours can be seen as one that shifts from an emphasis on interaction between the fiscal and monetary authorities toward an emphasis on the interaction between the monetary authority and wage and price contractors. We see this as a step forward but want to emphasize that the interaction between fiscal and monetary authorities continues to remain important and deserves more scrutiny than space has allowed us to provide here.

Finally, these findings have important implications for national policy makers. In particular, they suggest that enhancing the independence of the central bank may not be the economic panacea that many believe it to be. Central bank independence may provide the full gains promised for it only when it is combined with coordinated wage bargaining. But, unlike central bank independence, which can be legislated relatively easily, wage coordination is difficult to secure and substantially beyond the control of government policy. A nation's capacity for wage coordination depends on the character of a variety of social organizations, such as trade unions and employer confederations, which emerge out of a long historical process and may not be immediately amenable to political engineering (Levy 1993; Regini 1984). Thus, many governments that enhance the independence of their central bank may find the results somewhat disappointing.

VI. IMPLICATIONS FOR EUROPEAN MONETARY UNION

This analysis also has substantial implications for the monetary union that Europe is now entering. Economic and Monetary Union (EMU) is built around a central bank whose general structure and level of independence is modeled on the German Bundesbank. Many hope that, as a consequence, the new monetary union will achieve levels of economic performance equivalent to historic levels in Germany.

Our findings suggest that such aspirations are unlikely to be realized, because German levels of performance have depended not only on an independent central bank but also on a coordinated wage-bargaining system that was responsive to it. The European Union (EU) is unlikely ever to acquire Community-wide institutions for such coordination of wage bargaining. On the one hand, its leaders have yet to show any real interest in acquiring such institutions, as the halting nature of their steps toward a Social Charter indicates (Lange 1993; Leibfried and Pierson 1995; Streeck and Schmitter 1991; Streeck 1995). On the other hand, even if they sought more coordinated labor market institutions, the latter would be difficult to secure. Wide disparities in the way in which workers and employers are organized across the nations of the EU make it difficult to imagine how wage bargaining could be coordinated across the continent without large-scale reorganization; and the few efforts made by trade unions or employers to reorganize wage bargaining on a European level have been singularly unsuccessful (George 1992; Streeck and Schmitter 1991). As a result, in order to secure low rates of inflation, a European central bank may have to resort to relatively high levels of unemployment because it will lack the effective signaling process provided by a continent-wide system of wage coordination.[19]

More important yet, the common view that all nations will gain from European monetary union may be wrong (cf. European Commission 1989; Gros 1996: 26 et passim.). Our analysis suggests that the move to EMU may improve the economic performance of some nations relative to their past experience but could erode the performance of others. The precise effects experienced by each nation will be conditioned by the effectiveness of its existing institutions relative to those it acquires by virtue of joining the monetary union.

Some sense of these effects can be gleaned from Table 6.6, which reports the average postwar performance of nations possessing different combinations of institutions. Although realized performance under EMU will differ from these historical levels, the table does suggest how performance under the institutional conditions it provides is likely to compare with the performance that can be secured under the different institutional conditions found in its member states.[20] EMU will create an economic unit characterized by a highly independent central bank and uncoordinated wage bargaining. That is the situation represented by quadrant II in Table 6.6. Whether a nation will gain or lose over the long run from entry into EMU, in terms of inflation and unemployment, will depend on

19 This conclusion is reinforced by the finding that economies with more independent central banks tend to have higher sacrifice ratios. See, e.g., Walsh (1995).
20 Since we focus here on the economic effects of institutional context ceteris paribus, this analysis ignores other effects, both positive and negative, that the move to EMU may have, such as those following from lower transaction costs or the need to adjust to asymmetrical demand and supply-side shocks. On these and other effects, see Eichengreen (1992) and Kenen (1995).

Table 6.6. *National economic well-being under different institutional structures assessed by the inflation rate, the unemployment rate, and the Okun misery index, 1955–90*

		Level of central bank independence	
		Low	High
Degree of coordination in wage bargaining	Low	I MI: 12.2 π: 7.5 UE: 4.7	II MI: 10.9 π: 4.8 UE: 6.1
	High	III MI: 8.9 π: 6.2 UE: 2.3	IV MI: 7.6 π: 4.8 UE: 2.8

Notes: MI = misery index, π = inflation rate (%), UE = unemployment rate (%). See note to Table 6.1 for coding of CBI and CWB.

the quadrant of the table from which it is moving. Nations that have long had relatively dependent central banks and uncoordinated bargaining systems, such as Britain, Ireland, and France (in quadrant I), may gain slightly, at least as judged by the Okun misery index (i.e., the sum of inflation and unemployment rates), by virtue of acquiring a more independent central bank. Although they are not included in our empirical analysis, Greece, Portugal, and Spain probably also fall into this category. If they expect to replicate Germany's historic levels of performance, however, even these countries may be disappointed because they are moving to quadrant II rather than to quadrant IV, where Germany has been located.

By contrast, Table 6.6 suggests that virtually all other member states in the EU will experience pressures tending toward a deterioration in economic performance as a result of the move to monetary union because they are shifting from the institutional conditions of quadrants III or IV to those of quadrant II. Ironically, one of the biggest potential losers will be Germany, a prime mover behind the establishment of EMU. It has long benefited from the smooth interaction between its independent central bank and its coordinated wage-bargaining system. But this interaction will be disrupted because monetary policy will be controlled by a European central bank that faces a wide range of organizationally disparate and uncoordinated wage bargaining units. That bank cannot be expected to respond directly to German bargainers any more than to Danish or Spanish bargainers. Indeed, most nations that once had a coordinated wage-bargaining system may suffer because they will become part of a common currency area with a multiplicity of uncoordinated bargaining units. In the German case, Table 6.6 predicts a movement from an Okun score of about 7 to one that is closer to 11. Thus, the move to EMU may not be an unmitigated blessing, and its effects on national economic performance will be distributed unevenly across countries.

In addition to these national effects, the establishment of EMU may also have significant distributive consequences across different social groups inside each nation. It is well established that changes in the rate of inflation and the rate of unemployment have more adverse effects on some social groups than on others. Although it is difficult to identify all of these effects with precision, lower-skilled manual and clerical workers tend to suffer disproportionately from rising rates of unemployment (Wood 1994; Hibbs 1977). Thus, it is important that, even when the move to EMU improves the aggregate economic performance of a nation, as measured by the Okun index, it may shift the mixture of inflation and unemployment experienced there. Even those nations in quadrant I that should gain the most from entry can expect to experience higher levels of unemployment as a result. Indeed, from an institutional perspective, there is reason to expect EMU to conduce toward rates of unemployment higher than those most of its member nations have historically enjoyed, either because the new European central bank will be more independent than their own has been (and thus more likely to privilege inflation over unemployment) or because it will seek rates of inflation commensurate with past experience but without the efficient signaling mechanism provided by systems of coordinated wage bargaining. This suggests that those at the margins of the labor market may bear the greatest costs associated with the creation of European Monetary Union.

Of course, we emphasize that one must treat these inferences with caution. EMU is likely to have other economic effects not modeled here that could offset some of the distributive consequences on which we focus; and, because the figures in Table 6.6 are based on historical levels of performance, the actual levels of economic performance realized in the EMU are likely to diverge from them for a wide variety of reasons. In particular, since the inflationary increment built into wage bargains is greater in times of widespread inflation than in times of high unemployment, of the sort currently seen in Europe, both the credibility gains that can be secured via central bank independence and the corresponding costs of forgoing coordinated wage bargaining may be relatively low in the short term, showing up only if the European economy moves in a more inflationary direction. In the long run, however, the theory and evidence provided here suggest that European Monetary Union should have more uneven distributive effects within and across countries than is conventionally acknowledged.

To return finally to the German case, it may be that the best guide to what we can expect from EMU is not the familiar image of *Modell Deutschland* but the experience that Germany has had with unification after 1989. After all, the creation of a European monetary union is analogous in some respects to the process of German unification. High-wage and highly skilled economies will be joined to less developed regions under a single monetary authority. That authority will have to cope with a greater variety of economic shocks than did its national predecessors. New modalities for wage bargaining and fiscal coordination across the disparate regions of the union will have to be developed; and the various kinds of economic integration that should follow from monetary integration may generate substantial economic dislocation, as they did in Germany, albeit to a lesser degree because all member states are advanced capitalist economies.

In this context, the lessons that follow from the example of German unification are not altogether encouraging. The German system itself experienced severe strain as a result of unification. Two sources of strain deserve emphasis here. First, efforts to incorporate East Germany into the existing industrial relations system proved highly taxing and only partly successful. One result was high levels of industrial conflict, notably in the spring of 1993 when employers challenged the extension of the wage-bargaining system to the East (Locke and Jacoby 1995; Webber 1994; Silvia 1994). Second, unification also provoked conflict between the federal government and the Bundesbank, which customarily responds not only to wage bargains, as we have emphasized here, but also to the fiscal policies of the government. When the efforts of the latter to finance unification resulted in fiscal expansion, the Bundesbank responded with high interest rates to encourage fiscal restraint and dampen inflationary pressures. The consequences were far from ideal for the German or European economies.

European Monetary Union will pose similar, if less severe, challenges. It will disrupt the processes of signaling and coordination long established between central banks and wage bargainers in some nations, which may inspire broader changes in industrial relations systems (Soskice 1997). It will require the development of new relationships between the European central bank and the fiscal authorities of each nation, which have already been the subject of considerable controversy.[21] Moreover, in the context of continuing high unemployment, many member governments may seek more expansionary policies precisely when the new European central bank is seeking to establish its credibility with relatively rigorous monetary policies. One effect is likely to be higher levels of unemployment than many proponents of European Monetary Union currently envisage.[22] Another may be intensified pressure for institution-

---

21 At least some national governments have supported monetary union in the hope that it will allow them to implement more expansionary policies than were possible under a European Monetary System dominated by the Bundesbank, while others insist on greater fiscal and monetary strictness. See Fratianni and Von Hagen (1992:chs. 8, 9), Gros (1996:88 ff.), Frieden et al. (forthcoming), and Eichengreen (1992).

22 The case of the United States in the early 1980s, when the government ran high deficits while the Federal Reserve Bank pursued a tight monetary policy, suggests that significant employment effects, lasting up to ten years, can follow from this combination. See Krugman (1989), on the political

6.A. Data Appendix

We list here summary statistics and all the data necessary to replicate the postwar-average results presented in the text. Data analysis conducted in *Econometric Views* 2.0; *Stata* 5.0; and *Gauss-386i* v. 3.01. All data available from http://www-personal.umich.edu/~franzese.

Country	MI	UE	Infl.	CBI	CWB	GDP	Open	Uden	Lcab
United States	10.17	5.76	4.41	0.75	0.00	9.43	0.11	0.24	0.00
Japan	6.34	1.97	4.42	0.41	0.75	8.49	0.20	0.32	0.00
Germany	6.80	3.13	3.68	0.93	0.75	8.92	0.39	0.34	0.29
France	10.79	4.16	6.63	0.43	0.25	8.91	0.29	0.18	0.17
Italy	14.19	5.576	8.62	0.37	0.25	8.72	0.30	0.34	0.18
UK	12.25	4.88	7.37	0.42	0.00	8.95	0.37	0.43	0.33
Canada	11.49	6.43	5.06	0.61	0.00	9.25	0.39	0.30	0.00
Austria	6.57	2.18	4.39	0.65	1.00	8.71	0.46	0.55	0.65
Belgium	9.94	5.48	4.46	0.41	0.50	8.88	0.95	0.48	0.24
Denmark	11.51	4.85	6.65	0.53	0.75	8.94	0.52	0.67	0.64
Finland	10.75	3.10	7.66	0.49	0.75	8.78	0.43	0.54	0.39
Ireland	16.10	8.10	8.00	0.46	0.00	8.38	0.79	0.51	0.09
Netherlands	9.05	4.27	4.78	0.56	0.50	8.91	0.93	0.34	0.16
Norway	8.00	2.23	5.76	0.23	1.00	8.96	0.54	0.55	0.72
Sweden	8.46	1.73	6.73	0.30	1.00	9.03	0.45	0.73	0.85
Switzerland	5.00	0.89	4.11	0.84	0.75	9.32	0.53	0.32	0.23
Australia	10.56	3.95	6.61	0.47	0.25	9.10	0.28	0.46	0.22
New Zealand	9.22	1.34	7.88	0.14	0.25	8.97	0.43	0.58	0.27
Mean	9.96	4.01	5.96	0.50	0.49	9.15	0.46	0.44	0.31
Std. Dev.	2.88	2.038	1.578	0.20	0.37	0.20	0.23	0.15	0.24
Maximum	16.5	8.46	8.62	0.93	1.00	9.51	0.95	0.73	0.83
Minimum	4.98	0.87	3.68	0.15	0.00	8.60	0.11	18.3	0.00

Notes: MI = misery index; UE = unemployment; Infl. = inflation; CBI = central bank independence; CWB = coordination of wage bargaining; GDP = natural log of real GDP per capita; Open = (exports + imports)/GDP; Uden = fraction of labor force unionized; Lcab = fraction of cabinet seats held by left parties. See notes in the text for sources.

building to cope with the dilemmas of coordinating wage bargaining or fiscal and monetary policy in the new environment.

The larger point here is that the creation of a European monetary union will generate a variety of new coordination problems that will not automatically

economy of American monetary policy more generally Mayer (1990) and Wooley (1984), and on potential fiscal/monetary conflict under EMU, Kenen (1995:ch. 4) and Gros and Thygesen (1992:ch. 8).

be resolved by the presence of an independent central bank. The principal argument of this paper is that the resolution of such problems depends on the development of a larger system of institutional arrangements. An independent central bank trying to impose its will on a reluctant government or recalcitrant workforce is only a second-best solution to problems that could be tackled more effectively through a broader range of institutions. When contemplating institutional reform, it would be wise for national governments and European policy makers alike to consider the complete set of coordination problems they confront and the full range of institutional solutions that can be brought to bear on them.

References

Al-Marhubi, Farim and Thomas D. Willett. n.d. The anti-inflationary influence of corporatist structures and central bank independence: The importance of the hump-shaped hypothesis. Mimeo, Claremont McKenna College. Claremont, CA.

Alesina, Alberto. 1988. Macroeconomics and politics. *NBER Macroeconomics Annual*, 13–52.

Alesina, Alberto and Vittorio Grilli. 1993. The European central bank: Reshaping monetary politics in Europe. In *Establishing a central bank*, edited by Matthew Canzoneri, Vittorio Grilli, and Paul Masson. Cambridge: Cambridge University Press.

Alesina, Alberto and Lawrence Summers. 1993. Central bank independence and macroeconomic performance. *Journal of Money, Credit and Banking* 25(2): 151–63.

Alt, James and Kenneth Shepsle, eds. 1990. *Perspectives on Positive Political Economy*. New York: Cambridge University Press.

Alvarez, R. Michael, Geoffrey Garrett, and Peter Lange. 1991. Government partisanship, labor organization and macroeconomic performance. *American Political Science Review* 85(2):539–56.

Bade, Robin and Michael Parkin. 1982. Central bank laws and monetary policy. Mimeo, Department of Economics, University of Western Ontario.

Baglioni, Guido and Colin Crouch, eds. 1990. *European industrial relations: The challenge of flexibility*. London: Sage.

Barro, Robert and David Gordon. 1983a. Rules, discretion and reputation in a model of monetary policy. *Journal of Monetary Economics* 12:101–22.

——— 1983b. A positive theory of monetary policy in a natural rate model. *Journal of Political Economy* 91(4):589–610.

Beck, Nathaniel. 1982. Presidential influence on the federal reserve in the 1970s. *American Journal of Political Science* (August):415–45.

——— 1991. Comparing dynamic specifications: The case of presidential approval. *Political Analysis* 3:51–89.

Beck, Nathaniel, and Jonathan Katz. 1995. What to do (and not to do) with time-series-cross-section data in comparative politics. *American Political Science Review* 89(3):634–47.

200   UNIONS, EMPLOYERS, AND CENTRAL BANKS

Beck, Nathaniel, and Jonathan Katz. 1996. Nuisance *versus* substance: Specifying and estimating time-series-cross-section models. *Political Analysis* 6:1–36.

Beck, Nathaniel, Jonathan Katz, R. Michael Alvarez, Geoffrey Garrett, and Peter Lange. 1993. Government partisanship, labor organization, and macroeconomic performance: A corrigendum. *American Political Science Review* 87(4): 945–8.

Berghahn, Volker and Detlev Karsten. 1987. *Industrial relations in West Germany*. Oxford: Berg.

Bleaney, Michael. 1996. Central bank independence, wage-bargaining structure, and macroeconomic performance in OECD countries. *Oxford Economic Papers* 48:20–38.

Bruno, Michael and Jeffrey Sachs. 1985. *Economics of worldwide stagflation*. Cambridge, MA: Harvard University Press.

Calmfors, Lars. 1993. Centralization of wage bargaining and economic performance – a survey. Stockholm: Institute for International Economic Studies Seminar Paper # 536.

Calmfors, Lars and John Driffill. 1988. Centralization of wage bargaining. *Economic Policy* 6(April):13–61.

Cameron, David. 1984. Social democracy, corporatism, labor quiescence, and the representation of economic interest in advanced capitalist society. In *Order and conflict in contemporary capitalism*, edited by John H. Goldthorpe, 143–78. New York: Oxford University Press.

Canzoneri, Matthew, Vittorio Grilli, and Paul Masson, eds. 1993. *Establishing a central bank: Issues in Europe and lessons from the United States*. Cambridge: Cambridge University Press.

Carlin, Wendy and David Soskice. 1990. *Macroeconomics and the wage bargain*. Oxford: Oxford University Press.

Clark, W., U. N. Reichert, with S. L. Lomas, and K. L. Parker. 1998. International and domestic constraints on political business cycles in OECD economies." *International Organization* 52:87–120.

Crouch, Colin. 1993. *Industrial relations and European state traditions*. Oxford: Clarendon.

Cukierman, Alex. 1992. *Central bank strategy, credibility and independence: Theory and evidence*. Cambridge, MA: MIT Press.

Cukierman, A., 1997. Central bank independence, coordination of wage bargaining, inflation and unemployment. Mimeo, Tel-Aviv University School of Economics.

Eichengreen, Barry. 1992. Should the Maastricht treaty be saved? *Princeton Studies in International Finance*, 74:38ff.

1996. European Monetary Unification and International Monetary Cooperation. Paper prepared for the Council on Foreign Relations Study Group on Transatlantic Economic Relations.

Eichengreen, Barry and Jeffry Frieden, eds. 1997. *The political economy of European integration*. Ann Arbor: University of Michigan Press.

Eijffinger, S. C. W. and J. De Haan. 1996. *The political economy of central bank independence*, Special Papers in International Economics #19, International Finance Section, Department of Economics, Princeton University.

European Commission. 1990. One market, one money. *European Economy* 44 (October).

Ferner, Anthony and Richard Hyman, eds. 1992. *Industrial relations in the new Europe*. Oxford: Blackwell.

Flanagan, Robert J., David W. Soskice, and Lloyd Ulman. 1983. *Unionism, economic stabilization and incomes policies*. Washington, DC: Brookings Institution.

Franzese, Robert J., Jr. 1994. Central bank independence, sectoral interest and the wage bargain. Harvard Center for European Studies Working Paper # 56.

1996. *The political economy of over-commitment: A comparative study of democratic management of the Keynesian welfare state*. Ph.D. Dissertation, Harvard University.

1999. Monetary policy and wage/price bargaining: Macro-institutional interactions in the traded, public, and sheltered sectors. In *Varieties of capitalism: The institutional foundations of comparative advantage*, edited by Peter Hall and David Soskice. Forthcoming.

Fratianni, Michele, Jürgen von Hagen, and Christopher Waller. 1992. The Maastricht way to EMU. *Princeton Essays in International Finance*, (June):187.

Fratianni, Michele and Jürgen von Hagen. 1992. *The European monetary system and the European monetary union*. Boulder, CO: Westview Press.

Frieden, Jeffry, et al. (forthcoming). *Towards economic and monetary union: Problems and prospects*. Oxford: Oxford University Press.

Garrett, Geoffrey and Christopher Way. 1995. The rise of the public-sector unions and the decline of corporatism. Paper presented at the 1995 Midwest Political Science Association Conference, Chicago.

George, Michael. 1992. Euro-corporatism after 1992. Paper presented to the Annual Meeting of the American Political Science Association.

Golden, Miriam. 1993. The dynamics of trade unionism and national economic performance. *American Political Science Review* 87:439–54.

Golden, Miriam and Michael Wallerstein. 1999. Trade union organization and industrial relations in the postwar era in 12 countries. In *Continuity and change in contemporary capitalism*, edited by Herbert Kitschelt, Gary Marks, Peter Lange, and John Stephens. Cambridge: Cambridge University Press.

Goodhart, Charles A. E. 1995. The political economy of monetary union. In *Understanding interdependence*, edited by Peter B. Kenen, 448–506. Princeton, NJ: Princeton University Press.

Goodman, John. 1992. *Monetary sovereignty: The politics of central banking in Western Europe*. Ithaca, NY: Cornell University Press.

Grilli, Vittorio, Donato Masciandaro, and Guido Tabellini. 1991. Political and monetary institutions and public finance policies in the industrial countries. *Economic Policy* 1991:341–92.

Gros, Daniel. 1996. *Towards economic and monetary union: Problems and prospects*. Brussels: Center for European Policy Studies.

Gros, Daniel and Neils Thygesen. 1992. *European monetary integration.* New York: St. Martin's.

Hall, Peter A. 1986. *Governing the economy.* New York: Oxford University Press.

1994. Central bank independence and coordinated wage bargaining: Their interaction in Germany and Europe. *German Politics and Society* (Autumn): 1–23.

Hall, Peter A. and Robert J. Franzese, Jr. 1998. Mixed signals: Central bank independence, coordinated wage bargaining, and European Monetary Union. *International Organization* 52(3): 505–35.

Havrilesky, Thomas and James Granato. 1993. Determinants of inflationary performance: Corporatist structures vs. central bank autonomy. *Public Choice* 76: 249–61.

Hibbs, Douglas. 1977. Political parties and macroeconomic policy. *American Political Science Review* 71: 1467–87.

Hirsch, Fred and John Goldthorpe, eds. 1978. *The political economy of inflation.* London: Martin Robertson.

Iversen, Torben. 1994. Wage bargaining, monetary regimes and economic performance in organized market economies: Theory and evidence. Harvard Center for European Studies Working Paper #59.

1996. The real effects of money. Mimeo, Harvard University.

Iversen, Torben and David Soskice. 1997. Central bank–trade union interactions and the equilibrium rate of employment. Mimeo, Harvard University and Wissenschaftszentrum-Berlin.

Katzenstein, Peter. 1987. *Policy and politics in West Germany.* Philadelphia: Temple University Press.

Kenen, Peter B. 1995. *Economic and monetary union in Europe.* New York: Cambridge University Press.

Krugman, Paul. 1989. *Exchange-rate instability.* Cambridge, MA: MIT Press.

Kydland, Finn and Edward Prescott. 1977. Rules rather than discretion: The inconsistency of optimal plans. *Journal of Political Economy* (June): 473–86.

Lane, Jan-Eric, David McKay, and Kenneth Newton. 1991. *Political data handbook: OECD countries.* New York: Oxford University Press.

Lange, Peter. 1993. Maastricht and the social protocol: Why did they do it? *Politics and Society* 21(1): 5–36.

Lange, Peter and Geoffrey Garrett. 1985. The politics of growth: Strategic interaction and economic performance in the advanced industrial democracies, 1974–1980. *Journal of Politics* 47: 792–827.

Layard, Richard, Stephen Nickell, and Richard Jackman. 1991. *Unemployment: Macroeconomic performance and the labor market.* Oxford: Oxford University Press.

Leibfried, Stephan and Paul Pierson, eds. 1995. *European social policy: Between fragmentation and integration.* Washington, DC: Brookings Institution.

Levy, Jonah. 1993. Tocqueville's revenge: Dilemmas of institutional reform in postwar France. Doctoral Dissertation, MIT.

Lindberg, Leon and Charles Maier, eds. 1985. *The politics of inflation and economic stagnation.* Washington, DC: Brookings Institution.

Locke, Richard M. and Wade Jacoby. 1995. The dilemmas of diffusion: Institutional transfer and the remaking of vocational training practices in Eastern Germany. Mimeo, MIT, Cambridge, MA.

Lohmann, Susanne. 1992. Optimal commitment in monetary policy. *American Economic Review* 82: 273–86.

1994. Federalism and central bank autonomy: The politics of German monetary policy, 1957–1992. Mimeo, University of California at Los Angeles.

Markovits, Andrei S. 1986. *The politics of the West German trade unions*. New York: Cambridge University Press.

Mayer, Thomas, ed. 1990. *The political economy of American monetary policy*. New York: Cambridge University Press.

Milgrom, Paul and John Roberts. 1992. *Economics, organization and management*. Englewood Cliffs, NJ: Prentice-Hall.

Persson, Torsten and Guido Tabellini, eds. 1994. *Monetary and fiscal policy*. Cambridge, MA: MIT Press.

Posen, Adam. 1995a. Central bank independence and disinflationary credibility: A missing link? *Brookings Papers on Economic Activity.*

1995b. Is central bank independence (and low inflation) the result of financial opposition to inflation? *NBER Macroeconomics Annual* 253–74.

Regini, Marino. 1984. The conditions for political exchange: How concertation emerged and collapsed in Italy and Great Britain. In *Order and conflict in contemporary capitalism*, edited by John H. Goldthorpe, 124–42. New York: Oxford University Press.

Rogoff, Kenneth. 1985. The optimal degree of commitment to an intermediate monetary target. *Quarterly Journal of Economics* 11: 1169–90.

Scharpf, Fritz. 1988. Game theoretical interpretations of inflation and unemployment in Western Europe. *Journal of Public Policy* 7(1): 227–57.

1991. *Crisis and choice in European social democracy*. Ithaca, NY: Cornell University Press.

Silvia, Stephen J. 1994. A house divided: German employers' associations after unification. Paper presented to the Industrial Relations Research Seminar, MIT.

Soskice, David. 1990. Wage determination: The changing role of institutions in advanced industrialized countries. *Oxford Review of Economic Policy* 6(4): 36–61.

1991. The institutional infrastructure for international competitiveness: A comparative analysis of the UK and Germany. In *The economics of the New Europe*, edited by A. B. Atkinson and R. Brunetta. London: Macmillan.

1997. The future political economy of EMU: Rethinking the effects of monetary integration on Europe. Wissenschaftszentrum-Berlin, Discussion Paper.

Streeck, Wolfgang. 1984a. *Industrial relations in West Germany*. London: Heinemann.

1984b. Pay restraint without incomes policy: Institutionalized monetarism and industrial unionism in Germany. In *The return of incomes policy*, edited by Ronald Dore, Robert Boyer, and Zoe Marn, 118–140. London: Pinter.

1995. From market-making to state-building: Reflections on the political economy of European social policy. In *European social policy*, edited by Stephan

Leibfried and Paul Pierson, 389–431. Washington, DC: Brookings Institution.

Streeck, Wolfgang and Philippe Schmitter. 1991. From national corporatism to transnational pluralism. *Politics and Society* (June): 133–64.

Swank, Duane. 1989. Partisan policy: Political parties, economic interest representation, and fiscal policies in the capitalist democracies, 1970–85. Mimeo, Marquette University.

Swenson, Peter. 1989. *Fair shares.* Ithaca, NY: Cornell University Press.

Thelen, Kathleen. 1991. *Union of parts: Labor politics in postwar Germany.* Ithaca, NY: Cornell University Press.

1992. Union structure and strategic choice: The politics of flexibility in the German metalworking industries. In *Union politics in comparative perspective,* edited by Miriam Golden and Jonas Pontusson. Ithaca, NY: Cornell University Press.

1994. Beyond corporatism: Toward a new framework for the study of labor in advanced capitalism. *Comparative Politics* 27: 107–24.

Tsebelis, George. 1990. *Nested games.* Berkeley: University of California Press.

Visser, Jelle. 1992. Trade union membership data base. Department of Sociology, University of Amsterdam (as cited in Golden and Wallerstein 1999).

Walsh, Carl E. 1995. Central bank independence and the short-run output–inflation trade-off in the European Community. In *Monetary and fiscal policy in an integrated Europe,* edited by Barry Eichengreen, Jeffrey Frieden, and Jürgen von Hagen. Berlin: Springer Verlag.

Webber, Douglas. 1994. The end of solidarity: The German solidarity pact. *West European Politics.*

Woldendorp, J., H. Keman, and I. Budge. 1994. Party government in 20 Democracies. *European Journal of Political Research* 24(1): Special Issue.

Wood, Adrian. 1994. *North–south trade, employment and inequality.* Oxford: Clarendon Press.

Wooley, John. 1984. *Monetary politics: The federal reserve and the politics of monetary policy.* New York: Cambridge University Press.

DECENTRALIZATION, MONETARISM, AND THE SOCIAL DEMOCRATIC WELFARE STATE

Torben Iversen

One of the primary dilemmas facing social democracy in the 1990s is that governments have to increasingly choose between equality and employment. This marks a critical change from the 1960s and 1970s, when social democracy offered a viable political strategy to *simultaneously* promote equality and employment for all. The old strategy – epitomized by the Scandinavian countries – was premised on a combination of centralized and solidaristic wage bargaining, flexible monetary policies, and expansion of a labor-intensive and redistributive welfare state. In this chapter I argue that this strategy has been undermined by two broad developments.

First, the rise of new technology and growing competition from newly industrializing countries have caused a diversification of the unemployment risk structure and a bifurcation of the labor force into a highly qualified, secure, and world-market-integrated segment, and a less-qualified, insecure, and sheltered segment. This has shattered the consensus underpinning solidaristic wage policies and the universalistic welfare state. Second, capital market integration has constrained the capacity of governments to run deficits and pursue inflationary monetary policies, thus limiting the incentives for employers and better-paid workers to agree to centralized controls on wage increases. As a result of these changes, pressure is mounting on governments of all stripes to adopt nonaccommodating monetary and social policies with the purpose of *deterring* wage–price militancy and *inducing* wage flexibility. Such policies engender greater inequalities, however, leaving social democracy with the difficult dilemma of having to chose between more inequality and lower employment.

During the "golden period" of social democracy, the trend across partisan divides and advanced democracies was to strengthen institutions and policies that facilitated a coordinated accommodation of worker and business interests, thereby forging convergence around a social democratic model of economic and social policy-making. In the 1980s and 1990s, by contrast, convergence in Northern Europe appears to occur around a conservative or "Germanic" model of capitalism, by which wages are set below the peak level ("industry bargaining"), macroeconomic are tied to a strict nonaccommodating policy rule ("monetarism"), and social policies perpetuate status differentials and labor market dependence ("commodification").

The rest of this chapter is an attempt to substantiate these claims both theoretically and empirically, with a focus on Northern Europe and especially the changes that have occurred in Denmark and Sweden since the early 1980s. The first section outlines a conceptual framework for understanding the causal interactions between economic macroinstitutions and policies. The second section explores the empirical implications of this framework for understanding economic performance using a variable-oriented statistical approach. The third section focuses on institutional change and offers a more in-depth comparative analysis of institutional change in two Scandinavian countries: Denmark and Sweden. The final section concludes with a discussion of the strategic options open to social democracy.

A FRAMEWORK FOR ANALYSIS

The analysis focuses on the interactions of three macroinstitutions that *jointly* shape economic behavior and outcomes: *the collective bargaining system, the macroeconomic policy regime*, and the *welfare state*. This institutional nexus is characterized by a certain division of labor between actors that are particularly well-positioned to influence policies in each institutional domain. Organized groups of capital and labor are especially powerful in the collective-bargaining system, governments and bureaucrats tend to dominate the macroeconomic policy regime, while influence over welfare state policies tends to be shared more evenly among executives, parliaments, and service providers.

The existence of these interconnected institutions, and the political division of labor between them, creates a context of strategic interdependence where decisions in each domain shape, and are shaped by, decisions in other domains. There are two fundamental approaches to the study of these institutional interactions. One is to treat the institutions as exogenously given constraints on behavior and then hypothesize the economic and distributional consequences of such behavior. The other is to take the couplings between economic institutions and outcomes as given, and then hypothesize the likely structure of institutional preferences and probable institutional choices. In this "nested game" formulation, the choices in the higher-order institutional game depend on the equilibrium outcomes in each of the institutional subgames (Tsebelis 1990). Since this chapter is concerned with strategic options under different institutional constraints, as well as with institutional change, it is necessary to engage in both levels of analysis. I start the discussion with a characterization of the subgames, exploiting the insights into these in the recent political economy literature.

MACROINSTITUTIONS AND ECONOMIC OUTCOMES

Beginning with the macroeconomic regime, there are two dominant views. On the one hand, new classical economic theory implies that there are economic benefits to be achieved from the government credibly committing to an anti-inflationary, or nonaccommodating, policy rule.[1] According to this view, the ability of governments to pursue expansionary monetary policies raises inflation expectations and creates uncertainty about the future because governments face short-term political incentives to inflate (the so-called time-inconsistency problem). Institutionalization of a nonaccommodating policy rule is therefore required to stabilize expectations and to facilitate downward price–wage adjustments to external shocks. By contrast, new Keynesian economists argue that policy flexibility is important because imperfectly competitive product and labor markets preclude downward adjustment of prices and wages in the event of an external shock (prices are "sticky"). Under these circumstances, producers will be demand-constrained, and real-wage adjustment will be feasible only through expansionary fiscal and monetary policies.

Though hotly contested in the economic literature, the two positions are in my view compatible once the role of the wage-setting system is taken into account. Thus, in highly centralized systems, the privileged position of peak associations of unions and employers creates high capacity for real-wage restraint (Cameron 1984; Lange and Garrett 1985; Calmfors and Driffill 1988), but low capacity for nominal wage restraint (Hibbs and Locking 1996; Moene and Wallerstein 1993; Iversen 1996). The reason is related to the need for the confederal leadership to forge distributive compromises between high- and low-wage unions. Such compromises almost invariably lead to egalitarian wage policies because the bargaining position of low-wage unions is typically superior *inside* the confederal structure as compared to *outside* it.[2] In turn, solidaristic wage policies are linked to monetary policies via the incentives of peak-level bargainers to use inflationary wage demands as a "hedge" against inequalizing, market-generated wage-drift (i.e., wage increases above the negotiated rates).

1 Although there is an appreciation of the problem that a strict adherence to a rule has costs in the form of lost policy flexibility (see especially Rogoff 1985; Lohmann 1992).

2 In a decentralized bargaining system, by contrast, weak unions lack veto power over distributive outcomes and will be more vulnerable to slack labor-market conditions. In the jargon of bargaining theory, the "inside options" of low-wage unions tend to be superior to their "outside options," leading to a gradual compression of wages.

Because wage-drift tends to primarily benefit high-wage groups (whose wages are held back in the collective-bargaining process), it undermines the distributive terms of the centralized wage bargain. Confederal leaders are therefore prone to demand nominal-wage increases that lead to "excessive" total wage increases during periods of low to moderate economic growth. This kind of nominal-wage rigidity produces sticky prices that can be combined with real-wage flexibility only if some of the nominal increases are accommodated through growth in the money supply (as advocated by del Keynesians). Precisely because centralized unions understand the need for such real-wage adjustment, they are predisposed to accept inflation-induced cuts in real wages.

This situation contrasts to intermediately decentralized – that is, industry- or sector-based – bargaining systems in which there are strong incentives for unions (especially in the sheltered sectors) to free-ride on the restraint of others. Such incentives make it difficult to achieve the kind of mutual accommodation of wage and monetary policies that are feasible in centralized systems. Instead, restrained price–wage behavior can only be accomplished if unions and employers know with great certainty that militant price-wage behavior will be "punished" by nonaccommodating policy responses, which dampen demand and raise unemployment (Hall 1994; Iversen 1998; Soskice and Iversen forthcoming). Credible policy commitments thus help deter militant price–wage behavior, at the same time as nominal-wage adjustment is facilitated by lower pressures for wage solidarity (which is inversely related to decentralization). The new classical scenario of flexible downward wage–price adjustments in the context of a credible noninflationary policy rule is therefore better approximated in (semi)decentralized than in centralized bargaining systems.

It is important to point out that this logic does *not* extend to highly fragmented bargaining systems in which the behavior of wage setters is so poorly coordinated that externalities are completely discounted.[3] A monetary deterrence strategy is effective *only* if economic agents are sufficiently well-organized and coordinated to behave in a nonmyopic, strategic fashion – when agents possess "strategic competence in Fritz Scharpt's (1991) terminology." In bargaining systems in which neither employers nor workers possess such competence, collective restraint turns into a perverse collective-action problem. By implication, militant price–wage behavior in a fragmented system is tempered only by actual – as opposed to anticipated – demand constraints and unemployment. The distinction proposed by Soskice (1990) between coordinated market economies (where the coordinating capacity of employers and workers is high) and liberal market economies (where such capacity is absent) is thus highly salient for my argument.

---

3 An exception is feasible if economic conditions are stable over long periods of time since the use of contingent strategies and learning may lead to what Scharpf, following Dahl and Lindblom, has called ecological coordination (1991:177).

Turning now to the role of the welfare state, Esping-Andersen (1990) has convincingly argued that a very salient aspect of social policies is their capacity to "decommodify" labor by affording workers a guaranteed source of income outside the market. Welfare regimes thus have a direct influence on the incentives that individuals and groups face in the labor market. Theoretically, the welfare state intersects with the bargaining system and the economic policy regime in two principal ways. First, to the extent that publicly provided services and cash benefits are viewed by workers as part of their income – what is sometimes referred to as the *social wage* – the government can influence the behavior and incentives of unions by altering the size and composition of this wage. In centralized systems an expansion of solidaristic – that is, decommodifying and egalitarian – welfare benefits can help to contain the wage demands from especially low-wage groups. In this fashion, the government can potentially ameliorate the inflationary pressures from solidaristic wage policies, while at the same time contributing to wage leveling.[4] In (semi)decentralized bargaining systems, on the other hand, an egalitarian social wage will raise the wages of low-paid groups *without* ensuring compensating wage restraint among the better-paid. Contrary to the wage-dampening effects of solidaristic welfare policies in centralized systems, such policies are prone to *fuel*, rather than to contain, wage competition.

The second point of intersection between the character of the welfare state and the other parts of the macroinstitutional nexus pertains to the government's public employment policies. Class cooperation in highly centralized bargaining systems has always been premised on the capacity and willingness of the government to guarantee full employment and to compensate workers generously for temporary spells of unemployment. By *socializing the risks of unemployment* the government facilitates "responsible" union behavior (Esping-Andersen 1990: ch. 7). Such expansionary pressures on public-sector employment are amplified by solidaristic wage policies that foreclose growing employment in low-productivity private-sector service production (Iversen and Wren 1998). In decentralized systems, by contrast, upward solidaristic pressures on public employment are lower, and expansionary employment policies weaken the causal

---

4 The role of the state as a "compensator" for wage restraint has long been recognized in the neo-corporatist literature (e.g., Hibbs 1978; Cameron 1984; Robertson 1990). In return for wage moderation, unions are "rewarded" by an increase in the social wage. Yet the logic of this argument differs from mine, and its explanatory status is in dispute (Lange 1984). The problem is that the social wage is a public good from the perspective of unions, and hence cannot rationally forestall free-riding behavior. My argument, however, does not conceptualize the social wage as a compensation mechanism for labor as such, but rather focuses on its function in facilitating an internal distributive compromise between high- and low-wage constituencies. To the extent that the social wage can be viewed as an extension of the centralized bargaining system, therefore, the sectoral compromise underpinning solidaristic wage policies will contribute to an expansion of a redistributive welfare state. In this manner, the redistributive aspects of centralized bargaining transcend the narrow confines of the private bargaining system and "spill over" into welfare policies (the social wage).

linkage between wage behavior and unemployment – a linkage that is central to an effective deterrence strategy.

THE POLITICS OF INSTITUTIONAL CHANGE

Having described the strategic interaction between governments and private economic agents in different institutional domains, the question of institutional preferences and choices can now be addressed. The discussion will be brief because institutional change depends on a large number of contingent factors that are better addressed in the empirical analysis. A few important theoretical issues, however, can usefully be highlighted at this point.

Starting from the observation that the interest realization of different societal groups is affected in different ways by the distributive and economic outcomes of institutionally mediated microbehavior, organized groups and individuals will prefer institutions that produce favorable outcomes to themselves, subject to the constraint that the pursuit of such preferences does not lead to offsetting, and greater, losses in aggregate welfare. Two mechanisms in particular circumscribe distributive struggles from producing outcomes that are grossly inefficient.

The first is *sociotropic economic voting*, or the tendency of voters to support policies that have favorable macroeconomic consequences. This type of voting (as opposed to "pocketbook" voting) is known to have played a significant role in many of the elections held in industrialized democracies since the Second World War (see especially Lewis-Beck 1988, Powell and Whitten 1993). Sociotropic voting places a constraint on the extent to which political parties and partisan governments can pursue distributive/ideological goals that interfere with economic efficiency. Although voters may be mobilized to support an economic policy program that does not produce immediate results, and even if distributive preferences may interfere with concern for performance, policies that produce persistently poor performance are unlikely to be the most successful in mobilizing electoral support.[5] As Stephen Elkin notes, "sustained poor performance, and thus low or declining levels of material well-being, will mean electoral difficulties and possibly electoral rout" (1985:187).

The second mechanism, referring specifically to organized sectors of labor and capital, is the *macroeconomic context* in which institutional preferences are formed. Though both employers and workers are divided internally over the relative importance of wage restraint and wage flexibility, the relative salience

---

5 In a slightly different formulation, the median voter – who has a significant impact on policies because her support is crucial for legislative majorities – will typically be left relatively unaffected by redistribution, but will be affected by efficiency. Policies that do not pay close attention to efficiency will therefore be prone to defection by the median voter.

of these concerns is conditioned by the character of both the monetary regime and the welfare state. For example, in a macroeconomic environment in which the government pursues full-employment policies and in which welfare benefits are highly decommodifying, employers and workers in the exposed sectors are prone to support centralized bargaining institutions as a means to control wage costs, *even* if they oppose the distributive consequences that go along with such institutions. As in the case of governments, when distributional interests cannot be satisfied without substantial sacrifices in efficiency, rational behavior can compel groups to support institutions that are not their first preference.

On the notion that political battles over institutions tend to be constrained by a concern for efficiency, one may identify three prevalent "clusters" of institutions, or ideal-type institutional couplings: (i) one combining centralized bargaining and a flexible monetary regime with a universalistic welfare state (the "Scandinavian model"), (ii) one combining decentralized bargaining and a nonaccommodating regime with a corporatist welfare state regime (the "Germanic model"), and (iii) one combining a fragmented bargaining system with a means-tested and highly decommodifying welfare state (the "Anglo-Saxon model"). Underpinning these three clusters are causal mechanisms that link change in one institution to changes in others. Specifically, I argue below that the combination of capital–market integration, technological change, and electoral realignments over the past two decades have shifted the relative power of actors with conflicting institutional interests in such a way as to undermine the political and economic viability of the Scandinavian model.

The following empirical analysis is divided into two parts. In the first I test the implications of the institutional argument for economic outcomes (the "subgames"). Is it indeed the case that particular institutional couplings are systematically linked to certain economic outcomes and that some couplings produce superior performance? In the second section I discuss how changes in the political balance of power in each of the three semiautonomous institutional domains have undermined the political-economic viability of centrally coordinated political economies.

INSTITUTIONS AND ECONOMIC OUTCOMES: STATISTICAL EVIDENCE

The following analysis is based on time-series data for ten OECD countries in the period from 1973 to 1993. The ten countries – Austria, Belgium, Denmark, Finland, Germany, Japan, Netherlands, Norway, Sweden, and Switzerland – all belong to David Soskice's category of coordinated market economies for which it is reasonable to assume strategic competence (or capacity for coordination) on the part of the main economic agents.

OPERATIONALIZATIONS

Centralization is measured by a composite measure for the locus of bargaining authority and the number and size of bargaining agents. At any level of bargaining, the smaller the number of bargaining units, and the more uneven their size, the higher the degree of centralization. When several bargaining levels are involved (the national and industry levels, for example), centralization is a weighted average of the different levels, with weights determined by the relative authority over the wage-setting process wielded at each level. Specifically, centralization (CEN) is defined as $\Sigma_{ij} w_i p_{ij}^2$ where w_i is the weight accorded to each bargaining level i ($\Sigma w_i = 1$), and p_{ij} is the share of workers covered by union (or federation) j at level i.[6] The construction of the index is explained in detail in Iversen (1999:ch. 3).

The monetary regime is measured by a *hard-currency index* (CUR) that is based on the differential growth in exchange rates across countries.[7] The index is normalized to vary between 0 and 1, with low values reflecting a relatively depreciating currency and high values reflecting a relatively appreciating currency. The idea is that currency traders buy and sell according to their forecast of monetary policy conditions in different countries and that a relatively appreciating currency will reflect more restrictive, nonaccommodating monetary policies. The alternative to this policy-based measure is to use available indexes of central bank independence. These are all impressionistic in nature, however, and completely insensitive to changes over time – limitations that can be quite severe when using panel data for a small set of countries. Besides, even if we assumed that these indexes accurately measured central bank independence, we could not be confident that they accurately captured commitment to a nonaccommodating policy.[8]

The *welfare regime* is measured by unemployment compensation rates and public-sector employment. Both variables are highly salient indicators of decommodification, and since both are expected to have similar effects on labor market behavior and economic performance, they were combined into an *index of commodification* (COM) that is the average of unemployment compensation rates and total public-sector employment (after standardization of both variables).[9] The former is measured as the average unemployment compensation rate over a

---

6 The weighting of p by itself (p^2) ensures that a very uneven distribution of members (i.e., where a few unions are dominant) leads to a higher centralization score than if the unions were equally sized.

7 The index was created by partitioning the 1973–93 period into three subperiods of varying length. The rule for the partitioning was that within-period variance in growth rates should be minimized, while between-period variance should be maximized. No country exhibited more than three distinct subperiods, and in some cases there is little variance between the periods.

8 Still, central bank independence indexes are highly correlated with the hard-currency index, and Iversen (1998a) contains results for the former that are very similar to those reported below.

9 The index was normalized to have the same range as the hard-currency index.

three-year period for a representative 40-year-old unemployed person, taking into account different family circumstances (single or married, with or without working spouse) and previous levels of earnings.[10] The data for public-sector employment is based on OECD's standardized measures of government employment as a percentage of total employment. As a check on the validity of the index, the cross-time means were compared to the (static) decommodification index developed by Esping-Andersen (1990:52). It turns out that the two measures are tightly related with a correlation coefficient of $-.95$.

FINDINGS

Table 7.1 shows the results of a pooled cross-sectional time-series analysis using ordinary least squares estimation and panel robust standard errors.[11] In addition to the theoretical variables just discussed, several control variables were incorporated into the analysis. $LEFT_{i,t}$ measures the left partisan composition of governments and varies from 2 (government completely dominated by right parties) to 4 (government completely dominated by left parties). It is based on the distribution of cabinet positions between parties weighted by these parties' position on an ideological LR-scale obtained from Castles and Mair (1984).[12] The variable is designed to "pick up" any effects of partisan politics that are not passing through either monetary or social policies. $EXMAR_{i,t}$ is an economic control variable measuring the yearly growth in each country's export market. Higher growth obviously should be associated with lower unemployment. $UNOECD_t$ is the average rate of unemployment across OECD countries and is designed to remove any international diffusion effects from a general change in employment. $UN_{i,t-1}$ and $UN_{i,t-2}$ are lagged dependent variables with one- and two-year lags, respectively. The dummy variable called Fin_{91-93} is included to control for the collapse in the large Finnish trade with the former Soviet Union and the ensuing deep recession. Such cataclysmic events are neither anticipated by the model, nor do they raise serious theoretical questions about its validity.[13]

10 The data are biyearly and from the OECD Database on Unemployment Benefit Entitlements and Replacement Rates. The compensation rate for the first year of unemployment is weighted twice that of the second or third year since the compensation rates for the first year of unemployment are likely to influence union wage policies more than rates for the second and third year. Compensation rates beyond this three-year time horizon are assumed not to affect the wage behavior of unions. In one case, Sweden, the data were adjusted to take into account that unemployed in this country can reearn rights to full compensation by accepting a guaranteed employment offer in a labor-market program. The low legal compensation rates for the second and third years are otherwise highly misleading.
11 For an excellent discussion of pooled time-series regression, in particular the superiority of dynamic OLS techniques, see Beck and Katz (1995).
12 The index was constructed by Tom Cusack, and I am grateful to him for letting me use his data.
13 Additional variables, including one measuring dependency on energy imports and one measuring exposure to trade, were found to have negligible effects on the results. These variables were subsequently dropped from the analysis for the purpose of presentational economy.

Table 7.1. *OLS estimates of the effects of institutional variables on the rate of unemployment*

	Predicted sign	Regression estimates and *t*-statistics					
		Model I		Model II		Full model	
		b	t^a	b	t^a	b	t^a
a		2.00	4.28*	2.09	4.04*	2.32	4.27*
$CEN_{i,t}$	−	−3.47	−3.86*	−3.38	−3.38*	−4.04	−3.92*
$CUR_{i,t}$	−	−1.42	−3.63*	−1.26	−3.13*	−0.93	−2.04**
$COM_{i,t}$	−	—	—	—	—	−0.75	−1.65√
$CEN_{i,t}*CUR_{i,t}$	+	7.03	2.94*	—	—	4.50	1.35
$CEN_{i,t}*COM_{i,t}$	+	—	—	6.02	2.91*	3.63	1.33
$LEFT_{i,t}$		−0.10	−1.37	−0.13	−1.59	−0.14	−1.79√
$EXMAR_{i,t}$		−0.07	−5.44*	−0.07	−5.50*	−0.06	−5.45*
$UNOEDC_t$		−0.03	−0.91	−0.02	−0.62	−0.03	−0.76
$UN_{i,t-1}$		1.46	20.96*	1.47	21.49*	1.46	21.41*
$UN_{i,t-1}$		−0.53	−7.89*	−0.55	−8.36*	−0.53	−8.20*
Fin_{91-93}		2.88	6.16*	2.84	5.91*	2.86	6.11*
		Adj. R^2 = .971		Adj. R^2 = .971		Adj. R^2 = .972	
		N = 210		N = 210		N = 210	

^{a}Based on panel robust standard errors.
*Significance levels: *p < 0.01; ** p < .05; √ p < .10 (two-tailed tests).*

Table 7.1 shows the regression results from three different specifications of the statistical model. For easy reference, the predicted signs of the theoretical variables are indicated in the left column of the table. Model I shows the effects on unemployment of the interaction between bargaining centralization (CEN) and the monetary regime (CUR). Note that both variables have significant direct effects on unemployment, and that they interact in a way we would expect from the theoretical argument. Thus, the combination of *either* a highly centralized wage-bargaining system with a flexible and accommodating monetary policy regime, *or* a decentralized bargaining system with a nonaccommodating policy regime produce low levels of unemployment.

A similar conclusion is implied by Model II for which the monetary regime variable was substituted for the commodification variable (COM). Thus, low unemployment is achieved when *either* a centralized bargaining system is combined with decommodifying social policies, *or* a decentralized system is combined with low unemployment compensation and public-sector employment. This finding is consistent with the proposition that a unified and centralized union movement will exchange wage restraint for solidaristic and expansionary

Table 7.2. *The estimated rates of unemployment depending on the centralization of bargaining and the accommodation of monetary (top entries) and social policies (bottom entries)*

| | | Accommodation? | |
		Yes	No
Bargaining System	Centralized	2.9 ➔ 1.2	5.5 ➔ 6.5
		3.0 ➔ 1.6	5.0 ➔ 5.4
	Decentralized	5.9 ➔ 7.4	3.8 ➔ 3.1
		6.1 ➔ 7.5	4.1 ➔ 3.8

Notes: Numbers are predicted unemployment rates of a particular combination after four years and in the long run (starting from the overall mean level). Centralized bargaining systems refer to the mean score for the Scandinavian countries (in the case of Denmark and Sweden prior to the breakdown in the early 1980s); decentralized bargaining systems refer to all other countries and years. The high and low values on the policy variables ("accommodation") were defined as one standard deviation above and below their means. Control variables (not shown) were all held at their mean. See text for the operationalization of variables.

social policies, whereas in a decentralized bargaining system restraint is actually undermined by decommodifying policies.

Table 7.2 provides a more tangible impression of the results. It shows the predicted effects on unemployment of a particular combination of bargaining system and level of policy accommodation, where the latter is measured by both the index of monetary accommodation (the top entries) and the index of commodification (the bottom entries). The bargaining variable was divided into a centralized category that reflect the peak-level systems found in Scandinavia (prior to the breakdown) and a decentralized category characterized by the absence of peak-level bargaining. The left entries show the predicted level of unemployment after a four-year period, assuming that all countries started with the same average level of unemployment. The right entries (bolded) show what happens after unemployment has reached a stable (long-run) equilibrium level. Notice that regardless of whether focus is on the monetary policies or unemployment/public-employment policies, the effect of accommodation is lower unemployment in a centralized bargaining system, but higher unemployment in a decentralized system. *There thus appear to be two distinct paths to full employment: (i) one that combines peak-level bargaining with an accommodating monetary regime and de commodifying social/employment policies, and (ii) one that combines decen-*

Table 7.3. *The estimated rates of unemployment depending on the bargaining system, the monetary regime, and the degree of commodification (from time* t $= 4$ *to time* t $= \infty$ *in percent*

		Monetary regime			
		Accommodating		*Nonaccommodating*	
Commodification:		Low	High	Low	High
Bar-gaining System	*Centralized*	3.2 ➜ 2.1	3.9 ➜ 3.4	4.7 ➜ 5.0	5.4 ➜ 6.3
	Decentralized	6.3 ➜ 8.0	4.4 ➜ 4.2	5.0 ➜ 5.4	3.0 ➜ 1.7

Note: Same as for Table 7.2.

tralized bargaining with a nonaccommodating monetary regime and commodifying social/employment policies.

The results of the combined model – in which all variables were included simultaneously – reinforces these conclusions. Although collinearity makes it difficult to separate out clearly the effect of the monetary regime from the effect of commodification ($r = .75$), the results summarized in Table 7.3 paint a rather clear picture. As before, the table shows what would happen to unemployment and inflation over the short run ($t = 4$) and the long run ($t = \infty$) if countries with different combinations of values on the independent institutional variables started from the same (average) level of unemployment. The table brings out rather succinctly the strategic trade-offs faced by governments. For example, while it is not impossible for social democratic governments to combine full employment with decommodifying welfare policies, such a combination presupposes both an accommodating monetary regime and a highly centralized bargaining system – institutional prerequisites that have never been fully satisfied in countries such as Austria, Belgium, Germany, and the Netherlands.

One way of illustrating the dynamic implications of the model is by imagining what would happen if the bargaining system was decentralized in the context of an accommodating monetary regime and decommodifying un-employment/public-employment policies (moving from the top left cell to the bottom left cell). The likely consequence of such decentralization would be that a very low equilibrium rate of unemployment (2.1 percent) would gradually increase to a new equilibrium level of 8 percent. This is a scenario that few social democratic governments would find either ideologically acceptable or politically palatable. Yet there are no easy alternatives for social democracy in this scenario. Although a credible commitment to a nonaccommodating monetary regime can improve employment prospects, such a strategy would also involve a fundamental reordering of economic priorities and necessitate an end to government–union collaboration over economic policies. Even more problematic in ideological terms would be cutbacks in unemployment benefits and policies that increased inequality, despite the possible employment gains of such policies. Decentralization, in other words, presents social democracy with a politically unattractive trade-off between unemployment and equality.

Of course, just as social democrats would find it difficult to pursue flexible and redistributive social-economic policies in a decentralized system, so liberal-conservative parties would find it difficult to pursue antiinflationary policies in an entrenched centralized system. Not only would such policies clash with the distributive goals of the union movement (thereby engendering industrial unrest), it would also lead to considerable levels of unemployment. Under these circumstances, economic logic and political pragmatism may well impress liberal-conservative parties to adopt an essentially social democratic platform: flexible full-employment policies coupled with decommodifying welfare state policies. And this *was* essentially the experience of center-right governments in Scandinavia before the early 1980s. Since then, however, such governments have pursued more distinct "neo-liberal" economic policy agendas, and social democrats have seemed to follow suit.

The fundamental difference between the 1960s/1970s and the 1980s/1990s is that the social democratic dilemma has become politically dominant, while the liberal–conservative dilemma has receded. Today, social democratic governments increasingly mimic a neo-liberal economic policy agenda, while liberal and conservative parties have become more outspoken critics of the traditional social-democratic economic project. In the next section, I argue that this change coincides with the breakdown of centralized bargaining and the intensification of external constraints on macroeconomic policies.

INSTITUTIONAL ADAPTATION TO A NEW ECONOMIC ORDER

The argument advanced above implies that macroinstitutions are causally related: concerns over electoral support make democratic governments gravitate toward policies that facilitate full employment; similarly, concerns over costs and unemployment bring together pivotal sectors of employers and unions behind "efficient" bargaining institutions. This logic is particularly salient for the relationship between centralization and monetary regimes. Since partisan governments cannot control the structure of the bargaining system directly, monetary policies will affect distributive compromises only through the facilitation of distributive compromises within a centralized system. If organized capital and labor therefore refuse to support centralization, accommodating monetary policies will have few distributive effects, but will lead to higher levels of militancy, unemployment, and inflation.

In social and public-employment policies, the political choices are even harder because they will have direct distributional effects. In addition, the trade-off is magnified by the opposition governments are likely to encounter from entrenched groups of public-service producers and welfare recipients, themselves a product of the welfare state (Pierson 1996). Nevertheless, unless political parties have lexicographic preferences, if the equality–employment trade-off is strengthened by decentralization of bargaining, politicians have an incentive to produce an offsetting reduction in the decommodifying effects of social and employment policies. This is particularly true in the areas that are most salient for labor-market performance: unemployment compensation and public-sector employment. Changes in one institutional setting will therefore create pressures for changes in others – the central thesis of this section.

As a first cut to explain this proposition, Figure 7.1 maps the changing location of the ten cases on the three political–institutional variables. The figure shows the position of countries on the centralization and monetary regime variables for two subperiods (1973–83 and 1984–93), with the arrows indicating direction of change. The symbols associated with each observation represent the score of the different countries on the commodification index.

As expected, the cases cluster along the northwest–southeast diagonal with Nordic countries initially in the centralized/accommodating cell (and exhibiting very low levels of commodification), and with Germany, Japan, Switzerland, and the Netherlands in the decentralized/nonaccommodating cell (and exhibiting higher degrees of commodification). For the entire 1973–93 period, the correlation between centralization and accommodation is .85, between centralization and commodification .86, and between accommodation and commodification .91. In other words, there are very strong tendencies for clustering. The only country that consistently falls outside this pattern is Belgium, although the tightening of monetary policies since 1983 has moved it closer to decentralized/nonaccommodating cell. Consistent with the argument, Belgium has paid a very high price for this institutional "disequilibrium" in the form of the worst unemployment record among our ten countries.

Two cases – Denmark and Sweden – have experienced a decentralization of their bargaining systems over the 1980s and 1990s. These changes have been accompanied by a shift toward hard-currency policies in first Denmark and then in Sweden, by cuts in unemployment benefits, and by an end to public-sector employment expansion. In addition, new electoral cleavages have been emerging between public- and private-sector employees, and radical wage solidarism appears to be a thing of the past. In Norway, and to a lesser extent in Finland, these trends have been less visible during the 1980s due primarily to a combination of inflationary pressures from the oil boom (in Finland through expand-

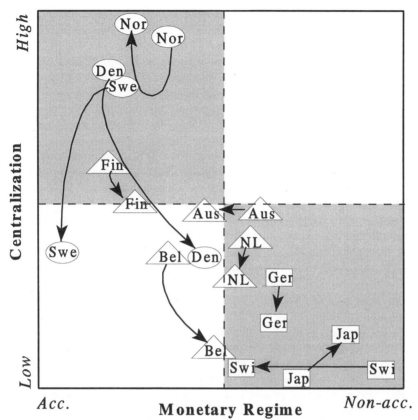

Note: Scores on the monetary regime and centralization variables are measured by the mean value on the CUR and CEN indexes the two periods 1972–83 and 1984–93. The symbols indicate the location of the ten countries on the COM index. An *oval* indicates low commodification, a *triangle* medium commodification, and a *rectangle* high commodification. The arrows indicate the approximate path and direction of change.

Figure 7.1. *The changing location of organized market economies on three economic – institutional dimensions (level of commodification is indicated by symbols).*

ing trade with the Soviet Union), and accommodating macroeconomic policies that helped to preserve a (tenuous) alliance behind centralization. Common forces of change are mounting on all centrally coordinated systems, however, pointing to an emerging pattern of convergence around some version of the "Germanic model." In the following I discuss the politics of convergence in two cases – Denmark and Sweden – focusing on the three political–institutional domains that have taken center stage in this study: the bargaining system, the monetary regime, and the welfare state.

NEW TECHNOLOGY AND GROWING PRESSURES FOR WAGE FLEXIBILITY

Recent changes in manufacturing technology have profoundly affected the parameters for the efficient organization of production and firm-internal incentive structures, and a consensus is developing that the widespread application of numerically controlled, multipurpose machinery during the 1970s and 1980s has placed a premium on shop-floor autonomy and intrafirm skill formation (e.g., Piore and Sabel 1984; Piore 1986; Sabel 1989, 1993; Streeck 1991). These changes have made monitoring of work effort more difficult, and it has increased the cost of dismissing workers, who often represent valuable assets in terms of skills and production-specific knowledge. As a result, higher wages for skilled employees and non-standard systems of remuneration have become popular managerial tools for achieving higher work performance and longer-term employee commitment to the firm (Pontusson and Swenson 1996; Iversen 1996). To the extent that centrally negotiated wage norms inhibit such wage flexibility, they constrain the pursuit of diversified quality production strategies. Technological change has therefore increased the attraction for leading firms of decentralized bargaining and simultaneously made wage costs a less crucial (though by no means insignificant) determinant of international competitiveness.

The transition toward more knowledge-intensive modes of production has also caused what I would call a bifurcation of the labor market risk structure. Thus, while well-trained and better-educated segments of the labor force face very secure employment prospects and can anticipate continuous skill upgrading and the associated monetary rewards, low- and semiskilled blue-color workers – once the backbone of the advanced industrial economy – face slack labor markets and insecure job prospects, partly due to competition from low-wage countries (Wood 1994). Evidence from nearly all OECD countries establishes a clear *negative* link between peoples' level of training/education and their risk of unemployment, and it shows that the rise in unemployment during the 1970s was disproportionally concentrated among low-skilled manual workers (see Streeck 1991; Glyn 1993; Wood 1994; OECD 1992, 1994:ch. 7).

The growing need among employers for in-house training and flexible incentive systems and the bifurcation of the labor force in terms of workers' ability to take advantage of these changes have stimulated the rise of new cross-class "flexibility coalitions" between diversified quality producers and better-trained segments of the labor force. In Denmark and Sweden such coalitions have opposed the labor associations' pursuit of solidaristic wage policies, and the centralized bargaining system has been undermined by their actions. Over the 1970s and 1980s many firms, especially in the engineering sector, began to introduce nonstandard forms of payment systems aimed at increasing labor productivity and long-term company loyalty (Standing 1988:56–63; Pontusson and Swenson 1996; Kjellberg 1992:107–12; Ibsen and Stamhus 1993; Due,

Madsen, Jensen, and Petersen 1994:157, 161). The increasing use of these new forms of remuneration were often supplemented by more traditional wage hikes that primarily benefited well-trained workers with scarce skills. In seeking more flexible wage systems many employers therefore became cooperative partners for those privileged groups of employees seeking to escape the constraints of solidaristic wage policies.

Attempts to solve this problem by allowing decentralized wage formation to play a greater role within the confines of centrally determined wage ceilings largely failed because they ran counter to the power structure within the established centralized system, and because wage ceilings served as focal points for across-the-board wage increases at the decentralized level. Instead, the centralized bargaining system was abandoned altogether through an institutional reform process led by an alliance of export-oriented engineering employers and unions dominated by highly skilled, and relatively well-paid, workers. In Denmark this movement away from centralization was greatly facilitated by rising unemployment and the new economic policy under the center-right government coming to power in 1982, while the Swedish devaluation-led, full-employment policy (the "Third Way" strategy) complicated the transition by creating tight labor markets. This tension now seems to have been resolved in favor of decentralization with the 1991 reversal of Swedish macroeconomic policies. In turn, the change in macroeconomic policy goals away from full employment and toward low inflation is related to the weakened capacity of governments to commit to full employment in increasingly integrated international capital markets. This is the topic of the next section.

CAPITAL MARKET INTEGRATION AND THE LOSS OF MONETARY POLICY AUTONOMY

A number of econometric studies have found a pronounced increase in capital market integration over the 1970s and 1980s (see Feldstein and Horioka 1980; Bayoumi 1990; Frankel 1991; Garrett 1995; Quinn and Inclan 1997).[14] Such integration undermines monetary flexibility because exchange rate uncertainty will lead to capital outflows. Although domestic monetary authorities can provide offsetting incentives to currency traders by raising real interest rates above the world level, such "risk premiums" dampen domestic investment to the detriment of growth and employment. The effects of expansionary fiscal policies are similar since deficits lead to higher inflation expectations and perceived exchange-rate risks. Low barriers to capital movement therefore reduce the

---

14 In turn, the increase in integration has been attributed to a complex set of factors – including changes in communication technology and the rise of the Euro-dollar market – which combine with widespread liberalization of financial markets (partly through the auspices of the European Community) to make it very difficult for individual countries to control cross-border capital flows (see for example Goodman and Pauly 1993; Frieden 1991).

government's capacity to effectively manipulate macroeconomic instruments, while investors will find it easier to escape costs that policymakers may otherwise impose. Capital market integration, in short, makes the government more vulnerable to the exit decisions of private investors, and it increases the costs of following even mildly inflationary full-employment strategies.

Because solidaristic and full-employment policies in Scandinavia were inflationary, globalization of capital posed a particularly difficult problem for governments in these countries. The problem of combining flexible monetary policies with integrated capital markets was particularly acute in Denmark, where credit markets had always been comparatively open and left to the oversight of the central bank. These monetary-policy constraints – which were exacerbated by EC membership and participation in the European currency arrangements (first the "Snake" and then the EMS) – created a double problem for the government. On the one hand, since Danish inflation was above the German level, there was a persistent expectation that the krone could not, over time, retain its value against the German deutschmark (DM). Consequently, Danish interest rates incorporated a substantial risk premium that compensated foreign investors for the loss they faced in the event of a devaluation, and the central bank had to accumulate large (and expensive) foreign currency holdings as a hedge against speculation.[15] On the other hand, LO defiantly refused to accept the limits for wage increases that the government – heeding the advice of its own economists – tried to impose. Although there were extensive consultations between the government and LO over wage policies, they could not come to any consensus and frequently clashed in very public ways. From the perspective of LO, the problem was that the government would no longer guarantee full employment (unemployment had reached nearly 10 percent in 1981), while from the perspective of the government the problem was that unions failed to appreciate the monetary constraints under which it had to operate and simply demanded too much.

Unable to reverse an increasingly desperate economic situation (the Finance Minister publicly described it as the country falling into an economic abyss), the Social Democrats abdicated from power in 1982 and turned over the reins to a bourgeois coalition government determined to pursue radical reforms. In short order the new government pegged the krone to the DM, liberalized capital markets, and suspended all cost-of-living (CoL) indexation. After a relatively short transition period, the lifting of capital controls and the initiation of dramatically restrictive fiscal policies (an 8 percent deficit was converted into a 4.5 percent surplus in the course of five years!) convinced markets that the

---

15 Real long-term interest rates in Denmark in the 1973–80 period were an average of 2.7 percent above those in Germany, while in a hard-currency country like Austria (where there was virtually no uncertainty about the value of the schilling) interest rates were held at (nearly) the same level as in Germany.

government meant business. In addition, by suspending the automatic CoL indexation, and by repealing a mechanism compensating public employees for private-sector wage increases, the government reduced the inflationary contagion from wage-drift.

Compared to Denmark at the time the first oil-price shock hit, the Swedish government was far better positioned to continue its full-employment policies. Swedish credit and currency markets were subject to extensive controls, and the central bank (Riksbanken) wielded considerable power over the credit-formation process. This combination allowed the government to pursue countercyclical monetary policies and to steer investments by means of credit rationing (Mjøset 1986:131; Scharpf 1991:205). During the 1970s and early 1980s the Swedish full-employment strategy was facilitated by exchange-rate devaluations that helped to boost the price competitiveness of Swedish industry. The key to the medium-term success of such policies, however, was that devaluations were accompanied by across-the-board wage restraint (Mjøset 1986:106, 258–9; Martin 1985). For example, despite substantial nominal wage increases, real wages *fell* following the devaluations in the mid-1970s, contributing substantially to the improvement in the current account. Similarly, the Third Way strategy of devaluation-led reflation after the election in 1982 was premised on an advance agreement by LO *not* to demand compensation for the CoL increases expected from higher prices on imports (Elvander 1988:291; Pontusson 1992:116–17).

During the 1980s, however, as the effects of the 1982 devaluation wore off, Swedish monetary policies ran into the same constraints as Danish policies had in the 1970s. Thus, when the current account drifted into deficit, confidence in the Swedish krona started to slip, and the Social Democratic government was faced with the choice of either making another devaluation or adopting a "Danish" solution of committing to a hard-currency regime. The difference between this situation and the one that preceded the devaluations in the mid-1970s and early 1980s was that the krona had become much more vulnerable to international currency speculations. With the expansion of world capital markets, the liberalization of capital controls in most OECD countries, and the revolution in information technology, Swedish currency markets had become deeply embroiled in global markets, and efforts to shield the economy against these markets were increasingly impeded by the rapid expansion of gray markets (Moses 1994:140–2). Instead of trying to go against the tide of these changes, the Swedish government decided in the mid-1980s to follow the examples of Norway and Denmark and liberalize capital markets.

With such liberalization, and probably without it as well, the integration of currency markets made a devaluation strategy a much more risky and uncertain proposition. Unless the government could convince speculators that it was able to effectively control nominal wages in the wake of a devaluation, another run on the currency was bound to happen in short order. Yet the government was in no position to make such guarantees. Not only had nominal wage restraint failed in the past, but the peak-level bargaining system that enabled policy coordination was in a state of disarray. Instead, the government gave in to the pressures of the market and pegged the value of the krona to the ECU in May of 1991. Like the Danish policy reversal in 1982, this was arguably the most important change in Swedish macroeconomic policies since the 1950s because it meant a de facto abandonment of the post–World War II commitment to full employment.

Despite deflationary polices and desperate interest rate hikes, the hard-currency policy did not survive the currency turmoil following the Kohl government's deficit-financed unification policy. Yet the Swedish policy reversal in 1991 was not merely cosmetic, but accompanied by a substantial and sustained discretionary tightening of fiscal policies, an increase in interest rates, reductions in unemployment benefits, and preparation for membership in the European Union and the EMS. Whether the Social Democratic government is fully committed to these policies is still an open question, but the central bank has been granted greater independence, and there have been no attempts at radical reflation.

WELFARE REFORMS AND ELECTORAL REALIGNMENTS

As I have argued, a nonaccommodating economic policy regime helps to deter militant behavior in a (semi)decentralized bargaining system by threatening unemployment, but a similar logic also applies to the welfare state – especially the size and character of unemployment compensation and financing. A coherent strategy to shift the macroeconomic policy regime in a monetarist direction would therefore involve reforms of social policies designed to concentrate the costs and risks of especially unemployment on the collective price–wage decision makers. Moreover, because tax-financed egalitarian welfare benefits induce compensatory demands from high-paid groups in a decentralized bargaining system, and because such egalitarianism undermines pay flexibility, social policies designed to increase economic efficiency would move toward a more earnings-graduated benefit system.

To the extent that voters are sociotropic, this logic would imply that decentralization undermines the electoral support for highly egalitarian social policies, at least in those areas of the welfare system that are most salient for the labor market. In addition, institutional changes may generate new electoral divisions over the welfare state. Thus, while the centralized-flexible social democratic model – with centralized, solidaristic wage bargaining, commitment to full employment, and a universalistic welfare state – engendered broad class solidarity, decentralization undermines the economic rationale for solidaristic policies and brings to the fore distributive divisions between low- and high-productivity labor and between those in secure market positions and those in insecure positions. Such divisions have been amplified by the transition to a post–industrial service economy, which widens the gap between a high-productivity, internationally oriented growth sector, and a low-productivity, more home-market based service sector.

In the Scandinavian context, the manifestation of these changes is particularly evident in a growing electoral division between low-skilled workers employed in the public sector and high-skilled workers in the private sector. The public–private sector division is both over pay relativities (i.e., over whether the pay of low-productivity public-service workers should follow those of their higher-productivity colleagues in the private sector) and over the need for wage restraint (with sheltered public-sector workers less concerned about this than exposed private-sector workers) (see Swenson 1991; Garrett and Way this volume). Empirically, a very similar pattern of change from the 1970s to the 1980s emerges in the two countries, although the magnitudes are considerably greater in Denmark. Thus, while in the early 1970s private-sector employees were slightly more likely than public-sector employees to vote for left parties, over time the "direction" of these differences has shifted, and their magnitudes have multiplied, so that by the end of the 1980s public employees were much more likely to vote for especially New Left parties, while private-sector employees were far more likely to vote for Right parties. The Social Democrats in both countries remained comparatively "neutral" in this transition, drawing support from both constituencies.[16]

The emerging realignment of Danish and Swedish electoral politics has been accompanied by welfare reforms in both countries. As in the case of the other institutional changes, and reflecting a more complete electoral realignment, these reforms have been more far-reaching in Denmark (though the process can in no way be considered complete in either case). The purpose of the reforms since 1982 in Denmark was not just to reestablish a balanced budget but also to signal to capital markets that fiscal and social policies were now subjugated to the requirements of restrictive monetary policies. With unemployment figures in double digits, a primary target for the reforms was the extremely generous unemployment benefit system.[17] The new government was particularly keen to eliminate what it regarded as union disincentives to responsible wage behavior, and to reduce the overall financial burden of the system. While a radical reform of the system proved politically infeasible at the time, the removal of the price indexation

16 During the 1980s the proportion voting for New Left parties in Denmark (especially the Socialist Peoples' Party) among public employees was about three times that among private employees. In Sweden, a public-sector employee was twice as likely to vote for either the Communists or the Greens by 1988, and 60 percent of these parties' support came from the public sector (based on data from Danish and Swedish national election studies).

17 Historically, unemployment insurance was established and financed by the unions, but in the postwar period much of the administrative and financial burden was taken over by the state, reaching nearly 90 percent in the 1970s.

of the upper limit for benefits caused the average compensation rate to fall markedly over the course of a few years from over 80 percent in 1980 to less than 60 percent in 1985. Without any major overhauls of the system, mandated unemployment insurance had quietly been reduced to the lowest level in Scandinavia. Though unions and employers could compensate for lost benefits by increasing member contributions, this implied a more income-differentiated system in which sectors with low unemployment rates would be "rewarded," thus creating the type of incentive structure the government was aiming for. Between 1982 and 1989 the share of benefits financed by the state fell from 88 percent to 65 percent (Scheuer 1992: 179).

Most of the cutbacks in the Swedish welfare state were also initiated in support of the hard-currency policy introduced by the bourgeois government in 1991. Similar to the situation in Denmark in 1982, the government deemed it necessary to commit to a fiscal-austerity package to convince capital markets that the pegging of the krona to the ECU was credible. Cuts in the compensation for sick leave, the introduction of a waiting day, reductions in pensions, and a general political resolve to scale back the public sector were measures that the government (with the *support* of the Social Democrats) announced to communicate its commitment to the new economic policy. With the collapse of the EMS exchange-rate system, and the resulting explosion of speculative capital movements, the basis for the proposals (which were premised on Social Democratic votes) fell through, but the political determination to continue the austerity policies persisted, and cutback have now been implemented in such areas as sickness benefits and parental leave (Stephens 1996). In addition, the progressivity of the tax systems has been notably reduced through cuts in marginal tax rates.

The most intensively contested reform in Sweden has been in the area of unemployment insurance. Under the conservative government increases were mandated in the unemployment contributions of employees, and the maximum duration of benefits was restricted to two periods of 300 days (previously there were no limits on the number of periods). Furthermore, the rate of compensation was reduced from 90 percent to 80 percent of previous earnings (subject to a ceiling). While the Social Democrats vowed to reverse these changes, in fact they did the exact opposite and compensation rates were cut further. Clearly, these reforms do not add up to anything that can be characterized as a fundamental transformation of the Swedish welfare state, but they *do* constitute real changes and they signal a shift to the right in terms of the political rhetoric, debate, and party platforms that shape social policies.

CONCLUSIONS

The combined effect of capital market integration and technological change during the 1970s and 1980s has been to increase the capacity, or power, of employers and unions in the exposed sector to commit to a decentralized system, while it has weakened the government's hand in maintaining a flexible, full-employment strategy. Similarly, the polarization of the unemployment risk structure and the market pressures for greater earnings equalities have splintered the old class consensus behind egalitarian welfare policies and public-sector expansion. In this concluding section I will briefly outline some of the implications of these changes for the strategic options that are open for social democracy.

The most immediate political dilemmas that social democratic parties face are in the electoral arena. In the private sector they are losing support from both high-skilled workers (who increasingly vote to the right of center) and from low-paid workers in the public sector (who tend to vote for New Left parties). Because the Social Democratic electoral support is built upon a broad class alliance *across* sectors, new cross-cutting cleavages polarize the parties' constituencies and chip off support at the margins. Yet if the parties were to shed their class character and adopt a clear sectoral profile (in either direction), it would only further alienate large portions of their traditional constituencies. Consequently, if the choice for the Social Democrats were between reaffirming themselves as "class-mass" parties, or becoming "sectoral" parties, the future of social democracy would look very bleak indeed. Instead, a viable strategy for the 1990s and beyond must be based on a new cross-sectoral compromise, but one that transcends class as an organizing principle. What are the components of such an alternative?

In my view, a viable political project would have to be based on the principle of economic efficiency coupled with an unorthodox and pragmatic approach to electoral alliance building. The success of the Social Democratic model in the past was always premised on the capacity of the government to expand profits and investment, while *simultaneously* promoting a fair distribution of income and life chances for a large portion of the electorate. Conversely, the failure of the model resulted from a perpetuation of egalitarian ideals that went beyond what was compatible with sustained international competitiveness and that ignored the shifting balance of power between different sectors of workers and employers. Only by promoting a high-efficiency economy, well aligned with the underlying cross-class coalition structure, can the Social Democrats hope to be a party of both prosperity and welfare.

If this diagnosis is correct, then there can be no way back in the foreseeable future to a class-based, centralized equilibrium with a highly egalitarian welfare state. Any concerted attempt to regain control over macroeconomic policy instruments through extensive capital controls would be a recipe for economic disaster, and technological change has made employers in the most dynamic sectors of the economy squarely opposed to such a strategy. If the principle of economic efficiency is going to continue to be a cornerstone in the social democracy strategy, therefore, it has to be recognized that decentralization and monetarist macroeconomic policies in the future must be part of the institutional foundation of social democracy, *despite* their antithetical relationship to traditional socialist ideals. High pay for unskilled workers in the public sector combined with generous and collectively financed flat-rate unemployment benefits also introduce rigidities into the wage structure that can be ill-afforded in a fiercely competitive international economy. Instead, the emphasis must be on continuous skill-upgrading, which depends not only on wage incentives, but also on legislated obligations of employers to provide opportunities for training and retraining for *all* their employees (the right to paid sabbaticals in Denmark is an example of this policy).

More generally, the emphasis much be on the creation of decentralized, high-quality production regimes in both the public and private economies. Social Democrats must acknowledge that the centralization that used to characterize the social democratic state in terms of the industrial relations system, the coordination of macroeconomic policies, and the welfare state can no longer play a constructive role in the political–organizational future of social democracy. The need as well as capacity for peak-level coordination in economic policies has disappeared along with growing capital-market internationalization and movement toward a postindustrial economy. In a similar vein, an improvement of both the quality and efficiency of public services will require continued decentralization of services, more consumer involvement in decision making, and more competition between providers. In short, Social Democrats must bring their political ambitions into line with an institutional and technological environment in which production of goods and services is becoming more knowledge-intensive, more internationalized, and more decentralized. The moderate left can either become an active and significant political force in this continuing structural transformation, or it can engage in a losing political battle to defend the interests of those who benefited most from the rise of the bureaucratic and centralized Keynesian welfare state.

References

Bayoumi, Tamin. 1990. "Savings-Investment Correlations: Immobile Capital, Government Policy or Endogenous Behavior?" *IMF Staff Papers*, 37, 360–87.

Beck, Nathaniel and Jonathan Katz. 1995. "What to Do (And Not to Do) With Time-Series Cross-Section Data." *American Political Science Review*, 89 (September), 634–48.

Calmfors, Lars and John Driffill. 1988. "Centralization of Wage Bargaining." *Economic Policy*, 14–61.

Cameron, David. 1984. "Social Democracy, Corporatism, Labor Quiescence, and the Representation of Economic Interest in Advanced Capitalist Society." In John H. Goldthorpe (ed.), *Order and Conflict in Contemporary Capitalism*. New York: Oxford University Press.

Castles, Francis and Peter Mair. 1984. "Left–Right Political Scales: Some Expert Judgements." *European Journal of Political Research*, 12, 73–88.

Due, Jesper, Jørgen Steen Madsen, Carsten Strøby Jensen, and Lars Kjerulf Petersen.

1994. *The Survival of the Danish Model. A Historical Sociological Analysis of the Danish System of Collective Bargaining.* Copenhagen: DJØF.

Elkin, Stephen. 1985. "Pluralism in Its Place: State and Regime in Liberal Democracy." In Roger Benjamin and Stephen Elkin (eds.), *The Democratic State.* Lawrence: University Press of Kansas.

Elvander, Nils. 1988. *Den Svenska Modellen: Lönforhandlingar och inkomstpolitik 1982–1986.* Stockholm: Allmanna Forlaget.

Esping-Andersen, Gøsta. 1990. *The Three Worlds of Welfare Capitalism.* Princeton, NJ: Princeton University Press.

Feldstein, Martin and Charles Horioka. 1980. "Domestic Savings and International Capital Flows." *The Economic Journal*, 90, 314–29.

Frankel, Jeffrey. 1991. "Quantifying International Capital Mobility in the 1980s." In B. Douglas Bernheim and John B. Stoven (eds.), *National Savings and Economic Performance.* Chicago: Chicago University Press.

Frieden, Jeffry. 1991. "Invested Interests: The Politics of National Economic Policies in a World of Global Finance." *International Organization*, 45, 425–51.

Garrett, Geoffrey. 1995. "Capital Mobility, Trade, and the Domestic Politics of Economic Policy." *International Organization*, 49, 657–87.

Glyn, Andrew. 1993. "Stability, Inegalitarianism and Stagnation: An Overview of the Advanced Capitalist Countries in the 1980s." Paper prepared for the WIDER Project on Savings, Investment and Finance.

Goodman, John B. and Louis W. Pauly. 1993. "The Obsolescence of Capital Controls? Economic Management in an Age of Global Markets." *World Politics*, 46, 50–83.

Hall, Peter A. 1994. "Central Bank Independence and Coordinated Wage Bargaining: Their Interaction in Germany and Europe." *German Politics and Society*, (Autumn), 1–23.

Hibbs, Douglas. 1978. "On the Political Economy of Long-Run Trends in Strike Activity." *British Journal of Political Science*, 8.

Hibbs, Douglas and Håkan Locking. 1996. "Wage Compression, Wage Drift, and Wage Inflation in Sweden." *Labour Economics*, 3 (September), 109–41.

Ibsen, Flemming and Jorgen Stamhus. 1993. *Fra Central til Decentral Lønfastsættelse.* Copenhagen: Jurist-og Økonomforbundets Forlag.

Iversen, Torben. 1996. "Power, Flexibility and the Breakdown of Centralized Wage Bargaining: The Cases of Denmark and Sweden in Comparative Perspective." *Comparative Politics*, 28 (July): 399–436.

1998b. "Wage Bargaining, Central Bank Independence and the Real Effects of Money." *International Organization*, 52 (Summer): 469–504.

1999. *Contested Economic Institutions. The Politics of Macroeconomics and Wage Bargaining in Advanced Democracies.* Cambridge: Cambridge University Press.

Iversen, Torben and Anne Wren. 1998. "Equality, Employment, and Budgetary Restraint: The Trilemma of the Service Economy." *World Politics*, 49 (July): 507–546.

Kjellberg, Anders. 1992. "Sweden: Can the Model Survive?" In Anthony Ferner and Richard Hyman (eds.), *Industrial Relations in the New Europe*, pp. 88–142. Oxford: Basil Blackwell Ltd.

Lange, Peter. 1984. "Unions, Workers, and Wage Regulation: The Rational Bases of Consent." In John Goldthorpe (ed.), *Order and Conflict in Contemporary Capitalism*, pp. 98–123. Oxford: Clarendon Press.

Lange, Peter and Geoffrey Garrett. 1985. "The Politics of Growth: Strategic Interaction and Economic Performance in the Advanced Industrial Democracies, 1974–1980." *Journal of Politics*, 47, 792–827.

Lewis-Beck, Michael. 1988. *Economics and Elections: The Major Western Democracies*. Ann Arbor: University of Michigan Press.

Lohmann, Susanne. 1992. "Optimal of Commitment in Monetary Policy: Credibility versus Flexibility." 1982 (March). *American Economic Review*, 273–86.

Martin, Andrew. 1985. "Wages, Profits, and Investments in Sweden." In Leon N. Lindberg & Charles S. Mair (eds.), *The Politics of Inflation and Economic Stagnation*. Washington, DC: Brookings Institution, 403–66.

Mjøset, Lars. 1986. *Norden Dagen Derpå*. Oslo: Universitetsforlaget.

Moene, Karl Ove and Michael Wallerstein. 1993. "The Decline of Social Democracy." In Karl Gunner Persson (ed.), *The Economic Development of Denmark and Norway since 1879*. Gloschester: Edward Elgar.

Moses, Jonathan. 1994. "Abdication From National Policy Autonomy: What's Left to Leave?" *Politics and Society*, 22, 125–48.

OECD. 1992. *From Higher Education to Employment*. Paris.

OECD. 1994. *The OECD Jobs Study. Evidence and Explanations*. Paris.

Pierson, Paul. 1996. "The New Politics of the Welfare State." *World Politics* 48, 2, 143–179.

Piore, Michael. 1986. "Perspectives on Labor Market Flexibility." *Industrial Relations*, 25, 146–67.

Piore, Michael J. and Charles F. Sabel. 1984. *The Second Industrial Divide, Possibilities for Prosperity*. New York: Basic Books.

Pontusson, Jonas. 1992. *The Limits of Social Democracy*. Ithaca, NY: Cornell University Press.

Pontusson, Jonas and Peter Swenson. 1996. "Labor Markets, Production Strategies, and Wage Bargaining Institutions: The Swedish Employer Offensive in Comparative Perspective." *Comparative Political Studies*, 29 (April), 223–50.

Powell, Bingham G. and Guy D. Whitten. 1993. "A Cross-National Analysis of Economic Voting: Taking Account of the Political Context." *American Journal of Political Science*, 37, 391–414.

Quinn, Denis P. and Carla Inclan. 1997. "The Origin of Financial Openness: A Study of Current and Capital Account Internationalization." *American Journal of Political Science*, 41 (3), 771–813.

Robertson, John. 1990. "Transaction-Cost Economics and Cross-National Patterns of Industrial Conflict: A Comparative Institutional Analysis". *American Journal of Political Science*, 34, 153–90.

Rogoff, Kenneth. 1985. "The Optimal Degree of Commitment to an Intermediate Monetary Target." *Quarter Journal of Economics*, 100, 1169–89.

Sabel, Charles. 1989. "Flexible Specialization and the Reemergence of Regional Economies." In Paul Hirst and Jonathon Zeitlin (eds.), *Reversing Industrial Decline*. Oxford: Berg: 17–69.

1993. "Learning by Monitoring: The Institutions of Economic Development." In Neil Smelser and Richard Swedberg (eds), *Handbook of Economic Sociology*. Princeton, NJ: Princeton University Press.

Scharpf, Fritz. 1991. *Crisis and Choice in European Social Democracy*. Ithaca, NY: Cornell University Press.

Scheuer, Steen. 1992. "Denmark: Return to Decentralization." In Anthony Ferner and Richard Hyman (eds.), *Industrial Relations in the New Europe*, pp. 298–322. Oxford: Basil Blackwell Ltd.

Soskice, David. 1990. "Wage Determination: The Changing Role of Institutions in Advanced Industrialized Countries." *Oxford Review of Economic Policy*, 6, 36–61.

Soskice, David and Torben Iversen. forthcoming. "The Non-Neutrality of Monetary Policy with Large Price and Wage Setters." *Quarterly Journal of Economics*.

Standing, Guy. 1988. *Unemployment and Labour Market Flexibility: Sweden*. Geneva: ILO.

Stephens, John D. 1996. "The Scandinavian Welfare States: Achievements, Crisis, and Prospects." In Gøsta Esping-Andersen (ed.), *Welfare States in Transition*, pp. 32–65. London: Sage.

Streeck, Wolfgang. 1991. "On the Institutional Conditions of Diversified Quality Production." In Egon Matzner and Wolfgang Streeck, *Beyond Keynesianism*. Aldershot: Edward Elgar: 2–61.

Swenson, Peter. 1991. "Labor and the Limits of the Welfare State." *Comparative Politics*, 23, 4, 379–99.

Tsebelis, George. 1990. *Nested Games. Rational Choice in Comparative Politics*. Berkeley: University of California Press.

Wood, Andrian. 1994. *North–South Trade, Employment and Inequality*. Oxford: Oxford University Press.

8

THE POLITICS OF MACROECONOMIC POLICY AND WAGE NEGOTIATIONS IN SWEDEN

Andrew Martin

As is well known, the proximate reason that the system of central wage negotiations between the Swedish Confederation of Labor (LO) and the Swedish Employers Confederation (SAF) was terminated in the 1980s was that employers, particularly the large multinationals dominating the engineering sector, wanted to terminate it. There are strong grounds, including the economic interests entering into the engineering employers' actions, for arguing that this is a sufficient explanation for the demise of the system (Pontusson and Swenson 1993; Swenson and Pontusson this volume). In this essay, I explore the possibility that it may not be sufficient. The alternative I suggest is that the macroeconomic consequences of policies implemented by Social Democratic governments during the 1980s made it very difficult if not impossible for those, including the governments, who sought to maintain centrally coordinated negotiations in at least some form to do so in the face of efforts by those who sought to end them. This implies that under different macroeconomic conditions, it might have been possible to maintain some form of centrally coordinated wage bargaining, though not without modifications that would have been necessary to satisfy the main economic interests of those who sought to abolish them. Accordingly, I attempt to show what this counterfactual scenario might have looked like, offering some evidence that policies producing different macroeconomic conditions could plausibly have been implemented and that the

The author thanks Ton Notermans for many stimulating discussions, which have helped him understand the course of economic policy in Scandinavia and elsewhere; Lars Jonung for supplying much of the material on credit market deregulation and its consequences used in this chapter; Jon Erik Dølvik, Lawrence Kahn, and Michael Wallerstein for material on Norway; the many persons interviewed in necessary modifications could plausibly have been made, and indeed were beginning to be made, so that the conditions for maintaining centrally coordinated wage negotiations would have been considerably more favorable.[1] I suggest, however, that the employers opposed to central negotiations might nevertheless have persisted in their determination to block their continuation in any form and that, if so, it would have been because they had political interests that would not have been satisfied by any modifications in the system of central negotiations short of its demise.[2]

This reexamination of the 1980s experience in Sweden does not offer an explanation of the demise of central negotiations that is radically different from that offered by others. It differs in putting more weight on two factors that the others treat more summarily or not at all: macroeconomic policy and the political interests at stake in centralized negotiations. With respect to macroeconomic policy, it calls for closer attention to the actual sequence of decisions and both the economic assumptions and political considerations that entered into them. As one observer put it, "My suspicion is that many economic problems in Sweden and Finland that are basically due to the failure of macroeconomic management in the 1980s have been falsely attributed to the assumed rigidities of labour market institutions" (Vartiainen 1995:25, note 20). With respect to political stakes, it recalls that unions are typically actors in the political as well as market arena and that there is no reason why this should not also be true of employers and their organizations. This suggests the need to take into account the connections between the structure of the relationships between unions and employers in the market arena and their respective activities in the political arena. Thus, this chapter shares with the others in this volume the emphasis on the "interaction across different political-economic arenas" pointed out in the Introduction. At the same time, this chapter explores chains of causality between macroeconomic policy and wage-bargaining structure as well as between wage-bargaining structure and electoral politics that run in other directions than those assumed in many of the other chapters.

Sweden for much of the information about government, union, and employer policies on which this chapter rests; and participants in a conference at Cornell University, October 1995, on Macroeconomic Regimes, Wage Bargaining and Institutional Change in an Integrating Europe for comments on an earlier version of this chapter. Errors and opinions remain the author's responsibility

1 The (inadequately recognized and understood) utility and logic of counterfactuals in social analysis are discussed in Tetlock and Belkin (1996).

2 I summarize the argument that Swedish employers had a political stake in depriving the Swedish Confederation of Labor (LO) of its wage-bargaining role, which I develop more fully in Martin (1992).

SOCIAL DEMOCRATIC MACROECONOMIC POLICY IN THE 1980S: THE FAILURE OF THE "THIRD WAY"

The pattern of macroeconomic policy pursued by Sweden's Social Democratic (SD) governments during the 1980s amounted to an attempt to maintain "social democracy in one country" at a time when governments in most of the countries with which Sweden was economically linked were rolling back and abandoning whatever approximations to social democracy had previously been established. The attempt failed. The failure precipitated the SDs' worst electoral defeat since 1928, followed by a sharp rise in unemployment to levels not seen since the Great Depression. In this context, a coalition of nonsocialist, or bourgeois parties, as they are known in Sweden, came into power and embarked on what they described as a "system change," through which social democracy would be supplanted by the kind of neo-liberal market-oriented policy regime being implemented in varying degrees in other advanced capitalist countries. That attempt was only partially successful, cut short by a decisive defeat in the 1994 election, which brought the SDs back into office. Paradoxically, the bourgeois coalition lost because it aggravated the economic crisis produced by the collapse of the macroeconomic strategy by which the SDs had sought to preserve social democracy in one country.

The SDs returned to office in 1982 after six years in which there had been four governments consisting of various combinations of bourgeois parties (the first since 1932). Those governments had tried without much success to cope with the problems afflicting the Swedish economy. Although the problems had structural roots going further back (dependence on a resource-based production chain – iron mining–steel production–shipbuilding – which came up against new international competition; on forest products as well but less challenged by new competition), they had been intensified by Swedish responses to the first OPEC price shock, first by the Social Democratic government prior to the 1976 election and then by the bourgeois governments that succeeded it. The latter initially felt compelled to prove that they could meet the standards of full employment and distributive justice set by the Social Democrats, while modifying things to satisfy values of individual choice and scope for innovation the SDs were accused of frustrating. The problems were aggravated, however, by the second OPEC oil-price shock and accompanying inflation and the very restrictive macroeconomic policies pursued in response, especially by the United States under Volcker, the head of the central bank under Carter and Reagan, by Britain under Thatcher, and to a somewhat lesser extent by the Federal Republic of Germany and its central bank. These policies have been described as a "monetarist shock" even more damaging to world growth than the oil shocks. By sharply increasing interest rates and cutting demand in the First World, the monetarist shock precipitated the debt crisis in much of the Third World, setting back its development, threatening the international financial system's collapse, and bringing unemployment in the First World to its highest level since the Great Depression (cf. Lipietz 1987). In this context, and following a highly expansionary election-year macroeconomic policy in 1979, Sweden's bourgeois government found itself facing growing budget and current account deficits, to which it responded with a policy of austerity that contributed to a rise in unemployment and included some minor reductions in social benefits (Martin 1985). The SDs won the 1982 election by attacking the bourgeois parties for all these things and claiming that they, the SDs, had a strategy for coping with what they described as an economic crisis in a way that would restore full employment and the welfare state. In short, they could restore the social democratic policy regime which they had constructed over their long period of rule from 1932 until it was interrupted in 1976.[3]

How were they to do so?[4] They had rejected the drastically restrictive strategy that relied on high unemployment to eliminate inflation, pursued by Volcker and Thatcher, to which the bourgeois government had apparently begun to turn. But they also rejected the strategy pursued by the French Socialists under Mitterrand, which relied on expansion of domestic demand to eliminate unemployment. That too was an attempt to pursue in one country a policy pattern that deviated from those carried out by the others to which it was linked. But the Swedish SDs rejected it on the ground that it was incapable of decreasing unemployment on a sustainable basis, something that was already becoming evident and soon confirmed by Mitterrand's abandonment of the strategy in favor of austerity.

Having rejected both of these two alternatives, the SDs proceeded to implement what they described as the "Third Way." The basic idea of the Third Way was to reduce unemployment by increasing demand, in contrast with the Volcker–Reagan–Thatcher strategy, but to do so in a way that would reduce rather than exacerbate the budget and current-account deficits, in contrast with the Mitterrand strategy, thereby assuring the sustainability of reduced unemployment. The way in which that was to be accomplished was by changing the composition of the growth in demand, so that most of the growth would come from foreign demand rather than domestic demand. The problem as it was perceived was how to do that when foreign demand was stagnant, as a result of the extremely restrictive policies being pursued elsewhere. In the past, SD

---

3 The Social Democrats' strategy for coping with the crisis was presented in Socialdemokraterna (1991). However, it made no mention of the devaluation which, as we shall see, turned out to be the cornerstone of the strategy that was actually implemented SD was once in office.

4 The following description of the Social Democratic government's economic policy is based primarily on the account provided by the Finance Minister, Kjell-Olof Feldt, in his book, Feldt (1991), supplemented by earlier interviews with Feldt and several of his associates. The analytic framework for the discussion draws heavily on Notermans (1999), Henrekson (1990), Bergström, (1989), and Wihlborg (1993).

economic policy, including the strategy for it known as the Rehn–Meidner (RM) model, was predicated on the assumption that international growth would provide sufficient demand most of the time and that any declines in growth would be brief and could be offset by temporary stimulus of domestic demand. But now that the world had been plunged into the worst recession since the 1930s, the conclusion was that that assumption no longer held and that stagnation in Sweden's export markets would persist for at least the next few years and possibly even for the rest of the decade.

Under these conditions, the only way to base an expansionary policy on foreign demand was to increase by a little bit Swedish industry's share of the stagnant world market. The only way to do that without relying on restrictive policies to reduce domestic demand and relative costs, thereby increasing unemployment, was by a devaluation. The preceding bourgeois governments had already devalued the krona a couple of times and the foreign exchange markets expected that the incoming SD government would carry out another devaluation rather than increase interest rates enough to avoid it, at the cost of increased unemployment. The markets were of course right, and in the usual self-fulfilling fashion, were abandoning the krona at a rate that made a devaluation, or a much less probable jump in interest rates, unavoidable. The only question facing the new government was how much to devalue: a defensive devaluation by just enough to offset the exchange markets' expectations about how much higher inflation would be in Sweden than elsewhere, or a larger offensive devaluation that would give Swedish exporters a definite competitive advantage. The new government opted for the latter, announcing a devaluation of 16 percent against a trade-weighted basket of Sweden's trading partners' currencies on the day it took office (it had intended a 20 percent devaluation but was talked out of it by a variety of foreign interlocutors). In this way, it believed, full employment would be restored on a sustainable basis because it would increase profits in the export and import competing industries, that is, the tradable goods or competitive sector, which would in turn induce increased investment in that sector. This would increase the capacity of the sector, thereby raising the level of economic activity that could be reached without leading to renewed balance of payments deficits, while at the same time directly increasing employment in the sector, thereby lowering the level of unemployment.

The Third Way was understood to be a risky option, for the conditions on which its success depended were inherently difficult to meet. As the Finance Minister, Kjell-Olof Feldt, put it, "The world was . . . full of failed devaluations" (Feldt 1991:91). The risk was that the change in the composition of demand that the devaluation was designed to achieve – that is, the decrease in the share of domestic consumption in GNP growth relative to the share of exports and industrial investment – would be reversed by successful efforts to secure increases in household income sufficient to offset the decline in purchasing power resulting from the devaluation. There were two main institutional

Table 8.1. *Shares of GNP components in total real GNP growth 1981–84 and 1985–88 (1985 prices)*

GNP components	1981–84 (%)	1985–88 (%)
Private consumption	0.7	83.5
Public consumption	16.8	18.4
Business gross investment		
Total	19.7	43.9
Tradables sectors	0.6	14.1
Nontradables sectors	16.2	28.2
Net exports	62.8	−45.8
Total	100	100

Source: Henrekson (1990:46 Table 1).

means available for preventing this. One was Sweden's system of wage bargaining with its elements of centralized negotiations between peak organizations of unions and employers. The other was the array of fiscal and monetary macroeconomic policy instruments at the disposal of the government. The functions each was relied on to perform were both necessary; neither alone could achieve the needed effect. It was not at all clear that the available means as they were constituted at the time were adequate to perform the functions on which success depended. But even if they had been, those institutional means were significantly impaired in the years that followed, and they ultimately proved inadequate to the tasks assigned to them, contributing to the failure of the Third Way. Even had they been at their best, however, the tasks assigned to them by the particular manner in which the Third Way was implemented might have been more than they could have carried out. By the same token, they might have been able to perform the functions required of them despite the extent to which they had been impaired if the burdens placed on them by the implementation of the Third Way had not been as great as they were.

For the first few years, it looked as if the Third Way was a brilliant success; the economy behaved exactly as it was supposed to, and Swedish economic policy won the accolades of such expert outside observers as the OECD, the Brookings Institution, and the *Economist* magazine. But then there was an abrupt reversal. This is strikingly clear if we look at the most relevant indicators (Table 8.1).

In the first period, nearly two-thirds of GNP growth is accounted for by net exports, with less than one percent accounted for by private consumption, and the addition of public consumption leaves just over a fifth of GNP growth accounted for by total consumption. Thus, the intended shift from consumption to exports seems to have been achieved to a remarkable degree. Especially striking is the success in holding back private consumption. Less success appears to have been achieved in the Third Way's goal of increasing investment, particularly in the tradables sector, where investment accounted for less than one percent of GNP growth. This is interpreted as indicating that the intended effect of increasing the tradable sector's share of GNP growth was as effectively achieved as it was almost entirely through a rapid increase in capacity utilization, which had to occur before investment in increasing capacity could occur. Once the slack in capacity had been taken up, investment in new capacity could be expected. In all, the data point to clear success for the Third Way.

In the second period, the picture is dramatically different. Private consumption accounted for an even larger share of GNP growth in this period than net exports accounted for in the preceding period. Adding the slightly increased share of public consumption, total consumption growth absorbed a bit more than the entire growth of GNP (102 percent) during the second period, while the share of net exports turned sharply negative (−46 percent). In terms of the Third Way's objectives, this was partly offset by the growth of investment, but even this turns out to have been twice as great in the nontradables sector than in the tradables sector, whose expansion the strategy was designed to achieve. Some dampening of the shift from domestic consumption to net exports seen in the first period should be expected in the second period, for even if expansion in the first period were entirely confined to the tradables sector, the resulting increases in income and employment (including that resulting from investment) would spill over into increased private consumption, imports, and domestic investment in the second. But nothing like the complete reversal shown by these data could be expected. Thus, they point to a complete breakdown of the Third Way in the face of an explosive boom in domestic consumption and investment in the non-tradables sector and a collapse of exports.

Why did it happen? Did it have to happen? Was the Third Way doomed to fail? Or were there policy choices that caused the strategy to fail? The case that failure was not inevitable rests on the argument that different choices could have been made, and that if they had been, the Third Way could have worked, at least well enough to avoid the crisis of the economy, of the SD labor movement, and of the social democratic model that was precipitated by the Third Way's failure.

Basically, what happened is that macroeconomic policy turned out to be much more expansive than was compatible with the structural shift in the pattern of growth, from the sheltered to the exposed sector, that was necessary for the strategy to work. There were two basic policy choices that proved to be excessively expansionary. The first was the size of the devaluation, which turned out to be too large. The second was the deregulation of the domestic credit market, whose timing unleashed a credit-based speculative boom. We examine each of these choices and the alternatives that were available.

THE DEVALUATION

The initial exchange rate policy choice can be partly attributed to a forecasting error. As indicated before, the decision in favor of a large offensive devaluation rather than a smaller defensive one was based on the assumption that world demand would be stagnant because policy in the major countries would continue to be very restrictive for at least a few years. What the Swedish policy-makers – the Finance Minister, Kjell-Olof Feldt, and a small group of economists around him – did not anticipate was that the U.S. economy would be given the largest expansionary fiscal stimulus in its history except for that provided by expenditures for the Second World War. That was the effect of the combination of the Reagan administration's big increase in military spending, the huge income tax cuts in which Reagan and the Congress outbid each other, and the impossibility of getting major offsetting cuts in domestic spending through Congress. Despite all of Reagan's supply-side talk, he proved to be the most expansionist Keynesian the United States ever had. In any case, this meant recovery in one of Sweden's most important markets. Swedish products became increasingly competitive in that market since there was a further effective devaluation of the krona relative to the dollar because the dollar appreciated against most other currencies as high U.S. interest rates attracted the capital inflows that financed the U.S. budget and current-payments deficits (which were increased in the process). The U.S. recovery, well on its way in time for Reagan's reelection campaign, also began the recovery in Sweden's European markets. However, the dollar's rise also pulled the krona up relative to European currencies (because of its weight in the currency basket against which the krona's rate was set), on top of which there was a real appreciation of the krona relative to those currencies because inflation rates declined more slowly in Sweden than in its European trading partners, so that Swedish competiveness in those markets declined (Wihlborg 1993:238).

Although the Swedish economic policymakers did not anticipate this, they saw it happening almost as soon as they announced the big devaluation, and they realized that the devaluation was larger than needed even for an aggressive ("beggar thy neighbor") effort to capture an increased market share for Swedish exports. Whether they realized it or not, this also made the conditions on which the success of the devaluation option depended, which were already difficult to meet, even more difficult to meet than they otherwise would have been. The devaluation had a greater inflationary effect, via increased import prices, than a smaller one would have had, making the task of reducing the difference between inflation in Sweden and Germany (and hence in its European trading partners generally) harder than it had to be.[5] Paradoxically, the gain in competitiveness

---

5 Consumer prices in Sweden in 1982–85 rose at annual rates of 8.9, 8.0, and 7.4 percent, while in Germany they rose at rates of 3.3, 2.4, and 2.2 percent, respectively (OECD 1993:140, Table A 15).

secured from a larger devaluation was probably more vulnerable to being eaten up by the resulting higher inflation than the gain from a smaller devaluation with a smaller inflationary effect. The higher inflationary impact meant that the real-income cut suffered by most of the population, and the redistribution of income from labor to capital, was larger than necessary, making the burden of securing agreement by organized claimants – mainly unions and pensioner organizations – to absorb it by abstaining from compensatory increases in wages and transfer payments larger than it had to be.

The initial mistake in exchange-rate policy was compounded by the failure to correct it once it was recognized. Having decided to use exchange-rate policy as a macroeconomic policy instrument, the government failed to use it consistently to try to hit the right level of stimulus – which would mean offsetting the initially excessive devaluation by a revaluation. When policymakers were asked why this was not done, the answer was that a revaluation would not be credible to the foreign-exchange markets. But both the Swedish policymakers and their vigorous critics in the IMF and other Nordic countries had agreed that the devaluation had been larger than it had to be to be sustainable, so it is hard to see why a revaluation that brought the exchange rate closer to what would have been sustainable would not continue to be credible. Indeed, precisely because a revaluation would have had a direct antiinflationary effect on import prices while at the same time signaling a willingness to bring inflation down, it probably would have contributed to the sustainability of the new exchange rate. Since competitiveness in U.S. markets would have been largely maintained by the dollar's sharp rise, while competiveness in European markets would have declined less to the extent that the inflation differential was diminished, the extent to which the recovery was export-led would probably have been nearly as great as it was. And as the extent of the export-led recovery became clearly evident, as it did during the following two years, the sustainability of a small revaluation would have been reinforced. Thus, a reduction in the scale of the devaluation was very unlikely to have significantly reduced the extent of the export-led recovery, while making its persistence more likely.

There was evidently more to the reluctance to correct the excessive devaluation by a revaluation than doubts about the markets' reaction to it, however. Since the devaluation was designed to induce increased investment in the tradables sector by boosting profits in it, a revaluation was viewed as defeating the whole point of the strategy. But this begs the question of how much increase in profits was optimal. Although, as a first approximation, the amount of investment might be expected to increase with the level of profits, the strategy is also exposed to risks that increase with the level of profits. The nature of these risks is familiar. For one thing, the higher the profits, the harder it is to secure wage restraint. Even if union negotiators, at whatever level, agree to rates of wage increases consistent with a ratcheting down of a wage–price spiral, workers' pressures for higher increases and employers' willingness to grant them can be expected to increase with the level of profits. The resulting wage-drift is likely to not only frustrate the intended wage restraint but also make it difficult for union negotiators to agree to wage restraint in the next round.[6] For another thing, the higher the profits, the less pressure there is for productivity-increasing investment. The expansion or preservation of existing plant, equipment, and product lines, including production that might no longer be profitable at exchange rates offering lower competitive advantages, rather than its replacement or modification in the quest for improved profitability, is encouraged (Erixon 1989).

Both kinds of risks are of course precisely what the RM model was designed to minimize through the maintenance of pressure on profits, biased against low-productivity production through standard-rate (solidaristic) wage policy (Martin 1984). The RM model leaves open the question of what the optimal level of profits is – the level that minimizes the risks stemming from high profits while inducing sufficient productivity-increasing investment to assure noninflationary full employment. As the level of profits rises, some point is reached where its negative effects outweigh its positive effects. The 1982 devaluation, under the unanticipated conditions that prevailed, probably pushed profits in Sweden's tradables sector beyond that point, to which they might well have been returned by a partial reversal. The optimum level undoubtedly differs under different conditions, and there may be conditions under which there is no trade-off that is satisfactory from a social democratic point of view; that may have been true in the 1980s, but not necessarily. The RM model was formulated at a time when profits in the tradables sector, measured in terms of the capital share of value added, were at exceptionally high levels, to which they briefly returned in the mid-1980s.[7]

It is also pertinent to recall that the RM model was framed in response to government pressures for wage restraint in the face of inflation and a profits boom, to which another large devaluation had contributed. That was the 1949 devaluation of the krona, following the British pound, by 30 percent against the dollar and Swiss franc, though only 13 percent on a trade-weighted basis. (Wihlborg 1993:205). It was credited with giving Swedish industry the advantage of an undervalued currency, which persisted for many years. Looking back at this precedent, the SD policymakers hoped that the 1982 devaluation would achieve the same kind of durable improvement in Swedish tradables' competitiveness.

They also repeated history by not subsequently revaluing in response to unanticipated changes when urged to by others. In the early postwar case,

6 This is a fundamental premise of the Rehn–Meidner model, which was given its classical formulation in the famous LO policy statement (LO 1951). For more recent discussions of the role of profits in wage formation, see Schager (1988) and Martin (1985).
7 For data on profits measured in terms of the capital share in value added in the tradables sector, see Martin (1984: 347, Table 3.5) and Konjunkturinstitutet (1987:118, Table 8:1).

revaluation was urged to blunt the domestic impact of the strong international inflationary pressures triggered by the Korean War. Having rejected that course, the government then sought exchange-rate stability (while preserving the undervaluation gained in 1949) by signing on to the Bretton Woods system in 1951, as the Korean War inflation died down. The designers of the Third Way anticipated a similar return to exchange-rate stability following what was to be a durable one-time shift in the terms of trade, to be accomplished by pegging the krona to the deutschmark. Originally intended to be immediate, this move was postponed indefinitely until its equivalent was adopted as a desperation measure when the krona was pegged (temporarily as it turned out) to the ECU in 1991. In any case, an immediate peg to the deutschmark would not have remedied the excessive devaluation unless it had been preceded by a revaluation. That, in turn, could have been done without pegging the currency to the deutschmark, even though doing so would undoubtedly have reinforced the credibility of the revaluation. Because the adoption of such a hard-currency policy could have signaled the replacement of full employment by price stability (as set by the Bundesbank) as the top policy priority, however, it was feared that it would alienate the unions, whose support was regarded as essential for the Third Way's success. Yet the continued utilization of exchange rates as an instrument of discretionary macroeconomic policy, implicit in the devaluation and equally consistent with any subsequent revaluation, would not have signaled an abandonment of full employment in the same way as adoption of a rule-based hard-currency policy would have, and would not have risked the loss of union support. On the contrary, both LO and the Central Organization of Salaried Employees (TCO) were the strongest advocates of a revaluation to correct the excessive devaluation, whose effects were making their efforts to secure wage restraint extremely difficult, precisely as the RM model described the effects of excessive demand on such efforts four decades earlier (Wihlborg 1993:239).

The differences between the situations then and in the 1980s made the case for consistent use of the exchange rate as a discretionary instrument of macroeconomic policy even stronger. The Korean War inflation was international, as prevalent in Sweden's trading partners as in Sweden, so inflation in Sweden did not threaten the competitiveness of its tradables, which helped make the 1949 devaluation's effects last. From 1983 through the rest of the decade (i.e., after the devaluation), on the other hand, Sweden' inflation rates tended to be around double those of the G7 countries and the EC (OECD 1993:140, Table A 15). This gap in inflation rates made it much more urgent to bring Sweden's rates down than in the 1950s by whatever means were available, including exchange-rate policy. At the same time, another difference between the two periods made any effort to secure exchange-rate stability futile and thereby risky. For in the 1950s, the Bretton Woods system into which Sweden entered provided relative stability for what turned out to be over two decades. The instability that set in once it broke down has proven to be inescapable. Though the efforts to establish a zone of stability in Europe may have been advantageous to Germany (and German manufacturers currently have strong doubts about that), they pose considerable risks to countries like Sweden whose markets are less concentrated in continental Europe. Continued discretion to vary the exchange rate against the deutschmark, to appreciate as well as depreciate against it, would thus be a valuable means for coping with those risks – which, of course, Sweden was forced to resort to anyway.[8] In all, it seems that Sweden's SD policymakers did have the option of quickly correcting what unexpectedly turned out to be an excessive devaluation through a revaluation, so that the failure to take that option was a mistake that did damage to their strategy that could have been avoided.

CREDIT MARKET DEREGULATION

The second basic policy choice that undermined the Third Way was the deregulation of the domestic credit market, particularly its timing in relation to changes in the tax system and elimination of foreign-exchange controls. The shift back from growth concentrated in the export sector to domestic consumption and investment in the sheltered sector shown so clearly in the data was to a large extent based on an explosive growth in borrowing, reflecting a total loss of control of the credit market. For a long time, Swedish economic policy had relied on an apparatus of credit controls both to curb inflation and to allocate capital, especially to housing, while keeping interest rates low. This apparatus operated mainly by credit ceilings and controls over the portfolios of banks and insurance companies. Over time, this apparatus eroded as people found various ways to circumvent the controls – new nonbank businesses and new practices for lending and borrowing developed – and it was difficult for the central bank to keep up with developments in this so-called gray market by extending the regulatory net to it. At the same time, the regulated sector – banks and insurance companies – complained that they were put at a competitive disadvantage. Finally, in keeping with the growing vogue of deregulation, economists were arguing that credit should be shifted to the market (Jonung 1993).[9]

So, during the early 1980s, the central bank was calling for deregulation.

---

8 In November 1992, the bourgeois government was forced to allow the krona to float, along with several other currencies, by the wave of disturbances in the European Exchange Rate Mechanism (ERM), thereby abandoning the effort to use the ERM as an external anchor for monetary policy begun by the Social Democratic government when it tied the krona to the ECU in May 1991.

9 An additional factor undermining the credit market regulatory system to which Jonung points was the state's efforts to meet its need to finance increased budget and current-account deficits after the late 1970s by attracting new buyers of government debt with market rates of interest that were higher than those given to the credit institutions that were required to purchase debt.

The Finance Minister agreed in principle but worried about its possible effects on consumption. He had good reason to do so, for an example of what could happen was near at hand in Norway, where a similar deregulation in 1984 was followed by a big burst in domestic consumption and asset price inflation (Rødseth 1994). But the central bank gave assurances that there would be no problem: The regulations were no longer working anyway, deregulation would simply shift borrowing back from the gray market to the banks, any net increase in borrowing would be temporary and small, and the central bank could handle it by limiting banks' borrowing at the central bank. With these assurances, the government gave its assent. The principal measure in the 1985 "November Revolution" was the abolition of quantitative ceilings on "nonpriority" lending by banks and mortgage institutions. In place of the quantitative controls, the central bank turned to interest charges on bank borrowing from the central bank, on a scale rising with the amount of borrowing relative to the borrowing bank's equity, as the principal instrument for controlling the volume of credit (Jonung 1993:312). As soon as the deed was done, it turned out that the central bank had been wrong in its assurances: There was a huge explosion of borrowing, it did not subside quickly, and the central bank could not handle it at all.[10]

After gently rising from about 72 to 77 percent of GDP during the first half of the 1980s (following two decades of virtual stability), the total volume of loans outstanding by all credit institutions more than doubled, to about 135 percent, between 1985 and 1990 (Jonung and Stymne 1997:25, Figure 1.2). The largest burst, in terms of the year-to-year change in loan stock, came immediately after the deregulation, with the biggest contributions coming from the banks and mortgage institutions, which had been most effectively regulated, while finance companies, which had grown up to evade the regulations and were less effectively regulated, made a much smaller contribution (Jonung and Stymne 1997:25, Figure 1.1). What this showed was that the controls had in fact been working to some extent even if they had not been working very well, for they had clearly dammed up a lot of demand for credit that flooded out once the controls were abolished.

That demand for credit was fueled by inflation, which was in turn accelerated by the credit-based boom, and by tax policy. Although the excessive stimulus as well as import price increases resulting from the large devaluation had made it difficult to bring inflation down, the government had achieved some success by 1985 (with considerable help from union wage restraint), after which the inflationary pressures that were building up anew were temporarily

10 The following account of the credit explosion relies heavily on Jonung and Stymne (1997), supplemented by Bäckström (1993) and Wohlin (1998). Some economists argue that deregulation contributed little to the boom that followed. Their arguments, which I find unconvincing, are summarized by Englund (1998).

offset (and obscured) by the sharp drop in oil prices – "OPEC III" – only to burst out in a sharp new acceleration of price increases beginning in 1987 (Jonung and Stymne 1997:29, Figure 1.5). Because nominal interest rates lagged behind inflation, real interest rates declined, becoming negative on one measure by 1991 (Jonung and Stymne 1997: 28, Figure 1.4). The incentive to borrow that this, together with expectations of continued inflation, provided was reinforced by the deductibility of interest on loans, not just for housing but any purposes, from taxable income. Earlier income tax reforms reduced but did not eliminate this possibility, leaving half of the interest still deductible when the domestic credit market was deregulated. This on top of inflation brought real interest rates even lower. On household bank loans, they fell to less than one percent in 1988 and 1989, dropping under zero in the following year (Jonung and Stymne 1997:30, Figure 1.6).

The result was a huge credit-based boom both in demand for consumer durables and in residential and commercial real estate, stimulating a construction boom. This put upward pressure on prices, not only of consumer durables but also real property and shares, especially the shares of banks, real estate, and construction companies (Jonung and Stymne 1997:36, Figure 1.12; 35, Figure 1.11). The upward pressure on asset prices was reinforced by the separation of domestic and foreign financial market deregulation. Though the domestic market was deregulated, capital controls that restricted investment in foreign securities and real estate by Swedish citizens (though they did not effectively restrict foreign direct investment by Swedish corporations) were left intact for another three years. In the interval, much of the increased demand for financial assets was confined to Sweden, creating a "hothouse" effect that pushed domestic asset prices up further. In turn, the rise in asset prices contributed to the further growth in the rate of borrowing as loans were secured with assets whose prices were increasing. The cumulative effect of all this was to make it possible for private consumption to sharply exceed disposable income in the years following the deregulation (Jonung and Stymne 1997:33, Figure 1.9). This meant that the household savings ratio became negative in those years (Jonung and Stymne 1997:37, Figure 1.14).

Thus, the extremely sharp rise in borrowing following deregulation of the credit market must have been largely, if indirectly, responsible for the abrupt shift in GDP growth from the tradables sector to domestic consumption and investment in the sheltered sector that so clearly signalled the breakdown of the Third Way. For the strategy to have worked, there had to be a shift in resources from the sheltered to the tradables sector, which was contingent on an increase in prices (including wages) and profits in the latter relative to the former, which in turn depended on concentrating demand growth in the latter and holding it back in the former. These requirements were met following the successive devaluations since 1977, but the trends in this direction were reversed and then moved sharply in the opposite direction following deregulation of the domestic credit market (Henrekson 1990: 32–7). The latter clearly undermined the Third Way by powerfully concentrating demand growth in the sheltered sector, as evidenced by the trends in consumption and asset prices. The credit-based domestic demand boom not only frustrated the Third Way but also increased the economy's financial fragility, and hence its vulnerability to a severe crash, for the boom was fueled by a classic speculative bubble. Released from their regulatory shackles, banks and their competitors fell all over themselves to lend – even issuing loans to customers as long as the customers did not specifically refuse the loans – so that the financial institutions loaded themselves up with loans that could only be serviced if the boom went on indefinitely, and real estate speculators – banks and construction companies – used loans to invest in projects that would also pay off only if the boom was perpetual. The speculative bubble thereby built up was bound to burst, and ultimately did, leading to a collapse of asset prices and a severe crisis in the Swedish banking system, which the next bourgeois government had to rescue with huge infusions of taxpayers' money.

Could the SD government have avoided, or at least mitigated, this source of the shift of demand growth back to the sheltered sector? It probably could not have avoided financial market deregulation indefinitely and completely. But it could have held on to the rickety system of controls longer since, as we at least know in retrospect, it was obviously having some effect. Even without the benefit of hindsight, however, the government might have acted differently, for the policymakers could have understood that timing was crucial from an elementary macroeconomic-policy perspective. Thus, it could have waited until the expansionary boom had been cooled down and then deregulated. That way, the deregulation could have been countercyclical instead of procyclical in its macroeconomic effect. Second, it could have waited until it had completed the tax reform it had planned anyway and entirely eliminated the deductibility of interest on loans. In other words, it could have done that first and then deregulated, rather than the other way around. Moreover, it might have delayed deregulation of the domestic credit market until it was ready to complete deregulation of international financial transactions. Finally, it could have taken more seriously the lesson to be learned by simply glancing over the border to Norway.

So why didn't the government at least eliminate the deductibility of interest before deregulating the credit market when it did? The main reason, apart from the failure of the central bank to anticipate the consequences of deregulation in the context of existing tax provisions, was that elimination of the deductibility of interest was considered part of a comprehensive tax reform package – referred to as the "tax reform of the century" – which was not yet ready to be launched. This was the Finance Minister's big project for improving the tax systems' long-term microeconomic effects, and he was afraid it would be politically vulnerable if done in bits and pieces. So he sacrificed macroeconomic policy to tax reform.

MACROECONOMIC POLICY IN SWEDEN

That was not the first time that had happened in Sweden; it had been done in 1970 by the Finance Minister's long-time predecessor, Gunnar Sträng, and the former was one of those who criticized his predecessor for doing so at the time. But there was an obvious way to have it both ways: Elimination of interest deductibility could have been kept in the tax package and still precede or be concurrent with credit market deregulation if the latter had been postponed, which would have been favorable in other respects as well. Unfortunately, the pleas by the banks and insurance companies and the naive assurances of the central bank obscured the risks. The conclusion seems inescable: The mistimed deregulation of the domestic credit market did severe damage to the SDs' economic strategy that could have been avoided.

MACROECONOMIC POLICY AND THE WAGE-BARGAINING SYSTEM

While the mistimed deregulation of the financial market directly undermined the effectiveness of monetary policy as an instrument for curbing the growth of domestic consumption, it indirectly undermined the effectiveness of the wage-bargaining system in making the contribution to the Third Way expected of it as well. That was to keep wage increases from offsetting the effect of devaluation in shifting demand growth from domestic consumption to exports and investment in the tradables sector. In doing so, as the Finance Minister put it, the Swedish model of wage bargaining, with its element of centralized negotiations, served as the "linchpin of the Third Way" (Feldt 1991:330). However, this was a burden that the wage-bargaining system could not bear in the face of the demand pressures generated by the combination of excessive devaluation and credit explosion.

It had long been understood by most actors in the Swedish political economy that the principal way in which unions could contribute to macroeconomic stability was by dampening inter-union wage rivalry through coordinated bargaining, thereby minimizing the extent to which such rivalry acted as an autonomous source of inflationary pressures in addition to those generated by a given level of demand. It had also been understood that the capacity of coordinated bargaining to keep inter-union wage rivalry from generating additional inflationary pressures varied with the level of demand, so that it diminished as increasing demand increased the tightness of labor markets. Thus, it could not be expected to counteract wage pressures generated by extremely tight labor markets in which employers drove wages far beyond negotiated rates by competing with each other for scarce labor. For unions to try to restrain wage growth in the face of such market pressures was bound not only to be futile but also to jeopardize their own internal cohesion. In other words, coordinated bargaining, for which central negotiations provided the underpinning, was limited in what it could do to curb inflation: it could supplement well-calibrated macroeconomic policy but it could not substitute for it.[11]

By the time the coordinating capacity of the Swedish model of wage bargaining was needed to support the Third Way strategy, however, that capacity had already been reduced – just as the effectiveness of credit market regulation had been. The function of inhibiting inter-union wage rivalry could be performed fairly effectively as long as wage bargaining was dominated by centralized negotiations between the confederation of blue-collar unions, LO, and the private-sector employers' confederation, SAF. However, the growth of separate white-collar unions, and the growth of both blue- and white-collar unions in the public sector, meant that LO–SAF negotiations covered a diminishing portion of the labor market (Calmfors and Forslund 1990:80–1, Tables 2 and 3; Elvander 1988). Wage rivalry between unions included in those negotiations and those outside them, as well as among the latter, made it increasingly difficult to curb the inflationary effects of wage rivalry.

Partly in response to this, powerful private-sector employers, notably the large multinationals in the engineering industry that were at the core of the economy, became disenchanted with central negotiations. This, as has been widely observed, was also partly because they felt that the standard rate or solidaristic wage policy on the basis of which LO unions agreed to coordinated wage bargaining limited their ability to differentiate wages to attract and retain skilled workers – a problem intensified by tight labor markets. The denouement is familiar (Swenson and Pontusson, this volume). The engineering employers withdrew from central negotiations in 1983, having induced Metall, the metalworkers union, to go along with them, and there were no central negotiations at all with SAF in the next wage round. After a partial and more complete restoration of centralized negotiations in the next two rounds, negotiations were again partially and then completely decentralized to industry level. By the end of the decade, SAF declared that it would never again engage in centralized negotiations, marking the definitive end of the Swedish model of wage bargaining as it had functioned since the mid-1950s. One more centralized agreement on the overall rate of wage increases, but no more, was reached, but only when the SD government set up a mechanism, the so-called Rehnberg commission, to perform the coordinating function that the peak organizations no longer could or would perform. This shift toward a state-led incomes policy proved to be a one-time event. By the time the contracts negotiated under the agreement expired, the bourgeois coalition was in power, and it was disinclined to extend the life of the commission in the face of renewed employer determination to

---

11 This understanding underlies the RM model as originally formulated in *Fackföreningsrörelsen och den fulla sysselsättningen* and has been articulated recurrently since. For further discussion see Martin (1984, 1985).

decentralize wage bargaining (Kjellberg 1998; Martin 1992; Pontusson and Swenson 1993).

Preserving coordinated bargaining in the face of these centrifugal forces on both sides of the labor market would have been difficult under the best of circumstances, so that it might simply have been impossible for this requirement of the Third Way to be met. On the other hand, the restoration of central negotiations in 1986 showed that there were strategies that the government and LO (including Metall) could use to bring SAF back to the bargaining table on behalf of the private-sector employers it represented (Martin 1992:61; Elvander 1988:220–30). But by then the boom that was already getting out of control, and the extremely tight labor markets that resulted, along with the intensification of distributive conflict fueled by increasing wage-drift and the growth of speculative wealth, created circumstances in which it was impossible for the government and LO to hold coordinated bargaining together.

Unemployment declined steadily from its 1983 peak of 3.5 to 1.9 percent in 1987, the second year of the two-year contracts negotiated in 1986. By the next year it was down to 1.6 percent and reached the extremely low trough of 1.4 percent in 1989. But these are national averages; unemployment was even lower in the metropolitan areas, especially Stockholm, where vacancies increasingly exceeded the number of unemployed workers in 1988 and 1989 (*Konjunkturldget* 1987:84; *The Swedish Economy* 1991:73, 77). Competition for labor among employers intensified as increasing proportions reported shortages of both skilled and other workers. More than three-quarters of engineering industry employers reported shortages of skilled workers by mid-1989, while there were even larger shortages of construction workers by then, reflecting the speculative real estate boom described earlier (*The Swedish Economy* 1990:71). The result, not surprisingly, was increasing levels of wage-drift, which exceeded negotiated increases for industrial workers in 1988 and 1989 (Figure 8.1). This had not happened since the 1974 wave of wildcat strikes accompanying the profits explosion that occurred then, and had not happened for two years in a row as far back as the records go. Thus, in these extremely tight labor markets, workers whose pay systems afforded opportunities for drift – primarily in the private sector – could cushion their wages against the inflation that had begun to increase rapidly in 1987 after falling markedly in the preceding years. This, as was to be expected, made distributive conflict among workers more intractable, particularly between those in the private and public sectors, and intensified the pressure on all unions, regardless of sector, to push for higher negotiated increases. Thus, whatever capacity the wage-bargaining system might have had to moderate the growth of wages was completely overwhelmed by the expansionary boom precipitated by the government's macroeconomic policy failures. What was remarkable is that the wage-bargaining system had been able to deliver as much wage restraint as it did, particularly in 1985 and 1986 when

Percent

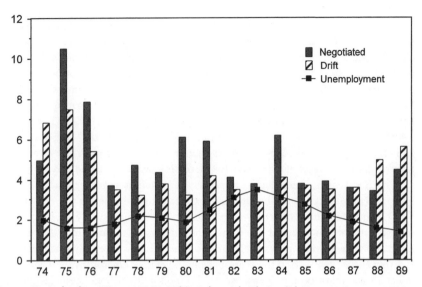

Source: *Konjunkturläget*, Hösten 1987, Table 5.6, p. 84; *The Swedish Economy*, Autumn 1991, Table 5.6, p.73 and Statistical Appendix, Table 18, p. 150.

Figure 8.1. *Wages and unemployment. Industrial workers' negotiated increases and wage-drift, and total unemployment, year-on-year percentage change, 1974–89.*

the government and unions succeeded in restoring some degree of central coordination, despite macroeconomic conditions that were already making it increasingly difficult (Figure 8.1).

If circumstances had been otherwise – in other words, if the government had not made the exchange-rate and credit-market policy choices that allowed the boom to get out of control – what difference might it have made to the wage-bargaining system's course of development? It seems at least possible that coordinated bargaining could have been held together beyond 1986 long enough to make the changes necessary for it to be acceptable to enough of the most powerful employers for it to be continued in some form, though almost certainly not in the form it had taken in the past. Such changes would have had to include a redefinition of the basis on which unions agreed to such bargaining. They would have had to make it possible to secure agreement to reverse the process of compression and standardization resulting from the form solidaristic wage policy had taken, allowing greater flexibility and differentiation. Could this have happened? There is evidence suggesting that it could, for such changes were already under way during the 1980s under the ideological cover of what was called "solidaristic work policy." Essentially, this is a formula for legitimating pay for knowledge, defining wage differentials based on skill differences as acceptable, providing that opportunities for learning skills were distributed in egalitarian (i.e., solidaristic) fashion through changes in the organization of training and work (Mahon 1991). This reformulation of solidaristic wage policy brings it closer to the way it was initially conceived in the RM model, emphasizing equal pay for equal work rather than generalized compression as it subsequently came to be understood. If, as argued, new production systems increased the need for such differentials, "solidaristic work policy" eased the adaptation of wage policy to that need.

While solidaristic work policy has been elaborated by LO and echoed in many of its affiliates as well as some of the white-collar unions, the initiative for it came from Metall. This is the metalworkers union, which joined with the engineering employers to break with the system of central negotiations in 1983. As importantly, however, it played a pivotal role in the temporary restoration of such negotiations in 1986 (Metall 1991). Metall's efforts to find a new basis on which unions could agree on coordinating wage bargaining, as well as its efforts to undo in 1986 what it helped to do in 1983, suggest that its interest in cross-class coalitions is limited and could be outweighed by the interest in intraclass coalitions that it evidently still has, so that it is not inevitably or unconditionally an ally of the engineering employers in their drive for decentralization. This is manifested most clearly in its bargaining coalitions and more permanent arrangements with other unions representing workers, white as well as blue collar, in the private sector, involving agreement on common new pay systems.

At the same time, by cutting across the confederal lines along which occupations have historically been organized in Sweden, the unions involved are facilitiating another change for which employers have been pressing: the replacement of separate agreements for workers belonging to different blue- and white-collar unions by single agreements that cover all workers, to which common pay systems apply without reference to organizationally defined occupational demarcations. The unions' response to the pressures for this kind of change has been to try to shape it rather than resist it. Thus, the unions seek to retain some control over the negotiation of single agreements through collective bargaining at the sectoral level in the face of employer efforts to confine their negotiation to the company level, in what appears to be a drive toward enterprise unionism (Martin 1995:281–82, Kjellberg 1998). While this gives the unions confronting the same employers a vital stake in cooperation, this does not preclude the identification of wider common interests, even across the more intractable private–public sector divide. What has made it so intractable are the claims for comprehensive sectoral pay parity advanced by the public-sector unions in the name of solidaristic wage policy. Even though the same conflicting claims can obviously be recast in terms of solidaristic work policy, the greater scope for knowledge-based differentiation inherent in that formula offers a more promising basis on which private- and public-sector unions might try to manage their conflicts so as to avoid mutually disavantageous political outcomes.

Even if that formula offers a more promising terrain for negotiations among unions as well as between unions and employers, it alone obviously cannot be expected to overcome the intra- as well as interclass conflicts that have been fragmenting the wage-bargaining system. Nevertheless, it along with the other changes that have been occurring suggests that it might have been possible to manage those conflicts in such a way as to permit centrally coordinated bargaining to continue in some modified form capable of performing the function of dampening interunion wage rivalry. It would probably have had to be organized by the government, perhaps along the lines of the Rehnberg commission or the even more active intervention by the Norwegian government, rather than by peak labor-market organizations as in the past (Dølvik, Bråten, Longva, and Steen 1997; Kahn 1996). And the content of the coordinated bargaining would also have had to be different. Agreements at the central level would probably have had to be confined to specifying overall rates of wage growth and, for example, general rules for assuring fairness in access to training and evaluation procedures, without detailed provisions governing the distribution of wage growth and configuration of pay systems, which would be left to bargaining at sectoral and local levels.

THE POLITICAL CONDITIONS FOR MAINTAINING CENTRALLY COORDINATED BARGAINING

Though it seems plausible to argue that the wage-bargaining system could have been modified in ways that might permit a measure of centrally coordinated bargaining to continue, this probably could have occurred only if three other basic conditions had been met. One is economic and the other two are political. The first is a macroeconomic environment that would have made it possible for wage increases to be set largely through central and sectoral collective bargaining, rather than market forces operating through competitive bidding among employers, essentially as prescribed by the RM model. In other words, it would have been necessary for the Third Way strategy to be successful. In the light of our analysis of why it was not successful, it seems plausible to argue that it could have been. There was nothing inevitable about the two major policy choices – the excessive devaluation and perversely timed domestic credit dereg-ulation – that combined to assure its failure. There were alternatives that could have been chosen; nothing in the domestic economy or politics or in the international economy blocked those alternatives. Accordingly, the first of these additional conditions probably could have been met.

If so, then there is a chance that the second condition could have been met.

That is the SDs' continuation in office. If social democratic control of governments has typically been a necessary, though not sufficient, condition for various forms of neo-corporatist bargaining structures in the past, it is probably even more necessary now, particularly insofar as governments need to intervene more actively to organize them than in the past. Swedish conservative governments were no more likely to do that than conservative governments were in Norway or elsewhere in the 1980s. So it is not surprising that the bourgeois coalition that came into power in Sweden in 1991 did not extend the Rehnberg commission's life, although by that time, the disintegration of centrally coordinated bargaining had probably gone too far, and the position of employers determined to push it further was too strongly entrenched to build on the alternative, which the Rehnberg commission embodied. Moreover, the sharp rise in unemployment following the collapse of the Third Way effectively eliminated any need for wage restraint to help curb inflation, at least for the foreseeable future. On the other hand, an SD government that had implemented the Third Way effectively, and had consequently been able to remain in office, would have had a strong stake in doing whatever was necessary to maintain a wage-bargaining structure capable of protecting noninflationary full employment from disruption by inter-union wage rivalry. In addition, SD parties that rely heavily on union mobilization of electoral support, as do the Swedish SDs, have another strong political stake in minimizing inter-union wage rivalry and the conflicts over economic policy with such parties it is likely to precipitate, in order to maximize the unions' political cohesion and hence their effectiveness in mobilizing support for the SDs (tacitly in the case of many TCO unions as well as explicitly in the case of most LO unions) (Martin 1992:chs. 2, 4, 5).

This suggests why the third condition might not have been met. That condition is a willingness on the part of employers to engage in centrally coordinated wage bargaining. Since it takes two to tango (or in this case three, with the government at least providing the dance lessons), such bargaining obviously could not take place unless the employers could be induced to come back to the table. And, of course, the Swedish employers, spearheaded by those in the engineering industry, were increasingly determined in their refusal to do so. But as we saw, it was possible that the changes under way in the structure and content of centrally coordinated bargaining were at least potentially capable of meeting the employers' essentially microeconomic objections to the system of centralized negotiations as they had functioned in the past. If this made coordinated bargaining more acceptable to the employers, a macroeconomic context in which such coordinated bargaining could also serve a useful stabilizing function might have made it even more acceptable.

All of this might nevertheless not have been enough to overcome employer opposition to the continuation of centrally coordinated wage bargaining, no matter in what form. It could well be that, in addition to the economic stakes employers came to believe they had in eliminating such bargaining, many of

them perceived a political stake in doing so. The very function of reinforcing
the unions' political cohesion and mobilizational effectiveness that coordinated
bargaining seems to have served, giving the SDs and their union supporters a
political stake in it, is precisely what could give employers a political stake in
terminating it. Whether this political function of coordinated bargaining did
give employers a stake in terminating it depends on whether they came to
believe that the disadvantages of SD governments, or at least SD governments
that remained strongly dependent on union support, outweighed any advantages
they might afford over the unstable coalitions of bourgeois parties. There is
some evidence to suggest that employer opinion did move strongly in this
direction in the 1970s.[12]

By the middle of the decade, the interaction of SD government and union
policies was being perceived as posing increasing threats to employer interests,
prompting an intensive internal review of SAF's role and strategy. These threats
included the growth of the public sector and its multiple impacts on wage
bargaining, directly through pattern-setting and indirectly through the taxation
to finance it, and increasing reliance on payroll taxation to offset income tax
concessions exchanged for wage restraint. Particularly disturbing, however, was
the unprecedented burst of labor legislation over the preceding half-decade. This
legislation significantly enlarged union and employee rights and correspondingly constrained those of employers, most notably with respect to employment
security, workplace health and safety, the rights of local union officials, and
union representation on company boards. The codetermination law (MBL) pending at the time would extend the pattern, giving unions a voice in work
organization matters that had hitherto been managerial prerogatives. Moreover,
an even more fundamental threat loomed ahead in the form of the proposal for
wage-earner funds (collective profit sharing) LO was preparing. This new and
still growing body of legislation was perceived in SAF, as it was in LO, as
demonstrating LO's ability to bring about changes in labor-market institutions
through the political process that it could not win through negotiations, and
that further reinforced the unions' power.

From SAF's perspective, the political route that LO took to achieve the
changes as well as the substance of the changes were both departures from the
"Swedish model" of industrial relations that had prevailed ever since it was

---

12 The following discussion is based on De Geer (1989:122–39, 222–4, 276, 289–321) and interviews
in 1989 and 1990 with SAF and industry executives who required anonymity. On the basis of his
own familiarity with the archives cited by De Geer, Peter Swenson has argued compellingly in
personal communications and conversations that there is little documentary evidence for the proposition that employers saw in the elimination of central negotiations a way to weaken LO's political
power. He acknowledges, however, that such views might be held even if not recorded in the archives
and that such views are at least consistent with the intensification of SAF's political activity in
response to the labor legislation sought by LO and enacted by Social Democratic governments in the
1970s.

enshrined in the Basic Agreement reached by LO and SAF at Saltsjöbaden in 1938. One of its central features was the regulation of industrial relations primarily through negotiations between the private parties in the labor market, without state intervention.[13] Another of its central features was that the counterpart of management's recognition of labor's right to organize was labor's recognition of management's right to manage. LO was now seen as abandoning the private regulation of industrial relations in favor of state intervention, relying on its power in the political arena to overcome SAF's efforts to uphold management's rights in the labor market.

To defend employer interests against these threats more effectively than it had, many voices within SAF urged it to take a more active political role. The organization had already begun to increase its efforts to influence public opinion. These efforts, which included the sharpening of its own membership's ideological awareness and confidence as well as building more favorable attitudes to private enterprise in the wider public, were initiated in response to the leftward shift in the political climate in the late 1960s. The radicalization of LO, parallel trends in TCO, and the readiness with which the political parties, primarily the Social Democratic Party but also the Liberal party, were willing to translate the unions' initiatives into policy were all interpreted as efforts to cope with the challenge from the left to which the parties themselves were exposed. SAF's campaign to reverse the shift and create a more favorable climate for private enterprise was intensified during the first half of the 1970s. But SAF's mid-decade review showed the need to do more to counter the threats.

Given the importance ascribed to the threats that flowed directly from LO's leverage in the policy arena, reducing that leverage would seem like an obvious way to counter the threats; and insofar as that leverage was based on LO's wage-bargaining role, a similarly obvious way to reduce LO's leverage would be to deprive LO of that role. These links between LO's political and wage-bargaining roles could hardly have gone unnoticed; in fact they were not. A participant in the SAF executive committee's discussion in late 1975 is described as urging "decentralized negotiations, which would obstruct solidaristic wage policy and weaken the centralized counterparts [i.e., LO and PTK]" (De Geer 1989:128). And in SAF's postmortem on the preceding wage round at the beginning of 1976, the likelihood that "a decentralization [of wage negotiations] would diminish the trade union movement's power" was explicitly cited as an argument for abandoning central negotiations. The threat of wage-earner funds and MBL legislation looming on the horizon are the only reasons indicated why the diminution of the union movement's power was held to be desirable (De Geer 1989:224). But that is perhaps enough, for it seems clear that LO's ability to

13 Except for a ban on strikes during the life of contracts, which was enacted into law by a bourgeois coalition government with the support of SAF in 1928, and which remains in force. For an excellent analysis of the system of "centralized self-regulation," see Kjellberg (1998).

secure passage of such legislation was perceived as a major threat to employer interests, that LO's ability to do so was ascribed to the wage-bargaining role that centralized negotiations gave it, and that decentralization of wage negotiations was viewed as a way of combating the threat by depriving LO of that wage-bargaining role.

Although the impulse to decentralize wage negotiations was evidently reinforced by the expectation that it would reduce LO's power in the policy arena, the impulse was inhibited by doubts that some had at that point in the 1970s about the economic consequences of a transition to decentralized negotiations. In any case, the urgency of diminishing the SD labor movement's political power was diminished when the SDs lost the 1976 election. The resulting formation of the first bourgeois government since 1932 was seen as creating the conditions for pursuing an alternative strategy for wage bargaining that relied on a greater centralization rather than decentralization. At the same time, this historic and possibly durable shift in the distribution of political power also diminished the force of the political argument for decentralized bargaining. MBL had been enacted near the end of the Social Democratic goverment, but its effects could be blunted now that the unions could no longer hold the credible threat of a "political alternative" to negotiations over the employers in the process of negotiating MBL's implementation. Moreover, the threat of wage-earner funds had been removed, at least for the time being and potentially forever. Not only would the stream of labor legislation be stopped, but the whole range of policy could be expected to be more favorable. With the SAP out of power, then, whatever political leverage LO might have derived from central negotiations was severely curtailed; such leverage was accordingly no longer a strong reason to end central negotiations.

When the expectations held out for the bourgeois governments were disappointed, however, the impulse to decentralization reemerged more strongly than ever. From the employers' perspective, centralized negotiations brought no better results under the bourgeois governments than they had under the Social Democrats.[14] Moreover, the divisions among the bourgeois parties that rendered them incapable of governing effectively assured the Social Democrats' return to power in 1982, and with it the renewed threat of legislative encroachment on employer interests. There is no reason to think that the links between LO's wage-bargaining role and such a threat, which had been observed in the mid-seventies, had been forgotten; that it had not been seems quite clear from the responses of those interviewed a decade and a half later.[15] On the contrary, in view of the establishment of wage-earner funds, albeit in much watered-down

---

14 The greatest disappointment was the government's failure to back SAF's massive lockout against all its LO union counterparts in 1980 (De Geer 1989:265).
15 Interviews conducted by the author during 1989 and 1990 with SAF and industry executives who required anonymity.

form, there was reason to attach renewed importance to LO's influence in the policy arena, and hence to consider ways of diminishing it when the SAP was back in power. If, as could be expected, it would be diminished by decentralizing wage bargaining, that could only reinforce the case for doing so. And if doing so would also contribute to a more durable shift in the distribution of political power by diminishing the intensity and effectiveness of the LO unions' mobilization of electoral support for the SAP, that could only add to the attractiveness of decentralizing wage negotiations, even if that could not be one of its explicitly avowed objectives.

Though the reduction of electoral support for the SAP was not an explicitly avowed objective of SAF's increasing efforts to influence public opinion either, any effects those efforts might have in improving the bourgeois parties' electoral fortunes could hardly be unintended. To be sure, much care was taken to uphold SAF's image of nonpartisanship. Thus, the need to do so was emphasized at the time SAF took its initial decisions to expand its political role. To that end, any impression of direct SAF support for the bourgeois parties was to be avoided. This was a view shared by those parties, leading them to decide to stop accepting financial support from business organizations or companies, the liberals doing so in 1971 and the conservatives in 1977 (Gidlund 1983:246–7). In addition, it was deemed important for SAF's positions to be formulated differently from those of the parties and to limit its efforts to the earlier months of election years, curtailing its activities as elections approached. Such dissociation of SAF and party activities was necessary to lend plausibility to the claim, made by SAF's executive director in 1982, that "we do not generally participate in election campaigns" (De Geer 1989:125, 276; Hansson and Lodenius 1988:22, 26–37). By then, however, SAF was abandoning this caution and extending its efforts closer to the elections, both in its own name and through a network of separate organizations, including publishing and public relations subsidiaries and associations that it supported or cooperated with.

Notwithstanding SAF's formal nonpartisanship, then, the main thrust of SAF's endeavors to influence public opinion was certainly complementary to the bourgeois parties' campaign themes, particularly those of the conservative party and, to a somewhat lesser extent, the liberals. This was the case not only with the issue of wage-earner funds but also the broader, less controversial but nevertheless contested features of Social Democratic policy, such as the growth of the public sector, the taxes to finance it, and its alleged insensitivity to individual choice. These themes came to be woven together within a broad neo-liberal ideology that called for a "system change" that would replace the bureaucratic social democratic order with the "market economic alternative" (Thimerdal 1985). This kind of fundamental system change was what the bourgeois government that came to power in 1991 promised to bring about.

SAF's long-term efforts to change the ideological parameters of Swedish politics in a neo-liberal direction were continued and given greater impetus under a new chairman installed in 1989. In addition to being the CEO of a major engineering-sector firm, he had also held leadership posts in the conservative party. Having declared "the so-called 'Swedish model' dead" as a result of SAF's commitment to decentralized bargaining, he went on to say in an open letter to the membership that:

> The center of gravity of SAF's work is shifting to idea and opinion formation. It is ideas that change the world. If SAF can successfully spread tomorrow's ideas about wage formation and economic policy issues and what concerns the very basis for a free and good society – the market economy – the association's role would be greater than ever. SAF is the motor of system change (*SAF Tidningen* 16 February 1990:11).

In effect, SAF took over from the bourgeois parties the task of formulating and articulating the ideology with which to mobilize support for the "market economy alternative." Even if it thereby becomes the motor of system change, however, it obviously cannot do without the parties to get the legislative measures needed to implement the alternative, such as "lowering tax pressure, opening the public sector to competition, and privatizing publicly owned enterprise" (*SAF Tidningen* 16 February 1990:11). To the extent that SAF does perform this task successfully, it is bound to weaken the SAP's appeal and improve the bourgeois parties' electoral prospects. This could hardly be unintended; nor would this, in turn, be in any way surprising. Given the wide variety of ways in which SD policy was judged contrary to the interests of the employers SAF was supposed to represent, particularly since the early 1970s, and the ideological orientation most employers presumably share, a very high proportion of them could obviously be expected to support the bourgeois parties, especially the conservative party.[16]

While Swedish employers' political sympathies undoubtedly lie overwhelmingly with the bourgeois parties, this entitles us to conclude no more than that the employers are likely to regard any weakening of the Social Democratic labor movement that might result from the decentralization of wage bargaining as a welcome by-product of it, without necessarily regarding it as an objective to be pursued through decentralization. If such sympathies alone determined employer attitudes to the structure of wage bargaining, it might never have been centralized to begin with. After all, it was SAF's insistence that brought the system of central negotiations into being, but there is no reason to think that employers' political sympathies were any less strongly with the bourgeois parties when SAF did so. Such evidence as we do have tells us that employers were, if anything, slightly more inclined to support those parties at the inception of centralized bargaining than they are now (Giljam and Holm-

---

16 There is not much empirical evidence to support this intuitively self-evident proposition but there is some. See Holmberg (1984:102) and Giljam and Holmberg (1990:220).

berg 1990:220). What evidently determined SAF's earlier preference for a centralized structure was its estimation of the direct effects of alternative bargaining
structures on wages rather than any indirect effects they might have on LO's
political role. Similarly, it might seem, what determined the more recent switch
in its preference to a more decentralized structure was the change in its estimation of those direct effects on wages rather than any indirect political effects.
What changed, apparently, was not the political sympathies of SAF's leaders
and members but their economic evaluation of centralized negotiations. Previously, any indirect political gains the Social Democratic labor movement might
have derived from such negotiations had presumably been deemed a price worth
paying for the direct economic benefits the employers derived from centralized
negotiations. Those political gains were presumably judged a price no longer
worth paying when central negotiations no longer yielded those economic
benefits.

The story may not be that simple, however. For one thing, it might not
have occurred to those involved in SAF's initial efforts to compel LO to engage
in central negotiations that they could contribute anything to LO's political
role. The possible connection might not have been noticed until much later,
perhaps not until the 1970s when LO's political role was increasingly perceived
as a threat. Alternatively, the connection might have been noticed but not
judged to be a cost or a price that was being paid until the 1970s. At least
during the prime years of the Swedish model, once the pension issue died down
and as long as LO and the Social Democratic government observed the spirit of
Saltsjöbaden as SAF understood it, whatever contributed to LO's authority and
influence might well have been viewed positively, contributing to the consensual governance of Sweden through cooperation between highly organized business and labor. Only when LO began using the political gains it derived from
centralized negotiations to win legislation that threatened employer interests
did those gains presumably come to be judged as costs. From this point of view,
the price paid for central negotiations could be said to be rising at a time when
the economic benefits they yielded to employers were declining.

The story is probably even more complicated than that, for the calculus in
terms of which the economic benefits yielded by central negotiations were
judged may well have been changing, quite apart from any decline in the
capacity of central negotiations to deliver what had earlier been expected of it.
Such a change could well have been expected from the increasing internationalization of Swedish industry. Sweden's large multinational firms, heavily concentrated in the engineering sector that has driven the decentralization of wage
bargaining, have become increasingly important to Sweden's economy at the
same time that the Swedish market has become less important for them. Thus,
they account for an increasing share of Sweden's exports while those exports,
and their sales in Sweden, account for a decreasing share of their total worldwide
sales (Swedenborg, Johansson-Grahn, and Kinnwall 1988).

As Swedish multinationals – or multinationals that still have operations in Sweden – come to depend decreasingly on sales in Sweden, the level of demand in Sweden becomes decreasingly important for them (Erixon 1985). What is important for them is the supply of whatever they need for whichever of their operations remain in Sweden. Paramount among such inputs is the skilled and adaptable labor that they are accustomed to having in Sweden. For them, it is important to secure such labor, and to be able to attract and keep it with wages relatively higher than needed to secure whatever less skilled and less scarce ancillary labor they need, without having their wage costs driven up by having to compete for its most sought-after labor in labor markets made tight by the quest for full employment, and without being forced to offset the reduction of differentials by solidaristic wage policy. This, of course, is what gives such firms an especially strong stake in a decentralization of wage bargaining that would render solidaristic wage policy impossible.[17]

But it also gives them a stake in the whole range of changes embraced in the "market economy alternative" promulgated by SAF and the conservative party, for it promises greater capacity to concentrate expenditures on labor costs where they are most needed from their point of view while slowing the overall growth of labor costs. Thus, rolling back the public sector and diluting the universalistic welfare state by private provision promises less need for financing by income and payroll taxes. The "tax wedge" between the firms' labor costs and the earnings of the workers they want to attract, and to keep in order to capture the returns on investment in training, could presumably be decreased correspondingly. While their labor costs would probably have to include the costs of generous "fringe benefits," they would presumably be limited insofar as they were confined to financing "private welfare states" for the firms' own employees instead of the universalistic welfare state built up over decades of Social Democratic rule.

If such a transformation of Swedish society is what is required for Sweden to remain an attractive site for some of the multinationals' operations, it can hardly be achieved without substantial political changes. The return of government by the bourgeois parties on a more durable basis would meet that need. If that is prevented by the continuing divisions among the bourgeois parties, the need might still be met by a Social Democratic party with sufficiently diminished electoral support to make it unable to govern except as a partner in coalitions with one or more bourgeois parties. If depriving LO of its wage-bargaining role contributes to that result by diminishing LO's capacity to maintain its affiliates' political cohesion and hence their effectiveness in mobilizing electoral support, bringing with it a diminution in LO's influence on policy, the decentralization of wage bargaining would be directly instrumental to

---

17 This is one of the central factors in the explanation for the decentralizaiton of wage bargaining advanced in Pontusson and Swenson (1993) and Swenson and Pontusson (this volume).

achieving the necessary political changes. The need might even be met by a Social Democratic Party able to garner enough electoral support to govern without entering into coalitions with any bourgeois parties by distancing itself from unions, like Britain's "New Labour," encouraged to do so by LO's declining mobilizational capacity. Thus, while reconfigured economic interests undoubtedly drove the Swedish engineering multinationals to reject the system of central negotiations they previously supported, they may well have done so because of the indirect political effects of central negotiations as well as their direct economic effects.

CONCLUSION

I have argued that the Swedish engineering employers' objections to the direct microeconomic effects of the system of centralized wage negotiations as it had come to operate are insufficient to explain their stakes in terminating the system and their success in doing so. Two other factors, I suggested, contributed to this outcome. One is the macroeconomic conditions under which the system operated as a consequence of two key policy decisions made by SD governments: an excessively large devaluation immediately upon returning to office in 1982 and an ill-timed deregulation of the domestic credit market in 1985. The combined effect of these decisions was to generate an explosive expansionary boom that undermined the SD's Third Way economic strategy and made it much more difficult than it otherwise would have been to resist the employers' drive to end centralized negotiations. The other factor is the effect of the wage-bargaining role such negotiations gave LO in reinforcing the LO unions' political cohesion, effectiveness in mobilizing electoral support for the SDs, and hence LO's influence on SD policy. Increasing opposition to the resulting pattern of policy since the 1970s by employers generally as well as the engineering employers in particular led to increased efforts to influence electoral outcomes, to which the elimination of the wage-bargaining role that contributed to the LO's mobilizational effectiveness could be instrumental.

The counterfactual scenario implied by these propositions is that centralized negotiations could have been maintained in some form providing that four conditions had been met: (i) a macroeconomic environment in which centralized negotiations could function effectively to moderate wage growth; (ii) modifications in the form of centralized negotiations along lines that would satisfy the employers' microeconomic interests; (iii) a continuation of SD control of the government; and (iv) a renewed willingness of employers to engage in centralized negotiations. I tried to show that the first three conditions could have been met. Alternative decisions with less-expansionary macroeconomic effects that could plausibly have been made could have met the first condition. This would have created a more favorable environment for the modifications in the form of wage negotiations that could have met the second condition. By permitting successful implementation of SD economic strategy, a less expansionary macroeconomic environment could have made it possible to meet the third condition. This leaves the question of whether the fourth condition could have been met, a question that shall be left open.

Organized employers, at least in Sweden and elsewhere in Europe, are typically more reticent about their partisan preferences than unionists, preferring to couch the policies they call on governments to pursue in terms of economic necessity – the word is "competitiveness" nowadays. However, since we know that unions are typically not merely economic actors, in the sense of confining their action to markets, but are also engaged in politics, it should not surprise us if employers too are engaged in politics. In either case, politics may be instrumental to economic interests or they may be driven as well, or more, by ideological commitments, and in either case the political implications of actions in markets may enter into the choices shaping those actions. It may accordingly be necessary to bring politics back into political economy to adequately understand the eminently political struggles over the shape of labor-market institutions as well as much else.

References
Bäckström, Urban. 1993. "Tillgångspriser och stabiliseringspolitik," Ekonomisk Debatt 21, 5.
Bergström, Villy. 1989. "Vårt ekonomiska läge." In Vårt ekonomiska läge. Stockholm: Sparfrämjandet.
Calmfors, Lars and Anders Forslund. 1990. "Wage Formation in Sweden." In Lars Calmfors, ed., Wage Formation and Macroeconomic Policy in the Nordic Countries. Oxford: Oxford University Press.
De Geer, Hans 1989. I vänstervind och högervåg: SAF under 70-talet. Stockholm: Almänna Förlaget.
Dølvik, Jon Erik, Mona Bråten, Frode Longva, and Arild Steen. 1997. "Norwegian Labor Market Institutions and Regulations." In Jon Erik Dølvik and Arnild H. Steen, eds., Making Solidarity Work? The Norwegian Labour Market Model in Transition. Oslo: Scandinavian Univeristy Press.
Elvander, Nils. 1988. Den svenska modellen. Stockholm: Allmänna Förlaget.
Englund, Peter. 1998. "Var avregleringen av kreditmarknaden en efterfrågechock?" Ekonomisk Debatt 26, 5.
Erixon, Lennart. 1985. What's Wrong with the Swedish Model? An Analysis of Its Effects and Changed Conditions 1974–1985. Institut för Social Forskning, Meddelande.
——— 1989. "Den tredje vägen – inlåsning eller förnyelse?" Ekonomisk debatt 17, 3.
Feldt, Kjell-Olof. 1991. Alla dessa dagar: I regeringen 1982–1990. Stockholm: Norstedts.
Gidlund, Gullan M. 1983. Partistöd. Lund: CWK Gleerup.
Giljam, Mikael and Sören Holmberg. 1990. Rött Blått Grönt: En bok om 1988 °ars riksdagsval. Stockholm: Bonniers.

Hansson, Sven Ove and Anna-Lena Lodenius. 1988. *Operation högervridning*. Stockholm: Tidens Förlag.

Henrekson, Magnus. 1990. "Devalveringnas effekter på den svenska ekonomins struktur." Forskningsrapport 34. Stockholm: Fackföreningsrörelsens Institut för Ekonomisk Forskning.

Holmberg, Sören. 1984. *Väljare i förändring*. Stockholm: Liber Förlag.

Jonung, Lars. 1993. "Riksbankens politik 1945–90." In Lars Werin, ed., *Från räntereglering till inflationsnorm: Det finansialla systemet och riksbankens politik 1945–1990*. Stockholm: SNS Förlag.

Jonung, Lars and Joakim Stymne. 1997. "The Great Regime Shift: Asset Markets and Economic Activity in Sweden, 1985–93." in Forrest Capie and Geoffrey Wood, eds. *Asset Prices and the Real Economy*. London: Macmillan.

Kahn, Lawrence M. 1996. "Against the Wind: Bargaining Recentralization and Wage Inequality in Norway 1987–91." Preliminary draft. Cornell University.

Kjellberg, Anders. 1998. "Sweden: Can the Model Survive?" In Anthony Ferner and Richard Hyman, eds., *Changing Industrial Relations in Europe*. 2nd ed. Oxford: Blackwell.

Konjunkturläget. 1987. Hösten.

LO. 1951. *Fackföreningsrörelsen och den fulla sysselsättningen*. Stockholm: Landsorganisationen i Sverige.

Lipietz, Alain. 1987. *Miracles and Mirages: The Crisis of Global Fordism*. London: Verso.

Mahon, Rianne. 1991. "From Solidaristic Wages to Solidaristic Work: A Post-Fordist Historical Compromise for Sweden?" *Economic and Industrial Democracy* 12, 3.

Martin, Andrew. 1984. "Trade Unions in Sweden: Strategic Responses to Change and Crisis." In Peter Gourevitch, Andrew Martin, and George Ross, eds., *Unions, Change and Crisis: The United Kingdom, West Germany and Sweden*. London: George Allen and Unwin.

———. 1985. "Wages, Profits, and Investment in Sweden." In Leon N. Lindberg and Charles S. Maier, eds., *The Politics of Inflation and Economic Stagnation*. Washington, DC: The Brookings Institution.

———. 1992. *Wage Bargaining and Swedish Politics: The Political Implications of the End of Central Negotiations*. Prepared for the Study of Power and Democracy in Sweden. Stockholm: Trade Union Institute for Economic Research; Cambridge: Harvard Center for European Studies Working Papers.

———. 1995. "The Swedish Model: Demise or Reconfiguration?" In Richard Locke et al., eds., *Employment Relations in a Changing World Economy*. Cambridge, MA: MIT Press.

Metall. 1991. *Solidarisk arbetspolitik för det goda arbetete*. Stockholm: Svenska Metallindustriarbetareförbundet.

Notermans, Ton. 1993. "The Abdication from National Policy Autonomy: Why the Macroeconomic Policy Regime Has Become So Unfavorable to Labor." *Politics and Society* 21, 2.

———. 1999 *Money, Markets and the State*. Cambridge: Cambridge University Press.

OECD. 1993. *OECD Economic Outlook 54*.

Pontusson, Jonas and Peter Swenson. 1993. "Varför har arbetsgivarna övergivit den Svenska modellen?" *Archiv för studier I arbetarrörelens historia*, 53/54.

Rødseth, Asbjørn. 1994. "Om konjukturane i Norge etter 1980: Vegen til høg arbeidsløyse." In Agnar Sandmo, ed., *Perspektiv på arbeidsledigheten* SNF-Årbok 1994. Bergen: Fagbokforlaget.

SAF Tidningen, 16 February 1990.

Schager, Nils Henrik. 1988. "Den svenska löneökningstakten," *Ekonomisk debatt* 16, 8.

Socialdemokraterna. 1991. *Framtid för Sverige.* Stockholm: Tidens Förlag.

Swedenborg, Birgitta, Göran Johansson-Grahn, and Mats Kinnwall. 1988. *Den svenska industrins utlandsinvesteringar 1960–1986.* Stockholm: Industriens Utredningsinstitut.

The Swedish Economy. 1990 (Autumn), 1991 (Autumn).

Thimerdal, Arne, ed. 1985. *MAS-Rapporten: Det marknadsekonmiska alternativet.* Stockholm: Timbro Förlag.

Tetlock, Philip E. and Aaron Belkin, eds. 1996. *Counterfactual Thought Experiments in World Politics: Logical, Methodological and Psychological Perspectives.* Princeton, NJ: Princeton University Press.

Vartiainen, Juhana. 1995. "Can Nordic Social Corporatism Survive? Challenges to the Labour Market." Discussion Papers 125. Helsinki: Labour Institute for Economic Research.

Wihlborg, Clas. 1993. "Växelkurspolitiken." In Lars Werin, ed., *Från ränteglering till inflationsnorm: Det finansialla systemet och riksbankens politik 1945–1990.* Stockholm: SNS Förlag.

Wohlin, Lars. 1998. "Bankkrisens upprinelse," *Ekonomisk Debatt* 26, 1.

PART III

MACROECONOMIC AND DISTRIBUTIVE OUTCOMES

9

PUBLIC-SECTOR UNIONS, CORPORATISM, AND WAGE DETERMINATION

Geoffrey Garrett and Christopher Way

A central tenet of the corporatism literature is that the Phillips curve trade-off between inflation and unemployment is mitigated in countries with powerful and centrally coordinated organized labor movements. Most empirical studies, however, are based on data about labor market institutions from the early 1970s and refer to macroeconomic outcomes in the decade following the first OPEC oil shock in 1973. Recent case studies, in contrast, suggest that corporatism broke down during the 1980s in its Scandinavian bastions, in a cycle of strikes, inflation, and ultimately higher unemployment (Iversen 1996; Pontusson and Swenson 1996). We argue that one important reason for the apparent economic problems of strong labor regimes in recent years has been the growth of public-sector unions. So long as public-sector unions are not "too strong" (this limit is estimated empirically), corporatist institutions continue to promote both price stability and low rates of unemployment.

Encompassing labor movements – those that cover large sections of the work force in a relatively small number of independent unions and in which authority is concentrated in the hands of leaders of a single trade union confederation – provide an organizational structure that is conducive to low inflation and low unemployment because they mitigate distributional conflict among all workers. There is a limit, however, to the ability of encompassing labor movements to perform this role. Where public-sector unions are extremely strong (as has recently been the case in Scandinavia), confederation leaders cannot stop public-sector workers from using their organizational power to bid up their

We would like to thank the anonymous reviewers, as well as, Torben Iversen, Jonas Pontusson, and Peter Swenson for very helpful comments. This chapter draws extensively on Garrett, Geoffrey, and Christopher Way. 1999. "The Rise of Public Sector Unions, Corporatism, and Macroeconomic Performance, 1970–1990," Comparative Political Studies 32:411–434. We thank "Comparative Political Studies" for permission to excerpt this article.

wages to levels that have deleterious consequences for the private sector – and especially for those industries that are exposed to international trade.

This chapter relies on three recent systematic studies of labor movements in Organization for Economic Development and Cooperation (OECD) countries that allow us to test the labor market institutions–performance nexus more precisely than has hitherto been the case. We use Visser's (1991) data on public-sector unions, Golden and Wallerstein's (1995) analysis of the structural attributes of organized labor movements, and Traxler's (1994) study of the coverage of collectively bargained wage contracts. These data sources allow us to construct time-sensitive measures of theoretically important attributes of organized labor movements.

To test the argument we proceed in two stages. First, the interactive effects of the encompassment of labor market institutions and the strength of public-sector unions on inflation and unemployment are estimated using panel data for 15 OECD countries at five-year intervals between 1970 and 1990.[1] Second, we focus on the intervening stage between labor market organization and macroeconomic outcomes by examining patterns of wage growth in the public and private sectors. Although we cannot compare the theoretically appropriate variable – wage growth above productivity increases – because meaningful data are not available for public-sector productivity, the analysis does provide evidence that is consistent with our argument.

The remainder of the chapter is divided into four sections. Section 1 develops the theoretical argument. Section 2 presents the data we use to operationalize the encompassment of labor market institutions and the strength of public-sector unions. The interactive effects of these two variables on inflation and unemployment are analyzed in Section 3. Section 4 discusses the implications of the chapter by way of conclusion.

1. CORPORATISM AND THE PUBLIC SECTOR

CHANGING CONCEPTIONS OF CORPORATISM

Much of the early work on corporatism posited a linear and positive relationship between the power of trade unions and the centralization of wage setting, on the one hand, and macroeconomic outcomes, on the other (Cameron 1984; Korpi and Shalev 1979). The basic claim of these studies is that the more the labor market is organized, the greater the incentives for union leaders to consider the health of the national economy. Hence, the more likely overall wage growth

---

1 The countries are Australia, Austria, Canada, Denmark, Finland, France, Germany, Italy, Japan, the Netherlands, Norway, Sweden, Switzerland, the United Kingdom, and the United States. This is the entire set of countries for which all the relevant data are available.

is to be restrained – in the name of higher total employment and moderate inflation.

There are significant limitations to this argument. Notably, the simple corporatism thesis does not take seriously the basic insight of neoclassical economics that labor markets would function efficiently in the absence of trade unions (resulting in both low inflation and low unemployment). Organization into trade unions allows workers to push their wages above market-clearing levels. Moreover, individual unions have strong incentives to maximize the wages of their members, even if this has negative externalities for the economy as a whole and other workers (Olson 1982).

The neoclassical and corporatist perspectives were synthesized by Calmfors and Driffill (1988). They differentiate cases in which organized labor movements have the beneficial effects highlighted in the corporatism literature from those where union power has deleterious consequences for economic performance. Calmfors and Driffill argue that the relationship between labor market institutions and economic performance is "hump-shaped." Three scenarios are considered with respect to the level at which most wage bargains are struck – in individual firms, at the industry level, or nationally.

First, Calmfors and Driffill argue that it is possible to generate low inflation and high levels of employment simultaneously in cases where wages are set predominantly at the firm level. This is because small and isolated groups of workers are not sufficiently strong to alter the market determination of wages. Second, where wages are primarily set at the industrial level (that is, labor market institutions are "stronger" on most indicators), wage-push inflation will result – irrespective of the deleterious consequences of this behavior for overall levels of employment. In this case, union leaders are tempted to use their organizational power to increase the wages of their members, but they have little incentive to care about the negative externalities of this behavior.

Finally, Calmfors and Driffill argue that wage militancy will be mitigated by national-level wage-bargaining arrangements. National union leaders have strong incentives to internalize the externalities associated with labor power – exercising wage restraint today to improve the material well-being of all workers in the longer run. In this final case, inflation and unemployment outcomes are expected to be just as good as in the case of the free labor market.

The Calmfors–Driffill hypothesis has been very influential. Their concentration on the level at which wage bargains are predominantly struck as the most important feature of labor market institutions, however, can be criticized. Golden (1993) argues convincingly that the internal structure of labor movements – and specifically the ability of central union leaders to coordinate the behavior of large sections of the work force – is more important to explaining economic performance than the level of wage bargaining per se. The reason for this is straightforward.

To be effective, centralized wage agreements must be adhered to at lower bargaining levels. But there are powerful incentives for groups of workers and their employers to free-ride on central agreements by making higher local wage settlements ("wage-drift"). The concentration of union authority in peak confederations whose constituents are spread throughout the economy mitigates wage-drift in two ways. First, the leaders of peak union confederations have strong incentives to coordinate wage restraint in all sectors (to increase the employment prospects of all workers). Second, they have the authority to sanction constituents that do not abide by such agreements.

As a result, one should expect in equilibrium that the presence of national wage agreements will covary with the encompassment of labor unions. Nonetheless, central wage setting may be imposed in cases where underlying structural conditions are inappropriate. In such cases, it is likely that the effectiveness of national agreements will be quickly undermined by wage-drift at lower levels of collective bargaining.

In this chapter, we follow Golden's lead and concentrate on the organizational structure of labor movements rather than the level at which wages are set.[2] Nonetheless, the consequences for economic performance of variations in labor movement structure can be mapped directly from Calmfors–Driffill. Workers face a pervasive collective-action problem. Maximizing wages is the objective of every worker. If all workers pursue this strategy, however, the collective outcome will be suboptimal. Nominal wage increases will be eroded by higher economy-wide inflation, and unemployment will increase.

Inflation and unemployment performance can be expected to be good in cases that approximate free labor markets, in which unions are not strong enough to bid up wages above market-clearing levels. In cases where individual unions are strong but numerous or they are not subject to the authority of a single peak confederation, macroeconomic outcomes will be considerably worse because of the negative externalities of union militancy. Finally, where most of the work force is covered by collective bargaining agreements among a small number of unions and authority is concentrated in a single peak confederation, performance will be similar to that in the free labor market case. In this case, labor leaders can be expected to internalize the externalities of wage increases.

Thus, the state of the theoretical art on labor market institutions concentrates on their internal organizational characteristics and asserts that their relationship to macroeconomic performance is not linear, but parabolic.

In recent years, however, the empirical veracity of this hypothesis has been questioned. The deleterious consequences of strong but decentralized unions

2 It should also be noted that it is extremely difficult to gather data that accurately reflect the effective level of wage setting in many countries (Golden and Wallerstein 1995). As a result, empirical studies of the effects of wage-setting levels, including that by Calmfors and Driffill, rely on relatively crude indicators whose validity is hard to ascertain. For a recent effort to derive more precise measures of the centralization of wage setting, see Iversen (1996).

continue to be felt. But the performance of some countries with relatively encompassing labor movements has manifestly deteriorated. The clearest example is the end of full employment in Scandinavia. As a result, it seems to many that today the relationship between labor-market institutions and economic performance is indeed linear – but negative. Contra the early corporatism literature, union power appears always to be bad for the economy.

In the remainder of the chapter, we take issue with this conclusion by distinguishing between the effects of the strength of public-sector unions on economic performance from those of the structural attributes of labor market institutions.

BRINGING IN THE PUBLIC SECTOR

Most existing analyses of the impact of labor market institutions on economic performance implicitly assume that the interests of all workers are the same. If this assumption was ever valid, it certainly has not been in recent years. Among other things, scholars have pointed to the destabilizing effects of increasing conflicts between unions in the sector of the economy exposed to international competition and those in industries whose products are not traded (Pontusson 1992; Swenson 1991; Wallerstein 1995).[3] The most important and readily identified component of the nontradables sector is the public sector.[4]

The strategic calculus of workers in the public sector is very different from that of those employed in the exposed sector of the economy. Wage growth has immediate consequences for the welfare of workers in the exposed sector. International market conditions determine the price of goods and services. Thus, the competitiveness of national producers in international markets – and in turn employment – is a function of changes in labor costs (relative to changes in productivity).[5] At a given world market price for a product, if workers push up their wages at a rate faster than their productivity increases, total employment in the firm or industry will decline. International market conditions thus place a strong constraint on labor militancy.

This relationship is much weaker in the public sector. There is nothing akin to a "world market price" for the bulk of public-sector services. The producers of these services – governments – are essentially free to set the price

---

3 Pontusson and Swenson (1996) argue that conflict between high- and low-value-added producers in the exposed sector put additional pressure on corporatism in the 1980s.

4 The relationship between the public sector and the portion of the economy insulated from international competition is not isomorphic. It is very difficult, however, to make judgments about precisely what is and what is not exposed to trade outside the public sector. Moreover, available data on the composition of trade unions is based on the distinctiveness of the public sector. As a result, we assume that public-sector unions are a good approximation for organized labor in the nontradables sector.

5 Assuming that other factors are constant, such as the exchange rate and supply and demand conditions in the international economy.

for them. The proximate determinant of employment and wages in the public sector is government preference rather than global competitiveness. Moreover, there are strong incentives for governments not to cut public-sector jobs (rather, they face incentives to expand them) to prop up overall employment levels – especially in hard times. This allows governments to reap the short-term benefits of lower unemployment while putting off the costs until the future (through borrowing). In the long run, of course, higher government spending must be paid for with higher taxes. But voters apparently suffer from fiscal illusion; survey data show that most citizens want government to spend more while simultaneously lowering taxes.

The political economy of government employment creates powerful incentives for public-sector workers to push up wages in the expectation that this will not adversely affect their job security – certainly not in the short term. Instead, they can expect that the costs of their wage militancy will be borne throughout society via larger budget deficits and higher inflation. The more extensively the public sector is unionized, the more powerful should be upward wage pressures, and the greater should be negative externalities of public-sector militancy.

Exposed-sector workers, in particular, will be adversely affected by wage militancy in the public sector. Higher deficits and inflation will put upward pressures on interest rates and the exchange rate, decreasing the competitiveness of national products in international markets. One should thus expect public-sector union strength not only to be inflationary, but also to increase unemployment in the exposed sector of the economy. In the end, governments will be unable to continue creating public-sector jobs at the same rate that they are lost in the exposed sector. Thus, over time one would expect public-sector unionism to push up economy-wide unemployment and to harm economic performance.

THE INTERACTIVE EFFECTS OF PUBLIC-SECTOR STRENGTH AND LABOR MARKET INSTITUTIONS

Up until now, we have discussed the macroeconomic effects of labor market institutions and the strength of public-sector unions as if they are independent of each other.[6] This subsection argues that the impact of labor market institutions on economic performance is likely to be conditional on the strength of public-sector unions. One of the primary objectives of organized labor movements in open economies is to ensure that wage developments in the whole economy are compatible with promoting the competitiveness of the exposed sector (Garrett 1998).[7] This entails reining in wage militancy in nontradables,

6 For an analysis of these independent effects, see Garrett and Way (1995).
7 In Scandinavia, "wage solidarity" – equalizing wages across all segments of the work force irrespective of their productivity, competitiveness, etc. – has also been an important goal of organized labor

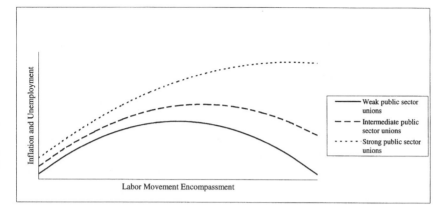

Figure 9.1. *The economic effects of labor market institutions conditional on the strength of public-sector unions.*

and in the public sector in particular. Ceteris paribus, the more powerful are public-sector unions, the more difficult it will be for central labor confederations to ensure that the exposed sector acts as the "wage leader" for the economy as a whole. What does this imply for the Calmfors–Driffill hypothesis?

When public-sector unions are very weak, the arguments made in the first subsection hold without modification. Hence, one should expect the parabolic relationship between labor organization encompassment and inflation and unemployment to obtain (the "weak public sector" curve in Figure 9.1). In this case, public-sector unions have little impact on wage setting. Workers in the exposed sector have incentives to push up wages, but these will be mitigated either by market forces when unions are very weak, or by the discipline imposed by confederation leaders when unions are encompassing. In intermediate cases, a spiral of wage-push inflation and higher unemployment will be generated by the inability of powerful but decentralized unions to act collectively to lessen the negative externalities arising from wage militancy.

As public-sector unions become stronger, it becomes more difficult for encompassing labor movements to coordinate the behavior of all their members. The hump-shaped relationship between labor organization and inflation can be expected to weaken, with the benefits of encompassing unions, in particular, becoming increasingly small (the intermediate case in Figure 9.1). The more powerful are public-sector unions, however, the greater their conflict of interests with those employed in the exposed sector, and the more difficult it becomes for labor leaders to restrain public-sector wage growth in the name of exposed-sector competitiveness.

Indeed, at some threshold of public-sector union strength, the hump-shaped

(Iversen 1996; Moene and Wallerstein 1992). But this has not been the case in other important examples of corporatist institutions, most notably in Germany and Austria.

relationship should disappear entirely and be replaced by an almost linear association between labor encompassment and higher rates of inflation and higher unemployment (the "strong public sector" case in Figure 9.1). The reason for this is that public-sector unions become increasingly effective in lobbying the central labor confederation to use its authority to push up public-sector wages at the expense of exposed-sector competitiveness – through a wage-leveling policy, for example. In the long run, this strategy would be untenable for even for the strongest public-sector unions because there must be a limit to the willingness of governments to increase public-sector employment to compensate for reduced competitiveness in the exposed sector. But in the short run, the notion that powerful public-sector unions would use their power within central labor confederations to erode the competitiveness of the exposed sector is highly plausible (Wallerstein 1995).

2. MEASURING THE ENCOMPASSMENT AND SECTORAL COMPOSITION OF LABOR MOVEMENTS

Most studies measure the encompassment of labor market institutions by using some combination of union density (the proportion of unionized employees in the labor force) and qualitative codings of the internal organization of labor movements that condense the last three decades or so into a single observation (see Alvarez, Garrett, and Lange 1991; Cameron 1984 for examples). In recent years, however, three research projects have collected data that allow the construction of more precise measures of theoretically important attributes of labor market institutions.

First, Visser (1991) collected annual cross-national data on the size and composition of trade union membership for the period 1970–89, including separate measures for public-sector unions. Second, Golden and Wallerstein (1995) compiled data on the structural attributes of national labor movements, including the size and composition of union confederations at five-year intervals from 1950 to 1990. Finally, Traxler (1994) gathered data on the portion of national labor forces covered by collective-bargaining arrangements in 1990.

We have used these data to construct time-varying indicators for two facets of national labor market institutions: the organizational capacity for collective action among the labor force as a whole, and the strength of public-sector unions. The public-sector variable expresses membership in public-sector unions as a proportion of total civilian employment.[8]

8 This measure was computed from Visser's (1991) data on public-sector union density and from OECD figures (various) for public-sector employment. Visser records a public-sector union density figure only for 1985 in Canada and only for 1988 in Finland. We have extrapolated to the other time periods by

The organizational-capacity variable consists of two elements designed to measure the encompassment of national labor movements. First, we use the coverage rate of collective bargaining to measure the portion of the labor force that is effectively organized by labor unions. This indicator is preferable to the more conventional union density because in some countries – most notably France – a large portion of the labor force who are not formally union members are nonetheless covered by the terms and conditions of union contracts (Traxler 1994).[9]

The organizational capacity of labor for collective action is measured using data on the distribution of union members across national-level confederations and the number of unions affiliated to those confederations. These two indicators tap *interconfederal* concentration and *intraconfederal* concentration, respectively.[10] The interconfederation indicator is a Herfindahl–Hirschman index:

$$interconfed = \sum_{i=1}^{i} (confed \div unions)^2$$

where *confed* is the membership of the ith confederation and *unions* is total union membership. The range of this measure is 0 to 1. A score of 1 could connote a union movement in which all members belonged to the same confederation (as was the case in Austria for the period under analysis in this chapter).

The number of affiliate unions in the main confederation provides the basis for the intraconfederation index. So that higher scores on this index indicate greater capacity for collective action (as is the case with higher scores for the interconfederation index and bargaining coverage), we based the intraconfederation measure on the inverse of the number of affiliates in the largest confederation. We then set the highest score in the data set equal to "1" and adjusted all other scores accordingly.

The data for the 15 countries over the past two decades on interconfederal and intraconfederal concentration, the coverage rate of collective-bargaining strength, and overall encompassment rank are reported in Table 9.1. Two main observations should be made. First, there is no evidence of a secular decline in confederation concentration from 1970 to 1990. With respect to interconfederation concentration, labor movements became increasingly fragmented in France, Canada, and Norway, while concentration increased in Australia, the Netherlands, and Japan. But on balance, average interconfederal concentration in our sample of countries did not change appreciably from 1970 to 1990. Similarly, changes in intraconfederal concentration between 1970 and 1990 reveal no decline in labor's capacity for collective action. There has been a steady decrease in the number of affiliate unions in nearly all countries in our sample.

assuming that the evolution of public-sector density in Canada and Finland matched the average changes across other OECD countries. In the data analyses we paid special attention to these countries to ensure that the results were robust to their exclusion.

9 The data for bargaining coverage rate are only for 1990.

10 These terms are those of Golden and Wallerstein (1995).

Table 9.1. *Measures of concentration of union membership, number of affiliate unions, and coverage of collective bargaining agreements*

	Interconfederation index in **Bold** Intraconfederation index in *Italics*					
Country	*1970*	*1975*	*1980*	*1985*	*1990*	Coverage
Australia	.57	.57	.62	.81	.81	.80
	.51	*.55*	*.56*	*.56*	*.57*	
Austria	1	1	1	1	1	.98
	.94	*.94*	*1*	*1*	*1*	
Canada	.54	.51	.42	.33	.35	.38
	.14	*.13*	*.17*	*.16*	*.17*	
Finland	.51	.51	.37	.41	.38	.95
	.48	*.54*	*.52*	*.54*	*.63*	
France	.30	.28	.24	.22	.22	.92
	.51	*.55*	*.56*	*.56*	*.57*	
Germany	.69	.72	.70	.70	.70	.90
	.94	*.94*	*.88*	*.88*	*.94*	
Japan	.18	.17	.18	.17	.39	.23
	.24	*.23*	*.30*	*.30*	*.19*	
Netherlands	.24	.24	.27	.42	.56	.71
	.75	*1*	*1*	*.88*	*.88*	
Norway	.58	.51	.48	.43	.42	.75
	.43	*.43*	*.44*	*.44*	*.52*	
Sweden	.52	.50	.49	.47	.45	.83
	.52	*.60*	*.60*	*.63*	*.65*	
Switzerland	.34	.32	.31	.30	.29	.53
	1	*.94*	*1*	*1*	*.94*	
United Kingdom	.71	.74	.88	.83	.72	.47
	.10	*.14*	*.14*	*.17*	*.20*	
United States	.40	.40	.42	.59	.69	.18
	.12	*.13*	*.14*	*.16*	*.17*	
Average	.51	.50	.49	.51	.54	.66
	.51	*.55*	*.56*	*.56*	*.57*	
Standard Deviation	.22	.23	.25	.25	.23	.28
	.35	*.36*	*.36*	*.34*	*.34*	

Sources: Data for the confederation indices are from Golden and Wallerstein (1995), except for Australia from Deery and Plowman (1985); period averages are entered for Australia and France for the intraconfederation index due to missing data. Data for the coverage of collective wage in 1990 are from Traxler (1994). Higher scores on all measures denote greater capacity for collective action in national labor movements as a whole. The encompassment rank is based on 1990 data (interconfed × 25 + intraconfed × .25 + coverage × .5).

Table 9.2. *Measures of labor movement encompassment and public-sector union strength*

Country	Encompassment rank	Public-sector strength rank	Change in public-sector strength, 1970
Australia	5	4	−1.1
Australia	1	6	+0.4
Canada	13	9	+5.3
Denmark	11	7	+8.6
Finland	3	3	+10.2
France	7	11	−7.2
Germany	2	10	+0.4
Italy	10	12	+2.3
Japan	14	15	−1.5
Netherlands	6	8	−1.2
Norway	8	2	+10.6
Sweden	4	1	+15.8
Switzerland	9	13	+0.5
United Kingdom	12	5	−0.6
United States	15	14	+0.3

Notes: Rankings are calculated for the 1990 scores on the encompassment index and public-sector union membership as a percentage of civilian employment. Increase from 1970 to 1990 is the increase in public-sector union membership as a percentage of civilian employment.
Source: See text for details.

The number of affiliates has declined or remained constant in 11 of the countries, with only Japan and Switzerland experiencing increased fragmentation on this measure.

The second thing to note from the table is that great cross-national variations persist in the structure of labor movements. On both of our concentration measures, Austria's labor movement is far better equipped to act collectively than is Japan's. Similarly, the variation in the coverage of collective bargaining in 1990 was great, with Austria again at the top of the table and the United States at the bottom.

Table 9.2 highlights these cross-national variations in 1990 with respect to an overall ranking of encompassment, derived from an index reflecting equally the coverage and organizational facets of union movements.[11] These rankings show important similarities with prior efforts to classify the internal organiza-

11 With all three components on a [0,1] scale, the index consists of a weighted sum with bargaining coverage receiving a weight of one-half whereas inter- and intraconfederation concentration each receive a weight of one-quarter.

tion of labor movements, but there are some significant differences as well. Austria, Germany, Sweden, and Finland receive the highest scores on the encompassment index for 1980, while the United Kingdom, Japan, Canada, and the United States fill out the bottom of the list. Few would quibble with the ranking of Germany or Austria, but the placement of Finland is slightly more contentious because most studies of corporatism rank it as a borderline case. Australian labor market institutions changed considerably between the early 1970s and the late 1980s with the incorporation of organized labor in economic policy-making under the Accord process (Stilwell 1986), a development that is consistent with its relatively high ranking. Among the weak union countries, the American, British, and Canadian cases are unproblematic. Japan's low rank can be faulted for ignoring informal coordination organized by business associations (Soskice 1990), but this is true for any indicator based on the organization of labor movements.

Finally, we rank Norway in the middle of our sample, while Sweden is located lower than on other indices. This diverges from the conventional view of these cases as exemplars of encompassing labor market institutions. The Golden and Wallerstein data make clear, however, that the concentration of unions in Norway and Sweden has always been lower than in Austria and Germany, among others, and that it has been declining since 1970. Moreover, this is consistent with recent case studies that describe a substantial breakdown in the capacity for collective action in the Swedish labor movement, in particular in the 1980s (Iversen 1996; Pontusson and Swenson 1996; Thelen 1993).

In contrast with the relative stability of the organizational capacity of labor movements for collective action, data on public-sector strength show that the sectoral composition of trade unions has changed considerably since 1970. The average strength of public-sector unions increased up until 1985 and then stabilized. Until 1980, much of the growth in these unions could be attributed to the expansion of public-sector employment. Membership in public-sector unions grew in the 1980s, however, even though public-sector employment was relatively stable. This suggests that the propensity for workers to join unions in recent years has been higher in the public than the private sector, perhaps reflecting the rapid growth in part-time work in the private sector (Traxler 1994).

As was the case for encompassment, the rankings in Table 9.2 also reveal important cross-country differences in the evolution and level of public-sector union strength. These unions grew very rapidly in Finland, Norway, and Sweden in the 1970s and 1980s, a development we consider to have boded ill for the ability of these labor movements to act in ways that are conducive to economic competitiveness. In contrast, the size of public-sector unions was quite stable in Austria, Germany, and the Netherlands. Finally, public-sector unions retreated in Australia, increasing the prospects for the behavior of all workers to have been coordinated in ways that are conducive to strong macroeconomic performance. Unsurprisingly, the United States, Japan, and Switzerland brought up the bottom of the list.

Taken as a whole, the data suggest that there were no great changes in the structural attributes of national trade union movements between 1970 and 1990. If the organizational structure of unions was conducive to corporatism in some countries in the 1970s, there is no reason to believe that this was not the case 20 years later. The sectoral composition of labor movements, however, did tilt considerably toward the public sector in many countries. We hypothesize that this change in the sectoral composition of power had profound consequences for the labor market institutions–macroeconomic performance nexus.

3. PUBLIC-SECTOR UNIONS, WAGES, AND ECONOMIC PERFORMANCE

Our attempt to evaluate the arguments laid out in Section 1 entails two steps. First, we explore the interactive effects on inflation and unemployment of the organizational structure of trade unions and their sectoral composition. Second, after establishing that broad macroeconomic outcomes are consistent with the argument, we examine patterns of wage growth across countries, which is the key intervening variable in our model between labor market institutions and macroeconomic outcomes. By doing so, we hope to establish the plausibility of our causal argument: Does the causal mechanism posited in this chapter account for the macrolevel outcomes?

ENCOMPASSMENT, THE PUBLIC SECTOR, AND ECONOMIC PERFORMANCE

To evaluate the interactive effects on inflation and unemployment of the orga-nizational structure of trade unions and their sectoral composition, we analyzed data for 15 countries and five time periods. Since our labor market observations are at five-year intervals from 1970 to 1990, we organized the economic perfor-mance data as five-year averages centered around these observations: 1968–72, 1973–77, 1978–82, 1983–87, and 1988–92.

Analyzing data that pool time series for a number of countries creates special statistical problems for ordinary least squares (OLS) regression estimates. Specifically, OLS is vulnerable to heteroskedastic errors across units, unit- or time-specific effects, and autoregression within countries. Nonetheless, relatively simple methods can avoid the problems inherent in pooled analysis. First, the use of panel-corrected standard errors – an extension of White's method for calculating heteroskedasticity-consistent standard errors to pooled data – amelio-rates problems arising from heteroskedastic errors. Second, the least-squares dummy variable (LSDV) model deals with unit- and time-specific effects by assigning a dummy variable to each time period and country case. Finally, including a lagged dependent variable usually eliminates autocorrelated errors (Beck and Katz 1995).

Interactive regression analysis facilitates the testing of the hypothesis that the effects of the structural attributes of labor market institutions on economic performance are contingent on public-sector union strength. Since our hypotheses suggest interactions generating parabolic relationships among continuous variables, we estimate models in which the shape – not just the slope – of the encompassment–performance relationship changes with different levels of public-sector union strength (Jaccard, Turrisi, and Choi 1990). The best way to test this argument is to interact public-sector union strength with both the encompassment index and its square:

$$Y_{it} = \beta_1 ENC_{it} + \beta_2 ENC_{it}^2 + \beta_3 PS_{it} + \beta_4 ENC_{it} \times PS_{it} +$$
$$\beta_5 ENC_{it}^2 \times PS_{it} + \beta_6 Y_{it-1} + \beta_7 CBI_{it} + \beta_8 NOBARG_{it} +$$
$$B_9 VULN_{it} + \Sigma\beta_z PERIOD_{zt} + \mu_{it} \qquad (1)$$

In this equation, Y is the dependent variable – inflation or unemployment. ENC is the index of the encompassment of labor market institutions described in the last section, and PS is our public-sector union strength variable. We also included a number of control variables. CBI is Cukierman's (1992) legal index of central bank independence. NOBARG is a dummy variable for countries that restrict the collective-bargaining rights of public-sector unions (Japan, Austria, and Switzerland). We would expect inflation and unemployment to have been lower under these conditions. VULN measures the economy's vulnerability to international economic conditions (exports plus imports as a share of GDP multiplied by the OECD growth rate). Higher scores on this variable should be associated with lower inflation and unemployment. Finally, PERIOD stands for five time-period dummy variables.

If the results were consistent with our hypotheses, we would expect the following pattern of coefficients for the variables that jointly operationalize the encompassment–public-sector unions interaction. The parameter estimates for ENC and PS should be positive but those for the ENC·PS interaction should be negative. In contrast, we anticipate negative coefficients for ENC^2 and positive estimates for ENC^2·PS. This pattern of results would produce the predicted conditional relationships. Taking inflation as an example, very strong and very weak union movements would produce lower inflation, and moderately strong labor movements higher inflation, but only when public-sector unions were weak. At higher levels of public-sector union strength, the ends of the parabola would flatten.

To see this algebraically, equation (1) can be rearranged thus:

$$Y_{it} = \beta_3 PS_{it} + (\beta_1 + \beta_4 PS_{it}) \times ENC_{it} + (\beta_2 + \beta_5 PS_{it}) \times ENC_{it}^2 + \qquad (2)$$

$$\beta_6 Y_{it-1} + \beta_7 CBI_{it} + \beta_8 NOBARG_{it} + B_9 VULN_{it} + \Sigma\beta_z PERIOD_{zt} + \mu_{it}$$

The terms in parentheses represent the conditional coefficients for the encompassment index and its square. If β_1 were positive and β_4 negative, then the conditional coefficient for ENC would be positive whenever $\beta_1 > (\beta_4 \cdot PS)$. Similarly, when β_2 is negative and β_5 is positive, then the conditional coefficient for ENC^2 is negative if $\beta_2 > (\beta_5 \cdot PS)$. This implies that the hump-shaped relationship is more pronounced the weaker are public-sector unions. As PS increases, the interaction effect pushes the conditional coefficients on ENC and ENC^2 in the opposite direction, dampening the hump-shaped curve.

Table 9.3 presents coefficients for the equations estimating the interactive models of inflation and unemployment. Diagnostic tests indicated the presence of time-specific effects (but not country-specific ones).[12] Thus, we included period dummy variables but did not use country dummies. Most of the control variables were appropriately signed and statistically significant. Our dummy variable NOBARG, which captures the fact that public-sector unions have few restricted bargaining rights in a handful of countries, was significant and negative in both equations. Thus, the remaining effects of public-sector union strength are not artifacts of the bargaining environment.

The coefficients for the encompassment index and its squared term were both statistically significant and had the signs implied by the Calmfors–Driffill hypothesis. The public-sector union strength variable had a positive coefficient in both the inflation and unemployment models and was statistically significant at the 5 percent level or better. As anticipated, greater public-sector strength was associated with higher inflation and unemployment. More importantly and quite strikingly – given the high level of multicollinearity built into the estimating equations by the use of multiplicative terms – all of the interaction variables were correctly signed and statistically significant in both the inflation and unemployment models.[13] The interaction term between public sector union strength and the encompassment index was negative, whereas the interaction between encompassment squared and the public-sector variable was positive.

These results imply that, as hypothesized, the macroeconomic effects of the

12 F-tests for time period effects clearly reject the null hypothesis of equal intercepts for different points in time. Considering unit effects, on the other hand, F-tests fail to reject the null hypothesis of equal constant terms for the inflation data. This test is described by Greene (1990). The same pattern held for the unemployment models.

13 Although multicollinearity introduces inflated estimates of variances, it does not degrade the desirable properties of OLS estimates of coefficients (Jaccard, Turrisi, and Choi 1990). Hence, the practical problem is that greater variance makes it more difficult to obtain statistically significant estimates by standard criteria.

Table 9.3. *The relationships between encompassment, inflation, and unemployment, conditional on public-sector union strength*

Independent variables	Inflation	Unemployment
Dependent variable lagged one period	0.38**	0.65***
	(0.15)	(0.10)
1968–72	−6.9*	−4.2*
	(4.1)	(4.32)
1973–77	−3.1	−3.4
	(3.9)	(4.31)
1978–82	−6.4*	−2.4
	(3.8)	(4.28)
1983–87	−9.5**	−1.8
	(3.9)	(4.18)
1988–92	−8.2**	−3.6*
	(4.1)	(4.05)
Vulnerability to OECD demand	−0.03***	−0.005
	(0.01)	(0.005)
Central bank independence	−3.7**	−2.1**
	(1.65)	(1.19)
No bargaining	−1.5**	−2.3**
	(0.68)	(0.86)
Encompassment	58.1**	25.5**
	(22.7)	(19.62)
Encompassment squared	−54.9**	−20.2*
	(21.6)	(19.03)
Public-sector union strength	126.4**	93.6**
	(55.6)	(46.75)
Encompassment × Public-sector union strength	−494.7**	−320.5**
	(209.2)	(179.62)
Encompassment squared × Public-sector union strength	460.5**	242.1**
	(189.6)	(166.01)
Adjusted R-squared	0.75	0.86
N	75	75

Notes: All entries are least-squares dummy variable estimates with panel-corrected standard errors in parentheses. Inflation and standardized unemployment data is from the OECD.
*$p < 0.10$, two-tailed test.
**$p < 0.05$, two-tailed test.
***$p < 0.01$, two-tailed test.

encompassment of labor are contingent on public-sector union strength, and that this interaction effect is nonlinear. Where public-sector unions were very weak, the predicted level of inflation increased steadily with increasing encompassment to a peak just short of the mean within-sample value of the encompassment index, but declined sharply thereafter. This produces the parabola predicted by Calmfors and Driffill.

In a typical linear-interaction model, the slope of a relationship changes as a function of the moderator variable. In contrast, our estimates allow us to demonstrate that the shape of the labor organization–performance relationship also changed with variations in public-sector union strength. The parabola flattened at higher levels of public-sector unionization. Eventually the curve flipped direction (and became U-shaped, rather than hump-shaped). Higher scores on the encompassment index were associated with higher, instead of lower, inflation. Specifically, the slope of the right-hand tail became positive and statistically significant when public-sector union membership was above about 18 percent of the labor force, a percentage reached by Finland, Norway, and Sweden in the 1980s. Above this threshold, increasing the encompassment of labor market institutions had deleterious consequences for inflation.

The unemployment results tell a similar story. Where public-sector unions were very weak, the hump-shaped relationship between encompassment and unemployment held. As with inflation, increasing public-sector union strength pushed the tails of the curve upward, altering the shape of the relationship between labor organization and unemployment. Finally, where public-sector unions were very strong (again, organizing around 20% of the labor force), the slope on the right-hand tail of the curve became positive: The greater the encompassment of labor market institutions, the higher was unemployment.

To sum up, the evidence presented in Table 9.2 is strongly supportive of our argument that the relationship between the encompassment of labor market institutions and economic performance is contingent upon the strength of public-sector unions. Where these unions are weak, a hump-shaped curve does describe the effects of encompassment on inflation and unemployment. Where public-sector unions are much stronger, however, increasing the encompassment of labor market institutions frequently leads to higher inflation and unemployment.

PUBLIC-SECTOR WAGE GROWTH

Skeptics might contend that although these macroeconomic outcomes are consistent with our argument, they provide no evidence to support our causal story in which wage growth is the central mediating variable between labor market organization and aggregate performance. The core of our argument is that public-sector employees can push up their wages above levels consistent with productivity increases, and that this effect is exacerbated when these workers are unionized. It is simply not possible for us to test this argument directly because there is no way adequately to measure public-sector productivity. In this subsection, however, we analyze the data that do exist to highlight two things. First, all else being equal, public-sector workers seem to earn more than their private sector counterparts. Second, wages of public employees have grown at a rapid rate over the past decades, especially given the consensual view that productivity growth in this sector has been, at best, very slow.

Labor economists posit several reasons for high wage-push pressures in the public sector. The first two we have already highlighted: the lack of effective competition for public services and the fact that governments face a softer budget constraint than do firms subject to the competitive pressures of national and international markets. Moreover, labor demand for public-sector occupations is relatively price inelastic (Ashenfelter and Ehrenberg 1975).[14] This allows government workers to push up their wages without fearing decreases in employment. As Richard Rose (1985:41–2) concludes, "all in all, public employees today are likely to be in a better strategic position to get what they want from their employer than are employees in the private sector."

Empirical work examining public-sector wages supports these assertions. Studies of public–private pay differentials in the United States consistently report a substantial public-sector wage premium (Belman and Heywood 1995; Freeman 1986). Furthermore, public-sector jobs typically provide greater fringe benefits than do private-sector positions, indicating that public-sector compensation advantages are even greater than suggested by wage data (Heywood 1991). Though the most detailed research focuses on the United States, sizable public-sector wage premiums have been reported for Italy as well (Bardasi 1996), and this finding has been corroborated for a broader cross section of OECD countries (Gornick and Jacobs 1997; Heller and Tait 1983).

We now use the OECD's International Sectoral Databank (1993) to explore differences in pay levels and trends across sectors from 1970 to 1990.[15] These data are not very precise – obscuring, for example, the variability of pay within sectors and not allowing comparison of precisely comparable occupations. Nonetheless, they do allow us to gain insights into wage determination in the public and private sectors.

Looking first at patterns in wage growth, we examine three sectors of the economy: government service providers; private-sector community, social, and personnel service providers (i.e., the closest competitor to government services in the private sector); and total industry averages. This data show that even though productivity growth has almost certainly been lower in the public than

14 The greater price inelasticity of demand for labor in the public sector derives from poor substitution possibilities facing consumers of government services.
15 This data set contains annual data covering 31 sectors of the economy for 14 countries: the United States, Canada, Japan, Germany, France, Italy, the United Kingdom, Australia, the Netherlands, Belgium, Denmark, Norway, Sweden, and Finland.

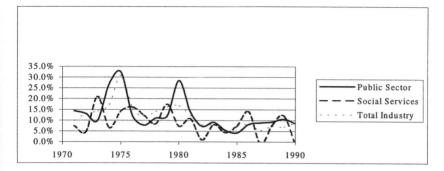

Figure 9.2. *United Kingdom: nominal wage growth in public and private sectors.*

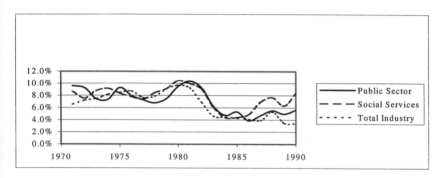

Figure 9.3. *United States: nominal wage growth in public and private sectors.*

in the private sector,[16] the wages of public employees have not lagged behind those in the other two sectors appreciably from 1970 to 1990. This implies that public-sector production has been beset in recent decades by steadily increasing unit labor costs. Figures 9.2–9.5 chart the evolution of wages in the three sectors in four countries that represent a cross section of economies of varying size and labor organization: the United Kingdom, the United States, Italy, and Norway. In all four countries, public-sector wages generally rose with those of total industry and private-sector social service providers, occasionally even outstripping the other sectors.

The fact that public-sector wage growth has matched that in other sectors is even more notable against the backdrop of high absolute wage levels in the

---

16 Productivity growth in the public sector should be low for several reasons. Public-sector production faces fewer of the competitive pressures that drive increases in private-sector productivity. Technological progress is less important in the labor-intensive activities characterizing most government service provision. And perhaps more importantly, the vast expansion in public-sector employment over the past three decades can only dampen productivity, barring massive capital infusions.

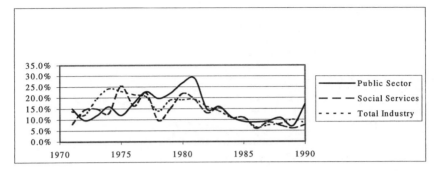

Figure 9.4. *Italy: nominal wage growth in public and private sectors.*

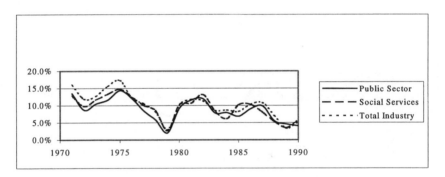

Figure 9.5. *Norway: nominal wage growth in public and private sectors.*

public-sector. Controlling for education, experience, and other aspects of human capital, public-sector workers in the United States earn more than their private-sector counterparts (Freedman 1986; Smith 1977). In all 14 countries for which we have data, average compensation was higher for producers of government services than for private-sector service providers.

UNIONS AND PUBLIC-SECTOR WAGE GROWTH

Economists believe unions should be particularly successful in pushing up wages and benefits in the public-sector (Freeman 1986). Since government employers face a weaker budget constraint than private firms, they may be less motivated to resist union demands. Moreover, the strike threat in the public-sector is often greater than in the private sector, since government officials may hesitate to risk a shutdown in essential services, and consequently give in to excessive union demands. Finally, the relative price inelasticity of the labor demand curve for

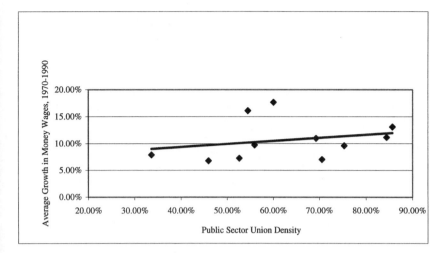

Figure 9.6. *Union density and growth of money wages in the public sector.*

government work leaves unions free to drive up compensation without fearing declines in employment.

In accord with these expectations, empirical studies report a substantial public-sector union wage premium.[17] Although the wage premium is substantial, it is not much greater than that found in the private sector. However, this is somewhat deceptive since unions in the public-sector raise benefits more than they raise wages. Consequently, the total impact of public-sector unions on labor cost is greater than looking at wages alone suggests.

Bearing this caveat in mind, we again turned to the OECD's International Sectoral Databank to examine the effect of union density on wages in the public sector. Figure 9.6 plots the average growth in nominal wages from 1970 to 1990 against union density in the public-sector for 11 countries. The plot reveals a slight positive relationship between the growth of money wages and unionization levels in the public sector. Since the public-sector union compensation premium is expressed in greater fringe benefits at least as much as it is in higher wages, the upward slope of the linear best-fit line is very supportive of our argument.

Figure 9.7 repeats the same exercise, but this time for real wages (i.e., controlling for inflation). As with nominal wages, the chart reveals a tendency for average real wages in the public-sector to grow more rapidly as unionization of government workers increases. Although the relationship is not exceptionally strong – Italy, for example, featured very high real-wage growth despite rela-

17 This summary is based on Freeman (1986).

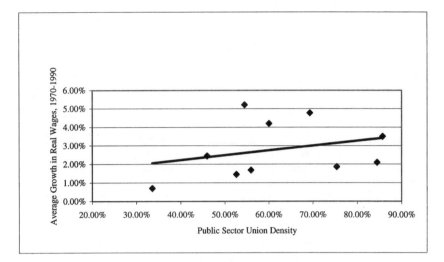

Figure 9.7. *Union density and growth of real wages in the public sector.*

tively weak public-sector unions – the positive association is consistent with our argument. Given that public-sector union density is weakly associated with greater levels of government employment, and that the public-sector wage premium tends to decrease with the size of the public-sector (Gornick and Jacobs 1997), the relationship may well be even stronger than suggested by Figure 9.7.

4. CONCLUSION

This chapter supplements the existing literature on the macroeconomic effects of labor market institutions by directly incorporating the effects of sectoral union strength on the propensity of labor movements to internalize the externalities of wage militancy. Our most important finding is that encompassing labor movements are only associated with desirable macroeconomic effects cases when public-sector unions are weak. Along with several other chapters in this volume, our analysis suggests a revision of the traditional focus of the corporatist literature on labor as a unified actor.

The corporatist literature of the 1970s and 1980s implicitly assumed the interests of all workers are the same. Instead, our argument emphasizes the importance of the sectoral composition of labor movements, and particularly of the distinctions between exposed and sheltered sectors and between private and public employment. This distinction suggests important differences between two sets of cases normally understood as "corporatist," the Nordic countries on the one hand, and Austria and Germany on the other. Macroeconomic performance deteriorated sharply in the former set of countries, and national institutions such as centralized wage setting with a wage solidarity norm fell by the wayside. Our chapter suggests that one important cause of the breakdown of corporatist arrangements in these countries was the rapid growth of public-sector unions.

Moreover, the shift of labor toward sheltered sectors in the Nordic countries has coincided with increasing exposure to the global economy. While this is likely to reduce wage militancy in the exposed sectors, globalization increases the incentives for governments to cushion dislocations and risk (Garrett 1998, Rodrik 1997). Expanding public-sector employment was been the classic Scandinavian means of domestic compensation in the 1970s and 1980s. It is thus not surprising that efforts to control the public wage bill – already prominent in efforts to decentralize pay determination, increase contract employment, and even to reduce the number of civil servants – have become central elements of policy reform in the 1990s.

References

Alvarez, R. Michael, Geoffrey Garrett, and Peter Lange. 1991. "Government Partisanship, Labor Organization and Macroeconomic Performance." *American Political Science Review* 85:541–56.

Ashenfelter, Orley, and Ronald G. Ehrenberg. 1975. "The Demand for Labor in the Public Sector." In Daniel Hamermesh, ed., *Labor in the Public and Nonprofit Sectors*. Princeton, NJ: Princeton University Press.

Bardasi, Elena. 1996. "Differenziali salariali tra i settori pubblico e privato: un'analisis microeconmetrica." *Lavoro E Relazioni Industirali* 3:4–59.

Beck, Nathaniel, and Jonathan Katz. 1995. "What To Do (And Not to Do) with Time-Series–Cross-Section Data in Comparative Politics." *American Political Science Review* 89:634–47.

Belman, Dale, and John S. Heywood. 1995. "State and Local Government Wage Differentials: An Intrastate Analysis." *Journal of Labor Research* 26:183–201.

Calmfors, Lars, and John Driffill. 1988. "Bargaining Structure, Corporatism, and Macroeconomic Performance." *Economic Policy* 6:13–61

Cameron, David. 1984. "Social Democracy, Corporatism, Labour Quiescence, and the Representation of Economic Interest in Advanced Capitalist Society." In John H. Goldthorpe (ed.), *Order and Conflict in Contemporary Capitalism*. Oxford: Oxford University Press.

Crouch, Colin. 1994. *Industrial Relations and European State Traditions.* Oxford: Clarendon Press.

Cukierman, Alex. 1992. *Central Bank Strategy, Credibility, and Independence: Theory and Evidence.* Cambridge, MA: MIT Press.

Deery, Stephen, and David Plowman. 1985. *Australian Industrial Relations.* New York: McGraw-Hill.

Freeman, Richard B. 1986. "Unions Come to the Public Sector." *Journal of Economic Literature* 24:41–86.

Garrett, Geoffrey. 1995. "Trade, Capital Mobility and the Politics of Economic Policy." *International Organization* 49:657–87.

1998. "Global Markets and National Politics: Collision Course or Virtuous Circle?" *International Organization* 52:787–824

Garrett, Geoffrey, and Christopher Way. 1995. "The Sectoral Composition of Trade Unions, Corporatism and Economic Performance." In Barry Eichengreen, Jeffry Frieden, and Jürgen von Hagen (eds.), *Monetary and Fiscal Policy in an Integrated Europe*. New York: Springer Verlag.

Golden, Miriam. 1993. "The Dynamics of Trade Unionism and National Economic Performance." *American Political Science Review* 87:439–54.

Golden, Miriam, and Michael Wallerstein. 1995. "Unions, Employers, and Collective Bargaining: A Report on Data for 16 Countries from 1950 to 1990." Paper presented at the Annual Meetings of the Midwest Political Science Association, Chicago.

Gornick, Janet C., and Jerry A. Jacobs. 1997. "Gender, the Welfare State, and Public Employment: A Comparative Study of Seven Industrialized Countries." Luxembourg Income Study Working Paper #168.

Greene, William H. 1990. *Econometric Analysis*. New York: Macmillan.

Heller, Peter, and Alan Tait. 1983. "Government Employment and Pay: Some International Comparisons." *Finance and Development* 20:44–7.

Heywood, John S. 1991. "Government Employment and the Provision of Fringe Benefits." *Applied Economics* 23:417–23.

Iversen, Torben. 1996. "Power, Flexibility and the Breakdown of Centralized Wage Bargaining." *Comparative Politics* 28:399–436.

Jaccard, James, Robert Turrisi, and Wan K. Choi. 1990. *Interaction Effects in Multiple Regression*. Sage University Paper series on Quantitative Applications in the Social Sciences, 07–072. Newbury Park, CA: Sage.

Korpi, Walter, and Michael Shalev. 1979. "Strikes, Industrial Relations, and Class Conflict in Capitalist Societies." *British Journal of Sociology* 30:164–87.

Moene, Karl-Ove, and Michael Wallerstein. 1992. "The Decline of Social Democracy." In Karl Gunnar Persson (ed.), *The Economic Development of Denmark and Norway since 1870*. Gloucester: Edward Elgar.

Olson, Mancur. 1965. *The Logic of Collective Action*. Cambridge, MA: Harvard University Press.

1982. *The Rise and Decline of Nations*. New Haven: Yale University Press

Organization for Economic Cooperation and Development. Various. *Labour Force Statistics*. Paris: OECD.

Organization for Economic Cooperation and Development. 1993. *International Sectoral Databank*. Paris: OECD.

Pontusson, Jonas. 1992. "The Political Economy of Class Compromise: Labor and Capital in Sweden." *Politics and Society* 20: 305–32.

Pontusson, Jonas, and Peter Swenson. 1996. "Labor Markets, Production Strategies and Wage-Bargaining Institutions: The Swedish Employers' Offensive in Comparative Perspective." *Comparative Political Studies* 29:223–50.

Rodrik, Dani. 1997. *Has Globalization Gone Too Far?* Washington, DC: Institute for International Economics.

Rose, Richard. 1985. *Public Employment in Western Nations.* Cambridge: Cambridge University Press.

Smith, Sharon P. 1977. *Equal Pay in the Public Sector: Fact or Fantasy?* Princeton, NJ: Industrial Relations Section, Princeton University.

Soskice, David. 1990. "Wage Determination: The Changing Role of Institutions in Advanced Industrialized Countries." *Oxford Review of Economic Policy* 6:36–61.

Stilwell, Frank. 1986. *The Accord and Beyond.* Sydney: Pluto Press.

Swenson, Peter. 1991. "Labor and the Limits of the Welfare State." *Comparative Politics* 23:379–99

Thelen, Kathleen. 1993. "European Labor in Transition." *World Politics* 46:23–49.

Traxler, Franz. 1994. "Collective Bargaining: Levels and Coverage." In *OECD Employment Outlook.* Paris: OECD.

Visser, Jelle. 1991. "Trends in Trade Union Membership." In *OECD Employment Outlook.* Paris: OECD.

Wallerstein, Michael. 1995. "The Impact of Economic Integration on European Wage-Setting Institutions." Prepared for the Conference on The Political Economy of European Integration. Berkeley, April 20–22.

10

LABOR MARKET INSTITUTIONS AND WAGE DISTRIBUTION

Jonas Pontusson

As noted in the introduction to this volume, common trends among OECD countries do not necessarily entail convergence. Thus the absence of convergence should not lead us to conclude that there are no common trends. Patterns of wage inequality illustrate this point. In virtually all OECD countries, wage differentials became more compressed in the 1970s, and this trend abated in the 1980s. In many countries, wage inequality has increased over the past 10 to 15 years. Yet the extent of wage compression in 1970–85 varies greatly across countries, and so does the extent of wage dispersion since 1980. Though some changes in relative country rankings occurred, cross-national variations in levels of wage inequality were as great at the end as they were at the beginning of each phase.

Several of the preceding chapters in this volume suggest that wage distribution represents a crucial dimension of the ongoing reconfiguration of wage bargaining, macroeconomic management, and public provision of social welfare in OECD countries. This is perhaps especially true for the Nordic countries, where wage restraint was explicitly linked to wage solidarity in the 1960s and 1970s, but trends in wage distribution appear to be closely related to institutional change in other countries as well. Before we can begin to grapple with contemporary dynamics, however, we need a better understanding of the determinants of cross-national variations in wage distribution or, in other words, a better understanding of how different varieties of capitalism produce distinctive wage-distributive outcomes. While the politics of wage distribution have fig-

This chapter forms part of a research project sponsored by the Twentieth Century Fund. For comments on previous drafts of this chapter, I wish to thank Jonathan Cowden, Alois Guger, Torben Iversen, Harry Katz, Franz Traxler, Lowell Turner, Chris Way, and the participants in the political economy research colloquium at Cornell University.

ured prominently in the literature on the Swedish model, they have been largely neglected by more broad-gauged approaches to comparative political economy.

Labor economists who study wage distribution from a comparative perspective typically end up arguing that institutions matter, that is, that supply and demand factors alone cannot explain observed variations in wage inequality across countries (see Rowthorn 1992; Freeman and Katz 1995; Blau and Kahn 1996; Gottschalk and Smeeding 1997). From a political-economic perspective, this literature is problematic in that it deals with the question of institutional context in either a reductionist or a residualist manner. To the extent that economists incorporate institutional effects into their models, they tend to reduce institutional context to a single, one-dimensional variable, such as the centralization of wage bargaining. More commonly, they invoke rather unspecified "institutional factors" to explain whatever variance remains when the effects of supply and demand factors have been taken into account.[1]

In comparative political economy, the study of wage distribution seems to have fallen between two stools: on the one hand, a research tradition concerned with (re)distribution, but focused on the welfare state and, on the other hand, a research tradition concerned with industrial adjustment, competitiveness, and macroeconomic performance. In addition to its substantive importance, the study of wage distribution provides an opportunity for comparative political economists to bridge these research traditions and to build on recent developments in labor economics.

The present chapter engages in an exploratory (and largely inductive) comparative analysis of the determinants of wage inequality, focusing on the role of political–institutional and economic–structural variables. I begin by presenting different measures of wage inequality and briefly discussing their meaning. The way in which OECD countries line up on these measures is often at odds with conventional typologies and country rankings. Most strikingly, a sharp contrast emerges between Sweden and Austria, commonly viewed as archetypical cases of social democratic corporatism (e.g., Cameron 1984). Although Sweden consistently stands out as the OECD country with the most egalitarian wage structure, Austria turns out to have the least egalitarian wage structure of any European OECD country.

In the second of the sections that follow, I review recent analyses of the Swedish case and discuss the extent to which contending explanations of wage compression fit the empirical evidence. I argue that the debate between those who emphasize union power and ideology and those who emphasize market forces and employer interests can be resolved (or dissolved) by recognizing two separate phases and types of wage compression, with their own distinctive causal

1 Another problem, from the perspective of comparative political economy, is that the labor-economics literature focuses heavily (sometimes exclusively) on the contrast between the United States and continental Europe.

dynamics. In methodological terms, this discussion amounts to a single case study in which change over time provides the basis for assessing causal claims.

The third section tackles the contrast between Sweden and Austria, engaging in a paired, qualitative comparison of "most similar cases." As it turns out, the two cases actually differ on a number of variables that might be construed as causes of divergent wage-distributive outcomes. Still, this comparison enables us to assess the plausibility of generalizing some of the arguments made in the literature about the Swedish case and also serves to generate new hypotheses. I argue that the Sweden–Austria comparison is consistent with the proposition that union strength and wage-bargaining centralization give rise to wage compression, and calls into question the relevance of Left government and the organizational cohesion of employers. Also, two economic–structural variables are relevant to the contrast between Sweden and Austria: the size of the public sector (much larger in Sweden) and the role of small business (much more important in Austria).

In the fourth section, I address the problem of assigning weight to equally plausible causal arguments by means of cross-sectional regressions. The regression results presented here suggest that unionization and wage-bargaining centralization promote the compression of wage differentials among men and women, and that female labor force participation has the opposite effect. None of these variables, however, predicts cross-national differences in between-gender differentials very well. The best predictors of between-gender compression are the size of the public sector and collective-bargaining coverage rates.

The final empirical section briefly explores the relationship between wage distribution and changing wage-bargaining institutions across OECD countries since the early 1980s, seeking to ascertain the extent to which the Swedish story of employer-initiated decentralization in response to wage compression (Swenson and Pontusson, this volume) can be generalized to other cases. Based on fragmentary evidence, I argue that (a) the countries that underwent decentralization of wage bargaining in 1980s experienced particularly sharp wage compression in the 1970s; and (b) decentralization and union decline both promoted wage dispersion in the 1980s.

1. MEASURES OF WAGE INEQUALITY

Table 10.1 presents aggregate measures of wage inequality in 1985 for seventeen countries. Referring to pretax income from employment, these measures do not take into account the redistributive effects of taxation and government spending. It should also be noted that the figures in Table 10.1 refer to the income of individuals rather than households and do not control for the effects of household size, as many measures of the distribution of disposable income do. And, finally, the population used to calculate these measures is restricted to full-time

Table 10.1. *Levels of wage inequality in 17 OECD countries, ca. 1985 (rankings from most to least egalitarian in parentheses)*

	90–10 ratios[a]			Rowthorn index[b]	Male–female ratio[c]
	Both sexes	Men	Women		
Australia	2.72 (9)	2.61 (8)	2.64 (9)	17.6 (12)	1.35 (9)
Austria	3.47 (15)	2.59 (6)	3.47 (12)	21.3 (14)	1.43 (13)
Belgium	2.39 (4)	2.39 (4)	2.21 (3)	14.8 (8)	1.30 (6)
Canada	4.45 (16)	4.03 (13)	4.24 (13)	22.5 (16)	1.56 (16)
Denmark	2.17 (3)			8.6 (3)	1.18 (3)
Finland	2.50 (5)	2.60 (7)	2.11 (2)	15.9 (9)	1.32 (8)
France	3.12 (14)	3.35 (12)	2.64 (9)	12.1 (5)	1.22 (4)
Germany	2.62 (8)	2.35 (3)	2.51 (6)	12.4 (6)	1.37 (10)
Italy	2.50 (5)	2.20 (2)	2.61 (8)	7.7 (1)	1.16 (2)
Japan	3.11 (13)	2.77 (10)	2.28 (4)	29.3 (17)	2.04 (17)
Netherlands	2.51 (7)			10.5 (4)	1.30 (6)
New Zealand	2.84 (11)	2.72 (9)	2.53 (7)	18.8 (13)	1.39 (12)
Norway	2.16 (2)			13.4 (7)	1.22 (4)
Sweden	2.07 (1)	2.13 (1)	1.74 (1)	8.5 (2)	1.15 (1)
Switzerland	2.72 (9)	2.44 (5)	2.70 (11)	16.3 (10)	1.43 (13)
United Kingdom	3.06 (12)	2.80 (11)	2.49 (5)	17.0 (11)	1.37 (10)
United States	5.30 (17)	5.53 (14)	4.45 (14)	22.2 (15)	1.47 (15)
Unweighted aver.	2.92	2.89	2.76	15.8	1.41

Definitions of measures and sources:
[a]The ratio of earnings at the lower end of the 90th decile to earnings at the upper end of the 10th decile, including all full-time wage earners. U.S. figures from OECD (1993:159–61); all other figures from OECD (1996:61–62).
[b]Coefficient of variation (standard deviation divided by the mean) of earnings across industrial sectors (manufacturing sectors plus mining and construction), weighted by employment; for most countries, blue-collar workers only. From Rowthorn (1992:92).
[c]Ratio of average male to average female hourly earnings. From Rowthorn (1992: 91).
Note: 90–10 ratios for Belgium, Canada, Finland, Italy, and New Zealand are based on 1986 data, for Austria and Norway on 1987 data, and for Switzerland on 1991 data.

employees. Thus the figures in Table 10.1 do not reflect cross-national variations in the incidence of part-time employment.

The measures presented in Table 10.1 are "aggregate" in the sense that they encompass multiple dimensions of wage distribution or, in other words, different forms of wage differentiation. Analytically, we can distinguish between, on the one hand, wage differentials associated with different characteristics of employees and, on the other hand, wage differentials associated with variations in profitability across firm or plants and variations in labor market conditions across regions or localities. The characteristics of employees that are associated with wage differentiation include (a) education and training, (b) age and experience; and (c) gender, race, legal status (immigrants), and any other characteristics that might constitute the basis for discrimination.[2]

Over-time and cross-national variations in wage distribution are a function of the size of these wage differentials, but also the distribution of the labor force by relevant characteristics and places of employment. If occupational (education-based) differentials are smaller among women than among men, as is the case in most countries, an increase of women's labor force participation would result in less wage inequality so long as within-gender and between-gender differentials remain unchanged. The same logic applies to cross-national variations: In this example, levels of wage inequality in countries with identical within-gender and between-gender differentials will vary depending on the gender composition of the labor force.

The most aggregate measure of wage inequality presented in Table 10.1 is the "90–10 ratio" for both men and women (first column). The 90–10 ratio is the ratio of earnings at the lower end of 90th decile to earnings at the upper end of the 10th decile. Whereas in the United States, a person at the bottom of the top 10 percent of the wage hierarchy earned 5.3 times as much as a person at the top of the bottom 10 percent, the equivalent person in Sweden earned only 2.07 times as much in 1985. Based on OECD data for all full-time wage earners, the figures in the first column provide a summary measure of the entire wage structure, encompassing all forms of wage differentiation. Reporting 90–10 ratios for men and women separately, the second and third columns take between-gender differentials out of the picture.

The fourth column reports a measure of intersectoral wage differentials in industry taken from Bob Rowthorn (1992). In terms of the analytical framework set out above, intersectoral differentials are a function of sectors (a) employing workers with different characteristics, (b) operating at different levels of (average) profitability, and/or (c) being concentrated in regions characterized by different labor market conditions. Using ILO data for blue-collar (hourly paid) workers, Rowthorn calculates the coefficient of variation of earnings (the standard deviation divided by the mean) across some 15 to 25 industrial sectors for each country. Rowthorn weighs each sector by its share of total employment and counts male and female earnings as distinct observations. By design, this

---

2 Within this analytical framework, discrimination can be defined as a wage premium associated with "maleness," "whiteness," etc., at a given level of education and experience. Differentials between blue-collar and white-collar employees fall under the first of the categories set out above. Skill-related differentials among blue-collar workers reflect what labor economists refer to as "returns to experience" as well as "returns to education."

last feature assigns more weight to gender differentials than previous studies of intersectoral differentials have done.

Based on Rowthorn's dataset, the last column of Table 10.1 measures gender differentials in terms of the ratio of average male to average female hourly earnings. Though narrower than the other measures, this too is a composite measure of wage inequality, for gender differentials are not simply a measure of economic returns to "maleness": They also reflect the fact that working women tend to be less educated and less experienced than working men. The Rowthorn index of intersectoral differentials correlates closely with the ratio of male-to-female earnings (a bivariate regression yields an adjusted R^2 of 86.6%). Based on individual-level data, Francine Blau and Lawrence Kahn (1995) also find a close correlation between gender differentials and the overall wage structure; they argue that this correlation primarily reflects the impact of the overall wage structure on gender differentials (rather than the other way around).[3]

Table 10.1 includes a wealth of information, to which I shall refer throughout the following analysis. A few preliminary remarks will suffice at this point. To begin with, Sweden clearly stands out as the OECD country with the most egalitarian wage structure in Table 10.1. On most measures, Denmark, Norway, and Finland follow Sweden rather closely. Belgium, the Netherlands, and Germany also belong in the egalitarian camp: In the case of Belgium and Germany, this is particularly true when between-gender differentials are left out of the picture. More surprisingly perhaps, Italy turns out to have a very egalitarian wage structure, especially within the industrial sector of the economy. Indeed, Italy ranks ahead of Sweden on the Rowthorn index.[4]

The United States and Canada consistently hold up the other end of the spectrum, but Japan has an even more inegalitarian wage structure by measures that weigh between-gender differentials heavily. By most measures, the UK and New Zealand also tend in an inegalitarian direction. The most surprising feature of Table 10.1, however, concerns the inegalitarian distribution of wages in Austria. On all measures but one, the 90–10 ratio for men only, Austria clearly stands out as the most inegalitarian of the European OECD countries, well "behind" the UK and France.

It should be noted that Austria does not stand out in this fashion and that the contrast between Austria and Sweden is much less pronounced in data on

3 According to Blau and Kahn's data for the mid-1980s (1995:108), the ratio of female to male earnings was 66.9% in the United States and 77.2% in Sweden, but the average female wage fell in the 33rd percentile of the male distribution in the United States, as compared to the 28th percentile in Sweden. Evidently, the 28th percentile was much closer to the median in Sweden than was the 33rd percentile in the United States.

4 Government statistics based on declared income probably overstate the wage compression that occurred in Italy in the period from the early 1970s through the early 1980s; see Erickson and Ichino (1995).

the distribution of disposable income generated by the Luxembourg Income Study. Measured in terms of disposable income "per equivalent adult," the 90–10 ratio for Austria was 2.89 in 1985, as compared to 2.58 for Sweden (OECD 1995:46). The discrepancy between these figures and those reported in Table 10.1 could be due to the effects of government taxation and spending, but I have found no evidence to support the claim that the Austrian welfare state is significantly more redistributive than the Swedish welfare state. Esping-Andersen and Korpi (1984) suggest that the opposite is the case. It seems more plausible to suppose that the discrepancy here reflects the fact that the figures for disposable income are based on households rather than individuals. To the extent that wage inequality is a function of between-gender differentials, a high level of wage dispersion may be compatible with a low level of household income dispersion.[5]

This chapter is not about social inequality per se. Rather, wage-distributive outcomes here serve as a window on labor markets and how they operate differently in different countries. This said, I hasten to add that income from employment accounts for the lion's share of income in all OECD countries and that the measures of wage distribution reported in Table 10.1 correlate rather closely with broader measures of income distribution (see Rueda and Pontusson 1997). Also, the OECD (1996:79–87) demonstrates that there is no straightforward correlation between wage dispersion in a single year and earnings mobility in the period from 1986 to 1991. Countries with more dispersion do not, as a rule, exhibit higher rates of earnings mobility. Hence "international comparisons of cross-sectional inequality probably provide a reliable indication of relative levels of inequality measured over longer periods" (OECD 1996:83).

2. THE SWEDISH CASE

As illustrated by Figure 10.1, the Swedish wage distribution underwent a drastic compression from the mid-1960s until the early 1980s.[6] The beginning of the "great compression" coincided more or less with the adoption of wage solidarity as a goal by Sweden's powerful confederation of blue-collar unions (Landsorganisationen, the LO), and so most of the literature on Swedish wage bargaining (e.g., Martin 1984) simply takes it for granted that union demands have been a major cause, if not *the* major cause, of wage compression. While Douglas Hibbs (1990, 1991) provides evidence in support of the conventional

5 In a similar vein, Burtless (1996) shows that rising inequality of household income in the United States is largely attributable to an increase in the correlation of spousal incomes (well-paid men being increasingly married to well-paid women).

6 Taken from Hibbs (1990), Figure 10.1 refers to the distribution of wages among private-sector blue-collar workers. Hibbs's figures for white-collar workers and white-collar/blue-collar differentials tell essentially the same story. See also Hibbs and Locking (1996:112) and Edin and Holmlund (1995).

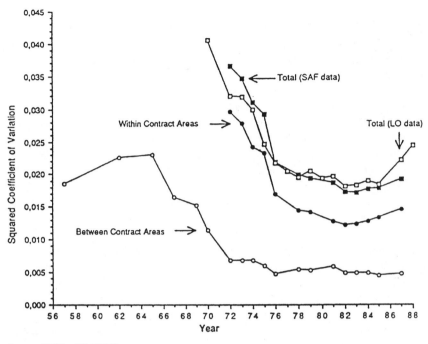

Source: Hibbs (1990:26).

Figure 10.1. *Wage dispersion among private-sector, blue-collar workers in Sweden, 1956–88*

view, other authors have recently sought to downplay the role of union policy in the evolution of the Swedish wage structure. This debate encompasses two distinct questions. The first question concerns the extent to which centralized wage bargaining "distorted" distributive outcomes determined by supply and demand in the labor market in the 1960s and 1970s. How much of the observed wage compression would have occurred in the absence of centralized bargaining or, perhaps, in the absence of any collective bargaining at all? The second question concerns the extent to which the market-distorting effects of centralized wage bargaining are to be attributed to union power and solidarity, as opposed to employer interests.

Ignoring the second question, Hibbs (1990, 1991) identifies the effects of centralized bargaining with the effects of union policy and provides two pieces of evidence in support of the contention that union policy has played a major role in Swedish wage formation. First, Hibbs uses microlevel survey data on the distribution of human capital among LO workers (the variance in years of formal education, vocational training, and work experience) to project wage dispersion

based on human-capital dispersion for the period 1968–86 and then compares
these projections to actual wage dispersion. The upshot of this exercise is that
wage inequality predicted by human-capital dispersion fell by 18 percent from
1968 to 1981, but actual wage inequality fell by more than three times as
much. Second, Hibbs compares the wage dispersion implied by central agreements between LO and its private-employer counterpart (Svenska Arbetsgivar-
föreningen, the SAF) with actual wage dispersion among LO workers, and finds
that "approximately 80 percent of the 'planned' compression of frame wages in
the SAF–LO area was achieved in the market" (Hibbs 1990:75).

As Per-Anders Edin and Bertil Holmlund (1995:331) put it, the latter of
Hibbs's results is indeed striking, but provides "no information on whether the
frame agreements were compatible with the fundamental demand and supply
forces." For their part, Edin and Holmlund deploy econometric models to argue
that supply factors provide considerable explanatory leverage on changes in
returns to different wage-earner characteristics. Specifically, their analysis shows
that (a) returns to education declined as the supply of gymnasium- and
university-educated labor increased in the 1970s, and increased as the expansion
of university education decelerated in the 1980s, and (b) the rise and subsequent
decline of relative youth wages (or, conversely, the decline and subsequent rise
of returns to age) can largely be explained by demographic changes.

Focusing on gender differentials, Lars Svensson (1995) also points to market
forces as a central determinant of wage-distributive outcomes. Svensson argues
that the conventional union-centered explanation of wage compression fails to
account for the timing of major trend changes. While LO and SAF agreed in
1960 to eliminate separate wage rates between men and women, this agreement
was not implemented until 1962 and, in Svensson's time series, the trend
toward compression of gender differentials begins in 1960. At the other end of
the great compression, the female–male wage ratio had clearly reached a plateau
by 1980, and a trend toward increased gender differentials can be observed prior
to the decentralization of wage bargaining in the 1980s. In addition, Svensson
(1995:128–9) observes that the evolution of gender differentials among white-
collar workers conforms closely to the pattern for blue-collar workers even
though the principal white-collar union organizations (Tjänstemännens Cen-
tralorganisation, the TCO, and its private-industry affiliate, Svenska Industritjänstemannaförbundet, the SIF) did not embrace a policy of wage equalization
until 1973.

In contrast to Edin and Holmlund's, Svensson's market-oriented account of
wage compression emphasizes changes in relative demand for different types of
labor and connects labor market conditions to industrial organization. According to Svensson, the compression of the 1960s and 1970s should be seen as a
consequence of (a) the expansion of female-intensive activities in the public
sector, and (b) the routinization of labor tasks associated with the expansion of
Fordist mass production and other forms of rationalization in the industrial

sector as well as the service sector. Rationalization enabled employers to substitute less skilled workers, often women, for more-skilled workers, and increased relative demand for less skilled labor in turn led to higher relative wages for these workers. While public-sector employment growth came to an end, employers embraced transformative production strategies that shifted demand in favor of more skilled/educated labor from the late 1970s onward (cf. Swenson and Pontusson, this volume).

Svensson also suggests that government policies to promote female labor force expansion counteracted the compression of wage differentials from the late 1960s onward. The logic underlying this argument is that women's entry into the labor force represents an increase in the relative supply of unskilled labor (cf. Topel 1994). Clearly, the Swedish case does not support this argument in any straightforward fashion, for Sweden has not only the most compressed wage structure, but also the highest rate of female labor force participation of any OECD country, and both features emerged in the 1960s and 1970s. The crucial role of the public sector as a source of employment for Swedish women appears to be the key to this puzzle. By 1985, women accounted for 47.1 percent of the total labor force, and a whopping 67.1 percent of government employees. Conversely, the public sector accounted for 32.7 percent of total employment, and 46.5 percent of female employment (OECD 1997; Esping-Andersen 1990: 202).

Though the available data on wage distribution in the public sector are fragmentary, there can be no doubt that public-sector wage agreements took on a particularly solidaristic cast in the course of the 1970s (cf. Swenson 1992b). Arguably, public-sector employers were more inclined than private-sector employers to accommodate union demands for compression because they were sheltered from competition in product markets and, at the same time, more directly exposed to the politics of egalitarianism, being directly accountable to elected officials (more often than not, social democrats). The remarkably low level of wage inequality among Swedish women (see Table 10.1) can thus be explained in terms of the concentration of female employment in the public sector.

The arguments and evidence advanced by Edin and Holmlund and by Svensson provide an important corrective to the union-centered account of changes in the Swedish wage structure championed by Hibbs and others. But their analyses hardly constitute a definitive refutation of the proposition that union policy or, more broadly, the politics of wage bargaining have had a major impact on wage-distributive outcomes. To begin with, Edin and Holmlund's discussion of the supply of university-educated labor has little direct bearing on the evolution of wage distribution *among blue-collar workers*. Hence their alternative to Hibbs's account of the compression and subsequent dispersion of blue-collar differentials hinges almost entirely on the movement of relative youth wages.

Since women constitute a much larger share of the labor force than youth, Svensson's analysis of female labor supply and demand captures a larger portion of the overall picture.[7] However, Svensson's argument about the timing of major trend changes invites the following question: In the absence of the implementation of the LO–SAF agreement to abolish separate wage rates for women and men from 1962 onward, would the increase of relative female wages in 1960–61 have been anything but a blip in the time series? In the case of an ongoing process such as wage compression, timing alone does not settle the weight to be assigned to different causal variables.

As for the reduction of white-collar gender differentials in the 1960s, in the absence of any clear policy commitment by white-collar unions, this development might at least partly be seen as a spillover from the LO–SAF arena. Through the labor market, any leveling of gender differentials that LO might have imposed on SAF in the 1960s would have created pressures on employers, especially SAF-affiliated employers, to raise relative female wages for white-collar workers as well. The notion of spillover also applies to the role of public-sector wage bargaining: Since private-sector employers compete with public-sector employers for labor, especially at the lower end of the labor market, wage compression in the public sector may lead to wage compression in the private sector.

Granted that some of the wage compression of the 1960s and 1970s can be attributed to the politics of wage bargaining, the question becomes, to what extent is this egalitarian effect of wage bargaining in turn attributable to union demands and, specifically, to LO's solidaristic wage policy? As part of a larger effort to reinterpret the experience of Swedish social democracy, Peter Swenson (1991, 1992a) argues that wage compression should rather be seen as a product of organized employer efforts to manage interfirm competition for labor. In Swenson's (1992a:350) words, "centralized solidaristic wage policy originated only when employers flexed their muscles against a labor movement divided on . . . centralization and redistribution."

Swenson's interpretation rests on the proposition that employers have a common interest in taking wages out of competition, that is, in curtailing each other's ability to bid up the price of labor, and that this interest comes to the fore under conditions of labor scarcity. At the same time, Swenson advances two arguments couched in terms of specific employer interests. First, Swenson (1991) argues that export-oriented employers pursued and successfully imposed more centralized forms of bargaining and standardized wage rates as a means to curtail wage growth in construction and other sheltered sectors of the economy. Second, Swenson (1992b:347) argues that in the 1950s employers in "structurally vulnerable low-wage industries like textiles" were not only the most eager

---

7 Edin and Holmlund (1995:329–30) also discuss changes in the supply and demand for female labor, but their analysis is indecisive on this score.

proponents of militant resistance to wage increases in general, but also "the most eager proponents of 'differentiated' pay increases for different industries, *so that they would be allowed by SAF to concede disproportionately high increases*" (emphasis in the original).

Like arguments emphasizing market forces, Swenson's employer-centered perspective represents an important corrective to conventional wisdom, but does not provide an entirely persuasive alternative account of wage compression in the 1960s and 1970s. For starters, policies pursued by union-supported social democratic governments must be invoked to explain the tightness of postwar Swedish labor markets, and the high degree of unionization must be invoked to explain why employers responded to labor scarcity with solidarism rather than segmentalism. More importantly for our present purposes, the theoretical rationale behind Swenson's account pertains primarily to interfirm wage differentials.

Although employers may favor standard wage rates to take wages out of competition, they also have an interest in maintaining unilateral control of intrafirm differentials. As commonly recognized, intrafirm leveling became an increasingly more important feature of solidaristic wage bargaining in the course of the 1960s and 1970s. Even with respect to interfirm differentials, it is questionable whether Swedish employers would have opted for such dramatic compression had they not been pushed by unions in this direction, and it is rather implausible that textiles and other structurally vulnerable low-wage industries dictated SAF policy in the 1960s. As Richard Freeman (1980:4–6) suggests, the need to sustain mobilizational capacity makes organized labor more deeply committed to interfirm wage standardization than organized capital.

To sum up, the arguments advanced by Hibbs, Edin and Holmlund, Svensson (Lars), and Swenson (Peter) all invoke variables that played a significant role in the process whereby the Swedish wage structure became so very compressed. The debate among these authors concerns the relative weight to be assigned to these different variables and how to conceive relationships among them. In my view, there are no clear winners in this debate and, indeed, there can be no clear winners so long as we conceive of the debate as a contest among causal models expected to explain the evolution of the Swedish wage structure over the entire postwar period. Focusing on the wage compression of 1960s and 1970s, we can distinguish two separate phases, each with its own distinctive causal dynamic (cf. Hibbs and Locking 1995).

The dominant conception of wage solidarity in the first phase, roughly from the late 1950s to the beginning of the 1970s, was "equal pay for equal work." This policy entailed the elimination of intraoccupational gender differentials as well as interfirm differentials determined by corporate profitability. Articulated by the LO research department in the 1950s, the principle of "equal pay for equal work" provided the basis for a working consensus between low-wage and high-wage unions within LO in the 1960s. It was also consistent with SAF's efforts to regulate interfirm competition for scarce labor and with the increase of relative demand for less-skilled labor associated with industrial rationalization. In short, solidaristic wage bargaining in the 1960s was largely consensual and essentially conformed to the trajectory of market forces, reinforcing market-driven compression.

From the late 1960s onward, the LO unions adopted a more egalitarian approach to the issue of wage solidarity, pushing for intraoccupational leveling within sectors and firms. This radicalization of union demands followed on the successes achieved in the 1960s and reflected a strengthening of the labor movement as a result of a long period of full employment and significant membership growth in the 1960s. To the extent that employers initiated or acquiesced in intrafirm leveling, such support came from large firms engaged in rationalization and expansion rather than the employer groups that Swenson designates as the principal proponents of wage solidarity.[8] By the mid-1970s, even these employers essentially adopted a defensive posture, conceiving new, more egalitarian and intrusive central-agreement provisions as necessary concessions to secure the exercise of wage restraint by the unions.

Though Söderström and Uddén-Jondal (1982) find no evidence that wage-drift served as a corrective to the distributive effects of central agreements for the entire period 1960–79, Hibbs and Locking (1996) show that wage-drift strongly counteracted centralized wage compression in the period 1972–82. These apparently conflicting observations suggest that the relationship between wage-drift and centrally negotiated compression changed at some point in the 1970s – that is, that wage-drift increasingly came to be at odds with the results of centralized bargaining.

Swenson's employer-centered perspective works best for the 1960s and Hibbs's emphasis on union ideology works best for the 1970s. For some period in the 1970s and 1980s, the distributive effects of wage bargaining ran counter to and prevailed over market forces. This said, the continuities between successive phases should also be recognized: as suggested above, the compression of the first phase set the stage for the second phase, and the tension between bargaining outcomes and market forces that emerged in the second phase in turn set the stage for the employer offensive to decentralize wage bargaining from the early 1980s onward.

---

8 Svensson's (1995:132) data on cross-sectoral variations in the evolution of female–male wage ratios in the first half of the 1960s are instructive in this regard. While the female-male ratio increased by an average of 6 percentage points for manufacturing industry as a whole from 1960 to 1965, much larger increases occurred in the metal industry (12.1%), the engineering industry (9.2%), and the electro-technical industry (7.2%). In the textile industry, on the other hand, the female:male ratio increased by only 1.2%.

3. SWEDEN AND AUSTRIA COMPARED

From the vantage of most accounts of Swedish wage compression, the high level of wage inequality in Austria is puzzling, for Austria apparently resembles Sweden on the variables emphasized by these accounts and, more generally, by the literature on social democratic corporatism: strong unions, Left government, and centralized wage bargaining. Arguably, the puzzle here stems from the fact that the literature on the Swedish case takes unions' preference for wage compression for granted. As noted by many observers (e.g., Flanagan, Soskice, and Ulman 1983:54, 76; Guger 1989:186, 1992:350; Walterskirchen 1991:55), the Austrian trade union confederation, the Österreichischer Gewerkschaftsbund (ÖGB), has never been consistently or strongly committed to the principle of wage solidarity. While affirming the principle that wage bargaining should be coordinated to ensure that wage increases are more or less the same across sectors, ÖGB has also affirmed the principle that wages must be allowed to vary according to corporate profitability to preserve employment. When these principles have clashed, the latter has evidently prevailed. Furthermore, the ÖGB has never pursued interoccupational wage compression in any conscious and systematic fashion.

In Rowthorn's (1992:125) words, the Austrian labor movement "has pursued a bargaining strategy which favors certain historically powerful groups of male workers," primarily skilled workers in nationalized industry. By contrast, the Swedish labor movement appears to have been more responsive to the interests of working women and other unskilled, poorly paid categories of wage earners. However, these observations amount to a reformulation rather than a resolution of the puzzle before us. The question becomes, why have Austrian unions eschewed wage solidarity while Swedish unions have pursued it with a vengeance? Or, in other words, why have "certain historically powerful groups of male workers" continued to dominate the Austrian labor movement, but not the Swedish? Let us begin with the variables emphasized by conventional accounts of Swedish wage compression and then turn to consider alternative, less "labor-centered" explanations.[9]

UNIONIZATION AND UNION ORGANIZATION

As noted by Richard Freeman (1980), there are two distinct dimensions to the relationship between unionization and wage structure (cf. also Blau and Kahn 1996). One dimension concerns wage differentials between union members and nonmembers or, in other words, the size of the wage premium associated with

---

9 See Kitschelt (1994), Kunkel and Pontusson (1998), and Traxler (forthcoming) for paired comparisons of Sweden and Austria that complement the following discussion. For descriptive materials on Austria, I have relied primarily on ILO (1986), Katzenstein (1984), Scharpf (1991), and Traxler (1991, 1992).

union membership for wage earners with equivalent qualifications, experience, and other relevant characteristics. The other dimension concerns the distribution of earnings among union members and how it compares to the distribution among unorganized wage earners. To the extent that unionized workers earn more than equivalent non-unionized workers, the wage-distributive effects of unionization will partly depend on the distribution of union membership across the wage hierarchy. Unionism would be a source of wage inequality if highly paid wage earners were better organized than low-paid workers, and the opposite would hold if low-paid wage-earners were better organized. In either case, however, unionization can be expected to reduce wage inequality to the extent that wages in the union sector are more compressed than wages in the non-union sector.

Freeman (1980, 1982, 1993) advances several arguments as to why we should expect wages in the union sector to be more compressed. To begin with, unions approximate the logic of democratic decision making (one person one vote) more closely than markets do, and whenever the mean wage exceeds the median wage, we would expect a majority of union members to favor redistributive wage demands. As organizations dependent on membership support in conflicts with management, moreover, unions have a strong interest in curtailing wage setting based on the subjective decisions of foremen or personnel managers. In unionized firms, job rates rather than individual rates tend to be the major determinant of pay. As noted above, unions also have an organizational interest in standardizing wage rates across plants and firms.

Though Austria is commonly described as a case of strong labor, the Austrian rate of union density is significantly lower than the Swedish rate, and comparing these cases in terms of change over time provides further support for the hypothesis that unionization reduces wage inequality. As measured by Rowthorn (1992:92), wage inequality declined by 28.4 percent from 1973 to 1985 in Sweden, as compared to a decline of only 3.2 percent in Austria. Over the same time period, Swedish union density increased from 72.2 percent to 83.8 percent, and Austrian union density fell from 57.7 percent to 51.0 percent (Visser 1996).[10] However, things are clearly more complicated than this simple comparison suggests. On the one hand, quite a few countries with more egalitarian wage structures than Austria's have lower rates of union density. On the other hand, union density figures probably exaggerate the differences in union strength between Sweden and Austria.

Two considerations, collective-bargaining coverage and the organizational cohesion of the unions, can be invoked to justify the conventional characterization of the Austrian labor movement as comparable to the Swedish labor movement in strength, despite a lower level of unionization. As highlighted by

---

10 These figures refer to "net union density," i.e., unemployed and retired union members have been subtracted from total union membership. According to Traxler (1992:285), gross union density held steady at 60% in Austria from 1973 to 1985.

a recent OECD report (1994), the percentage of the labor force covered by collectively bargained agreements exceeds the union density rate in many countries. With a coverage rate of 98 percent, Austria figures among the countries where this gap is particularly large. In Sweden, by contrast, the coverage rate is identical to the union-density rate (i.e., only union members are covered by collective agreements). The high rate of bargaining coverage in Austria derives from the fact that, while union membership is voluntary, the unions bargain with employer organizations based on mandatory membership (primarily affiliates of the *Bundeskammer der gewerblichen Wirtschaft*, BWK). Thus there can be no wage premium associated with union membership in Austria, and any wage compression negotiated by Austrian unions automatically extends across the entire economy. As these features would lead us to expect greater wage compression at any given level of union density, the high level of wage inequality in Austria becomes even more puzzling.

The wage-distributive effects of unionization are likely to depend on how unions are organized as well as whom they organize. Setting aside the question of centralization for the time being, the way that union organization relates to the blue-collar–white-collar divide constitutes a striking point of contrast between Sweden and Austria. In Sweden, like the other Nordic countries (see Wallerstein and Golden, this volume), there is a strict separation between blue-collar unions and white-collar unions, and the latter have their own peak organizations (TCO and SACO-SR). In Austria, by contrast, ÖGB-affiliated unions organize both blue-collar and white-collar employees in the public sector, and though there is a separate union for white-collar employees in the private sector, it too belongs to ÖGB. Accounting for about 21 percent of total ÖGB membership, the Gewerkschaft der Privatangestellten is by far the largest of the ÖGB's 15 affiliates.

Arguably, the lack of a strong commitment to wage solidarity by the ÖGB reflects the influence of an intraorganizational coalition of well-paid industrial workers and well-paid white-collar employees. In the absence of white-collar allies, skilled workers simply did not constitute a constituency powerful enough to resist the redistributive demands of low-wage workers in the Swedish LO. The fact that the Swedish TCO unions began to pursue wage compression among their own constituencies in the 1970s adds an interesting twist to the argument: Organizationally separated, neither skilled blue-collar workers nor well-paid white-collar employees (both, of course, principally male constituencies) were able to resist redistributive pressures, and wage rivalries across the blue-collar–white-collar divide pushed organizations on both sides of the divide to pursue solidaristic wage policies.

LEFT GOVERNMENT

There are several reasons to expect durable control of government by labor-affiliated Left parties to be associated with wage compression. First, such an association would arise if Left governments promote unionization, and unioni-zation in turn leads to wage compression. A second line of argument hinges on the proposition that Left governments prioritize the achievement and mainte-nance of full employment. Full employment strengthens the bargaining power of wage earners and, to the extent that they are organized, we might again expect that this would result in wage compression. Moreover, the effects of employment levels on bargaining power are likely to vary across the wage hierarchy. Typically, unemployment weakens the bargaining power of unskilled, low-paid wage earners more than it weakens the bargaining power of skilled, high-paid wage earners.[11] In a similar vein, the welfare policies commonly associated with Left parties – a high "social wage" – might be expected to strengthen the relative bargaining power of low-paid wage earners. Finally, one might suppose that Left governments would be more inclined than Center-Right governments to pursue wage compression through minimum-wage and equal-pay legislation.

The point here, of course, is that the Austrian case does not fit any of these expectations, since it leads the league on most measures of Left control of the government (e.g., Cameron 1984:160). To some degree, the connection between Left government and wage compression might be salvaged by arguing that conventional measures, typically based on the distribution of parliamentary and cabinet seats, exaggerate the political dominance of Austrian social democracy, and that Sweden in fact represents a purer case of durable Left government.

Several features distinguishing the Swedish and Austrian cases deserve to be mentioned here, however briefly. First, the Austrian Social Democratic Party (SPÖ) did not become the dominant party of government until 1970, several decades later than its Swedish counterpart (SAP), and the period of social democratic majority government only lasted until 1983. Second, the SPÖ has always had to contend with one principal rival on the Right (Österreichische Volkspartei, the ÖVP), a party with a strong popular base, whereas the Swedish "bourgeois bloc" has been notoriously divided (cf. Esping-Andersen and Korpi 1984). Third, the presence of the Communist Party, with a stable electoral base in the 4–6 percent range, has contributed to the ability of the Swedish social democrats to govern effectively without parliamentary majorities of their own. In Austria, by contrast, the social democrats have been forced to seek coalitions to their Right whenever they have lacked a parliamentary majority of the own. The *Proporz* system of allocating political appointments and the federal structure of the Austrian state have also constrained the SPÖ's political dominance. Throughout the period of social democratic majority government, the ÖVP retained control of a majority of state governments.

---

11 At the same time, increased unemployment tends to be associated with less wage inequality to the extent that job losses are concentrated at the bottom of the wage hierarchy. See Rueda and Pontusson (1997).

With respect to the mechanisms whereby Left government might cause wage compression, two things should be noted. First, the issue of minimum-wage legislation is irrelevant to the Sweden–Austria comparison, since neither country has a legislated minimum wage. Second, average unemployment rates for Sweden and Austria were identical (2.4%) over the period 1960–93. To the extent that Left control of the government matters, the Sweden–Austria comparison suggests that this variable operates through its effects on unionization, the social wage, or equal-pay legislation. The Austrian case casts serious doubts on the relevance of this variable, however: A more fine-tuned assessment of Left control of the government might lead us to expect greater wage inequality in Austria than in Sweden, but it surely would not lead us to expect greater wage inequality in Austria than, say, Germany or the Netherlands.

CENTRALIZATION OF WAGE BARGAINING

The corporatism literature commonly invokes centralization of wage bargaining and other forms of "interest intermediation" as a source of variation among advanced capitalist political economies. Much of this literature (see Golden 1993 for a review) shows that more centralized forms of bargaining are associated with wage restraint, and possibly a better trade-off between inflation and un-employment. The theoretical rationale behind this association is familiar and straightforward: wage restraint is essentially a public good, and centralization enables unions to overcome associated collective-action problems. Wage-distributive outcomes cannot as readily be analyzed in these terms, however, for we cannot say that one particular wage distribution is more "rational" than another from the point of view of all wage earners or, for that matter, all employers. If the politics of wage restraint are about coordination, trust, and perhaps sanctions to realize a Pareto-optimal outcome, the politics of wage distribution are more accurately described in terms of a continuous process of negotiating temporary settlements among competing interests. Why, then, might we expect centralization to matter?

Centralization facilitates the reduction of interfirm and intersectoral wage differentials since it means that more firms and sectors are included in a single wage settlement, but this presupposes that at least one of the parties of central-ized bargaining wants to achieve a reduction of interfirm or intersectoral differ-entials. Like institutional arrangements that provide for the extension of con-tracts to non-union wage earners (sectors), centralization might be conceived as a facilitating factor – a necessary but not a sufficient condition for wage com-pression.

In a somewhat different vein, one might argue that institutional arrange-ments affect the distribution of power among actors and thereby affect wage-distributive outcomes. In the Swedish case, low-wage unions affiliated with LO insisted on solidaristic measures as a condition for their participation in peak-level bargaining sought by employers in the 1950s (Swenson 1989:56–8). But why should centralization systematically strengthen the relative bargaining of low-wage unions? Michael Wallerstein (1997) suggests that the logic of a single union, which formulates wage demands on the basis of some form of majoritarian decision making, also applies here: If low-wage and high-wage unions bargain jointly, organizational politics will influence the demands that they pursue, and market forces will be less influential in determining the distribution of wage increases (cf. also Moene and Wallerstein 1997). Finally, one might suppose that centralized bargaining – in the extreme, a single settlement for all wage earners – renders wage differentials more transparent and politicizes wage-distributive outcomes. According to this argument, centralization not only empowers low-wage unions but also makes them more likely to demand redistributive measures.

Virtually all accounts of the Austrian case subscribe to Franz Traxler's characterization of the ÖGB as the most centralized union movement in Western Europe (1992:277) as well as his characterization of its employer counterpart, the BWK, as "Europe's most comprehensive, well-resourced and politically influential association" (1992:287). Under Austrian law, the unions affiliated with the ÖGB are considered subdivisions of the ÖGB, rather than independent associations, and as such cannot enter into legally binding agreements with other parties. In marked contrast to the Swedish case, where LO bargained on behalf of its affiliates in the era of peak-level bargaining (1956–83), individual unions bargain on behalf of ÖGB. Moreover, the opening of wage negotiations requires the approval of the Parity Commission for Prices and Wages (more precisely, its Subcommittee on Wages), based on a presentation of union wage demands by the ÖGB. Thus the ÖGB serves as the "gatekeeper" for union wage demands. The authority that these arrangements vest in the ÖGB is further reinforced by its complete control over union financing, including strike funds, and personnel.

The centralization of the ÖGB certainly exceeds that of LO, let alone Sweden's white-collar confederations. Yet much of the literature ignores (or downplays) the fact that the ÖGB has not engaged in direct wage bargaining with its employer counterpart since the 1940s, and that there has never been a Swedish-style peak-level agreement in Austria. Throughout the postwar period, national-level wage bargaining has been organized on a sectoral basis, and the "frame agreements" struck at this level appear to have been less substantive than their Swedish counterparts. In many sectors, contractual wage rates have been set through regional (state-level) negotiations. To the extent that informal discussion in the context of the Parity Commission can be said to have served to coordinate wage bargaining, this coordination has focused entirely on macroeconomic parameters. There is simply no evidence to suggest that wage-distributive issues have been a subject of negotiation at this level. By contrast, wage-distributive issues were from the beginning a core feature of peak-level bargaining between LO and SAF in Sweden.

In sum, we ought to distinguish between (a) centralization of authority within union and employer organizations, and (b) centralization of bargaining between them. The Sweden–Austria comparison suggests that if centralization has anything to do with wage compression, it is the latter dimension that matters. Had the ÖGB leadership wanted to push wage solidarity on its affiliated unions, it certainly had the authority to do so. Along the lines suggested above, however, the absence of peak-level bargaining might explain the absence of strong rank-and-file pressures on the ÖGB leadership to pursue such a policy.

EMPLOYER ORGANIZATION AND INDUSTRIAL STRUCTURE

The high level of wage inequality in Austria represents a puzzle, not only from the vantage of conventional, labor-centered accounts of Swedish wage compression, but also from the vantage of the employer-centered alternative proposed by Swenson. As noted above, Austrian employers are exceedingly well-organized, at least as capable of solidaristic behavior as Swedish employers, and labor markets were exceedingly tight in both countries in the period 1960–90. So why didn't Austrian employers also respond to postwar conditions of labor scarcity in ways that yielded intersectoral wage compression?

Variations in the internal organization of employer associations – the way they aggregate individual employer interests – provide part of an answer. Within the complex Austrian system of business chambers, state-level sectoral organizations constitute the basic unit. The decision-making bodies of these organizations are elected every five years by direct vote of all firms that belong to the organization in question and, regardless of size, each member firm has one vote in these elections (ILO 1986:36). In Sweden, by contrast, the statutes of the SAF and its sectoral affiliates provide for plural voting based on firm size (number of employees). Though neither set of organizations relies strictly on majority voting to determine their wage-bargaining stance, the Austrian system obviously favors small business and the Swedish system favors big business.

This basic difference between employer organizations is closely linked to differences in industrial structure. While most accounts of the Swedish political economy emphasize the role of large, export-oriented private companies, it is commonplace to observe that small business, often domestically oriented, occupies a very prominent place in the Austrian economy and that large-scale export-oriented industry is dominated by foreign-owned and, above all, state-owned companies (e.g., Katzenstein 1984, 1985; Kurzer 1993). The prominence of small business in the Austrian case cannot simply be explained in terms of a large private-service sector associated with tourism: It is also an attribute of the industrial sector, which accounts for a larger share of total employment in Austria (36.8% in 1990) than in Sweden (29.1%). As Table 10.2 shows, small firms (especially very small firms) account for a much larger percentage of the

Table 10.2. *The distribution of establishments or firms by size in Sweden and Austria, late 1970s*

No. of employees	Sweden (establishments) (%)	Austria (firms) %
<5		50.5
<10	22.5	
<50	75.6	92.8
50–99	11.1	3.5
100–499	10.9	3.2
>499	2.3	.5

Note: Swedish figures refer to 1977; year of Austrian figures not specified.
Sources: SCB (1979:138–139) and Vak (1982:166).

total number of industrial firms/establishments in Austria than in Sweden.[12] For our present purposes, the distribution of employment by firm or establishment size represents a more meaningful statistic. Unfortunately, the only Swedish data I have been able to find on this variable are restricted to the industrial sector, while the only Austrian data I have found refer to both services and industry.[13] As the German data included in Table 10.3 illustrate, industrial employment tends to be more concentrated than service employment, and hence it may be misleading to compare the Swedish and Austrian figures in this table. Still, the figures are consistent with the claim that the small-business sector is larger in Austria than in Sweden and also point to bifurcation (relatively less employment in medium-sized establishments/firms) as a distinctive characteristic of the Austrian employment structure.

As with unionization, there are two dimensions to the relationship between firm size and wage distribution. One dimension concerns wage distribution within firms. In general, union density tends to be higher and unions tend to be better organized in large-scale industries. Workers in large plants also tend to be more class conscious and more likely to support solidaristic union policies (Pontusson 1995a). For either or both of these reasons, we might expect more within-establishment wage compression in large establishments, and hence more

12 The figures in Table 10.2 are not strictly comparable: while the Swedish figures refer to establishments (workplace sites), the Austrian figures refer to firms. Very few industrial firms with less than 50 employees, however, are likely to be "multiestablishment firms."

13 Note that both sets of figures refer to establishments (not firms), and that the Austrian figures do not include public services.

Table 10.3. *The distribution of employment by establishment size in Sweden, Germany, and Austria, late 1980s*

	Industry only		Industry and services	
No. of employees	Sweden	Germany	Austria (%)	Germany (%)
<50	17.3%	28.2%	40.4	47.8
50–199	45.8	33.8	33.7	31.4
>199	36.9	38.1	25.9	20.8

Note: Swedish figures for 1989, German figures for 1987, and Austrian figures for 1988.
Sources: SCB (1991), StBA (1991), and Austria (1991).

economy-wide compression where a larger proportion of the labor force works in large establishments. Svensson's (1995) account of Swedish wage compression as a consequence of the routinization of work associated with the expansion of Fordist mass production is also germane here. Arguably, the size of the small-business sector restricted the scope of work routinization in Austria in 1960s and 1970s.

The other dimension of the relationship between firm size and wage distribution concerns wage differentials between small and large firms. In most if not all OECD countries, large firms on average make higher profits and pay higher wages than small firms (Loveman and Sengenberger 1990). Ewald Walterskirchen (1991:57) suggests that wage differentials between small and large firms are particularly large in Austria.[14] Even if the differentials were the same as in Sweden, the greater bifurcation of the Austrian employment by firm size should be associated with greater (economy-wide) wage inequality.

As commonly noted, solidaristic wage policy was conceived by the LO leadership in the 1950s, not only as a means to redistribute income, but also as a means to promote economic restructuring by squeezing the profits of less efficient firms while boosting the profits of more efficient firms. The above-noted differences in industrial structure might be viewed as a consequence of the fact that Swedish unions have pursued a solidaristic approach to wage bargaining, and Austrian unions have not. As the basic contrast between Swedish and Austrian industrial structure seems to predate the LO's pursuit of wage solidarity (cf., e.g., Traxler 1992:271), however, it is equally if not more plausible to argue that Swedish industrial structure promoted while Austrian industrial structure hindered wage compression in the 1960s and 1970s.

14 See Reiterlechner (1992) for detailed statistics on wage costs by establishment size in Austria.

RELATIVE SUPPLY OF UNSKILLED LABOR AND PUBLIC-SECTOR EMPLOYMENT

The comparison of Sweden and Austria clearly does not support the contention that women's entry into the labor force increases the relative supply of unskilled labor, and thereby promotes wage inequality. In 1960, working women accounted for 50.1 percent of the female population aged 15 to 64 years in Sweden, and 52.1 percent in Austria. While female labor force participation in Sweden had increased to 78.1 percent by 1985, it had declined slightly in Austria (51.0 percent). In 1985, women accounted for 47.1 percent of the total labor force in Sweden, as compared to 39.5 percent in Austria (OECD 1997).

As noted above, the concentration of female employment in the public sector appears to have attenuated the wage-distributive effects of female labor force participation in Sweden. The comparison with Austria strongly supports this line of argument, for the expansion of the public sector has been much weaker and less closely linked to female labor force participation in Austria. In 1985, public-sector employment accounted for 19.6 percent of total employment, as compared to 32.7 percent in Sweden, and women accounted for 36.9 percent of the public-sector labor force, as compared to 67.1 percent in Sweden (OECD 1997; Austria 1991; and Esping-Andersen 1990:202).

The contrast between Sweden and Austria in terms of women's role in the labor movement is equally stark. Though the gender gap in union density rates remains very large in Austria, the female rate of union density in Sweden surpassed the male rate in the 1980s. In Sweden, 85.9 percent of working women were union members in 1985, as compared to 83.3 percent of working men. For Austria, the corresponding figures were 36.7 percent compared to 56.8 percent (OECD 1991:116). As women account for less than one-third of total ÖGB membership, it is perhaps not surprising that Austrian unions have not pushed very hard for the compression of gender differentials. There can be little doubt that the high rate of union membership (and involvement) among Swedish women derives in part from their employment in the public sector. Also, it should be noted here that the wage gap between men and women is significantly smaller in the public sector than in the private sector in Austria (Mesch 1990).[15]

The argument behind the expectation that the entry of women into the labor force would give rise to wage dispersion applies to immigration as well and, in this case, public-sector employment is not likely be a confounding factor. For Austria, Wolfgang Pollan (1980) shows that foreign workers' share of the labor force provides a strong predictor of relative wage movements

---

15 Drawing on data collected for the Luxembourg Income Study, Gornick and Jacobs (1997) show that this also holds for Belgium, Canada, Germany, the Netherlands, the UK, and the United States.

between industrial sectors over the period 1962–76. Might immigration and the place of immigrants in the labor market explain some of the contrast between Austria and Sweden? Space does not permit a careful analysis of the issues involved here. Suffice it to note that, contrary to common preconceptions, Austria's reliance on immigrant labor has not been that much greater than Sweden's. In 1990, foreign-born workers accounted for 6.7 percent of the Austrian labor force, as compared to 5.6 percent of the Swedish labor force. Also, the ratio of unemployment for immigrants to the national unemployment rate was only slightly higher in Austria, 2.44 as compared to 2.35 (SOPEMI 1993). Especially by comparison to gender, immigration plays a relatively minor role in the political economy of wage inequality.

5. CROSS-SECTIONAL REGRESSION ANALYSIS

Starting the previous section with a most-similar-cases design, looking for one or two variables that might explain the variation in outcomes between two otherwise similar cases, we ended up with an embarrassment of riches: The Swedish and Austrian cases differ on many variables that can plausibly be invoked to explain wage-distributive outcomes, and the causal influence of these variables may be construed in different ways.

How can we choose among the variables identified above or, at least, order them according to relative significance? Faced with equally plausible explanations of divergent outcomes in two cases, we would prefer the explanation that is more generally applicable, and so one way to tackle this problem is to explore the extent to which the variables in question are associated with levels of wage inequality across the entire set of OECD countries. Such an exercise enables us not only to gauge how the variables perform as predictors of wage inequality but also to gauge the extent to which Austria is an exceptional case.

Several caveats are in order before we venture down this path. First, the number of observations of any given measure of wage inequality presented in Table 10.1 is very small by statistical standards (ranging between 14 and 17) and this severely restricts the possibility of testing complex causal models. With so few cases, regressions with more than two or three variables rarely yield any statistically significant results.[16] Second, data availability restricts the choice of independent variables. In particular, I do not have any comparable data on the size of the small-business sector or the distribution of employment by firm size across a significant number of OECD countries. Third, regression analysis does not enable us to discriminate between different causal mechanisms, and hence does not quite settle the question of causality.

16 Pooling of cross-sectional and time-series data provides the most obvious solution to the small-N problem. See Rueda and Pontusson (1997) and Wallerstein (forthcoming).

Table 10.4. *Bivariate regression results*

Independent variable	90–10 men only (14 cases)	90–10 both sexes (17 cases)	Male – female ratio (17 cases)
UNION	−.2756**	−.2547**	−.2340**
	(.1155)	(.1263)	(.0710)
COVER	−.2024**	−.2161***	−.2409***
	(.0760)	(.0687)	(.0698)
CENTR	−.5775**	−.4881***	−.4525**
	(.2583)	(.1558)	(.1912)
GOVEMP	−.2354	−.4546	−.9968***
	(.4011)	(.3093)	(.2610)
LEFT	−.1557*	−.1336	−.1335
	(.0902)	(.0790)	(.0889)
FEMEMP	.7151	.1270	−.4302
	(.6736)	(.5502)	(.6005)
IMMIG	−.1941	.1952	.7668
	(.4249)	(.3915)	(.4487)

See Table 10.1 for cases and values of the dependent variable; see the text for specifications of the independent variables. For lack of observations on the independent variables, the regressions with COVER do not include Italy, the regressions with CENTR do not include Australia and New Zealand, the regressions with LEFT do not include New Zealand, and the regressions with IMMIG do not include Australia, Canada, Finland, Italy, Japan, New Zealand, and the U.S. Standard errors in parentheses.
$*p < .10$, $** p < .05$, and $*** p < .01$ (two-tailed tests).

Finally, we must keep in mind that this type of exercise rests on the questionable premise that the causal relationship between independent and dependent variables is constant across countries (i.e., countries vary only on the values that these variables assume). To return to my previous discussion of the Swedish case, what I propose to do here is akin to a time-series regression for the entire period 1960–82. The notion of two separate phases of wage compression implies that separate regressions for, say, 1960–72 and 1970–82 would yield significantly different results (e.g., different β coefficients for union density). A single regression for the entire period obviously misses the "regime change" that occurred in the early or mid-1970s (cf. Western 1997).

Some insight might nevertheless be gained by engaging in a cross-sectional regression analysis of available data. As a first cut, Table 10.4 reports the results of a series of bivariate regressions with three different measures of wage inequality – the 90–10 ratio for men only, the 90–10 ratio for both sexes, and the ratio of average male to average female earnings – as the dependent variable. No matter which measure of wage inequality we use, union density (UNION) and Torben Iversen's index of wage-bargaining centralization (CENTR) are consistently and quite strongly associated with lower levels of wage inequality.[17] Despite the fact that these regressions include the Austrian case, we also observe a consistent and strong association between wage compression and collective-bargaining coverage rates (COVER), as measured for 1990 by the OECD (1994: 173). Significantly, the egalitarian effects of unionization and centralization tend to diminish the more gender-sensitive the measure of wage inequality, while the opposite is true for collective-bargaining coverage.

The signs of the coefficients for Left control of the government (LEFT), using Cameron's (1984) measures, and government employment as a percentage of total employment (GOVEMP), are consistently what we would expect, but these coefficients are, at best, statistically significant in only a couple of instances.[18] The coefficients for women as a percentage of the labor force (FEMEMP) and immigrants as a percentage of the labor force (IMMIG) are never statistically significant, and the signs for these coefficients change depending on the measure of wage inequality that we use.[19] Ignoring the lack of statistical significance, Table 10.4 indicates that female labor force participation is associated with more wage inequality among men and women, but also with less wage inequality between men and women.

Table 10.5 reports the results of a series of multiple regressions with both-gender 90–10 ratios as the dependent variable, and Table 10.6 reports the results of a series of multiple regressions with male–female ratios as the dependent variable. Both sets of regressions include a dummy variable for Austria. Whereas all of the regressions reported in Table 10.5 include FEMEMP, all of the regressions reported in Table 10.6 include GOVEMP. The regressions of Table 10.5 then test for the effects of any and all pairs of the political–

---

17 See Iversen's contribution to this volume for a detailed exposition of this index, which combines data on levels of bargaining with data on the concentration of union membership to yield year-by-year observations of wage-bargaining centralization. Because 1985 levels of wage inequality are the cumulative product of many rounds of wage bargaining, I here use the average score for each country for 1973–80. Although Austria ranks as a case of very high centralization in most indices that attempt to measure institutional arrangements of wage bargaining, it ranks near the middle of Iversen's index (see Table 10.8). Taken from OECD (1991:101), the union density rates used in the regressions reported here are net density rates (cf. note 10) for 1985 and correspond closely to the union density data presented in the introductory chapter of this volume.

18 In Tables 10.4–10.7, asterisks are used to indicate when the probability that the true value of the coefficient falls outside the 95% confidence interval is less than .1, .05, and .01. It is conventional to treat .05 as the threshold of statistical significance, but this is an entirely arbitrary standard and, given the small number of observations, a somewhat less stringent standard might be in order here.

19 Note that the regressions with IMMIG as the independent variable include only 10 countries.

Table 10.5. *Multiple regression results with both-gender 90–10 ratios as the dependent variable*

Independent variable	(1)	(2)	(3)	(4)	(5)	(6)
FEMEMP	1.4529***	.9484**	1.4671***	.9777**	1.2289**	.6892
	(.4533)	(.4094)	(.4549)	(.4011)	(.4538)	(.4618)
UNION	−.2225	−.2545**	−.3331**			
	(.1430)	(.0865)	(.1108)			
CENTR	−.4111*			−.4969***	−.5784**	
	(.2273)			(.1410)	(.2009)	
COVER		−.1743**		−.1566**		−.196(
		(.0605)		(.0599)		(.0687)
LEFT			−.1112		−.0806	−.167(
			(.0849)		(.0956)	(.0783)
AUSTRIA	10.8494*	13.3888**	14.8601*	14.3162**	14.0940*	20.894(
	(5.642)	(5.387)	(6.975)	(5.220)	(7.345)	(7.014)
Adjusted R^2	64.3	67.3	59.4	74.2	58.6	58.7
N	15	16	16	14	15	15

See Table 10.1 for cases and values of the dependent variable; see the text for specifications of the independent variables. For lack of observations on the independent variables, the regressions with COVER do not include Italy, the regressions with CENTR do not include Australia and New Zealand, and the regressions with LEFT do not include New Zealand. Standard errors in parentheses.
*$p < .10$, **$p < .05$, and *** $p < .01$ (two-tailed tests).

institutional variables discussed above: UNION, CENTR, COVER, and LEFT. In Table 10.6, pairs that include LEFT have been dropped because the coefficient for this variable is never statistically significant.[20]

Table 10.5 shows that so long as we control for either union density or wage-bargaining centralization, female labor force participation is strongly associated with wage inequality as measured by both-gender 90–10 ratios. According to these regressions, a one percentage-point increase of women's share of the labor force is associated with an increase of wage inequality in the range of .98 to 1.47 percentage points.[21] Controlling for Austrian exceptionalism, Left government is associated with a more egalitarian wage distribution when this variable is paired with collective-bargaining coverage, but the coefficient for

20 If we substitute GOVEMP or IMMIG for any one of the terms in the Table 10.5 regressions, the substitute variable is not statistically significant. The same holds if we substitute LEFT, FEMEMP, or IMMIG for any one of the terms in the Table 10.6 regressions.
21 To create comparable units of measurement, the wage ratios in Table 10.1 and Iversen's index figures have been multiplied by 100; i.e., ratios have been converted into percentages. It should also be noted that multiple regressions with 90–10 ratios for men only as the dependent variable yield results that are very similar to those of Table 10.5.

Table 10.6. *Multiple regression results with male – female ratios as the dependent variable*

Independent variable	(1)	(2)	(3)
GOVEMP	−1.0801**	−.9058***	−.8642**
	(.4734)	(.2702)	(.2771)
UNION	.0851	.0627	
	(.2005)	(.0848)	
CENTR	−.1474		−.0044
	(.3457)		(.1562)
COVER		−.1652**	−.1580**
		(.0603)	(.0608)
AUSTRIA	5.3994	8.4424	9.0923
	(8.078)	(5.176)	(5.122)
Adjusted R^2	58.9	73.8	77.9
N	15	16	14

See Table 10.1 for cases and values of the dependent variable; see the text for specifications of the independent variables. For lack of observations on the independent variables, the regressions with COVER do not include Italy, and the regressions with CENTR do not include Australia and New Zealand. Standard errors in parentheses.
$*p < .10$, $**p < .05$, and $***p < .01$ (two-tailed tests).

Left government loses its statistical significance when we introduce either union density or centralization into the regression. While collective-bargaining coverage has an egalitarian impact that is statistically significant in all of these regressions, the coefficients for union density and centralization are considerably larger than the coefficients for coverage when these variables are paired.

So long as they are not paired with each other, both union density and centralization are strongly associated with wage compression. However, the effects of these variables tend to cancel each other out (indicating a serious problem of collinearity). In the regressions that do not include centralization, a one percentage-point increase of union density is associated with decline of wage inequality in the range between .25 and .33 percentage points. With the scale of centralization measures being more compressed than the scale for union density, the corresponding range for centralization is .5 to .58. Finally, it should be noted that the coefficients for the Austrian dummy are statistically significant in every one of these regressions. Austrian wage inequality is significantly greater than we would predict based on the variables included in these regressions. (Not surprisingly, Austrian exceptionalism is especially pronounced when the regression includes LEFT and/or COVER.)

Turning to Table 10.6, the determinants of between-gender differentials are strikingly different from the determinants of overall wage inequality. In these regressions, the coefficients for union density and wage-bargaining centralization are invariably smaller than their standard errors (and, indeed, the sign of the coefficients for union density is positive, suggesting that union density might be associated with greater between-gender differentials). The Austrian dummy variable is also insignificant. Two variables, GOVEMP and COVER, alone constitute reliable predictors of the ratio of average male to average female earnings and, taken together, they predict roughly three-quarters of the observed variance on this measure of wage inequality. According to these regressions, a one percentage-point increase of the public sector's share of total employment is associated with a decline of between-gender differentials in the range between .87 and 1.08 percentage points, and a one-point increase of collective bargaining coverage is associated with a decline of between-gender differentials in the .16 to .17 range.

That the egalitarian effects of collective bargaining coverage operate primarily (perhaps entirely) through gender differentials makes good sense since coverage rates in excess of union density rates imply that union-negotiated wages are extended to non-union workers and, in most OECD countries, women are less likely to be union members than men (see OECD 1991). Similarly, the gendered impact of government employment can be explained by the fact that a large percentage of working women are employed by the public sector in most of these countries. With respect to the latter point, the results reported in Table 10.6 are all the more striking given that the measure of gender differentials used here is based on industrial workers only. It would appear that between-gender compression in the public sector has spilled over into the private sector.

The fact that female labor force participation is associated with smaller between-gender differentials in a bivariate regression and drops out of the picture in the multiple regressions of between-gender differentials, while being strongly associated with higher 90–10 ratios for men and women combined, remains something of a puzzle. Though only some of the coefficients are statistically significant, the regression results reported in Table 10.7 suggest that this puzzle might be resolved by taking into account the interaction of female labor force participation and the size of the public sector. With either 90–10 ratios for both men and women or male–female ratios as the dependent variable, both female labor force participation and government employment are associated with more wage inequality, but the interaction effect of these two variables is egalitarian. Thus our assessment of the egalitarian impact of government employment also needs to be qualified.

Table 10.7. *The interaction of government employment and female labor force participation*

	Dependent variable	
Independent variable	Both-gender 90-10 ratios	Male–female ratios
FEMEMP	4.3491**	2.7503*
	(1.645)	(1.517)
GOVEMP	6.6653*	3.0122
	(3.241)	(2.989)
GOVEMPxFEMEMP	−1.7648**	−1.0143
	(.7712)	(.7113)
Adjusted R^2	31.6	52.6
N	17	17

See Table 10.1 for cases and values of the dependent variable; see the text for specifications of the independent variables. Standard errors in parentheses.
$*p < .10$, $**p < .05$, and $***p < .01$ (two-tailed tests).

6. WAGE DISTRIBUTION AND INSTITUTIONAL CHANGE

In the course of the 1980s, Swedish employers began to push for a far-reaching restructuring of the system of wage bargaining, involving the abandonment of peak-level (confederal) negotiations and a much wider scope for firm-level bargaining. By the early 1990s, Swedish employers had pretty much achieved what they wanted (Swenson and Pontusson, this volume). While a trend toward more decentralized wage setting may be observed in a number of countries, Sweden stands out as an extreme case of institutional change (cf. Golden and Wallerstein 1996; Wallerstein, Golden, and Lange 1996).

The idea that wage differentials had become excessively narrow and rigid figured very prominently in the rhetoric of the Swedish employers' campaign to decentralize bargaining. It is tempting to suppose that the high degree union- or public-sector-led wage compression in the preceding decade explains the radicalism of the Swedish employer offensive. The absence of any serious effort by Austrian employers to dismantle the existing system of coordinated industry-level bargaining supports this line of thinking (Traxler et al. 1995). From a broader comparative perspective, the question becomes, do we observe a pattern of association between wage compression in the 1970s and decentralization in the 1980s?

Table 10.8. *Wage compression in the 1970s and decentralization in the 1980s*

	Iversen centralization score			% change in Rowthorn index from 1973 to 1985
	Ø1973–77	Ø1989–93	Change	
Decentralized				
Canada	.01	.01		−16.5
France	.02	.02		−5.4
Italy	.054	.04	−.01	−49.8
Japan	.053	.112	+.59	8.1
Switzerland	.063	.063		3.5
United Kingdom	.09	.03	−.06	−13.5
United States	.01	.01		−16.8
Centralized-stable				
Austria	.18	.18		−3.2
Finland	.176	.173	−.003	−21.6
Germany	.159	.1	−.059	−7.9
Netherlands	.138	.121	−.017	19.2
Norway	.303	.319	+.016	−6.6
Decentralizing				
Belgium	.24	.083	−.157	−27.9
Denmark	.385	.1	−.285	−22.8
Sweden	.345	.116	−.229	−28.4

Sources: Centralization scores provided directly by Iversen; wage data from Rowthorn (1992:92).

Based on data used in the preceding analysis, Table 10.8 represents a first stab at an answer to this question. The table is organized as follows. Using Iversen's centralization scores, I first distinguish between OECD countries with and without systems of centralized or coordinated wage bargaining in the mid-1970s. I then make a second distinction within the group with centralized systems, between those countries that underwent significant decentralization from the mid-1970s to the early 1990s and those that did not.[22] For each country, the percentage change in Rowthorn's gender-weighted index of inter-sectoral wage inequality from 1973 to 1985 is recorded in the last column of Table 10.8.

Perhaps because of the difficulties of measuring decentralization in a decen-

22 At the margins, any classification of this sort is necessarily arbitrary, but in this case, the cutoff points seem rather natural: The difference between the most centralized of the decentralized systems and the most decentralized of the centralized system in 1973–77 is large, and so is the difference in magnitudes of change between Germany (a moderate decentralizer) and Belgium (the most moderate of the large-scale decentralizers).

tralized setting, the countries with decentralized systems are as a group characterized by institutional stability (with Japan as a significant exception). With respect to changes in the wage structure, however, this group of countries is characterized by great diversity: Some underwent fairly major wage compression (extreme in the case of Italy) from 1973 to 1985 while the intersectoral wage spread actually increased in others (most notably Japan).[23]

Comparing centralized systems that have undergone decentralization with those that have not, Table 10.8 suggests an association between wage compression and institutional change, for the countries in which far-reaching decentralization has occurred experienced more extensive wage compression from 1973 to 1985 than any of the countries with stable bargaining systems. If it were not for Finland, characterized by extensive wage compression *and* institutional stability, the divergence of wage-distributive outcomes in these two groups of countries during the 1970s would be very striking indeed.

The data presented above also enable us to address the question of the wage-distributive consequences of decentralization in the 1980s. Did employers who successfully imposed more decentralized wage bargaining achieve the wage-distributive changes they wanted? In Table 10.9, the OECD countries are divided into the same three groups as in Table 10.8: countries with decentralized systems of wage setting, countries with centralized and stable systems, and countries with centralized systems that have undergone major decentralization. On the vertical axis, this table in turn distinguishes between countries in which a major decline of union density occurred in the 1980s and countries in which this was not the case (using data presented by Iversen and Pontusson, this volume). For each country, the table then reports the percentage change in 90–10 ratios for both sexes and for men only from the earliest to the most recent observations available (over the period 1979–95).

Because the evidence is fragmentary and the patterns by no means clear-cut, Table 10.9 must be read with care and caution. The following observations can be made. First, the countries that experienced neither decentralization nor union decline are the only countries in which wage compression continued through the 1980s. Second, with the exception of France, the group of countries that is characterized by decentralized wage setting and major union decline stands out as the group that experienced the most extensive wage dispersion in the 1980s.[24] Third, none of the countries characterized by decentralization also experienced major union density decline, and in terms of the extent of wage

23 Iversen's coding of the Italian case is questionable: Taking the *scala mobile* into account (a legislative form of wage regulation), most observers characterize Italy as a case of relatively centralized wage setting in the 1970s, and as a case of decentralization in the 1980s (Erickson and Ichino 1995; Baccaro and Locke 1998). Suffice it to note here that this alternative characterization turns Italy into a case that strongly confirms the hypothesis that wage compression in the 1970s led to decentralization in the 1980s.

24 The French exception is largely attributable to minimum wage legislation passed by socialist governments in the early 1980s; see Katz, Loveman, and Blanchflower (1995).

Table 10.9. *Decentralization and wage dispersion in the 1980s*

| | Major union decline[a] | | | | | |
| | Yes | | | No | | |
	Country	B90–10[b]	M90–10[c]	Country	B90–10[b]	M90–10[c]
Decentralized systems	UK	+18.6%	+32.2%	CAN	+4.7	+9.0
	US	+13.7	+18.0			
	ITA	−4.8	+15.3			
	JPN	+0.3	+6.9			
	FRA	+1.2	+1.2			
Centralized- stable systems	NTH	+17.2	+3.6	FIN	−3.3	+3.7
	AUS	+6.1	+3.0	NOR	3.9	
				GER	−13.8	+2.7
Decentralizing systems				SWE	+4.4	+4.3
				DEN	+1.4	
				BEL	−4.4	−2.1

[a]In countries classified as cases of major union decline, the 1990 union density rate was at least 17% lower than the 1980 rate; in the other countries, the 1990 rate was never more than 8% lower. Based on OECD (1994:184).
[b]The percentage change in 90–10 ratios for both sexes from first observation (never prior to 1979) and most recent observation (never later than 1995) reported by OECD (1996).
[c]The percentage change in 90–10 ratios for men only (same specifications).

dispersion these countries do *not* stand out. In fact, wage dispersion in stable centralized systems with major union decline was greater than in any of the cases of large-scale decentralization. If it were not for Canada, it would indeed be tempting to infer that union decline provides a better predictor of wage dispersion in the 1980s than decentralization. Suffice it to conclude here that both variables appear to be independently associated with wage dispersion.

7. CONCLUSION

In this chapter, I have engaged in four analytical exercises, all revolving around the problem of explaining broad patterns of wage distribution – why the degree of wage inequality varies across countries and/or over time. All four suggest that politics and institutional arrangements shape wage-distributive outcomes; supply and demand factors alone do not provide the basis for an adequate explanation of the variations across countries and over time that we observe (cf. Blau and Kahn 1966). This said, I want to make three points that run somewhat against or takes us beyond the "historical–institutionalist" approach to comparative political economy (cf. Pontusson 1995b).

First, the claim that "institutions matter" is too broad to be very meaningful. We need to specify which institutions matter and how they matter and, of course, this in turn depends on what it is that we want to explain. The point here is perhaps best illustrated in terms of the distinction made earlier between, on the one hand, the organizational centralization of unions and employers' associations and, on the other hand, centralized bargaining between unions and employers. Comparing Sweden and Austria, it would appear that peak-level bargaining creates conditions conducive to wage compression whereas industry-level bargaining between centralized labor-market parties does not.

Second, we should avoid the juxtaposition of politics/institutions and market forces. As suggested at several points in the course of this chapter, these "variables" interact continuously. Institutionalized wage bargaining in general, and peak-level bargaining in particular, is likely to yield more egalitarian wage-distributive outcomes than market forces would yield on their own, but market-driven wage-drift will correct for some of these egalitarian "excesses," and large discrepancies between bargained outcomes and market pressures can be sustained for only so long. At the same time, it is crucial to recognize that bargained outcomes shape market forces. Under conditions of full employment, wage compression agreed to by unions and employers in the public sector creates market pressure on private-sector employers to raise the relative wages of unskilled workers.

Third, economic–structural variables matter along with institutions and supply-and-demand considerations. The argument about spillover of wage compression from the public sector to the private sector points to the size of the public sector as an important source of variation among OECD countries (cf. Garrett and Way, this volume), and this hypothesis is supported by some of my regression results as well as the comparison of Sweden and Austria. The size of the small-business sector constitutes another economic–structural variable with potential significance for wage-distributive outcomes. From an analytical point of view, economic–structural considerations provide at least a partial answer to the question that labor economists raise, but seldom address explicitly: Why does relative demand for different types of labor vary across countries or over time?

Another theme that emerges from the preceding discussion concerns the need to distinguish different types of wage compression (or dispersion), and to recognize that there may be more than one path to a certain level of wage inequality as measured by, say, 90–10 ratios. As we have seen, the Swedish experience of wage compression can be divided into two distinct phases with quite distinctive causal dynamics – one dominated by interfirm compression and the other by intrafirm compression. In addition, the regression results presented above suggest that the determinants of within- and between-gender wage inequality are quite different. Perhaps most strikingly, strong unions seem to be more apt to promote within-gender than between-gender compression.

Working men are still more likely to be union members than working women, and it may be that the gendered impact of unionization on wage distribution diminishes as the gender gap in union density diminishes. Unfortunately, available cross-national data on union density by gender are fragmentary and do not allow us to test this hypothesis in any systematic fashion. We also lack comprehensive data on the distribution of male and female employment between private and public services in the OECD countries. These types of data are sorely needed to advance the comparative study of wage inequality.

To conclude, it should be clear that the distribution of wages is an object of intraclass distributive conflict and cross-class alliances – themes stressed by Swenson in his effort to recast the politics of social democratic corporatism. However, the distribution of wages should also be seen as an outcome of conflict and bargaining between labor and capital. This is most obviously true for occupational, intrafirm differentials. Though employers have a common interest in maintaining their ability to manipulate intrafirm differentials in response to labor market conditions, unions have an interest in restricting the scope of intrafirm differentiation. Also, it is crucial to recognize that the compression of interfirm (or intersectoral) differentials involves a rather special kind of cross-class alliance, quite different from firm- or sector-based alliances associated with trade and industrial-policy issues. According to the conventional view of the Swedish experience, the principal beneficiaries of solidaristic wage policy on the employer side were the most profitable firms, but on the labor side, the principal beneficiaries were the employees of the least profitable firms. This interpretation may need qualifications, but the general point still holds: The politics of wage distribution involves *both* class conflict and compromise *and* intraclass conflict and cross-class alliances.

References

Austria. 1991. *Statistisches Handbuch*. Vienna: Österreichisches Statistisches Zentralamt.
Baccaro, Lucio and Richard Locke. 1998. "The end of solidarity? The decline of egalitarian wage policies in Italy and Sweden." *European Journal of Industrial Relations*, 4:283–308.
Blau, Francine and Lawrence Kahn. 1995. "The gender earnings gap." In Richard Freeman and Lawrence Katz, eds., *Differences and changes in wage structures*, 105–44. Chicago: University of Chicago Press.
Blau, Francine and Lawrence Kahn. 1996. "International difference in male wage inequality." *Journal of Political Economy*, 104:791–836.
Burtless, Gary. 1996. "Widening U.S. income inequality and the growth in world trade." Washington DC: Brookings Institution.

Cameron, David. 1984. "Social democracy, corporatism, labour quiescence, and the representation of economic interest in advanced capitalist society." In John Goldthorpe, ed., *Order and conflict in contemporary capitalism*, 143–78. Oxford: Clarendon Press.

Edin, Per-Anders and Bertil Holmlund. 1995. "The Swedish wage structure." In Richard Freeman and Lawrence Katz, eds., *Differences and changes in wage structures*, 307–44. Chicago: University of Chicago Press.

Erickson, Christopher and Andrea Ichino. 1995. "Wage differentials in Italy." In Richard Freeman and Lawrence Katz, eds., *Differences and changes in wage structures*, 265–306. Chicago: University of Chicago Press.

Esping-Andersen, Gösta. 1990. *The three worlds of welfare capitalism*. Princeton: NJ: Princeton University Press.

Esping-Andersen, Gösta and Walter Korpi. 1984. "Social policy as class politics in post-war capitalism." In John Goldthorpe, ed., *Order and conflict in contemporary capitalism*, 179–208. Oxford: Clarendon Press.

Flanagan, Robert, David Soskice, and Lloyd Ullman. 1983. *Unionism, economic stabilization and incoomes policies*. Washington, DC: Brookings Institution.

Freeman, Richard. 1980. "Unionism and the dispersion of wages." *Industrial and Labor Relations Review,* 34:3–23.

———. 1982. "Union wage practices and wage dispersion within establishments." *Industrial and Labor Relations Review,* 36:3–20.

———. 1993. "How much has de-unionization contributed to the rise in male earnings inequality?" In S. Danziger and P. Gottschalk, eds., *Uneven tides,* 133–159. New York: Russell Sage.

Freeman, Richard and Lawrence Katz, eds. 1995. *Differences and changes in wage structures*. Chicago: University of Chicago Press.

Golden, Miriam. 1993. "The dynamics of trade unionism and national economic performance." *American Political Science Review,* 87:439–54.

Golden, Miriam and Michael Wallerstein. 1996. "Postwar industrial relations in non-corporatist countries." Paper presented at the Tenth International Conference of Europeanists, Chicago, March 14–16.

Gornick, Janet and Jerry Jacobs. 1997. "Gender, the welfare state and public employment." Luxembourg Income Study Working Paper no. 168.

Gottschalk, Peter and Timothy Smeeding. "Cross-national comparisons of earnings and income inequality." *Journal of Economic Literature,* 35:633–87.

Guger, Alois. 1989. "Einkommensverteilung und Verteilungspolitik in Österreich." In Hans Abele et al., eds., *Handbuch der österreichischen Wirtschaftspolitik,* 3rd ed., 183–202. Vienna: Manz.

———. 1992. "Corporatism: Success or failure? Austrian experiences." In Jukka Pekkarinen, Matti Pohjola, and Bob Rowthorn, eds., *Social corporatism,* 338–362. Oxford: Clarendon Press.

Hibbs, Douglas. 1990. "Wage compression under solidarity bargaining in Sweden." Working paper, Trade Union Institute for Economic Research, Stockholm.

———. 1991. "Market forces, trade union ideology, and trends in Swedish wage dispersion." *Acta Sociologica,* 34:89–102.

Hibbs, Douglas and Håkan Locking. 1995. "Wage dispersion and productive efficiency." Working paper, Trade Union Institute for Economic Research, Stockholm.

Hibbs, Douglas and Håkan Locking. 1996. "Wage compression, wage drift and wage inflation in Sweden." *Labour Economics*, 3:109–41.

ILO. 1986. *The trade union situation and industrial relations in Austria*. Geneva: ILO.

Katz, Lawrence, Gary Loveman, and David Blanchflower. 1995. "A comparison of changes in the structure of wages in four OECD countries." In Richard Freeman and Lawrence Katz, eds. *Differences and changes in wage structures*, 25–66. Chicago: University of Chicago Press.

Katzenstein, Peter. 1984. *Corporatism and change*. Ithaca: Cornell University Press.

1985. *Small states in world markets*. Ithaca: Cornell University Press.

Kitschelt, Herbert. 1995. "Austrian and Swedish social democrats in crisis." *Comparative Political Studies*, 27:3–39.

Kunkel, Christoph and Jonas Pontusson. 1998. "Corporatism vs. social democracy: Divergent fortunes of the Austrian and Swedish labor movements." *West European Politics*, 21:1–31.

Kurzer, Paulette. 1993. *Business and banking*. Ithaca, NY: Cornell University Press.

Loveman, Gary and Werner Sengenberger. 1990. "Economic and social reorganization in the small medium-sized enterprise sector." In Werner Sengenberger, Gary Loveman, and Michael Piore, eds., *The re-emergence of small enterprises*. Geneva: International Institute for Labor Studies, 1–61.

Martin, Andrew. 1984. "Trade unions in Sweden." In Peter Gourevitch et al., eds., *Unions and economic crisis*, 189–359. London: George Allen & Unwin.

Mesch, Michael. 1990. "Einkommensverteilung und Branchenstruktur in Österreich," *Wirtschaft und Gesellschaft*, 16(3):333–78.

Moene, Karl Ove and Michael Wallerstein. 1997. "Pay inequality." *Journal of Labor Economics*, 15:403–30.

OECD. 1991. "Trends in trade union membership." *Employment Outlook* (July), 97–134.

OECD. 1993. "Earnings inequality." *Employment Outlook* (July), 157–84.

OECD. 1994. "Collective bargaining: Levels and coverage." *Employment Outlook* (July), 167–94.

OECD. 1995. *Income distribution in OECD countries: Evidence from the Luxembourg income study*. Paris: OECD.

OECD. 1996. "Earnings inequality, low-paid employment and earnings mobility." *Employment Outlook* (July), 59–108.

OECD. 1997. *Historical statistics*. Paris: OECD.

Pollan, Wolfgang. 1980. "Wage rigidity and the structure of the Austrian manufacturing industry." *Weltwirtschaftliches Archiv*, 116:697–726.

Pontusson, Jonas. 1995a. "Explaining the decline of European social democracy." *World Politics*, 47:495–533.

1995b. "From comparative public policy to political economy: Putting political institutions in their place and taking interests seriously." *Comparative Political Studies*, 28:117–147.

Reiterlechner, Christine. 1992. "Der Einfluss der Betriebsgrösse auf die Lohnhöhe." Working paper, Kammer für Arbeiter und Angestellte, Vienna.

Rowthorn, Bob. 1992. "Corporatism and labour market performance." In Jukka

Pekkarinen, Matti Pohjola, and Bob Rowthorn, eds., *Social corporatism*, 82–131. Oxford: Clarendon Press.

Rueda, David and Jonas Pontusson. 1997. "Wage inequality and varieties of capitalism." Working paper no. 97.6, Institute for European Studies, Cornell University.

SCB. 1979. *Statistisk årsbok*. Stockholm: Statistiska centralbyrån.

SCB. 1991. *Statistisk årsbok*. Stockholm: Statistiska centralbyrån.

Scharpf, Fritz. 1991. *Crisis and choice in European social democracy*. Ithaca: Cornell University Press.

Söderström, H. T. and E. Uddén-Jondal. 1982. "Does egalitarian wage policy cause wage drift?" Institute for International Economics, University of Stockholm.

SOPEMI. 1993. *Trends in international migration* (OECD).

StBA. 1991. *Statistisches Jahrbuch für die Bundesrepublik Deutschland*. Stuttgart: Statistisches Bundesamt.

Svensson, Lars. 1995. *Closing the gender gap*. Lund: Ekonomisk-historiska föreningen.

Swenson, Peter. 1989. *Fair shares*. Ithaca, NY: Cornell University Press.

——— 1991. "Bringing capital back in, or social democracy reconsidered." *World Politics*, 43:379–399.

——— 1992a. "Managing the managers." *Scandinavian Journal of History*, 16:335–356.

——— 1992b. "Union politics, the welfare state and intraclass conflict in Sweden and Germany." In Jonas Pontusson and Miriam Golden, eds., *Bargaining for change*, 45–76. Ithaca, NY: Cornell University Press.

Topel, Robert. 1994. "Wage inequality and regional labor market performance in the United States." In Toshiaki Tachibanaki, ed., *Labour market and economic performance* 101–32. New York: St. Martin's Press.

Traxler, Franz. 1991. "Gewerkschaften und Unternehmerverbände in Österreichs politischen System." In Herbert Dachs et al., eds., *Handbuch des politishen Systems Österreichs*, 335–52. Vienna: Manz.

——— 1992. "Austria: Still the century of corporatism." In Anthony Ferner and Richard Hyman, eds., *Industrial relations in the new Europe*, 270–97. Oxford: Blackwell.

——— Forthcoming. "European transformation and institution-building in East and West." In David Good and Randall Kindley, eds., *Internationalization and institution-building*. Boulder, CO: Westview Press.

Traxler, Franz et al. 1995. "Labour market regulation and employment in Austria." Department of Sociology, University of Vienna.

Vak, Karl. 1982. "The competitiveness of the Austrian economy." In Sven Arndt, ed., *The political economy of Austria*, 156–175. Washington, DC: American Enterprise Institute.

Visser, Jelle. 1996. "Unionization trends revisited." Centre for research of European Societies and Industrial Relations, Amsterdam.

Wallerstein, Michael. Forthcoming. "Wage-setting institutions and pay inequality in advanced industrial societies." *American Journal of Political Science*.

Wallerstein, Michael, Miriam Golden, and Peter Lange. 1996. "Unions, employers associations and wage-setting institutions in North and Central Europe, 1950–1992." Department of Political Science, Northwestern University.

Walterskirchen, Ewald. 1991. *Unemployment and labour market flexibility: Austria.* Geneva: ILO.

Western, Bruce. 1997. "Wage growth and labor decline in the advanced capitalist countries, 1965–1993." Department of Sociology, Princeton University.

INDEX

Basic Agreement, LO-SAF (1938), Sweden
Swedish model of industrial relations in,
254–5
borrowing/lending, Sweden (1980s), 243–7
bourgeois parties, Sweden
differentiation within, 308
monetary policy of government under,
222–3
SAF takes formation of ideology from,
257–8
Bundesbank. *See* central bank, Germany.

Calmfors-Driffill model, 10–12, 48–9, 269
criticism of, 48–51
measures of centralization and employer
coordination, 52–3
capitalism, Germanic model of, 206
capital markets
capital flows related to integration of,
221–2
contagion with capital mobility, 23–4
effect of integration, 226–8
increase in integration, 221–2
internationalization, 22, 222
with and without capital controls, 23
central bank, Germany
independence of, 16
interaction with wage bargainers, 182–3
operation of ERM under hegemony of, 67
signaling by, 182–3
central bank, Sweden

credit market deregulation (1980s), 243–
7
tax reform policy (1980s), 246–7
using interest rates to control credit volume (1980s), 244–5
central bank, U.S.
lack of interaction with wage bargainers,
182
central bank independence
argument for, 173–5
deficiencies in conventional theory, 175–
7
effect on wage bargaining coordination,
183
European Central Bank, 173, 193–4
Germany, 180–3
index (Cukierman), 49–50
influence in cross-national analysis on
inflation and unemployment, 183–91
rational-expectations perspective, 176
signaling, 174–6, 179–80, 182–4
theory of, 174–7
centralization
related to employer coordination, 52–3
relation to inflation, 18–19
See also wage bargaining, centralized
class
class compromise in Sweden, 77
conflict and compromise, 31–2
cross-class realignment in Sweden, 91–7
effect of changes in labor market governance on, 100–3

331

in Sweden, 298–305
Sweden and Austria compared, 305–26
wage drift
Germany, 156
market-driven, 325
Sweden, 249, 81, 86–7, 156
wage distribution with, 21
wage policies
of centralized bargaining systems, 209
of decentralized bargaining system, 209
effect on wages of solidaristic, 21
Swedish solidaristic, 6, 85–7
wages
determinants of public sector, 272
growth public sector, 283–8
social wage, 209
wage restraint, 80
See also wage compression; wage distribution; wage drift; wage policies
wages, real
determinants of, 40–1
in neoclassical model, 40–3
in new Keynesian model, 43–53
wage setting
differences in Nordic country practices, 109–14
effect in Sweden of decentralized, 78–9
effect in Sweden of technological change on, 88–91
effect on aggregate demand of new Keynesian model, 47
government role in Swedish private-sector, 118
impact of public-sector unions on, 272–4
industry- and firm-level, 10
measures of centralized, 109–14
Swedish employers' push for decentralized, 77–9, 81–4, 88–97
trend toward decentralization, 108
trend toward decentralization in Nordic

countries, 108–9
See also wage bargaining
wage solidarity
defined, 80
policy in Sweden (1950s-1970s), 303–4
wage structure
in OECD countries (1985), 295t, 297
relationship to unionization, 305–6
variables in compression of Swedish, 298–303
Wallerstein, Michael, 27, 30, 101, 274
Walterskirchen, Ewald, 313
Way, Christopher, 27–8
welfare state
intersection with bargaining system and macroeconomic policy, 209
link to other macroinstitutions, 206
reforms in Denmark, 225–6
reforms in Sweden, 225–6
women
in labor force in Sweden and Austria (1960–1985), 314
participation in labor movement in Austria and Sweden, 314
public sector employment in Austria and Sweden, 314
workers, foreign
labor force share in Austria and Sweden, 314–15
Works Constitution Act, Germany, 160–1
works councils, Germany
codetermination rights of, 158–61
in dual system of industrial relations, 159
employer relations with, 142, 145, 158–9, 162
plant-level role of, 181
wildcat cooperation with employers, 147, 153

Zysman, John, 167